In memory of my father, Richard Hammer,
who inspired me to go places and to write about them

CONTENTS

GREECE
AND
THE ORIENT
(About B.C. 1250)

Aryan Peoples
Semitic   "
Hamitic   "

SCALE OF MILES
0   100   200   300   400

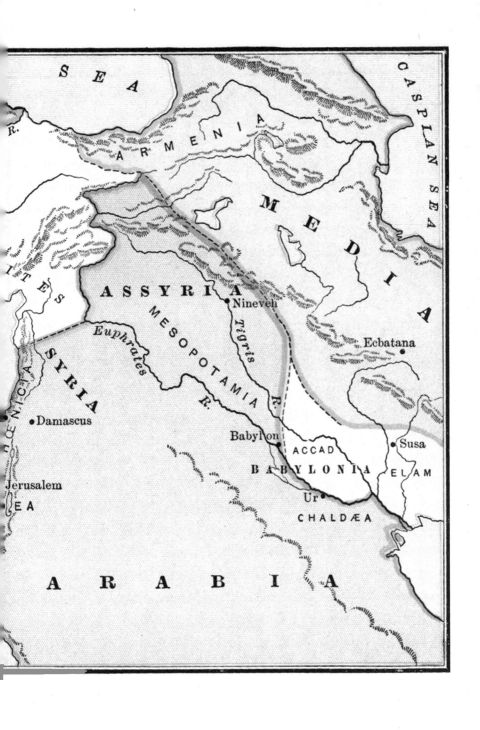

TIMELINE

705–681   Reign of Sennacherib, who moves the capital to Nineveh and launches the Samaria campaign, but fails to take Jerusalem

681–669   Reign of Esarhaddon, conqueror of Egypt

668–627   Rule of Ashurbanipal, last great king of Assyria, and plunderer of Babylon

612   Medes and Babylonians invade Assyria, destroy Nineveh, Nimrud, Ashur, and Dur-Sharrukin, and bring down the Assyrian Empire

538   Cyrus the Great, first king of the Achaemenid Empire, conquers Babylon

330   Alexander the Great and his army destroy Persepolis, putting an end to the Achaemenid Empire

PREFACE

QAL'AT SHERQAT,
NORTHERN MESOPOTAMIA, 1853

The mound stood on a bluff high above a bend in the river. Excavation teams had peeled off densely packed layers of wind-borne sand, exposing an ancient field of stonework and mud-brick masonry. Fragments of human-headed lions and bulls and smashed bas-reliefs lay strewn across the ruins, evidence that the city had come to some apocalyptic end.

As the sun rose over a landscape of riverine tamarisk trees, thorn bushes, and desert grass, workmen gathered around a square brick platform at the center of the mound. Once, experts believed, it had been the foundations of a temple or a palace. Inscribed relics had been discovered buried deep beneath structures such as this one. One theory held that the ancients had planted them there like time capsules, preserving royal annals for future monarchs to discover. Or perhaps they were messages to be read only by the gods.

Carrying pickaxes and shovels, faces covered with handkerchiefs to protect themselves from dust, the workmen positioned themselves at a corner of the platform and began to dig. They burrowed with difficulty through the concrete-like material, keeping watch all the while for anything unusual camouflaged amid the dun-colored brick.

Four feet below the surface, they had still found nothing. Six feet down, they gazed into an empty hole. But at eight feet, an object caught their attention.

It was a terra-cotta octagon, about the size of a coffeepot. Some pieces had broken off, and a portion had crumbled into powder. A scribe had gouged hundreds of tiny signs into each of its eight sides, squeezed so close together that the markings could barely be distinguished by the naked eye. The diggers clustered around the artifact in curiosity. Its arrowhead-like characters surely conveyed a message: a glimpse of life early in recorded history, when men first formed sophisticated urban centers, made observations of the heavens, and produced an outpouring of written accounts to explain the world. But over the thousands of years that the cylinder had been sealed in darkness, empires had risen and fallen, conquering armies had swept across the land, 150 generations had lived and died, and the meaning of the markings had been lost.

The lead archaeologist—born just miles away, and now one of a handful of men engaged in a race to unearth the secrets of his mysterious forebears—cradled the pieces. He observed how the fragments fit together and noted the deep gouges in the hardened clay.

Who, he wondered, would induce it to tell its stories?

The
MESOPOTAMIAN
RIDDLE

A CONTEST ON NEW BURLINGTON STREET

On a late-summer day in 1856, a letter carrier for metropolitan London's Post Office stepped from a mail coach in front of a three-story town house in Mayfair. Crossing the threshold, the courier—nattily attired in a black-silk top hat, scarlet frock coat, black-and-white-checkered vest, and dark gray trousers—handed a wax-sealed envelope to a clerk. The missive was addressed to Edwin Norris, the secretary of the Royal Asiatic Society of Great Britain and Ireland.

The anonymous postman had no way of knowing that the envelope he was bearing would help rewrite the story of civilization's origins and ignite a neck-and-neck contest for international renown. At stake: the immortality conferred on those who make once-in-a-century intellectual breakthroughs.

Though none had written the letter, three men—driven by boundless curiosity, a love of risk, and the distinctive demons of aspiration and ambition—were most responsible for making the contest possible.

One, Austen Henry Layard, was the son of an English colonial civil servant. At age twenty-two, he had fled the drudgery of clerk-

Victorian postman on his rounds

ship tasks in his uncle's law office for a life of adventure on the lawless backroads of the Ottoman Empire. Bandits robbed him three times and once left him to wander half-naked and barefoot through the desert. He joined a rebellious mountain tribe in Persia and spied in the Balkans for the British ambassador in Constantinople. At last he reached the mounds of Mesopotamia, where he transformed himself into the most celebrated archaeologist of the age.

Henry Creswicke Rawlinson, living in the shadow of a rich and influential father and an accomplished older brother, had decided that he could carve out his own identity only in exile. As a twenty-three-year-old military officer of the East India Company, he found himself in Persia. There he demonstrated a flair for languages, a skill at scaling heights in search of millennia-old inscriptions, and a powerful yearning, he confided to his sister, to do something to attract the world's attention. In his early thirties, he deciphered the writing of the ancient Persian Empire. The achievement, considered as fantastic in his time as mapping mitochondrial DNA in ours, brought Rawlinson his first taste of fame. And more dead languages were waiting to be understood.

Finally, there was Edward Hincks, a country parson in a remote corner of Ireland: brilliant, tormented by crippling anxiety and the specter of financial ruin, hungry for peer recognition of his linguistic gifts, and principled to a fault. Huddled for endless hours over his desk in his rectory, Hincks had tested his formidable intellect and escaped his many troubles by translating obscure texts written in Egyptian hieroglyphs and ancient Hebrew. Eventually he set his sights on the most tantalizing prize of them all.

By 1856 the paths of these three men had converged in a sometimes friendly, often combustible *pas de trois*. Now, with Layard watching from a judicious distance, Hincks and Rawlinson were about to become the prime contestants in a challenge to determine, once and for all, whether the oldest writing system in the world could be deciphered. However esoteric this might sound, the question was the subject of intense public debate in capitals on both sides of the Atlantic. For mid-nineteenth-century Britons, proving that this elusive script could be understood meant pulling back the curtain on a distant, vanished, yet hauntingly familiar world, one that had given birth to humanity's modern mind.

◄────────►

Until the 1840s, few people had known anything about the great civilizations that had begun their rise along the Tigris and Euphrates Rivers about 2000 BCE and endured for more than 1500 years. Assyria and its vassal state (and sometime rival) Babylon had once dominated the Near East and beyond. Classical writers described Assyria, which reached its zenith about 700 BCE, as the first true empire; the ancient Greek historian Herodotus wrote that Babylon "surpasses in splendor any city in the known world." But a coalition of enemies had destroyed Assyria in the late seventh century BCE, and Babylon was neglected, ransacked, and left to die out five hundred years later. "Today the greatest world city of antiquity is a mound of desert earth," one theologian wrote. By the mid-1800s, these societies had been almost entirely forgotten. At the British Museum, the world's preeminent repository of antiquities, the relics of Assyria and Babylon, including writings inscribed on clay bricks and stone, filled one three-foot-by-three-foot-by-three-foot cabinet.

But the excavations of Pompeii and Herculaneum in the mid-1700s had inspired a new science: investigating antiquity by digging objects out of the earth. And Layard was its most spectacularly successful practitioner. Enduring lethal epidemics, stultifying heat, vermin-infested camps, and the hostility of Ottoman authorities, he made a series of remarkable discoveries beginning in the mid-1840s: 2,500-year-old Assyrian palaces paneled with exquisite alabaster bas-reliefs and guarded by stone gods and monsters. In vivid and often shocking detail, the friezes depicted corpse-covered battlefields, battering-ram-wielding soldiers breaking down city ramparts, archers in stallion-drawn chariots, lines of bedraggled captives, vassals bearing tributes, kings attended by a retinue of eunuchs, and royal lion hunts in the bush. Unreadable inscriptions swirled around the carvings. Layard and his protégé, a Christian Arab from Mosul named Hormuzd Rassam, had also recently unearthed thousands of inscribed clay tablets in the royal library of the burned Assyrian capital, Nineveh: the tablets seemed to be filled with information about astronomy, medicine, religion, politics, laws, and everyday life.

The rediscovery of this lost civilization, which had controlled the Near East like no other empire before or since, seized the public's imagination. Hundreds of thousands of people flocked to the Crystal Palace in south London in 1854 to gaze at the "Nineveh Court," a fanciful reinvention of the royal palace, with lotus gardens, multicolored bas-reliefs, and blue-headed bull capitals perched atop Doric columns. Newspapers chronicled the arrival in England of giant winged lions and other stone colossi that testified to Assyria's artistic mastery and rich mythology. "The monuments [Layard] has sent home from the plains of Assyria . . . excited a livelier interest than anything else I saw in the Museum," proclaimed an American visitor in the *Natchez Courier* in Mississippi. "There they are, disinterred from the oblivion of ages, the last survivors, the sole historic monuments of Nineveh, her kings, and her people, and her glory!"

For the first time, too, museumgoers and newspaper readers could examine large samples of the vanished civilization's writing, which had predated Egyptian hieroglyphs by centuries. Assyrian and Babylonian scribes had ingeniously utilized the thick stem of a reed that grows in the wetlands of the Middle East, the *Arundo donax*, and split these stalks to create a trapezoidal tip. Then they pressed signs into damp clay and fired the inscribed tablets in a kiln, making them almost indestructible. Over time, scribes also carved the characters into copper and stone.

Cuneiform (the term derives from the Latin *cuneus*, or "wedge," referring to the characters' distinctive shape) lacked the beauty of hieroglyphs. One jokester would say that the signs looked like "what you might get if a flock of birds with obsessive-compulsive disorder took a walk across wet clay." But the writing system had taken over the ancient world. From Mesopotamia, cuneiform had traveled east to the Kingdom of Elam, on the plains of Persia. The Kingdom of Urartu, southeast of the Black Sea and dominated by the biblical Mount Ararat (where Noah's ark came to rest after the flood), adopted the writing for its language isolate, as did the Hittite Empire, an Indo-European power in Anatolia (present-day Turkey) that had reached its zenith during the mid-fourteenth century BCE. A simplified form took hold in Ugarit, a prosperous city-state on the Mediterranean coast, and finally in the Persian-speaking Achaemenid Empire, which, under Kings Cyrus, Darius, and Xerxes, had ruled Central Asia and parts of Africa and Europe from the sixth century to the fourth century BCE.

The wedge-based script endured for some 2,500 years. But papyrus gradually supplanted clay, new scripts made cuneiform obsolete, and the fifteen languages that used it died out. (The last datable cuneiform tablet is an astronomical almanac predicting the appearances of stars, planets, and other heavenly bodies inscribed around 79 CE; it was found in the early 1900s in Southern Mesopotamia.) By the second century CE, knowledge of the phonetic values and meaning of the characters had faded away.

In the 1820s the Englishman Thomas Young and his rival, the Frenchman Jean-François Champollion, had solved the riddle of the hieroglyphs. Scholars could now read the love poetry and funerary texts of the ancient Egyptians, study the military campaigns of the pharaohs, and learn how the dwellers along the Nile treated toothaches, performed surgeries, and measured time. With Layard's finds, the public now clamored for linguists to unravel the mysteries of cuneiform too. Believers were thrilled by the possibility that the royal annals of Nineveh, Nimrud (another destroyed Assyrian capital), and Babylon might corroborate tales from the Old Testament. The Hebrew Prophets had described Assyria's deportation of the ten Jewish tribes from Samaria in 721 BCE and the siege of Jerusalem twenty years later. Unfortunately, these accounts weren't corroborated by any other surviving records, which made them suspect to nineteenth-century historians. At a time when atheists, agnostics, and other skeptics were casting doubt on Scripture, the writing on the walls could turn out to be nothing less than proof of the veracity of the word of God.

Cuneiform also dangled the possibility of peering back even further in time. New excavations along the Euphrates River in Southern Mesopotamia had turned up tablets written in cuneiform that appeared to predate the finds at Nineveh by nearly 2,000 *years*, originating around 2500 BCE. The characters were familiar, but the language seemed different. If this far more ancient script were deciphered, it would offer insights into the very cradle of civilization— a place nearly as remote from the time of Assyria and Babylon as those city-states were from the Victorian era. In this flat, fertile zone humans established the first permanent communities, developed agriculture, scratched out pictures of objects that became writing, and slowly organized themselves into the types of complex hierarchical societies that remain recognizable today. Here also lay the supposed birthplace of Abraham, who had founded a new nation in the land of Canaan around 2100 BCE. Could it truly be possible to read records preserved from this distant time?

◄─────►

After going down blind alleys and stumbling into dead ends for years, Rawlinson and Hincks both claimed by the 1850s to be making great progress understanding the "arrowhead script." Academics, literary journals, and the public marveled at their apparent insights. But there was a problem. The rival philologists concurred on one thing: the writing of Babylon and Assyria was bewilderingly complex. Its most striking characteristic was what was called *polyphony*: many characters, they maintained, could be read in six, seven, even *eight* different ways.

Critics reacted "with shouts of incredulity," wrote the Oxford historian A. H. Sayce. Under the supposed rules of the Assyrian and Babylonian script, the *Dublin University Magazine* declared, "[a] modern decipherer could . . . make out any proposed name whatever from any assigned group of [characters]." Charles Wall, a professor of Hebrew at Trinity College Dublin, analyzed the signs said to make up the name of the Babylonian king who had captured Jerusalem in 597 BCE and marched the Jews into captivity. "[T]he various values capable of being assigned to the eight characters which are supposed to form the name of Nebuchadnezzar," he had calculated, "are such that the word might be read 393,216 different ways."

The American newspaper *The National Era*, founded in 1847 by the abolitionist editor Gamaliel Bailey, suggested that the so-called experts were perpetrating a hoax to cover up their befuddlement: "[I]t has now come to a question whether this system of translations be not altogether arbitrary, or, in a word, no translation at all," the journal proclaimed. The French Academy in Paris, it reported, "laughs at all decipherments, and treats the so-called translations as pure quackery."

Some academics were convinced that the writing would never be cracked. History is filled with examples of dead scripts that couldn't be deciphered, leaving their creators a blank slate. The Phaistos Disc, a fired-clay plate from a Bronze Age palace in Crete, contains forty-five distinct pictograms—a plumed head, a bell, a building shaped like a beehive—in a 242-character text that spirals across the surface like the pattern of a nautilus. The inscription has mystified philologists for more than a century.

At least one hundred would-be decipherers have offered theories about the Indus script, created by a proto-Indo-European civilization in what is now Pakistan and northwest India around 2500 BCE. Some have linked the writing, found on stone seals and pottery, to the still-undeciphered rongorongo runes on Easter Island. The celebrated Egyptologist Sir Flinders Petrie surmised that the seals were the stamps of high officials. One, he claimed, meant "the agent of the registrar of timber," another "the agent of irrigated land." None of this proved to be anything more than wild conjecture, and the writing remains an enigma. Was cuneiform destined for the same fate?

◄————►

In 1854, a unique opportunity presented itself. Austen Layard's protégé, Rassam, had discovered a relic buried beneath a temple in what was believed to be the oldest Assyrian capital, Ashur, in the semi-desert forty miles south of Rassam's hometown of Mosul. Nineteen inches tall and 2.5 inches wide, the octagonal column, known as a "prism," was inscribed with eight hundred lines of tiny cuneiform characters. It was believed to date to 1100 BCE—around the time that war was raging between the Trojans and the Greeks, and the prophet Samuel led the Israelites to victory against the Philistines. The mystifying cylinder was now in the custody of the British Museum. Rawlinson, who had close ties to the museum, was working on an official translation; the institution planned to publish it as soon as it was done.

As Rawlinson proceeded, a wealthy inventor with a passion for intellectual puzzles burst onto the scene. William Henry Fox Talbot had made his name two decades earlier by devising a method for fixing images from life onto chemically treated, light-sensitive paper. The breakthrough had earned him the title—shared with the Frenchman Louis-Jacques-Mandé Daguerre—the "father of photography." Talbot had lately devoted himself to a new enthusiasm: Assyro-Babylonian decipherment. He was pained to think that some of his peers were dismissing it as "quackery." Nearing sixty, he was determined to put doubts to rest about the passion that was consuming him in semi-retirement.

Talbot dispatched a letter—the letter that would change everything—to the Royal Asiatic Society, one of the leading research institutions of the day, offering to send in his own translation and have a panel of judges compare his with Rawlinson's. If the versions turned out to be identical or even close, he wrote from his estate, Lacock Abbey, a former nunnery 85 miles west of London that Henry VIII had confiscated and sold to one of Talbot's ancestors, "it must indicate that they have Truth for their basis." After a negotiation with Rawlinson and the British Museum, Talbot received a lithograph copy of the inscriptions in January 1857 and got to work.

Six weeks later, Talbot placed six notebooks in an envelope, sealed the package with wax, and dispatched it to the Royal Asiatic Society in Mayfair. To assure the public that he had prepared it "*before* the appearance of Sir H Rawlinson's translation," Talbot gave instructions to the society's secretary, Edwin Norris, to guard it. "Our next meeting is on the 21st . . . when I shall have much pleasure in presenting your sealed packet to the meeting of Council," Norris wrote back on March 13. "I will then lock it up in a strong box, of which I keep the key."

Eight days later, on March 21, two dozen members of the society converged on 5 New Burlington Street for their regular Saturday conclave. Hansom cabs clattered along the narrow lane, a few blocks east of Grosvenor Square, depositing the men before a three-story town house designed in the early eighteenth century by Nicholas Hawksmoor, a partner of Sir Christopher Wren. A discreet brass nameplate on the front door identified the building as the society's headquarters. They filed through the spacious interior, checked their topcoats and hats, and made their way to a ground-floor gallery.

Sitting in the room that afternoon was another man whose name would soon be linked to Rawlinson's and Talbot's by history: a thirty-one-year-old classicist and adventurer named Jules Oppert. Oppert was a descendant of Samuel Oppenheimer, a wealthy Jewish banker in Hamburg and the financier of the seventeenth-century Holy Roman emperor Leopold I. After being denied a position at German universities because of institutional antisemitism, Oppert had joined a three-year French archaeological expedition in Babylon and Northern Mesopotamia. Now his was a star on the rise. "His spontaneous wit, his extraordinary memory, and ready erudition . . . made companionship with him a delight," gushed a *Times* correspondent. The charming Parisian boulevardier asked if he could undertake a translation as well. "By affording three independent versions of the same document," he argued, an agreement among the decipherers could be even more persuasive.

But what about Edward Hincks? The churchman's fraught relationship with Henry Rawlinson had been marked by backstabbing, filched notebooks, accusations of stolen credit, withering reviews, infuriating discrepancies, and a snub by the British Museum that had cost Hincks a good part of his livelihood. Carrying a perennial chip on his shoulder, Hincks could be cantankerous and sharp-tongued, especially if he felt he wasn't being treated with sufficient respect. Determined to give the man his due, Edwin Norris recommended that the society dispatch lithographs of the texts at once to the reclusive pastor at his rectory in the village of Killyleagh, south of Belfast. It would be impolite to leave him out.

And so, after a decades-long saga of global adventures, near-death experiences, and eureka moments, the hour of reckoning was at hand. Now Rawlinson, Hincks, Talbot, Oppert, and eager bystanders—philologists, historians, theologians, literary editors, and other enthusiasts from London to Paris to New York—would discover whether the secrets of the most powerful ancient empire could be verifiably understood. And yet what the four would be undertaking wasn't any ordinary race to the finish line. To convince the public that their translations weren't hoaxes, they'd *all* have to be right. Each still hoped to be the *most* right, but each knew that his competitors couldn't be far behind, or his brilliance would be laughed off as a scam.

The stakes, they knew, were huge: A positive outcome had the potential not only to silence doubters and immortalize their names in the field of linguistic archaeology but also to confirm their insights into the thoughts, myths, preoccupations, calculations, and achievements of some of the first literate human beings in history. Failure would leave the scholars humiliated before their peers, their government—Queen Victoria's husband, Prince Albert, was a principal patron of the Royal Asiatic Society—and a global public. They would have to accept that they'd been fooling themselves for years—in Rawlinson's case, for decades. Deciphering these characters had become his life.

Now that two more decipherers had been added to the challenge, Norris proposed a deadline for all the submissions two months away, at which point a panel of judges "whose names it was thought would command general respect" would compare the four translations. Norris fixed another meeting of the Royal Asiatic Society for Wednesday, May 20, when the four sealed packets would be opened before witnesses and the "literary inquest" could take place.

The game was on.

CHAPTER ONE

◄◄———————————————►►

RAWLINSON

On an early July day in 1827, dozens of cadets stood on the deck of the *Neptune* in Portsmouth Harbour, excited and, in many cases, filled with trepidation about the voyage that lay ahead. Resplendent in red jackets with golden-tasseled epaulets and white trousers, the young men took the measure of one another and of the ship that would be their home for the next four months: a six-gun, three-mast, triple-deck East Indiaman merchant vessel chartered by the East India Company. Each had come with a steamer trunk packed with the requisite items for his new life, including black silk neckerchiefs; kid gloves; merino jackets; dressing gowns; a sword with a sword bag; toothbrushes and powder; a telescope; and a copy of John Doyle's *Military Catechism for the Use of Young Officers and Serjeants of Infantry*. And each had come with his own motives for traveling to a distant and potentially dangerous land: the promise of adventure, the pride of sharing in a patriotic enterprise, the prospect of making a fortune. Most had never left home before. None could be certain he would see England again.

Standing on a dock at the edge of the harbor, Henry Creswicke Rawlinson waited for the launch that would carry him to the *Neptune*. Seventeen years old, broad-shouldered, with long brown hair, dark eyes, and a pointed chin, the man who would become known as one of history's greatest scholar-adventurers scanned the dozen ships moored offshore. Rawlinson had spent the previous day at a racetrack in the Cotswolds, cheering on his father's Thoroughbreds, before receiving word from a messenger that the *Neptune* had embarked early from London and was on its way down the Thames to make a short stop at Portsmouth. With little time to spare, Rawlinson had ridden first to London for some last-minute provisioning, then galloped much of the ninety-six miles from London to the coast. He had arrived hours before the ship was to set sail. Now, as the reality of the journey sank in, he was overcome by doubt and regret.

Rawlinson had rarely had much to worry about before. He had been born in April 1810 on a country estate in Chadlington, twenty miles north of Oxford, the seventh of eleven children of Abraham Tyack Rawlinson, a wealthy landowner descended from a political ally of King Charles II, and his wife, Eliza Eudocia Albinia Creswicke Rawlinson. Abraham Rawlinson bred racehorses, hunted with hounds, oversaw his seven-hundred-acre property, served as a magistrate, and kept watch over poorhouses and lunatic asylums. It was a life of power, privilege, and noblesse oblige. From the terrace of the family mansion "the eye ranged . . . across fields and copses and the Evenlode River to the smart slope beyond," wrote Henry's younger brother George, "crowned . . . by the extensive woodland of Wychwood forest."

At thirteen Rawlinson had entered the Great Ealing School in London, founded in 1698. He read Homer, Aeschylus, and Euripides, wrote classical poetry, and excelled at cricket, football, and fives, a sort of handball played on a walled tennis court. Academic excellence came easy to him. Once he planted a dummy in his bed and snuck out with a classmate to attend an opera. The schoolmaster uncovered the scheme and sentenced the boys to memorize the *Ars Poetica* of Horace and recite it flawlessly within two weeks. The classmate failed and was expelled; Rawlinson succeeded and escaped punishment. Rawlinson "grew to be six feet high, broad chested, [and] strong-limbed . . . with a steady head, a clear sight, and a nerve that few of his co-mates equaled," his brother George wrote. His siblings, whom Rawlinson referred to as his "happy, happy, happy circle," admired his military bearing and called him "the General."

In 1826 Rawlinson attracted the notice of the East India Company, the ruthless trading firm founded by a group of London merchants in 1600. Eight years after its creation, the firm had gained its first foothold in India, and within a century and a half came to dominate global trade in opium, cotton, indigo, tea, and half a dozen other commodities. Parliament retained the right to renew or cancel its charter every twenty years, but the company raised a private army, crushed Indian resistance from Bengal to Mysore in the south to the Himalayan foothills, and built extraordinary wealth and power. The firm served as a proxy government, operating embassies and consulates in the subcontinent and Middle East, even making foreign policy, since its primary interests—geographic expansion and economic exploitation—aligned closely with those of the British Foreign Office. One Welsh castle owned by an East India Company commander became a repository for loot seized from the Mughal emperor in the early 1800s. "The riches include hookahs of burnished gold inlaid with empurpled ebony; superbly inscribed spinels and jewelled daggers; gleaming rubies the colour of pigeon's blood and scatterings of lizard-green emeralds," the historian William Dalrymple wrote. By 1802, "when the EIC captured the Mughal capital of Delhi," noted Dalrymple in *The Anarchy*, a history of the firm, "the Company had trained up a private security force of around 200,000—twice the size of the British Army—

and marshaled more fire power than any nation state in Asia." To gain admission to this corps of legalized pillagers required personal recommendations, testimonials, and an interview in Surrey with the Military Seminary committee, which approved cadets for the cavalry and infantry. Rawlinson passed—and received an officer's rank; months of military, surveying, mathematics, and language training at Blackheath in London; and a passage to India.

On the dock at Portsmouth Harbour, Rawlinson shook hands with his older brother, Abram, who had come from London to see him off, and stepped into the launch. As he watched his brother recede and the East Indiaman draw nearer with every stroke of the oarsman's blade, he felt "an intensity of grief" at the prospect of exchanging "the society of parents, friends, brothers, and sisters whom I love . . . for a life of misery and sorrow among strangers and barbarians." He clambered up a ladder to the *Neptune*'s main deck, passed a dozen white lifeboats mounted on wooden racks, maneuvered around midshipmen, gunners, carpenters, armorers, coopers, caulkers, cooks, quartermasters, and other crewmembers, and found his cramped aft cabin.

Surrounded by "laughing and joking" young cadets who appeared "totally unconcerned about their recent separation" from their families, the homesick youth stood alone as the vessel raised anchor and sailed out of the harbor past hundred-gun frigates and smaller sloops-of-war. "When I sit by myself on the poop [deck] and view the moonbeams glancing on the silvery sea," he wrote that evening, "I am wretched, miserable, alone in the world . . . I am an exile."

◄◄———►►

Once the initial wave of homesickness had passed, though, Rawlinson settled in for the long voyage around the Cape of Good Hope to

Bombay. As usual, he took charge. He edited a handwritten periodical called *The Herald of the Deep*, raised a glass of claret with fellow
cadets to celebrate his brother Abram's twenty-second birthday in
September, and organized shipboard auctions, adding to his library
for £10 handsome editions of Horace, Virgil, Catullus, and Cicero.
One stiflingly hot afternoon near the Equator he led a group of cadets on an unauthorized dip in the Indian Ocean that turned terrifying. Spotted by a great white shark, they had to swim frantically
back to the ship. "We . . . found the man-ropes thrown down for us,
caught them, eluded the shark, and were hauled up the side of the
vessel," he wrote, "much to the perturbation of a young lady who
was looking out of her cabin window and was not a little shocked
at seeing such a strange [group] of unclothed beings swarming up
past the Porthole!"

   He also befriended the figure that would awaken his fascination
for ancient civilizations: Sir John Malcolm, a diplomat, soldier, and
expert in Persian languages—a "pleasant, good-natured old gentleman," as Rawlinson described him—who was traveling to Bombay to serve as the colonial governor. The son of destitute Scottish
farmers, Malcolm had joined the East India Company as a fourteen-
year-old ensign, fought bloody battles against Indian armies, led
the British delegation to the shah's court, wrote a 1,100-page volume called *The History of Persia*, and took on promising cadets
as protégés. "He lent them books . . . invited them into his cabin,
and watched their progress with the deepest interest," wrote John
William Kaye in his 1856 *Life and Correspondence of Major-General
Sir John Malcolm*. "Malcolm employed some of his young friends
in copying his manuscripts, and . . . it is not difficult to conjecture
where [Rawlinson]"—by 1856 something of a national hero—
"took his first lesson in deciphering strange hieroglyphics."

   Rawlinson's dreams of adventure faded once he reached India.

The epic battles that had cemented the firm's control over India had subsided, and what became known as "the great calm" had taken hold. Assigned to the First Bombay Grenadiers in Allahabad, he settled into a predictable and often dreary routine. "Parade at sunrise . . . play billiards, go out visiting, idle or sleep . . . Out riding until dark, and in the evening sometimes cards. I am really quite sick of it," ran one typical diary entry. But in 1833, Rawlinson joined seven fellow East India Company officers and a contingent of Indian troops to serve as military trainers for the Persian ruler Fath-'Ali Shah Qajar. Thirty-three years earlier, Malcolm, then an East India Company diplomat, had arrived in Teheran laden with pistols, jeweled watches, telescopes, and other gifts, and accompanied by one hundred troops and three hundred servants, and made an alliance with the shah. Now, Imperial Russia was seizing Persian territory, and both the shah and the East India Company felt the need to shore up the relationship. Rawlinson arrived by ship in Bushire, on the southwest coast, that October; he called what would follow "the most momentous change" of his life.

The royal court in Teheran dazzled the now twenty-three-year-old Rawlinson. "A crystal bath . . . occupies the center of the apartment; magnificent chandeliers depend from the ceiling," he wrote about a visit to the shah's reception room. "Cashmere shawls, richly hued, carpet the floor; each recess around the walls holds the most splendid specimens of bijouterie in alabaster, ormolu, and bronze." Rawlinson took a deepening interest in Persia's history, culture, languages, and ancient writing—the long-extinct cuneiform signs that the first Persian kings had used to carve their inscriptions into stone. Before Rawlinson had arrived in Persia, "[a]ll that he knew was, that somewhere in the East there were inscriptions . . . in a strange character," George Rawlinson wrote, "commonly called 'the arrow headed,' that had . . . baffled inquirers, and was generally spoken of as a hopelessly insoluble problem." He had caught a brief glimpse of some ancient inscriptions during the ride north from the coast to Teheran, and he became obsessed with finding more. He wouldn't have to wait long.

In 1834 the aging shah died and his twenty-six-year-old grandson Mohammad Mirza took the throne. The next year, the new Persian ruler designated Rawlinson to act as a military adviser to his brother, the governor of Kermanshah, a province in northwest Persia, the heart of the ancient Achaemenid Empire founded by Cyrus the Great, about 310 miles from Teheran. Kurdish rebels were attacking the governor's troops in the Zagros Mountains, a 990-mile range that runs through what are today Iran, northern Iraq, and southeast Turkey. Rawlinson, for his part, appeared to be more ex-

Henry Creswicke Rawlinson

cited about the opportunity to study a lost writing and language than about rushing to the defense of the shah's brother. He felt a "thrill of satisfaction," George Rawlinson wrote, at the prospect of being posted "in a region richer in antiquarian treasures than almost any other in Persia."

Still, Rawlinson dutifully pursued the rebels through the mountains. "[C]aught the mutineers on the Turkish frontier," he wrote in a diary, and "persuaded them to come back [and] swear allegiance to the Shah." But what satisfied him most was a journey he made to nearby Hamadan, known in ancient times as Ecbatana, the mile-high summer residence of the Achaemenid kings. Close to Hamadan, in a boulder-strewn gorge at the bottom of 11,750-foot Mount Alvand, part of a subrange of the Zagros, stood two panels carved into a slab of granite. Each panel was inscribed with sixty lines of cuneiform, divided into three sections of twenty lines each. Judging from the variations of the signs, they were written in three different languages. The locals believed the more than two-millennia-old inscriptions, which remained undeciphered, contained the directions to a cache of gold and jewels hidden in the mountains. They called the tablets Ganjnameh: the treasure book.

⤙————⤚

Rawlinson didn't know it then, but those enigmatic signs engraved on the rock had their origins in a civilization that was far more ancient than Old Persia. The city-state called Uruk lay in a sunbaked region of plains, marshes, lagoons, and estuaries known as "the land of the black-headed people," the ug-Sag-Giga, five hundred miles south of Hamadan. Modern archaeologists would know the region as Sumer. By 3400 BCE, when the very first pictographs appeared here, the city contained about forty thousand people living closely together in one- and two-story mud-brick houses with reed roofs supported by wooden beams. They cultivated wheat, barley, lentils, dates, sesame, and cotton in the irrigated fields outside a fifteen-foot-high city wall; raised livestock for meat, skins, wool, and milk; and fished in the Lower Euphrates on skiffs made of braided reeds or wood. Traders brought back tin and semiprecious stones from the Iranian plateau, cedar from Lebanon, and copper from Cyprus and Bahrain, known then as Dilmun. Residents used grain, wool, or copper rings to buy goods at street cafés and groceries. Looming over the city was a forty-foot pyramidal structure with exterior staircases called a ziggurat. Atop the ziggurat stood what archaeologists named "the White Temple," covered in reflective gypsum and dedicated to the sky god, Anu.

What was life like for these early urban dwellers? The archaeological evidence suggests that it was surprisingly egalitarian and civic-minded. "[F]ew of these early cities contain signs of authoritarian rule," write the cultural anthropologists David Graeber and David Wengrow in *The Dawn of Everything: A New History of Humanity*. Citizens of Sumer "built spaces in harmonious and often beautiful patterns, clearly reflecting some kind of planning at the municipal scale," and carried out projects "united by devotion to [the city's] founding ancestors, its gods or heroes." Sumerian cosmology was filled with deities responsible for sickness, death, the netherworld, thunder, rain, crops, war, fertility, childbirth, healing—every aspect of life. The primary purpose of mortals, according to Sumerian origin stories, was to plant crops, raise livestock, and build so that the divinities could live in leisure. To that end, temple priests and administrators organized the production of beer, bread, and wine for human consumption and offerings for the gods, owned warehouses where crops were stockpiled, managed farmlands, operated factories and foundries, and oversaw a permanent temple staff and seasonal workforce of hundreds.

In the early 1900s, an archaeological team from the Deutsche Orient-Gesellschaft—the German Oriental Society, founded in Berlin in 1898—excavated hundreds of clay tablets from an ancient refuse dump near Uruk's White Temple. Several fragments, dating to around 3400 BCE, were divided into lined segments. Into each field scribes had etched, using a pointed instrument that predated the trapezoidal stylus cut from a reed, an array of images: human mouths, bowls, stalks of barley, flasks of beer, and numerical signs. These appeared to be records of payments to temple workers—the first known examples of proto-writing. (Uruk had also produced the world's first cylinder seals, rounded semiprecious stones depicting a crouching ram, the head of a lion, a loping gazelle, and other pictograms, worn around the neck to affix one's "signature" to property.) Life had grown complicated in this urban world: commercial transactions could no longer be tracked by memory alone. The early tablets had no grammar, no tenses, no attempts to replicate speech. They consisted of receipts, lists of rations, and other types of bookkeeping, gradually expanding to include names and titles of officials ("leader of law . . . leader of the plow . . . leader of the lambs").

What defined Sumerian writing most was its flexibility. This image of a roasting spit, for example, meant "to cook" or "to roast," or *muhaldim*—a character that appeared in ancient recipes ⚷.

But the sign also came to stand for the truncated *mu*, a word that meant both "name" and "year." A profile of a head with hatching at the point of the mouth could be *dug*, to speak; *inim*, word; *ka*, mouth; or *zu*, tooth ⚐. In contrast to these polyphonic signs, Sumerian had a number of different characters that all made the same sound. Fourteen pictograms had the phonetic value *gu*, including thread ⧨, ox ⧓, and shouting ⧠.

There were unspoken signs, too, known as determinatives, such as the star ✳, which was used to indicate that the following character would be a deity, known in Sumerian as *digir*, or alternatively, *an*.

The critical turning point in writing's development came when scribes realized that pictograms could be separated from the objects they represented and become pure sounds. The pictogram for barley, *she* ⨸, could combine with the sign for milk, *gah*, to connote *she-gah*, which had nothing to do with barley or milk but were simply the sounds that made the Sumerian word for "pleasing." Scribes strung together pictograms that allowed them to conjugate verbs and represent speech: *Ba* joined with *an*, a representation of a sun that meant "heaven," and *du*, a builder's nail, to make *ba-an-du*, "he built." A picture of a tree, *mu*, a stone, *nan*, and *du*, the nail again, made *mu-nan-du*, "he built it for him." With that innovation, scribes could capture language, record history, and write stories that would last. "Men separated by hundreds of miles could now communicate their thoughts," wrote H. G. Wells in his 1920 *The Outline of History*. "An increasing number of human beings began to share a common written knowledge and a common sense of a past and a future . . . [I]t is like a mere line of light coming through the chink of an opening door into a darkened room; but slowly it widens, it grows."

In the middle of the third millennium BCE, schools of writing known as *edubba* sprang up across Southern Mesopotamia. Aspiring government or temple scribes copied and memorized phrases and names of trees, animals, countries, cities, villages, stones, and minerals. They wrote essays describing their daily routine. "I recited my tablet, ate my lunch, prepared my new tablet," declared one fragment from about 2000 BCE, by which point the pictograms had assumed a distinctly wedge-like shape. "When school was dismissed, I went home . . . I told my father of my written work, then recited my tablet to him, and my father was delighted."

Sumerians invented the written contract to confer ownership of slaves, houses, and other property. They created epics, fables, and essays that predated the *Iliad* and the Bible by a thousand years and devised legal codes to protect people from oppressive debt and to punish criminals. Over time literacy spread into every corner of the Southern Euphrates region. Archaeologists have found tablets with writing in the majority of the houses in Nippur, Isin, and other Sumerian cities.

Newcomers from the west pushed aside the people of Sumer at the end of the third millennium BCE. These settlers, who became Babylonians and Assyrians, adapted the Sumerian signs to serve their own language, which would become known as Akkadian. (Modern philologists named the language after Akkad, a Southern Mesopotamian civilization that had thrived for two hundred years after the collapse of Sumer.) The Assyrians and Babylonians rotated the signs ninety degrees, so that by 900 BCE, the roasting spit looked like this: . Similarly, the Sumerian pictogram that meant both "mountain" and "foreign land," , evolved into this Akkadian cuneiform character: . The Akkadian signs acquired new phonetic values, while retaining some of the original Sumerian ones. Here lay the roots of the confusion that would one day come to torment decipherers.

Akkadian cuneiform had, in turn, inspired Old Persian: the simplified combinations of wedges that Rawlinson was now examining on a slab at the base of Mount Alvand near the Turkish frontier. And because texts meaning the same thing in Akkadian and Old Persian often appeared side by side in ancient inscriptions, cracking the Persian code would be the essential first step in gaining the bigger prize: the vastly more complicated and historically more significant writing of the Assyrians and the Babylonians.

As Rawlinson stood alone in the rocky gorge, gazing at the

inscription that supposedly pointed to riches hidden deep in the mountains, he must have been exhilarated by the thought that he had gone where almost no Westerner had ventured before. But Rawlinson was not the first would-be decipherer to take a shot at these baffling signs. The modern race to understand Old Persian, the key to opening the whole linguistic system and recovering the long-hidden past, had actually begun more than fifty years earlier, five hundred miles to the southeast, in the ruined capital of a once-glorious, nearly forgotten empire. So no, Rawlinson wasn't first. But he would soon catch up.

◄◄───────────────►►

CHAPTER TWO

PERSEPOLIS

The wind was howling. In the rain and sleet of a winter night, the *Greenland*, a Danish man-o'-war, forced its way northward through the Kattegat strait, trying to reach the safety of a Norwegian port. Six-foot swells battered the three-mast, square-rigged wooden ship. Norwegian pilot vessels tried to approach to guide it to a harbor, only to disappear in an impenetrable fog. Two sailors fell from the yardarm into the heaving sea and vanished in the darkness. Huddled below deck, seasick and terrified, Carsten Niebuhr, a twenty-seven-year-old cartographer and draftsman from a prosperous farming family in Hanover, prayed that he would make it through the night. "I surrendered myself completely into the hands of the almighty," Niebuhr wrote in his diary on February 8, 1761, "and I . . . retired to my bed for the duration of the gale, while the others had to labour above . . . to ensure the safety of the ship."

Niebuhr had joined four other young scholars from German principalities and Scandinavia on an adventure that had no precedent: a state-sponsored scientific research trip to the Middle East that was expected to last at least five years.

The project was named the Royal Danish Expedition. Its participants were to gather botanical samples, sketch Egyptian hieroglyphs and other ancient writing, draw maps, and search for scientific explanations for scriptural phenomena. They would measure Red Sea tides to understand the exodus of the Israelites from Egypt and identify flora and fauna mentioned in the Bible. Their ultimate destination was to be Arabia Felix, or "Happy Arabia," modern-day Yemen, a terra incognita that was known only as the source of frankincense and myrrh, tree resins used to make incense, medicine, and perfume.

Niebuhr and his fellow adventurers barely made it out of Europe. Five more Danish sailors fell overboard and drowned before the storms subsided in mid-February. The Seven Years' War was raging, and British privateers, believing that the *Greenland* was running contraband, chased it through the Aegean Sea. After gathering plants, studying hydrology, and sketching hieroglyphs along the Nile, the expedition reached the southern Arabian Peninsula on December 31, 1762. That's when an already difficult journey turned into a nightmare. Niebuhr was "affected with a severe rheum, vomiting, and excessive thirst," he wrote, and barely survived a fifteen-day bout of dysentery. Then Danish philologist and theologian Friedrich Christian von Haven fell ill on the Red Sea coast. On May 24, 1763, "[his] fever was become doubly violent, and he was delirious by the evening," Niebuhr remembered. "He then fell into a deep lethargy and expired in the night."

Seven weeks later Swedish natural scientist Peter Forsskåal became desperately sick and died en route to Arabia Felix's highland capital, Sana'a. Niebuhr watched in horror as a mob pried open his coffin in the burial ground and ransacked the corpse in search of hidden valuables. Sticking to a diet of bread, rice, and tea, Niebuhr managed to make the journey on foot back to the coast to meet a ship to Bombay—the easiest means of escape from the toxic environment. The others had to be carried down mountain paths in stretchers. Georg Wilhelm Bauernfeind, a German artist and engraver, and a Swedish servant named Berggren died of cholera or malaria one day apart aboard the vessel; both were buried at sea. The expedition's Danish doctor, Christian Carl Kramer, perished after reaching Bombay. That left Niebuhr alone, filled with grief, four thousand miles from home.

But after slowly regaining his strength in India, the sole survivor of the Royal Danish Expedition made a resolution: he would continue the mission on his own. He had pledged his loyalty to the Danish king; he had worked out a strict dietary regimen that he was confident would keep him alive; and he was insatiably curious about ancient Persia. From India he made his way to Oman, and then sailed through the Persian Gulf to Bushire on the southwest coast. In Shiraz, renowned for its poets and its landscaped gardens, he hired a local Armenian Christian as a servant and guide. The two departed in mid-March 1765 on horseback through the mountains

The ruins of Persepolis, from a history book published in 1885

for a ruined city forty miles away: Takht-e Jamshid, the capital of the first Persian kings, known in Greek as Persepolis.

◄◄───────►►

The name Pars, the ancient heartland of Persia, probably derives from *parça*, or rib cage, referring to the Zagros range that straddles modern Iran's western frontier. Around 900 BCE, a warrior named Achaemenes—reared, according to legend, by an eagle atop a mountain peak—began uniting the tribal chiefs of Pars. Three and a half centuries later a charismatic and ambitious Achaemenid khan, Cyrus, built alliances with the nomadic Medes, who dwelled in the mountains and valleys between the Black and Caspian Seas, and the sedentary Elamites, who lived on the plains, spoke a language with no certain relatives, and had been writing in cuneiform since 2300 BCE.

Cyrus was a fearsome-looking warrior who wore a heavy sheepskin coat, high leather boots, and black kohl, or mascara, smeared around his eyes. In 539 BCE, he led Pars horsemen, along with Medes and Elamites, toward Babylon. "Look! A great army is coming from the north," warned the prophet Jeremiah. "They are armed with bows and spears. They are cruel and show no mercy. As they ride forward on horses, they sound like a roaring sea."

Long gone were the days when Uruk's modest mud-brick houses made the city-state a sophisticated regional power. The early sixth-century Babylonian king Nebuchadnezzar II had created a dazzling metropolis of broad boulevards, palaces with lapis-lazuli facades, fortress-like temples, sumptuous gardens, and bustling marketplaces, bisected by the Euphrates River. "The most famous and strongest" city in Mesopotamia, Herodotus wrote in *Histories*, around 430 BCE, "lies in a great plain, and is in shape a square, each side a hundred and twenty furlongs [fifteen miles] in length. Round it runs first a fosse deep and wide and full of water, and then a wall of fifty royal cubits' thickness [86 feet] and two hundred cubits' [343 feet] height." An azure-and-gold mosaic archway with inlaid golden bulls and dragons, the Ishtar Gate, marked the entrance to the walled Processional Way, lined with 120 glazed-brick lions, bulls, and dragons. At the end stood Babylon's inner fortress, surrounded by a moat and dominated by the bastioned temple of the divine protector, Marduk.

Cyrus's soldiers dug a diversion channel and drained the Euphrates to waist level. Then they waded through the waterway, entered Babylon without a fight, and took prisoner Nabonidus, the city-state's last independent king. Forty thousand Jews, descendants of those taken captive after Nebuchadnezzar II's destruction of Jerusalem almost fifty years earlier, trekked home in joy, celebrating their freedom march as the "second Exodus." Claiming the mantle of Ashurbanipal, an Assyrian ruler who had plundered Babylon in 648 BCE, Cyrus called himself the "king of the universe . . . king of Babylon, king of Sumer and Akkad, king of the four corners of the world." From that point until his death in 530 BCE, he would be known as Cyrus the Great.

Cambyses II, Cyrus's son, expanded the borders of the nascent Achaemenid Empire to include Egypt. Then Darius, a bodyguard in Cambyses II's court and the son of a satrap, or appointed governor, in Bactria, in what is now Afghanistan, seized the throne. The king conquered much of Eastern Europe, coined money, standardized laws, and expanded the highway network created by Cyrus: eight thousand miles of groomed, policed roads extending from the Aegean Sea to the Indus Valley, with supply stations and fresh horses posted every twenty miles to speed the delivery of messages and booty. Two dozen governors collected tributes from vassal states—34,000 kilograms of silver a year from Babylon (according to Herodotus), 23,800 kilograms from Egypt and Libya, 12,240 kilograms from Bactria—and passed the proceeds to the king.

Much of that wealth would fund the ultimate vanity project of the ancient world. In 518 BCE, slaves and prisoners of war began to build a ceremonial capital at the foot of the Kuh-e Rahmat, "the Mountain of Mercy," in Pars. Darius named it Takht-e Jamshid, "the Throne of Jamshid," after a mythical Persian ruler from the dawn of history. "The wealth of this city eclipsed everything in the past," recorded Herodotus, even that of Cyrus's capital, Pasargadae, fifty miles north. "Into it the barbarians had packed the riches of all Persia."

The king covered its palaces and reception halls with inscriptions that described for posterity his noble lineage and his military victories. At the time, the literate elite of Persia wrote their language in Aramaic script, derived from the twenty-two-letter Phoenician alphabet. But Darius would boast that he had invented a new form of writing. Darius simplified the cuneiform of his vassal states, Elam and Babylon, designing characters with wedges that never intersected, making them easier to chisel into lustrous marble walls. The Old Persian cuneiform would remain limited to royal inscriptions, but, because it was always written side-by-side with Akkadian, it would prove to be of vital importance to future philologists. When Darius died in 486 BCE, attendants placed his body in a chariot drawn by sixty-four mules and led it past awestruck subjects to Naqsh-e Rustam, a crypt carved high into a cliff near Persepolis. It, too, was covered with cuneiform inscriptions.

Persepolis kept growing. Darius's son Xerxes I added a gleaming enamel facade to his father's audience salon; built his own palace emblazoned with cuneiform; and started work on the Hall of a Hundred Columns, a cavernous reception area where he received military delegations. His son Artaxerxes I finished Xerxes's reception hall and constructed yet another palace. Later kings added staircases, tombs, and an enigmatic bas-relief of a bearded Egyptian

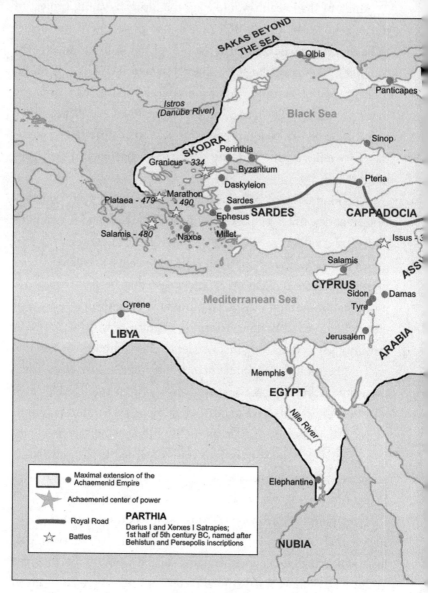

Map of Persia's Achaemenid Empire, showing scenes of significant battles and a section of the Royal Road mentioned by Herodotus in the fifth century BCE

MENIA

Caspian
Sea

Oxus River

Van

Gaugamela - 331

Tigris River

Euphrates River

HYRCANIA

MEDIA

PARTHIA

Behistun   Ecbatana

ARIA

ELAM

BABYLONIA

Cunaxa - 401   Susa

SAGARTIA

Babylonia

PERSIA

Pasargadae

Persepolis

Persian
Gulf

M A K A

sphinx. A huge archive in the city's vaults held all Achaemenid records, written in Elamite, Greek, Akkadian, Demotic Egyptian, Aramaic, and other languages of the ancient world.

⊷————————⊶

The beginning of the end for the Achaemenids came in 334 BCE, when Alexander the Great, hailed by many scholars as a second Achilles, marched east from Macedonia to avenge a massacre at the Parthenon and the burning of Athens in an invasion led by Xerxes's general, Mardonius, 145 years before. Four years after Alexander set out, his thirty-five-thousand-man army climbed through the Zagros Mountains and approached the gates of Persepolis, where they encountered some eight hundred Greek slaves who had been kidnapped over the years and recently released from captivity. "All had been mutilated, some lacking hands, some feet, and some ears and noses . . . [Alexander] was unable to restrain his tears," wrote Diodorus Siculus, a first-century BCE Greek historian. The king described Persepolis to his men "as their worst enemy among the cities of Asia, and he gave it over to the soldiers to plunder."

Bursting through the gates, Alexander's soldiers looted houses, killed every male inhabitant, rounded up the women as slaves, and broke into the "treasure house" and seized 2,500 tons of gold and silver; vessels made of alabaster, marble, lapis lazuli, and turquoise; cylinder seals; jewels; carpets; and ritual incense holders. With a blow of his sword, a soldier lopped the head off the Penelope in Persepolis, a statue of Odysseus's wife brought home by Xerxes after sacking Athens. "A quantity of torches was collected," Diodorus wrote. Alexander and a favorite courtesan, Thaïs, threw in the first incendiaries, and "the whole area of the royal palace was quickly engulfed in flames." The days of Achaemenid glory were over, Alexander declared. Darius III, the defeated king, was hunted down and stabbed to death.

And so the Achaemenid kings disappeared from history, their writing also consigned to oblivion. Local rulers stripped Persepolis of much of its stonework for their own palaces. A new power, the Parthians, moved into southwestern Iran around 140 BCE, determined to restore Persian glory. They ruled for almost five hundred years, then surrendered to the Sassanian dynasty, adherents of the Zoroastrian faith. In 651 CE the Sassanian Empire fell to the Arabs, and Persia became an Islamic state. The seventeenth-century historian Mahmud Harvai visited Persepolis, but made no mention of Darius, who seemed largely forgotten. "In a mountain cleft . . . the building of the *chihil minar* [Persian for "forty minarets"] is one of the wonders of the age," he wrote. "Its builder was Jamshid and Eskander-e-Rumi [Alexander the Great] . . . ordered its demolition."

◄◄─────►►

Carsten Niebuhr "could not rest until he reached Persepolis, and the last night he did not sleep," wrote his son, Barthold Georg Niebuhr, in *The Life of Carsten Niebuhr, the Oriental Traveller*, in 1836. As he and his servant descended through the Zagros Mountains toward a 5,600-foot-high plateau on the morning of March 17, 1765, the sunbathed ruins of Takht-e Jamshid came suddenly into view. Hours later he was walking among marble portals, staircases, lintels, and other remains of temples and palaces spread across a terraced platform a mile long and two-thirds of a mile wide, about one and a half times the size of London's Hyde Park. Niebuhr admired the complex's dozens of fluted gray-limestone columns, topped by twin-bull and twin-lion capitals, probably symbols of the triumph of spring at Nowruz, the Persian New Year. A set of marble steps led to the royal complex of Xerxes. A pair of fantastical creatures—winged, human-headed bulls, which archaeologists would later determine had been inspired by lamassus, Sumerian protective deities—stood guard at the gate.

Nearby, at the Audience Hall of Darius, dominated by thirty-six decorative columns and a portal guarded by two more of these colossal beasts, a profusion of bas-reliefs on the walls captured the splendor and breadth of the Achaemenid Empire: gift-bearing delegations of Egyptians, Parthians, Arabs, Babylonians, Nubians, and Ethiopians paid homage to the king. (Most exotic were the Ethiopians who, clad in leopard and lion skins and painted with vermilion and chalk, had joined the Persian army when Xerxes invaded Greece in 480–479 BCE. "These Aethiopians wore on their heads the skins of horses' foreheads, stripped from the head with ears and mane," Herodotus wrote in the *Histories*. "For shields they had bucklers [worn on the forearm] of cranes' skin.") The vassals bore as tributes okapis, one-humped and two-humped camels, a lion and her cubs, elephants, and other exotic animals from Africa and the steppes of Asia. Surviving flecks of color derived from minerals— Egyptian blue, azurite, malachite, hematite, cinnabar, yellow ochre, and the rare green tyrolite—hinted at the friezes' original opulence. "The image of these ruins remained indelible his entire life," Barthold Georg Niebuhr wrote. "They were the jewel of everything he had seen."

Niebuhr recorded the dimensions, construction materials, and architectural flourishes of columns and portals, and took notes about the attire, weaponry, jewelry, facial hair, and other characteristics of hundreds of procession members. But the inscriptions on the walls, doorways, and bases of platforms intrigued him even more. Unlike the Egyptian hieroglyphs that he had sketched in temples and tombs along the Nile, the signs seemed to bear no connection to physical objects. Perhaps they had originated as pictograms, he thought, but they'd turned into pure abstractions.

＊＜────────＞＊

Niebuhr was not the first Westerner to find himself pondering the meaning of these strange, wedge-shaped characters. In 1618, Garcia de Silva y Figueroa, a Spanish soldier and diplomat, had arrived in Persia under orders from King Philip III to strengthen a military alliance with the shah against the Ottoman Empire. "This place, without any doubt, must be the ancient Persepolis," he wrote that April, comparing it to descriptions by the Roman historian Quintus Curtius Rufus, Diodorus Siculus, and Plutarch. Figueroa provided the first recorded mention of the characters on the city walls. "There is a remarkable inscription carved on black jasper," he wrote to the Spanish ambassador to Venice. "Its characters are still clear and sparkling, astonishingly free from damage or deterioration despite their very great age. The letters . . . are neither . . . Hebrew nor Greek nor Arabic nor of any people that can be discovered now or to have ever existed."

Four years before Figueroa's visit, an Italian aristocrat, Pietro della Valle, had embarked on a pilgrimage to the Holy Land. He traveled on to Baghdad, where he wooed and wed a young Syrian Christian woman, and then journeyed with her on a sort of extended honeymoon to Persepolis. The inscription in the Palace of Xerxes "occupies the entire height of the wall from top to bottom," he wrote back in Europe many years later. "One cannot tell in what language or letters the inscriptions are written, because the characters are unknown." Della Valle sketched five characters, giving Europeans their first look at the written language of ancient Persia.

〈𐎢 𝀇 𐊫 〵 《𐎢

He was "induced to believe" from the "slope" of the characters that the script should be read from left to right. Others believed—wrongly, it would turn out—that it should be read from right to left, like Arabic and Hebrew, or from top to bottom, like Chinese or Japanese. The Italian nobleman's study of the writing came to a tragic end when his bride gave birth to a stillborn child and died near Persepolis. Unwilling to bury her in "the land of infidels," della Valle embalmed her corpse in camphor, and lugged it in a coffin around Asia for five years. He returned to Rome with the mummified remains in 1626 and interred them in the family sepulcher on the Capitoline Hill.

Thomas Herbert, a courtier to King Charles I, was equally mystified by the writing. "In part of this great roome (not farre from the portal)," he wrote around a decade after a 1628 visit, "wee noted above a dozen lynes of strange characters, very faire and apparent to the eye, but so mysticall, so odly framed as [to resemble] no Hieroglyphick." He believed that the writing would be "well worth" the scrutiny of those dedicated to "the dark and difficult Art or Exercise of deciphering." A Middle Eastern languages scholar named Anton August Heinrich Lichtenstein soon took up the challenge. Convinced for some reason that the wedges concealed messages written in Kufic Arabic—an elegant, angular script used in Quranic calligraphy—Lichtenstein translated one inscription as "The King, the Sovereign, Prince of all Princes, the Lord Saleh, Jinghis, son of Armerib, governor-general for the Emperor of China, Orkahn Saheb." It was an ambitious effort—but pure fantasy.

For a century the biggest debate over the writing at Persepolis concerned the very nature of the signs. Were they vowels and consonants? Syllables? Logograms, with each sign representing a word or an idea? In the mid-1600s, Jean Chardin, a French Protestant who had fled to England to escape religious persecution and served as the court jeweler to King Charles II, counted a total of fifty different characters in one lengthy inscription. That was close to the size of the English alphabet or the thirty-character German alphabet (which also includes the letters *ä, ö, ü,* and *ß*). Chardin reasoned that the system had to be phonetic. But when Engelbert Kämpfer, a German Orientalist and naturalist, looked at a different inscription, he counted hundreds of unique characters. The writing, he concluded, had to be composed of logograms.

Kämpfer, who had spent two years studying local plants and acupuncture in Nagasaki and Edo, imagined that he was eyeing something like Japanese, a hybrid consisting of two thousand regularly used logograms that every sixth-grader needs to know, along with two syllabaries. (In syllabaries each sign consists of a consonant-vowel combination; alphabets use separate signs for vowels and consonants and form syllables by joining the two.) A purely logographic system akin to Chinese requires a knowledge of many more characters—around eight thousand. They range from the two-stroke *rén,* meaning "man" 人, to the awesomely complex, sixty-two-stroke *biáng,* a noodle dish 𰻞. But Kämpfer saw no evidence to suggest that the Persian system had anywhere near as many logograms.

As these early decipherers debated, some linguists argued that the script had no meaning whatsoever. Thomas Hyde, the Regius chair of Hebrew and Laudan professor of Arabic at Oxford, dismissed attempts to decipher the characters as a "waste of time" in his 1700 book, *On the Ancient Religion of the Persians.* Hyde inspected two rows of characters from Persepolis sketched by an agent for the East India Company and concluded that the signs— which he named *ductuli pyramidales seu cuneiformes,* the "wedge-shaped" script, coining a term—couldn't constitute real writing. The inscriptions were obviously "an experiment," he said—"graffiti" dreamed up by ancient Persian scribes to see how many combinations of wedges they could invent.

-◄-————➤-

At eight o'clock on his second morning at Persepolis, Niebuhr, carrying his sketchpad and pencils, hiked from his guesthouse to the ruins in the chill of late winter. Frost covered the surrounding fields, burning off around 11 a.m. For the next twenty-four days, he labored in near-constant sunlight, interrupted by brief thunderstorms, drawing until it grew dark. Niebuhr focused first on pillars, capitals, and bas-reliefs. But soon his attention turned to the inscriptions. Sitting and standing for hours before cuneiform-covered slabs of marble, Niebuhr drew the characters with near-perfect fidelity. "These are all broken lines," he wrote about one damaged fragment. But, he added, "even this little bit can acquaint the scholar with the alphabet that was used in Persia at the time, and who knows whether we might be able to learn something from it."

By late March the frigid morning temperatures and drenching rain had given Niebuhr a miserable cold and cough. Worse, copying the inscriptions with the sun's glare reflecting off the marble was afflicting his eyes. "Those inscriptions on the higher parts of the walls could be distinctly traced only when the sun's ray fell upon them," Niebuhr's son wrote, "and, in this atmosphere, the hard and originally polished black marble does not decay so as to lose its polish. The eyes of the traveler, already strained by his incessant labor, became dangerously inflamed." One morning, Niebuhr woke up blind. He was forced to remain in bed until his sight returned twenty-four hours later. The next day he returned to the ruins and continued his work, with the blazing sun shining off the polished walls and white paper and beaming directly onto his retinas.

In early April, Niebuhr's Armenian servant became sick and,

a few days later, died. Shocked by the death, Niebuhr gathered up nearly a month's work—a forty-three-page report about the architecture; eighty-nine illustrations; and copies of hundreds of lines of inscriptions—saddled his horse, and departed Persepolis for Shiraz. He wasn't ready to go. "If my servant had stayed fit and well I would gladly have stayed at the ruins," he wrote, "but my eyes had suffered so much, and my health was . . . so weak that there was no room for taking excessive risks." (He would be plagued by eye trouble for the rest of his life and would die, at eighty-two, almost totally blind.)

Niebuhr made it back to Copenhagen in November 1767. He had been gone for nearly seven years. He returned with hundreds of hand-drawn regional and city maps from across the Orient, one of the largest contributions to cartography of the eighteenth century. But his greatest legacy was stirring up interest in the Achaemenid Empire and shedding light on the writing. Niebuhr's sketches of cuneiform signs, reproduced in his two-volume memoir, *Travels to Arabia and Other Countries in the East*, published in 1774 and 1778, allowed armchair-bound scholars across Europe to try their hand at deciphering this seemingly impenetrable script. Many couldn't resist the challenge, and over the next half century would rely on Niebuhr's skillful drawings to try to pry open the history and culture of the Persian kings.

Equally important, Niebuhr was the first to see that the inscriptions were written not only in Old Persian but also in two other languages. All three used wedges, but the characters were different: Niebuhr found only a single sign in the Old Persian that was replicated in the other two. The number of signs also varied from script to script. Old Persian was the simplest; by Niebuhr's count it contained forty-two unique characters. The other two languages each employed hundreds of unique signs—probably combining a

phonetic alphabet with logograms. This would explain the opposite conclusions reached by Jean Chardin and Engelbert Kämpfer:
Chardin was looking at Old Persian; Kämpfer was examining one
of the others.

Niebuhr was also convinced that the trilingual inscriptions all
said the same thing. A decade earlier, a French Oriental-languages
scholar, Abbé Jean-Jacques Barthélemy, had observed inscriptions
written in both classical Greek and an undeciphered script, on columns in the ancient desert city of Palmyra, in Syria. Barthélemy,
who read Greek, made the assumption that they were identical
texts. He compared the Greek inscriptions—eulogies for local
dignitaries—with the unknown parallel texts and deciphered the
local writing, known as Palmyrene, related to Aramaic, in forty-
eight hours. If the Persepolis scribes had written their multilingual
inscriptions with the same intention, then one set of texts could be
used to unlock the meaning of the others.

But Niebuhr didn't go any further. He considered himself a ge-
ographer, a scientist, and an artist, not a decipherer. It would be left
to others to coax the first sounds and meaning out of the cuneiform
inscriptions—to hear the Achaemenid kings speak after more than
two thousand years of silence.

CHAPTER THREE

BEHISTUN

W hen Henry Rawlinson first set his eyes on the cuneiform inscriptions known as Ganjnameh, "the treasure book," in 1835, he knew he faced a problem that had perplexed scholars and travelers for centuries. Rawlinson had no background in decipherment, and he was dealing with, wrote one academic, "a species of Asiatic writing of the most remote antiquity . . . the alphabet, the language, and the contents, were equally unknown." But he was a natural linguist: his facility with Hindustani had earned him a job as an interpreter for the First Bombay Grenadiers. Also, he had become deeply acquainted with Persian history on the passage to India with the soldier-scholar Sir John Malcolm and during his years in Teheran. As he made progress, he was likely to note references and patterns in the signs that other scholars wouldn't catch. Robert William Rogers, a professor of theology and Hebrew at Drew Theological Seminary, would write in the early twentieth century that the best decipherers demonstrated "the patience, the persistence, the power of combination, the divine gift of insight, the historical sense, [and] the feeling for archaeological indications." Rawlinson had both the historical sense and a feeling for archaeology; he was about to discover whether he had patience, persistence, and insight.

Now he stood beneath snow-capped mountains in a remote canyon in northwest Persia, a few miles from Kermanshah, studying two panels carved in a granite boulder. Each panel contained sixty lines of cuneiform, divided into three sections. And each section was written with distinctively different signs from the others. Rawlinson was seeing what Niebuhr had noticed in Persepolis: evidence that the ancient scribes had employed three cuneiform-based languages.

Rawlinson focused on the first and what seemed simplest of the three writings: Old Persian. It was known among scholars by now that King Darius had introduced cuneiform in the sixth century BCE, and that it had endured until the destruction of the dynasty by Alexander two hundred years later. The twenty lines of text, he reasoned, should be filled with praises of Darius and, perhaps, other Achaemenid kings. He noted that the two Old Persian texts were identical, except for three distinct groups of characters. These groups were placed in a different order in each inscription: "It was only reasonable to suppose," he wrote, "that the groups which were thus brought out and individualized must present proper names."

ⵌ. ⵍ. ⵓⵏⵞⵔ. ⵟⵟ. ⵏⵥⵞ
ⵔ.ⵟⵟ. ⵓⵏ. ⵏⵞⵔⵓⵟⵞⵡ.
ⵘⵟⵟ. ⵡ. ⵏⵞⵔⵟⵟ. ⵓⵏⵡⵟⵟ

Returning from the canyon to his base in Kermanshah, Rawlinson consulted the authoritative narrative of the Achaemenid dynasty, *The Histories of Herodotus*, which he'd brought with him, and made another conjecture: the jumble of signs made up the names of three consecutive rulers, grandfather, father, and son. "At hazard," he wrote, he applied the names of an Achaemenid satrap named Hystaspes; his son Darius; and Darius's son Xerxes. Rawlinson believed that Old Persian was alphabetical, and noticed that the number of characters in the names roughly matched the number of Greek letters.

It was a decent place to start. In 1713, the German polymath Gottfried Wilhelm Leibniz had proposed that the best strategy for deciphering an unknown writing system and language was to first identify proper names. By lining up the unfamiliar characters with their equivalents in a known alphabet, one could approximate their phonetic values. (The Japanese, for instance, spell Joseph Biden in katakana, a special syllabary for foreign words: ジョセフ·バイデン, which comes out as Ji-o-se-fu Ba-i-de-n. Russians, who use the Cyrillic alphabet, write Джозеф Байден, pronounced *Djoʒef Bayden*.) The problem, Rogers noted in *A History of Assyria and Babylonia*, was that the Greeks "were not careful to reproduce exactly the names of other peoples who were, in their view, only barbarians." So "Hystaspes," "Darius," and "Xerxes" were unreliable reference points. To obtain the true sounds made by the Old Persian letters, Rawlinson needed to recover a language that hadn't been spoken in over two thousand years.

Rawlinson found the answer in Avestan, a living language spoken by the Zoroastrians, followers of the prophet known to the Greeks as Zoroaster—Zarathustra in Old Persian. A camel herder in either Afghanistan or Azerbaijan around 1000 BCE, he had traveled across the Persian plain to preach a doctrine based on the worship of a benevolent god, Ahura Mazda, the "Wise Lord." Zoroaster's religious incantations, commentaries, and teachings were disseminated orally at first by priests known as magi, who performed their rituals while imbibing a hallucinogenic drink made from the mashed twigs of the haoma plant, most likely the stimulant *Ephedra sinica*. But a written Avestan alphabet with thirty-seven consonants and sixteen vowels developed during Persia's Sassanian era between the third and seventh centuries CE. The Islamic conquerors drove most followers of Zoroaster out of Persia, and they took refuge in India, where they continued to practice their monotheistic religion, known in India as Parsee. (The Parsees are best known for placing their dead to decompose and be devoured by vultures on raised, circular "towers of silence" rather than burying them.) Parsees still use Avestan in religious ritual and study, carefully preserving the language and writing in their sacred book, the Avesta.

While in India in the 1750s and early 1760s a Parisian Orientalist, Abraham Hyacinthe Anquetil-Duperron, collected copies of the Avesta, which had never been seen in Europe. Nine years after his 1762 return to Paris, he published a French translation, with a dictionary of hundreds of words, including names of Persian kings. Avestan and Old Persian were not perfect matches, and Anquetil-Duperron's transliterations of the Avestan words were often imprecise. Nevertheless, the dictionary provided Rawlinson with a good idea of how the Achaemenids would have pronounced the kings' names. To back up the dictionary research, Rawlinson consulted, he wrote, "a few Zend [manuscripts] obtained in Persia and interpreted for me by an ignorant priest of Yezd [sic]," an ancient desert city near Isfahan famed for its Zoroastrian fire temple—in which a sacred flame, symbolizing purity, has burned for over 1,500 years. (The name "Zend" was often used incorrectly to mean the Avestan language; in fact, the term referred to the annotations, commentaries, and translations of Avestan texts.)

Looking at the seven characters that composed the name he believed was Darius, he came up with DARAYAVAUSH, assigning tentative phonetic values to each sign.

𐏐𐏐𐏐 𐏐𐏐 𐏐 𐏐𐏐𐏐𐏐 𐏐𐏐𐏐𐏐𐏐
D   A   R(A)   YA   VA   U   SH

He did the same with Xerxes and Hystaspes, which Anquetil-Duperron's Avestan dictionary transliterated, respectively, as

KHSHYAARSHA and GOSHTASP. He aligned the transliterations with the cuneiform characters and obtained phonetic values of a dozen signs. These transliterations would prove to be somewhat off the mark. But it was a beginning, and it would soon be followed by a more significant breakthrough.

◂———▸

In the spring of 521 BCE, on his way home after defeating a rebel army in the far western corner of Persia, King Darius came upon a cliff located at the end of a range twenty miles east of Kermanshah. Flush with pride after his latest military triumph, the king chose the site, on a busy stretch of the Silk Road, to celebrate his subjugation, torture, and execution of those who had risen against him.

Three hundred thirty feet above the plain, Darius's sculptors carved on the smooth rock face a colossal bas-relief showing the Persian king, armed with a bow, representing his sovereignty, and accompanied by two attendants, with ten captured rebel leaders from across the Achaemenid Empire. One prisoner lay face down under Darius's left foot. Nine lined up behind the first, connected to one another by a rope around their necks, hands tied behind their backs. (The first prisoner would be gouged out of the rock at some point in antiquity, leaving only a ghostly impression.) The *faravahar*, a winged sun disk with a seated male figure in its center, hovered above the monarch: the figure was possibly Ahura Mazda, the supreme god of the Achaemenid pantheon, who had the sun as his eye, and, with the aid of six "bounteous immortals," protected humanity from Ahriman, the leader of demonic hordes. (The monotheistic Zoroastrians, who were contemporaneous with the Achaemenid kings, used the same name for their deity.)

Below, above, and to the left and right of this bas-relief, scribes etched on the rock wall approximately 1,120 lines of cuneiform

The carvings of Darius the Great at Behistun, from an
1863 issue of the French publication *Le Tour du Monde*

in the three primary languages of the empire, now known to be
Elamite and Akkadian as well as Old Persian. These inscriptions
stood side by side, proclaiming Darius's triumphs to countless pilgrims and traders on the Silk Road over the centuries.

After the Achaemenids fell from power, the meaning of the cuneiform writing was lost, and Darius's imagery sank into obscurity.
The carving became a kind of Rorschach test, reflecting the back-
grounds and biases of its observers. The Greek historian Diodorus
Siculus, writing around 60 BCE, called the cliff "Bagistana"—"the
place of the gods." He declared that the bas-relief was a self-portrait
done by the mythical Assyrian queen Semiramis, who, he said, had
climbed to the rock face by piling up the packs and saddles of her
beasts of burden. In his interpretation, the eight figures lined up ab-

jectly before her became "one hundred lance-bearers." Ibn Hawqal, an Arab traveler who saw the bas-relief in the mid-900s, believed it represented a teacher punishing his pupils. An eighteenth-century French diplomat concluded that the figures were Jesus Christ and the twelve apostles being blessed by the divine light of God.

The Scottish artist and traveler Robert Ker Porter, who visited in 1818, contended that the figures represented the Assyrian king Shalmaneser V from the Old Testament, and the ten Jewish tribes that his army expelled from the Kingdom of Israel. John Macdonald Kinneir, a Scottish East India Company officer who passed by Behistun in 1810, thought the frieze resembled bas-reliefs that he'd seen inscribed on the walls of the palaces at Persepolis, particularly "the floating intelligence in his circle" hovering above. Kinneir was on the right track and by the 1830s, a consensus was building among travelers and scholars that the bow-carrying figure was Darius the Great, and that the men lined up before him were defeated insurrectionists. But close-up scrutiny of the Behistun images and inscriptions would be difficult, Porter warned: "At no time can [the climb] ever be attempted without great personal risk."

In July 1840, a French painter and archaeologist, Jean-Baptiste Eugène Flandin, tried to reach a ledge just below the frieze to sketch the Old Persian characters arranged neatly underneath the image. Removing his shoes to avoid slipping on "the polished and perpendicular rocks," he would recount in his memoir, *Voyage en Perse*, he hauled himself up the cliff, seeking foot- and handholds in a few crevices. "I feared with every movement that I'd plunge to the bottom," he recalled. After some minutes, "[m]y tired, scratched fingers no longer had the strength to hoist me up and I was about to let go." Flandin's hand gripped the rock protrusion. He summoned his last strength, and scrambled onto the ledge. Then he realized that sketching the inscriptions—or even obtaining a decent view of them—was out of the question. "The height of the inscriptions, the narrowness of the ledge, forced me to press myself against the rock, without being able to step back," he wrote. "I had climbed for nothing."

The descent was just as perilous. Grabbing on to the cliff face with his fingernails and working his way down was like doing "lizard gymnastics," Flandin remembered. "I was bruised, cut by the sharp angles of the stones, all torn and bleeding." In the end, he wrote, "the study of antiquity is assuredly a noble pursuit, but what do we have to put ourselves through in the process?" The French antiquarian commission that Flandin had been a part of concluded that climbing Behistun was "impossible."

◂—————▸

Henry Rawlinson had ridden to Behistun for the first time in the winter of 1836—four years before the Frenchman. (It seems that neither Flandin nor anyone on the French commission was aware of that visit.) Arriving at the foot of the cliff from Kermanshah, accompanied by a few Persian servants, he set up camp beside some springs and a stream that paralleled the old caravan route. The camping was rough and primitive, but Rawlinson was accustomed to an unadorned lifestyle: an inventory of his expenses for daily life in Kermanshah, the northwestern Persian city where he'd gone to fight a Kurdish rebellion, includes little more than "lump sugar, tea, milk, charcoal and wood, shoes, boots, thread, candles, handkerchiefs, sealing wax and slippers" as well as "barley straw" and "three sets of horseshoes." Also listed were salaries for three full-time servants, plus a coffeemaker and a "waterman." He and his team had to be entirely self-sufficient: the bas-reliefs of Behistun drew occasional curiosity-seekers, but the remote area had just one nearby village with few permanent inhabitants.

With the uprising in the Zagros Mountains suppressed, Rawlinson felt free to throw himself wholeheartedly into his scholarly passion. Which, for him, meant risking life and limb. "The rock was bare, slippery, in places almost precipitous," recounted his brother George. Rawlinson scaled the cliff, presumably with a ladder on his back, and propped it against the rock face on the narrow ledge. Rawlinson managed to maneuver the ladder and twist his body in such a way that, unlike Flandin, he could obtain clear views of both the inscriptions at eye level and the frieze above.

From this precarious perch, he obtained the first intimate look at the bas-relief since Achaemenid times. Darius's carvers had used molten lead to fill in holes in the rock surface, he noticed, and coated each character with silicon-based varnish to provide a sheen. The varnish "had been washed down . . . by the trickling of water for three-and-twenty centuries," George Rawlinson wrote, "and it lay in flakes upon the foot-ledge like thin layers of lava." The scribes, Henry Rawlinson believed, must have erected scaffolding to reach the heights, "unless there were secret staircases, known to the guardians, of which there is at present no appearance."

Balanced on the top rung, steadying his body against the escarpment with his left arm, and holding his notebook in his left hand, he began by copying a series of short cuneiform texts contained in comic-strip-like bubbles around the prisoners' heads above him. "The interest of the occupation entirely did away with any sense of danger," Rawlinson wrote. It was a challenge, "such as any person with ordinary nerves may successfully encounter." Though Flandin would struggle four years later, Rawlinson made the climb, his brother wrote, "three or four times a day for many days together without any assistance whatsoever."

Rawlinson's primary interest—the main body of the text—lay just below the bas-relief. It consisted of five columns of Old Persian. Four columns contained 96 lines each, while the fifth had 32, making 414 lines in total. Rawlinson sketched with growing confidence. An "immense advantage . . . is obtained," wrote Thomas Young, the English scholar who made the first inroads into hieroglyphs, "by the complete sifting of every letter which the mind involuntarily performs, while the hand is occupied in tracing it." Rawlinson made one important observation early in his sketching: the Persian scribes appeared to separate words with a diagonal wedge ◣.

(Niebuhr and other scholars had made the same discovery, but Rawlinson at the time was unaware of their work.)

Some signs were already familiar to him. The first word of the first column he recognized from the inscriptions of Ganjnameh: it was the Persian king Darius. 𒊗𒆷𒁷 𒀹𒐊𒁹𒐊.

If the rest of the script followed the usual template, a list of the king's ancestors came next. After returning to Kermanshah, Rawlinson again consulted the *Histories*. In the seventh chapter he found what he was looking for: a quote from Xerxes as he prepared to lead his army into Greece to avenge the Persians' defeat under his father, at the Battle of Marathon in 490 BCE, ending an ill-fated invasion. Xerxes invoked eight forebears: Hystaspes, Arsames, Ariaramnes, Teispes, Cyrus, Cambyses, a second Teispes, and the founder of the dynasty: Achaemenes. It was a trove of proper names.

He studied his sketches. At the end of line four of the first column, Rawlinson spotted a word consisting of five characters. From DARAYAVAUSH he thought he knew the values of four of them: *A, R, SH*, and the same character *A* again. This, he conjectured, ought to be Arsames—or ARSHAM, as it would have been pronounced in Old Persian, according to the Avesta. He filled in the value of the new character: *M*. Further along he thought he saw the Old Persian version of Teispes: TISHPAISH. That provided him with the cuneiform characters *T* and *P*. He repeated the method for all eight of Darius's ancestors, picking up the values of another half dozen Old Persian characters.

In a letter to his sister, Rawlinson reported that he had made "considerable progress." He reminded her gleefully that she had once mocked him as "an ignoramus . . . attempting to decipher inscriptions which had baffled for centuries the most learned men of Europe." Yet Rawlinson made it clear that deciphering Old Persian was only the first step on a long journey. Certain that they were three versions of the same text, he believed the trilingual inscriptions of Behistun could function like the Rosetta Stone, the stele that bore the same inscription in three ancient writings of second-century BCE Egypt: classical Greek, hieroglyphs, and Demotic, a simplified version of ancient Egyptian.

If he could understand the Old Persian, which contained just a few dozen characters, he could then attempt to match proper names, per Leibniz, and pry out the sounds and meanings of the other two cuneiform scripts of the Achaemenid Empire. "I aspire to do for the cuneiform alphabet what Champollion has done for the hieroglyphics," Rawlinson wrote, bursting with self-confidence. "My character is one of restless, insatiable ambition—in whatever sphere I am thrown my whole spirit is absorbed in an eager struggle for the first place."

◄─────►

Back in Teheran for a respite, Rawlinson learned that a number of others were competing for first place. Inspired by a German academic, Georg Friedrich Grotefend, and relying on Niebuhr's Persepolis sketches, several of Western Europe's most distinguished philologists were making progress solving the Old Persian conundrum.

Grotefend, a high school Latin teacher in Göttingen in Lower

Saxony, had by his admission lacked "any profound acquaintance with oriental languages." Yet he had had a "remarkable aptitude for the solution of riddles," one biographer wrote. In 1802, Grotefend had a brilliant idea: he studied short texts on royal tombs dozens of feet below the crypt of Darius at Naqsh-e Rustam near Persepolis. These were written for kings of the Sassanian dynasty, the final monarchy to rule Persia before the Arabian caliphate conquered the land in the seventh century CE. The writing and language were known to be Pahlavi, closely related to Aramaic, a language still spoken by several hundred thousand people, including Kurdish Jews and Mandaeans, a sect of monotheists who worshipped John the Baptist.

The Pahlavi inscriptions, which had been deciphered years earlier, always began with the template: "X, king, great king of kings, king of nations." Grotefend conjectured that the Sassanians had simply borrowed the phrase from the Achaemenids. He then selected two short inscriptions sketched by Niebuhr at Persepolis, both the exact same length as the Sassanian ones. Grotefend noticed immediately a seven-character sequence that recurred eight times in the two Old Persian inscriptions. ⟨⟨Ⲓ. ⧖. ⪆⸱Ⲕ⸲.ⲔⲒ . ⨼.Ⲓ⪇

"I felt convinced," he recounted in his memoir, "that [any] word so often repeated must signify 'King.' " Grotefend consulted the Avesta, acquired the Old Persian name for "king," KH-SCH-E-H-I-O-H, and thus obtained the phonetic values of the seven cuneiform characters. In all, Grotefend deciphered thirteen Old Persian characters, including those that spelled Darius and Xerxes, and translated several lines of Persepolis texts. One biographer would call Grotefend's work "a gem of brilliant simplicity," while Kevin Cathcart, emeritus professor of Near Eastern languages at University College Dublin, hailed Grotefend's achievement as a profound "leap of the imagination."

Others had expanded on and tweaked Grotefend's discoveries. French philologist Antoine-Jean Saint-Martin obtained the phonetic values of half a dozen characters, which he revealed in the 1822 edition of the *Journal Asiatique*. The German scholar Christian Lassen published more in *The Old Persian Cuneiform Inscriptions of Persepolis*. Lassen's friend and rival, the Danish professor Rasmus Rask, put out a partial translation of the Ganjnameh inscriptions in 1823. The scholars quibbled with one another over the precise phonetic values of characters, the prevalence of diphthongs (sounds formed by two adjacent vowels), the total number of signs in the alphabet, the nature of the writing system (was it purely alphabetic or partly syllabic?), as well as the origins of the Old Persian language. Yet all were inching close to Rawlinson.

Around 1827 Rask had a breakthrough. The Dane noticed that the Old Persian word for "king" in the Persepolis inscriptions was often followed immediately by a second "king"—though the second time it always had four extra characters appended to it. Rask deduced that he was looking at a possessive ending, making the phrase "king of kings." Through trial and error, he deciphered the ending as *an-am*. 𒌝 𒅍 . 𒌝 . 𒀀𒅀 .

That happened to be identical to the possessive ending in Sanskrit, the sacred language of Hinduism that had arisen in India around 1500 BCE. Was Sanskrit an even closer relative of Old Persian than the language of the Zoroastrians? Certainly, Avestan and Sanskrit shared grammatical structures and had many cognates (words that have the same linguistic derivation): *nara* and *nar* for "man," *âsmi* and *ahmi* for "I am," *mantra* and *manthra* for "utterance," *yajna* and *yasna* for "sacrifice," *asura* and *ahura* for "lord," and hundreds more. So it was possible Old Persian had much in common with both.

Rask's discovery reflected a growing fascination with languages and the relationships among them. In the early eighteenth century Gottfried Wilhelm Leibniz posited that the descendants of the three sons of Noah—Ham, Shem, and Japhet—had spread three linguistic groups around the world. He named one "Japhetic," for European, and the second "Aramaic," for Semitic tongues. A third would be called "Hamitic," for some languages found across Northern Africa. William Jones, a Bengal Supreme Court judge and the founder of the Asiatic Society in Calcutta, the precursor of the Royal Asiatic Society of Great Britain and Ireland, found that language families didn't conform so easily to geographic areas. Regarded as the founder of philology, Jones discovered connections between Sanskrit, which he called the "great parent of Indian languages," and European tongues, including Greek, Latin, German, Lithuanian, and English. Later philologists would identify 265 words in modern Persian, also closely related to Sanksrit, with cognates in European tongues, including *pedar* ("father," Latin *pater*), *mader* ("mother," Spanish *madre*), *dokhtar* ("daughter," *Tochter* in German), and *div* ("devil," *diavolo* in Italian). Jones called these the "Indo-European family" of languages and suggested that all of them had come from one proto language in Central Asia many thousands of years earlier. Now, it seemed Rawlinson needed to understand as many of them as possible.

From Teheran, Rawlinson contacted booksellers in Europe. Reference materials, transported through the Mediterranean and the Black Sea and on horseback across the mountains and plains of Asia Minor, arrived at his residence. He also studied the methodologies of his growing number of competitors. Eugène Burnouf, a young French Orientalist, would choose a character he didn't recognize, randomly assign it an alphabetic value, plug it, *Wheel of Fortune*–style, into a word the rest of whose characters he understood, and then pore through Avestan and Sanskrit dictionaries to see if the result made sense. Burnouf assigned the letter *b* to a character he had found in Persepolis, for example, and came up with *Bakhtroch*—the Persian form of "Bactria," a satrapy, or province, below the Hindu Kush mountain range in Afghanistan that served as an early center of Zoroastrianism. Burnouf then took that *b*, plugged it into a specific word in the Ganjnameh inscription, and came up with *bu*—a slight variation on the Sanskrit *bhu*, which means "to be." Both words made sense in context. Rawlinson applied similar methods and began building up his knowledge.

He studied grammar and vocabulary in the Oxford professor Horace Hayman Wilson's *Sanskrit-English Dictionary*, which offered a wealth of information about the ancient Indian tongue. The University of Berlin philologist Franz Bopp had recently confirmed Jones's theory that ancient Greek belonged to the same Indo-European family as Sanskrit and Avestan, so Rawlinson immersed himself for the first time since his school days in the language of Herodotus. He committed to memory the entire geography of the Achaemenid Empire—every province, town, mountain, and river—to better recognize proper names in the inscriptions. He went word by word through the paragraphs from Behistun, filling notebooks with observations about etymology (the study of word origins) and orthography (the reasons that words are spelled the way they are). Slowly, the Achaemenid Empire, the dominant power of Western Asia for two centuries, was revealing its secrets.

←——→

In January 1838, Rawlinson introduced himself to the Royal Asiatic Society. Founded in 1823 at the Thatched House Tavern (a onetime favorite of Jonathan Swift's) near Piccadilly Circus by fifteen retired officers of the East India Company, the society reflected the growing European fascination, stirred up by Niebuhr and a handful of other adventurers and travel writers, for the culture, languages, and ancient civilizations of "The Orient," especially those of the Indian subcontinent. Fifteen years on, the group was still small, with about 350 members, but it had become one of the most distinguished scientific and educational institutions in Great Britain. Queen Victoria was a patron, and half a dozen former prime ministers and many other luminaries were on its membership rolls—Sir Moses Montefiore, George Everest, Belgium's king Leopold I, the shah of Persia, the maharajah of Travancore, and US president Martin Van Buren. In its fifteen short years of existence, the society had already supported investigations by German naturalist Alexander von Humboldt into South Pacific languages; an exploration of the kurgans, or Neolithic burial mounds of southern Russia; and the preservation of illuminated manuscripts in the Coptic monasteries of Upper Egypt. Society-backed scholars published their reports in the quarterly *Journal of the Royal Asiatic Society*.

Rawlinson was twenty-seven years old, unknown, with no academic credentials, yet his introductory letter exudes self-assurance, even a certain cockiness. "On my arrival in Persia about four years ago, I applied myself with diligence to the study of the history, geography, literature and Antiquities of the country," he wrote to the society's secretary, Captain Henry Harkness. "I accordingly applied myself (with no very sanguine hopes of success however) to the task of deciphering these inscriptions." After working on the Old Persian for two years, he added, he was writing to share "some very interesting researches which I am now enjoy[ing] in the country . . . the results of which I am anxious to communicate to the world thro' the Journal of the Royal Asiatic Society." His work was all original, he assured the society, "grounded solely on my own copies of the inscriptions at Hamadan and Bisitoon [*sic*]."

The society's linguists could see that Rawlinson had made more progress than any of his peers. He identified not simply the names of Persian rulers but also many ordinary vocabulary words, like the Old Persian for "fire," *athash*, as in "[t]he fire-worshipping king." (Avestan and Sanskrit provided him with *atash*, allowing Rawlinson to recognize the Old Persian cognate.) Transliterating what he could of the Old Persian signs and searching for the likely Avestan and ancient Greek equivalents, he found a string of kings and places: "king of kings, king of Persia, king of Media, son of Hystaspes, grandson of Circsames . . . [descendant of] Achamaneus . . . Darius is the heavenly king, sprung from Hystaspes." He prepared two more articles and promised to deliver a translation of the entire ninety-six-line first column inscription from Behistun as soon as possible. "If I keep my health, I should certainly be able by next month to send the packet off to you," he assured the secretary in 1839. To his sister he gloated again: "You remember laughing at me for trying to read these arrow heads, do you now? Let him laugh who wishes. Depend on it I shall only be a short way in hind of Champollion . . . some day." (Champollion, who had died six years earlier, had been immortalized as "the father and founder of Egyptology," though he had never made a stab at cuneiform.)

Then, politics and war intervened.

CHAPTER FOUR

KANDAHAR

In 1807, alarming intelligence reached the Foreign Office in London. An informant had eavesdropped on secret talks between Emperor Napoleon Bonaparte and Tsar Alexander I aboard a river barge in the Russian town of Tilsit. According to the spy, purportedly a disaffected Russian nobleman, Napoleon had proposed marching fifty thousand French troops across Persia and Afghanistan to join forces with Russia, and seize India from the British. The two despots soon fell out, and in 1815 Napoleon met his decisive defeat at Waterloo. But over the next two decades, the Russians inched closer and closer to the subcontinent. They seized much of the Caucasus, including Georgia, Armenia, and Dagestan, from Persia, marched to within forty miles of Constantinople, and cemented their hold over the ancient khanates, or tribal kingdoms, along the Silk Road in what are now Uzbekistan and Turkmenistan.

John Macdonald Kinneir, one of several prominent Scottish soldier-scholars of the era, argued in influential books such as *A Geographical Memoir of the Persian Empire* and *A Journey Through Asia Minor, Armenia and Kurdistan, in the Years 1813 and 1814* that Russia would scheme to enter India overland by one of several routes in Central Asia. The only way to stave off an invasion, Lord

Ellenborough, a member of the Duke of Wellington's cabinet, said, was to monitor and counter Russian moves in the vast no-man's-land between the two empires. "Indian army officers, political agents, explorers and surveyors were to criss-cross immense areas of Central Asia," wrote Peter Hopkirk in *The Great Game: On Secret Service in High Asia*, his classic account of the imperial rivalry, "mapping the passes and deserts, tracing rivers to their source, noting strategic features, observing which routes were negotiable by artillery, studying the languages and customs of the tribes, and seeking to win the confidence and friendship of their rulers."

It was a soldier-scholar-adventurer named Arthur Conolly who in 1840 had coined the phrase "the Great Game" to describe the intrigue, competition, and skullduggery between the British and the Russians. In his *Journey to the North of India, Overland from England, through Russia, Persia, and Afghanistan*, Conolly predicted that if the tsar's army invaded, it would establish a foothold on the subcontinent through Herat, an ancient city in northwest Afghanistan that lay on a caravan road a few dozen miles across the border from Persia. Alexander the Great, the Sassanians, and the Mongols had all captured the city; Persia had held it from the mid-sixteenth century until 1746. Conolly warned in his book, informed by his own journey along the route, that if Herat ended up in Russian hands, or was annexed by a pro-Russian Persia, the Russian army "might be garrisoned there for years, with every necessity immediately within its reach." The only way to prevent that from happening, he argued, was by ensuring that Britain had a strong ally in Afghanistan who would resist all invaders.

At the royal court in Teheran, the young shah Mohammad Mirza had once confided to Rawlinson that his goal was to rebuild the Persian army into a force of "100,000 disciplined troops and . . . revive the days of Nadir [*sic*] Shah," the powerful founder of the

Afsharid dynasty. (In 1739 an invading army led by Nader Shah stole the Peacock Throne, the bejeweled royal seat built for the Mughal emperor Shah Jahan, from the Red Fort in Delhi; the original throne, embedded with the famous Koh-i-Noor diamond, disappeared and was probably dismantled after Nader Shah's assassination by his own men thirteen years later.) In 1837, without warning, he sent an eight-thousand-man army across the Afghan border to capture Herat. The Persian troops dug trenches around the walled city, dodging Afghan sharpshooters on the ramparts, and the shah showed up at the scene to try to rally his troops and convince the Afghans to surrender. The British, unsure about Mirza's ultimate goal, saw the invasion as a destabilizing move and demanded that the Persian invaders withdraw.

Rawlinson soon found himself drawn deep into Great Game intrigue. On a 750-mile horseback ride from Teheran to Herat to assess the shah's intentions, he encountered "men in Cossack dress" on "the broken plain." Rawlinson followed them to camp and met their commanding officer, "a young man of light make, very fair complexion, with bright eyes and a look of great animation." The man, he learned to his alarm, was a Russian agent, Yan Vitkevich, carrying presents from the tsar to Mohammad Shah to cement a Russian-Persian alliance.

Vitkevich's next destination, Rawlinson ascertained, would be Kabul, where he was to meet Dost Mohammed Khan, the British-supported ruler of Afghanistan. Menaced by rival warlords and worried that the British might switch their loyalties, Dost Mohammed had become receptive to Russia's attempts to lure him to their side. If Vitkevich could win him over, nothing would stand between the tsar and India. Rawlinson rushed back to Teheran to warn the British legation.

A Scottish agent named Alexander Burnes was soon dispatched

to the king's Kabul fortress, Bala Hissar, on the back of an elephant, with a warning not to deal with the tsar. But in April 1838, Dost Mohammed met with Vitkevich at the fortress and fatefully sealed an alliance.

As tensions in the region grew, the governor-general of India withdrew the British ambassador from Teheran and directed Rawlinson to leave Persia at once for Ottoman-controlled Baghdad. For Rawlinson, this geopolitical brinksmanship meant the end—at least temporarily—of his cuneiform studies. "In the state of public affairs in Persia since I last wrote to you," Rawlinson informed the Royal Asiatic Society secretary, "I have found it quite impossible to fulfill my promise of forwarding you a copy of the great Behistun Inscription." Soon Britain broke off relations with the shah.

In July 1839 a twenty-one-thousand-man British-Indian force, including regular troops and the East India Company's private army, marched from the Indian Punjab through the Bolan Pass toward Kabul to unseat Dost Mohammed. Rawlinson's chance encounter on the Persian plain had touched off a war. The troops captured Kandahar without a fight. They overran the fortress at Ghazni in a bloody battle, stormed Kabul, and forced Dost Mohammed into exile. The British restored a ruler more to their liking, the former Afghan king Shah Shuja Durrani, who delighted in hacking off the noses, tongues, penises, and testicles of courtiers and slaves who displeased him.

In January 1840 the British government ordered Rawlinson to Kandahar, a mud-walled city sitting between Herat and Kabul, to serve as political agent for the East India Company in southern Afghanistan. For the next two years, alongside the chief of the British garrison, General William Nott, Rawlinson would help hold off hostile Pashtun warriors determined to expel the British invaders. Fiercely protective of their economic interests, both the firm and the British government regarded the continued occupation of Afghanistan as essential to protect India from Russian expansionism.

The First Anglo-Afghan War would illustrate the dual nature of Rawlinson's character—the British imperialist who exulted in killing Afghan fighters and the scholar who found delight exploring the arcana of Avestan and Sanskrit. In this, he was part of a grand tradition of soldiers who lived second lives as men of letters. The line stretched back to Cato the Younger, the great Roman politician, Stoic, and military leader in the first-century BCE war against the Thracian gladiator and escaped slave Spartacus; and Niccolò Machiavelli, the Florentine writer-diplomat who organized an army of citizen-soldiers loyal to the pope to capture Pisa from the Holy Roman Empire in 1509. Less than a century after Rawlinson would come T. E. Lawrence, the archaeologist, writer, and leader of the Arab Revolt against the Turks in World War I. All would later be held up as the very pinnacle of masculinity.

Rawlinson's illustrated stories for his two sons, written decades after the Afghan war, stressed his military escapades. He described with relish a battle outside Kandahar in 1842, in which he led troops up a hill on horseback in pursuit of a force of Pashtun warriors: "Away I went on my black Arab [steed] and they followed at a tremendous pace. One poor fellow was killed by my side. We routed them and I pursued the Chief . . . up the hills till we came to the pass. Any Afghans I met I cut down with my sword, but the chief got away." Galloping far ahead of his men, Rawlinson found himself face-to-face with a gray-bearded fighter. The Pashtun raised his blunderbuss, but the gun misfired. "I dropped my sword, seized one of those very pistols you have seen in my room, and bang it went, one bullet in the forehead and one in the head, and down he dropped dead," he wrote. "I turned round, [and] to my horror found my Afghan servant had brought me the heads of three of my victims."

While Rawlinson held off Pashtun warriors in Kandahar, the British forces in Kabul faced a rebellion they couldn't suppress. In January 1842, twelve thousand British soldiers under the command of Major-General William Elphinstone, along with their Afghan allies and dependents, began a ninety-three-mile retreat from Kabul toward the British garrison at Jalalabad through the snow-bound Hindu Kush. There, they came under attack from Afghan guerrillas. Thousands in the column died of exposure or starvation, or were killed during the fighting. Only one European, a British army doctor, made it out alive. "Army destroyed on Retreat from Cabul," Rawlinson wrote tersely in a diary. His position grew increasingly fragile. "Night attack on the town of Candahar," he recorded. In September, Rawlinson and his troops received an order from Lord Ellenborough, the governor-general of India, to evacuate Kandahar "and retire by Cabul to India."

◄◄————►►

And so, in the summer of 1843 Rawlinson found himself on a steamboat on the Ganges River, recovering from what he called "a severe attack of brain fever." Demoralized by the Afghan debacle, he had been grappling for the past half-year with another crisis: a fire had broken out on a boat transporting Rawlinson's records of the East India Company's expenses and provincial revenues in Kandahar. "Nothing remained of the papers but a mass of blackened scraps and half-burnt fragments," one biographer later recounted of the blaze that burned the vessel "to the water's edge" as it descended the Sutlej River in Punjab. Rawlinson's superiors in Bombay and London, who accepted no excuses for failure, had ordered him to reconstruct every expense, totaling £1 million (today worth about $159 million), obliging him to patch it all together from charred receipts and interviews with everyone with whom he'd engaged in a financial transaction. The "lamentable accident," the biographer wrote, "caused him six months of the most intense anxiety, and threatened to bring his official career to a disastrous end." Rawlinson managed to complete the task and get himself off the hook. But the Great Game had stopped feeling like a game, and he was contemplating a return to England.

Yet, as the 120-foot vessel steamed downriver from Allahabad, passing sand banks, gaudy Hindu temples, and cremation pyres, a chance encounter with a fellow passenger—none other than Edward Law, Lord Ellenborough—once again determined his future. Charmed by the younger man's good manners and grasp of geopolitics—and doubtless impressed by his family background— Ellenborough offered Rawlinson his pick of any open diplomatic post in the region. Rawlinson turned down the Residency in Nepal. "He was somewhat weary of governing half-civilised Orientals," his brother George would explain, in the casually racist language of nineteenth-century Britain. "[He] longed to get back to those linguistic and archaeological investigations which had engaged his attention . . . in Persia."

That left Rawlinson with only one option: the head of the "political agency" in Ottoman, or Turkish, Arabia, based in Baghdad, a backwater of the Ottoman Empire. The job, in a city surrounded by Bedouin tribes agitating to free themselves from Turkish rule, had such marginal importance that the East India Company had considered eliminating it. Rawlinson regarded it as the perfect assignment. The British had few vital interests in Turkish Arabia, also referred to as Mesopotamia. As long as war didn't break out, his job would principally consist of showing the flag and creating financial opportunities for British traders and other businessmen. And Behistun, with its hundreds of lines of undeciphered cuneiform, was just a 258-mile horseback ride away. Rawlinson was an expert horseman who, as a teenage soldier in India, had once covered the seventy-three miles between the towns of Poonah (Pune) and Panwell (Panvel) in three hours and seventeen minutes, a regimental record. He could make that journey to Persia in just three days.

But as Rawlinson contemplated resuming his work at Behistun, the attention of linguists and archaeologists was shifting to the deserts of Northern Mesopotamia. There, thanks to the efforts of a pair of adventurers, one French and one English, an unprecedented variety of Akkadian inscriptions—older and vastly more complex than the Old Persian—was beginning to emerge from the earth.

CHAPTER FIVE

ON THE
MESOPOTAMIAN PLAIN

I n early spring 1840, two bedraggled English travelers climbed
onto the roof of a house in Mosul, a decrepit trading center
and regional hub on the west bank of the Tigris River. Austen Layard and Edward Mitford had been on the road for nearly
six months and were now, they guessed, about halfway through an
overland journey to Ceylon. After encounters with brigands, rebels, and warlords in the Balkans and Asia Minor, the companions
had just arrived atop their half-dead horses in a region that had once
been the heart of ancient Assyria, the vanished empire whose triumphs and collapse had been chronicled by Old Testament prophets and Greek historians. "From the top of the houses the view of
the river and the Koord Mountains to the north is very fine," wrote
Mitford, "and in front spread the numerous mounds forming the
tomb of the Glories of Nineveh."

According to the ancient Greeks, Nineveh, the last capital of the
Assyrian kings, had been sacked and torched in the summer of 612
BCE. The remains of the city disappeared beneath layers of sand
and debris, swept over by desert winds. Whatever treasures Nineveh
once held, it was almost universally believed, had burned to ashes

during the invasion or later decomposed. "Desolation meets desolation," Layard wrote. "A feeling of awe succeeds to wonder; for there is nothing to relieve the mind, to lead to hope, or to tell of what has gone by." Yet Layard was not convinced that the glories of Assyria had simply crumbled into dust. The huge mounds, or tells, of Nineveh might have served as a protective cover, sealing off a civilization's wonders for millennia. The mounds, he wrote, "made a deeper impression upon me, gave rise to more serious thoughts and more earnest reflection, than the temples of Balbec and the theaters of Ionia," a center of Hellenistic culture during the third and fourth centuries BCE.

◂─────▸

Henry Austen Layard had been born in March 1817 in Paris, where his father, of Huguenot descent, had moved the family in the hope of recovering his health after contracting asthma—often a death sentence—in the British civil service in Ceylon. Later they relocated to Pisa, then Florence. Young Layard spent his days being homeschooled in a rented fifteenth-century palace and wandering the halls of the Uffizi Gallery, where he marveled at the works of Giotto, Martini, Bronzino, Titian, and other masters of the Italian Renaissance. In the evenings, curled up on a rug beneath a gilded table in the living room, he read and reread The Arabian Nights, the Middle Eastern folktales narrated by Scheherazade for the Sassanian king Shahryar. "My imagination became so much excited by it that I thought and dreamt of little else but 'djinns' and 'ghouls' and fairies and lovely princesses," he recalled many years later.

The idyll ended when Layard was thirteen. His parents moved back to London and placed him under the guardianship there of his mother's brother, Benjamin Austen, a prosperous lawyer who believed that his nephew needed discipline and a proper education. In

France, still anti-British in the wake of the Napoleonic Wars, Layard's Catholic classmates had regarded him with "hatred and contempt" and tormented him as "a Protestant and a heretic." At the Richmond School in London, his peers bullied him over his knowledge of French and Italian, and his continental airs: "We had little or nothing in common," he recalled. "I had tastes which seemed repugnant to them, and my head was crammed full of things and ideas which they despised." Layard's invalid father died of asthma in October 1834, when he was seventeen, and his uncle offered him a clerkship in his law office. The job held little interest for him, but Layard knew he had no choice. His widowed mother lacked the money to send him to university.

In Benjamin Austen's chambers, Layard carried out clerical tasks in equity, contract, and tax law. In the evenings he sat alone in his room in a Bloomsbury boardinghouse, thumbing through English common law tracts such as *Commentaries by Blackstone* and *Coke upon Littleton*. But he often put aside those books to play the flute, read Petrarch and Boccaccio, and daydream about walking in the Tuscan hills. While in Paris, Layard had met Henry Crabb Robinson, a former *Times* of London correspondent, a friend of Johann Wolfgang von Goethe, and a member of a literary circle that included William Wordsworth. The older man invited Layard to gatherings, and regaled him with stories of covering the Battle of Waterloo. Benjamin Austen would accuse Crabb Robinson, Layard wrote, of "having unsettled my mind, and of having encouraged in me pursuits and tastes entirely opposed to the serious study of law . . . The charge was perhaps well founded." Layard had changed his first name to "Austen" in gratitude to his uncle, but legal study, he wrote, "became repugnant to me, and all my efforts to persevere in it were in vain."

In 1838 another uncle—his father's younger brother—arrived in London from Ceylon, on leave from his position as a district judge in Colombo. Confronting his nephew's unhappiness, Charles Edward Layard proposed that he move to the colony; if practicing law there didn't work, he told him, he could always try his hand at coffee planting in the countryside. When Layard broke the news to Austen that he was quitting and heading to try his luck in the east, the older man reacted with relief. By now he had become convinced, Layard wrote, "that I . . . should make a very bad lawyer."

Before he could set out for Colombo, friends introduced him to Edward Ledwich Mitford, six years Layard's senior, who had just left his job with a mercantile house in Morocco and planned to start a new life growing coffee in Ceylon. Fearful of traveling by sea, Mitford proposed they ride horses together along an overland route through much of the Ottoman Empire, then across Persia, Afghanistan, and India. It would be a one-year journey on the cheap, with only a compass to guide them. In the best case, it would enable Layard "to realise the dreams that had haunted me from my childhood, when I had spent so many happy hours over *The Arabian Nights*," he wrote. But "[m]y relations looked upon the scheme as a somewhat insane one."

Layard left England by steamer on July 10, 1839. He carried a double-barreled shotgun, a pair of pistols, enough clothes to fit into one portmanteau, a cloth sleeping sack with an attached mosquito net, and a silver watch painted black to avoid arousing "the cupidity of the wild tribes through which we were to pass." He had a modest inheritance from his late father, and a £200 advance, worth about $24,000 today, to write a travel memoir—a booming new genre in the publishing industry.

Books such as John Hawkesworth's 1773 *An Account of the Voyages Undertaken by Order of His Present Majesty for Making Discoveries in the Southern Hemisphere*, chronicling Captain James Cook's Pacific journeys, and the German naturalist George Forster's

1777 *A Voyage Round the World* had fueled a fascination for stories of global adventure; William Daniell and Richard Ayton's eight-volume 1814–25 *A Voyage Round Great Britain*, meanwhile, heightened the appeal of the peripatetic life closer to home. "Narratives of voyages and travels . . . are of all books, perhaps, the best calculated to excite a strong and general interest in reading on the part of the community," the *Annual Review* had declared in 1805. With road networks improving and ordinary citizens enjoying more leisure and greater mobility, the English poet Samuel Taylor Coleridge in 1825 captured the restless spirit of the time: "Keep moving!" he urged in "The Delinquent Travellers." "Tour, Journey, Voyage, Lounge, Ride, Walk / Skim, Sketch, Excursion, Travel-talk— / For move you must! 'Tis now the rage / The law and fashion of the Age." In the 1830s the publishers John Murray and Karl Baedeker produced the first travel guidebooks to Continental Europe. Around the same time, Lord Byron's journeys on horseback and on foot through the eastern Mediterranean and Albania created a vogue for getting "off the beaten track" and escaping what the English travel writer Alexander William Kinglake called "the stale civilization of Europe."

Layard's own travel reading of choice for his journey was a ninety-page article in the *Journal of the Royal Geographic Society of London* by one Henry Creswicke Rawlinson, whom he had never met but who would soon play a transformative role in Layard's life. *Notes on a March from Zohab, at the Foot of Zagros, along the Mountains to Khuzistan (Susiana), and from Thence through the Province of Luristan to Kirmanshah, in the Year 1836* was filled with richly detailed accounts of Rawlinson's treks into remote Persian valleys and up fourteen-thousand-foot peaks on the hunt for ancient inscriptions. It was the kind of exploration of Eastern antiquity that Layard himself imagined making. (Mitford was less enthusiastic, dreaming more about coffee plantations in the verdant Ceylonese

Portrait of Austen Henry Layard

hills.) As the steamer pulled out of Portsmouth, Layard experienced a wave of euphoria at what lay ahead. "I was now independent," he wrote, "and no more exposed to the vexatious interference and control . . . that I greatly resented."

◂───────▸

By the time Layard and Mitford set out for Ottoman territory, the sultans had ruled a huge swath of Asia and Southeast Europe for about five hundred years. The early-fourteenth-century conqueror Osman I, the self-described "marchlord of the horizons, hero of the world," had led his Muslim holy warriors out of the steppes of Anatolia and defeated the Byzantines at the Battle of Dimbos in what is now western Turkey in 1303. Then the Asian army crossed the Dardanelles into the Balkans, gaining a European foothold. Bulgaria,

Thessaly (part of modern Greece), Serbia, Macedonia, and Albania all fell. His descendant Mehmed II's armies swept over Constantinople in 1453. By the late 1830s, the sultan ruled from the Persian Gulf to Bosnia, and from the north coast of the Black Sea to Yemen. But in recent years the Empire had begun to lose its grip. Catherine the Great had seized Crimea and regions around the Black Sea in a war with the Ottomans in the 1780s. Two decades later "Black George," the son of a Serbian peasant, took to the mountains and began chopping the heads off the hated Janissaries, a once-elite Turkish military force that had turned into a gang of lawless thugs. In 1821 the Greeks revolted after years of brigandage by Turkish security forces; a combined English, French, and Russian fleet fighting for the Greeks annihilated the Turkish fleet at Navarino Bay in 1827, and Greece was granted independence. In the Middle East, a charismatic Egyptian governor named Muhammad 'Ali, one of seventeen children of an Albanian night watchman, defeated an Ottoman force in Syria and declared his region independent in 1838. The "ferocious conqueror has degenerated into a torpid barbarian," the British historian William Eton had written as far back as 1798.

For Layard, seeking an escape from the stifling orthodoxy of Victorian England, Ottoman territory marked the transition point. In Montenegro, a mountainous Adriatic enclave allied with the Serbs, Layard and Mitford visited the *vladika*, or prince-bishop, at his palace in the ramshackle capital, Cetinje. "On a low round tower . . . was ranged a horrid array of forty-five human heads stuck on lances and blackening in the sun," Mitford observed. Trophies of a raid on the Turks, who were brutally keeping the Montenegrins under their control, the heads had, Layard noted, "long tufts of hair waving in the wind." As Layard and Mitford watched in horror, a gang of Montenegrin fighters soon arrived, opened a sack, and dumped another pile of bloody heads, including those of children, at the prince-bishop's feet.

The companions crossed Albania, another Balkan backwater on the edge of rebellion. They rode through the barren Judean Hills to Jerusalem, from which Layard, breaking off temporarily from Mitford and ignoring the warnings of local Arabs, traveled with guides and camels to Petra in modern-day Jordan. Carved out of red sandstone, the fortress city had been the capital of the ancient Nabataean kingdom, a Bedouin Arab state that controlled vital trade routes from Damascus to Arabia from the third to the first century BCE. In a desolate canyon near the ruins a Bedouin gang attacked Layard and his guides and robbed them of everything they had. Still, Layard kept going, meeting up again with Mitford in Aleppo, Syria, and dragging his increasingly dubious companion with him. Impulsive, headstrong, and heedless of danger, he seemed to be driven by a sense of destiny—a belief that he had been chosen to accomplish something grand.

After descending the Zagros Mountains and splashing through flooded meadows abundant with wildflowers, Layard and Mitford arrived in Mosul, the gateway to the mounds of Assyria, in the spring of 1840. Located on trade routes between China and the Mediterranean, the city had prospered as an outpost of ancient Persia and again during the Rashidun Caliphate that began in 632 CE. Except for a few opulent villas, medieval mosques, and handsome churches, it now had "a mean and poverty-stricken appearance," observed Layard. Windowless, mud-walled hovels lined the alleys, and whole neighborhoods lay wrecked and abandoned. Stagnant pools of water and rotting corpses of camels and cattle filled the open ground between city walls and the town. "[It] is enough to breed a pestilence," wrote Mitford. At dusk, the sky, he observed, "is alive with bats, which fly high, and afford sport to numerous kestrels, that pick them off, and eat them while hovering in the air."

Layard and Mitford took a ferry from the waterfront toward the main mound of Nineveh, known as Tell Kuyunjik, passing a collapsed bridge across the river that the Ottoman government had neglected to repair for years. A smaller mound known as Tell Nabi Yunis, the site of a mosque supposedly containing the remains of the prophet Jonah, or Yunis in Arabic, lay nearby. Layard took measurements of Kuyunjik and picked up fragments of cuneiform-inscribed brick but found nothing that suggested substantial remains of palaces lay buried underneath the soil. It is "one of the most remarkable facts in history," he observed, "that the records of an empire, so renowned for its power and civilization, should have been entirely lost."

He and Mitford spent a week exploring inscription-covered debris on the surface but lacked the money to hire workers. Plus, Mitford wanted to keep moving: his destiny, he believed, lay in the tropics. "A deep mystery hangs over Assyria," Layard wrote, before setting off down the Tigris with Mitford on a twelve-foot-by-eight-foot raft—"our frail and strange vessel," as Layard called it—fashioned from fifty inflated goat and sheep skins stitched together by willow twigs. As the companions oared toward Baghdad, Layard resolved to return to the mounds. "I was convinced that they must cover some vestiges of the great capital," he wrote, "and I felt an intense longing to dig into them."

◂———▸

The book of Genesis contends that Ashur, a son of Shem and a grandson of Noah, left Sumer in the third millennium BCE and founded a city at Qal'at Sherqat, forty miles south of Mosul. On a rocky crag 120 feet above the Tigris, he erected a ziggurat, dedicated to the goddess Ishtar. Diodorus Siculus contended that it was a king known as Ninus who had founded Assyria in 2189 BCE. Ninus conquered all the lands between the Nile and the Don Rivers, the Greek historian claimed, and met his queen, Semiramis, during a siege in modern-day Afghanistan. Born in Ashkelon, it was said, to a fish goddess and a mortal, and then abandoned in the wilderness, Semiramis was nurtured by doves and rescued by shepherds and took the throne of Assyria after Ninus's death. A commander of armies and an irresistible seductress, she became "the most renowned of all women of whom we have any record," Diodorus declared.

Modern archaeologists offer yet another version of the empire's origins. They believe that a trading settlement called Ashur began to thrive on the Tigris around the nineteenth century BCE. After several hundred years under the rule of the Mitanni Kingdom in Anatolia, the city gained independence around 1300 BCE and began to expand its territory. The Ashur kings seized lands east of the Tigris and as far west as the Zagros Mountains, exacting tributes of gold, livestock, slaves, and crops from their vassal states. Assyria became a nation-state devoted to war and conquest, backed by a huge army of professional soldiers, supplemented by seasonally levied troops, and marked by lethal innovations that gave it a technological advantage over its enemies.

Corps of engineers traveled with the soldiers to battlefields across the Near East, deploying mobile ladders to cross moats, and turreted "siege engines" with battering rams to punch through ramparts. Two-wheeled chariots, drawn by four horses, smashed enemy formations. After cities fell, the Assyrian troops rounded up tens of thousands of captives and deported them to other territories. This strategy weakened potential opposition to Assyrian rule and distributed labor around the realm. "The king . . . carried the Israelites away to Assyria," 2 Kings declared, after the conquest of Samaria in 722 BCE, begun by Shalmaneser V and completed by Sargon II. "He placed them in Halah, on the Habor, the river of Gozan, and in the cities of the Medes." By then, Assyria had seventy-five provinces and a Royal Road, a well-kept unpaved trail that stretched from western Anatolia to Afghanistan.

Soon, all roads led to Nineveh. In 705 BCE, King Sargon II was killed at around the age of sixty while leading a military campaign in Anatolia. A monarch needed to be buried in a sealed stone sarcophagus and placed with lavish offerings deep in the subterranean tombs of Ashur, to prevent the corpse from haunting the living. But the Assyrians never recovered his body, and his son and successor, Sennacherib, feared that his reanimated corpse might roam his capital, Dur-Sharrukin, searching for discarded food. The *Epic of Gilgamesh*, the Babylonian narrative from 1800 BCE, with which Assyrian kings would have been familiar, described the unburied dead chasing "scrapings from the pot and crusts of bread that are thrown away in the street."

To escape his father's ravenous spirit, Sennacherib relocated the capital thirteen miles south, to a then-modest settlement that had been populated for six thousand years. He built an eighty-room palace adorned with bas-reliefs, and filled Nineveh with orchards and landscaped gardens, kept lush by an aqueduct that transported water from the hills. He constructed inner and outer walls pierced by fifteen gates, dug eighteen canals, and laid out grand avenues and squares. For a hundred years, Nineveh was the largest urban center in the world.

It was also a constant instigator of violence. One frequent target was Babylon, located 340 miles to the south, which had fallen under Assyrian control toward the end of the thirteenth century BCE but was rarely comfortable in the subordinate role. Both cities were populated by Semitic peoples who shared a script and a language—noted by an early-nineteenth-century European adventurer who compared the writing on Babylonian bricks and the Akkadian inscriptions at Nineveh. Babylon's grandiose, glazed mud-brick architecture; its latticework of irrigation canals that sliced through the alluvial plain; and its patron god, Marduk, ruler of the universe and slayer of the sea monster-goddess Tiamat, the incarnation of chaos, captivated the Assyrian kings. In 729 BCE Tiglath-Pileser III proclaimed himself "King of Babylon," and walked at the head of a New Year's procession to honor and renew Marduk's power.

Twenty-five years later Sargon II covered his palace walls with allusions to the Babylonian creation myth, which celebrates Marduk's destruction of Tiamat with a huge gust of wind that inflated the monster's body. An arrow then cleaved her in two, creating heaven and earth.

But whenever Babylon tried to wrest itself from Assyrian domination, the kings made their displeasure known in brutal ways. In 698 BCE, Sennacherib put down an uprising with what he called "an orgy of destruction," then he tore out the religious heart of the city. Assyrian soldiers absconded with the cultic bed of Marduk, which the god shared with his wife, Zarpanitu, and his golden statue from the Ésagila temple, near Babylon's ziggurat. The priests of Ashur offered the bed to Assyria's eponymous supreme god and his wife, Mullissu. The relics remained in Ashur until Sennacherib's son Esarhaddon rebuilt Babylon and restored them to the temple.

Esarhaddon's son Ashurbanipal, who rose to power in Nineveh in 669 BCE, took uglier revenge on his vassal state. When his jealous older brother, Shamash-shum-ukin, Babylon's governor, organized a rebellion, Ashurbanipal surrounded the city's walls with troops and starved its population. "They ate dogs and mongooses," his inscriptions declared. "They gnawed on animal hides, leather straps, shoes, and sandals. Instead of bread they ate the flesh of their sons; instead of beer they drank the blood of their daughters. They became like corpses." In 648 BCE, after a two-year siege, the Assyrian army captured Babylon, murdered thousands of starving people, fed their bodies to "dogs, to pigs, to wolves, to eagles, to birds of the heavens," and plundered the governor's palace. Shamash-shumukin died in a raging conflagration, according to Ashurbanipal's annals, though it is unclear whether he was killed by the conquering army or took his own life.

Stories like these gave the Assyrians a reputation for unparalleled brutality among ancient conquerors. In 1918 Albert T. Olmstead, an American historian of the Near East, compared the atrocities inflicted on subdued peoples by Ashurbanipal and other Assyrian kings to the wanton slaughter of the Great War. Nearly a century later the British historian Paul Kriwaczek wrote that the empire "must surely have among the worst press notices of any state in history . . . their famous rulers . . . rate in the popular imagination just below Adolf Hitler and Genghis Khan for cruelty, violence, and sheer murderous savagery." But the British military expert Simon Anglim insisted that the Assyrians needed to be examined in the context of their time. The Romans, he wrote, "made a point of lining their roads with . . . victims of crucifixion dying in agony."

Some Assyriologists argue that practices of seemingly gratuitous cruelty turned out, upon closer examination, to be surprisingly merciful. For all the trauma the policy of deportation caused, they say, the defeated took their families, farm animals, and other belongings with them; received ample food and water on their long journeys; and if they were single, were even matched with spouses in their new locations. And the empire valued attributes beyond military might. Stephanie Dalley, an Oxford Assyriologist, maintains that Assyria's brutality was balanced by its imaginative literature, art, and religion—although this view is far from universal. The nineteenth-century historian Jacob Burckhardt, in his *Reflections on History*, criticized the "utterly uncouth royal fortresses of Nineveh, the meanness of their ground-plan and the slavishness of their sculptures."

The Old Testament prophets foretold Nineveh's destruction. Nahum spoke of "the bloody city, all full of lies and booty." Zephaniah, who followed Habbakuk in the line of the twelve minor Hebrew Prophets, predicted that God "will stretch out his hand against the north and destroy Assyria, and he will make Nineveh a desolation." In 612 BCE, the Babylonians, joined by other former vassal states, came for revenge. By the time the assailants had left, the world's most powerful city had been reduced to piles of corpses and smoldering ashes.

Over two hundred years later, in 401 BCE, a Greek mercenary army, the Ten Thousand, attempted to overthrow the Persian king Artaxerxes II, and put his brother, Cyrus the Younger, on the throne. But Cyrus was killed in a battle near Babylon, and the mercenaries beat a desperate retreat through the Mesopotamian desert. As they hurried along, the Athenian general and historian Xenophon, who had been recruited to serve as a leader of the Ten Thousand, observed a "large unoccupied fortress city . . . the Medes had formerly inhabited it." He called the deserted city Mespilla, from *Meso-pulai*, or "middle pass," which might have referred to the Tigris as it flowed between Mosul and the destroyed city. "The foundation of its wall was of polished stone full of shells, the breadth fifty feet and the height fifty feet," Xenophon noted. "[O]n it was constructed a wall of bricks, fifty feet broad and a hundred high; the circumference of it was six parasangs [twenty-one miles]." That was almost certainly a wild exaggeration, but Xenophon was surely looking at the remnants of a once-mighty capital.

Over time, sand, earth, and debris formed a mound, or a tell—from the Arabic for "small elevation"—that encased the ruins. Five hundred years after Xenophon passed through, Lucian, the Hellenized Syrian satirist, wrote that Nineveh "is so completely destroyed . . . that it is no longer possible to see where it stood." James Felix Jones, an English steamboat captain and draftsman who surveyed the region in the mid-nineteenth century, described the principal tell, Kuyunjik, as a ninety-six-foot-high "irregular oval" that covered 1,800 acres and formed a "total circuit" of seven miles. "Its sides . . . are deeply furrowed by the rains of succeeding winters, forming broken ravines, at uncertain intervals, in the steep declivities . . . from the summit to the adjoining plain," Jones wrote.

Claudius Rich, the East India Company's diplomatic resident in Baghdad, passed by Nineveh in 1820 on the way back from a journey to Kurdistan. He found pottery shards among piles of rubbish and turned up "a piece of fine brick . . . covered with exceedingly small and beautiful cuneiform writing," he wrote in *Narrative of a Residence in Koordistan, and On the Site of Ancient Nineveh*. Rich had encountered the same script on bricks that he'd picked up near the site of ancient Babylon in 1811. He'd heard that locals had discovered "an immense bas-relief, representing men and animals, covering a grey stone of the height of two men." Thrilled by this glimpse of a lost civilization on their own home ground, the entire population of Mosul had turned out to see it. But the city's ulema, or experts in Islamic law, had warned that the figures were idols of the infidels, "and in a few days it was cut up or broken into pieces." Rich located a part of the mound that he suspected concealed "either the citadel or royal precincts." But, in fragile health, he didn't attempt to dig. Besides, he wasn't sure there was anything left to be found. (Rich would die of cholera ten years later, at thirty-four, in the Persian city of Shiraz.)

⤛────────⤜

Layard and Mitford turned from the plains and the river and headed back to the Zagros Mountains, joining a caravan of Shia pilgrims returning home to Persia from the holy Mesopotamian cities of Najaf and Karbala. Arriving in Behistun, they had a chance encounter with the artist Eugène Flandin, who was planning his scramble up the cliff to copy the Old Persian inscriptions. Shortly afterward, in late 1840, Edward Mitford tired of his impetuous companion, who intended to linger in the Zagros region. Mitford was sure that Layard would get them killed, or at least robbed of all they had, and broke away to resume his journey to Ceylon. Though they would eventually resume contact, he fails to mention Layard once in the four-hundred-page memoir he wrote about their journey.

Layard now decided to follow alone in the footsteps of Rawlinson. In his ninety-page travel memoir for the *Journal of the Royal Geographic Society of London*, which Layard had just finished reading, Rawlinson had written of the mysterious inscriptions he encountered across the Zagros range. In one remote gorge he found a tablet "sculptured upon the face of the rock," showing a victorious king, armed with an axe, a strung bow, and a dagger, trampling his "prostrate foe of pigmy dimensions." The tablet bore a cuneiform inscription divided into three compartments of four lines each, "and written . . . in the complicated Babylonian character." In Rawlinson's second memoir for the society, about his trek through Persian Kurdistan in 1838, he wrote of climbing deep into the mountains to inspect the "Keli-Shun," a six-foot-tall pillar of dark blue stone located near a fourteen-thousand-foot-high pass, and inscribed with forty-one lines of cuneiform. The Kurds believed that a "potent magician" had created the pillar "to afford protection against danger . . . but [it] only serves to lure fresh victims to destruction." Rawlinson had to scrape away a sheet of ice to copy the inscription, only to find that most of it had eroded into illegibility.

Then, before drifting snows could strand him in the subfreezing heights, Rawlinson made a dangerous descent, pausing for a moment to take in the panorama. "The view from the summit of the pass was most magnificent—mountains towering over mountains, all heaped about in a chaos of disorder," Rawlinson wrote. "The huge masses of vapour left by the storms of yesterday, here hanging heavily upon a rocky crest, and there boiling up from the abysses that yawned beneath my feet, gave . . . an appalling grandeur to the scene."

To reach the most remote corners of the Zagros Mountains meant crossing the territory of the Bakhtiari people, a highland tribe with ten thousand armed men, a reputation for, Layard wrote, "treachery and murder," and a long-running feud with the shah's army. Layard obtained a laissez-passer (permit) from the Persian governor, Manuchehr Khan, a sadistic despot who had built a tower out of three hundred prisoners, mortared together like bricks, watched them suffer agonizing deaths, and left their corpses glued in place for days. When Layard rode up steep forested trails to the castle of the Bakhtiari chieftain, Mehmet Taki Khan, he found the warlord's young son dying of a fever. "The father appealed to me in the most heartrending terms, offering me gifts of horses and anything that I might desire if I would only save the life of his son," he recounted. Layard gave the patient a heavy dose of quinine. Within hours the boy broke into "a violent perspiration." By dawn he had recovered.

Overjoyed, Mehmet Taki Khan welcomed Layard into the tribe,

had him outfitted in traditional clothing, and offered him a bride on the condition that he convert to Islam. (Layard declined, though he may have had a love affair with the warlord's sister-in-law.) It was one of many examples of Layard's forming bonds with and earning the trust of strangers, thanks to his ebullience, linguistic skill, and endless curiosity about other cultures.

But Layard had to cut short his sojourn in the Zagros. The Persians now considered him an enemy because of his association with the Bakhtiari leader. When the army moved in to capture the warlord, Layard fled by raft down a river and rode two hundred miles across the desert to the relative safety of Ottoman territory. "That man! Why, if I could catch him, I'd hang him," the vizier in Teheran exclaimed to the British ambassador.

Layard later wrote to his uncle Benjamin Austen that he was "happier under a black Bakhtiari tent with liberty of speech and action and nobody to depend on, no-one to flatter, certain that I shall have dinner tomorrow—for there is always bread and water—and without need of that source of all evil, money." Now, on the lam, his money was running out, and his options were narrowing. On the desert track back to Baghdad, he was robbed and nearly murdered by rebellious Bedouins who mistook him for an Ottoman official. Staggering into the capital, barefoot and in rags, he soon learned that the Afghans had wiped out the British force near Jalalabad in early 1842, making it impossible for him to carry on through Afghanistan to Ceylon. He tried to persuade a wealthy British merchant to finance an archaeological dig at Nineveh, but the negotiations fizzled. "I scarcely know which way to turn," Layard admitted in a letter home, "and I feel so miserable that I would willingly return and live among the wild tribes of the mountains, cursing the name of England." He bleakly suggested to his mother that she and his younger brother Edgar come away with him and "colonize some uninhabited island." Reluctantly, he began planning his voyage back to London, though he had no prospects there either. Benjamin Austen wrote that he did not consider his nephew "a sober citizen" and would not welcome him home.

Then, in one of those twists of fate that reverberate in unexpected directions across decades, a geopolitical crisis intervened. In 1842, Persian troops seized from the Ottoman Empire a disputed border territory in the Zagros Mountains, an area that Layard now knew well. With war looming, the British ambassador in Constantinople, Stratford Canning, was looking for an expert who could provide intelligence, assess each side's claims, and present to him enough information to mediate the dispute. Robert Taylor, the British Resident in Baghdad, suggested that Layard detour through the Ottoman capital and offer his services. Layard accepted the proposal and, accompanied by an Ottoman postman, again set off through the desert.

Fifty hours and 250 miles later, Layard reached Mosul. He planned to spend a couple of days back in the city before moving on. His timing was fortuitous. Another recent arrival was Paul-Émile Botta, the French consul, a gregarious nomad who shared Layard's fascination with Near Eastern antiquity. Botta had just opened the first archaeological trench at Kuyunjik. Thus far, the consul had found little evidence of Nineveh—a few kiln-burnt bricks and fragments of alabaster, inscribed with cuneiform—but he had energy and the backing of the French government. Layard explored the mound with him for a full day. "M. Botta was a delightful companion," he wrote, gracious though disappointed that Botta had gotten there first. "He was liberal in his views, large-minded, willing to impart what he knew, and ready to acknowledge the merit of others."

Botta was also a troubled soul: he had become addicted to opium in China in 1829 during a scientific voyage around the Pacific. It "ruined his health," Layard observed, "and rendered him liable to occasional fits of melancholy and despondency." For his part, Botta praised opium as "an unlimited source of comfort and happiness," and urged Layard to take up the habit. Always eager to try new experiences, Layard had a few hits from Botta's pipe, but then developed a fierce headache and became severely nauseated. He would never take the drug again.

Before Layard left for Constantinople, he asked Botta to keep him informed of his progress on the mound. Then he continued his ride with the postman to the Black Sea coast, heading for a meeting that would change everything.

CHAPTER SIX

THE PALACE ON
THE TIGRIS

Henry Rawlinson departed from Calcutta in November 1843, bound for an open-ended term in Baghdad as the political agent of the East India Company, the equivalent of the British ambassador. Approaching the city by steamboat on the Tigris River, Rawlinson confronted an oasis filled with remnants of a glorious past. "The pendant branches of the graceful date tree, and the refreshing green of the pomegranate, with its bright red flowers, become more and more frequent," wrote one British rafter, "until . . . the river flows through one continuous grove." Edward Mitford, Layard's companion, described floating by a fragrant orange plantation, and then passing the four golden minarets and domes of the sixteenth-century Al-Kadhimiya Mosque, containing the tombs of two Shia imams. The river narrowed "to just 220 yards across, but not enough to destroy the grandeur of the noble stream," he wrote. For some the scene conjured up the eighth-century golden age, when the Abbasid caliphs founded their new capital in Baghdad (relocating it from Damascus) and swiftly transformed the city into the world's center of culture and learning. "He must be . . . void of poetry and sentiment, in whom the first glimpse of those shining domes does not excite some spark of emotion," one English visitor enthused. "Who is there that does not exclaim, 'Is this the Baghdad of [Caliph] Harunu-al-Reshid and the "Arabian Nights"?' "

The British Residency, a former palace overlooking the Tigris, evoked similar wonder. "The Residency is a magnificent house, decorated in geometric patterns and looking glass," wrote Henry James Ross, a Malta-born trader and British consular official in Mosul, who frequently turned up at the villa. A vaulted entrance, guarded by a white-uniformed sepoy—an Indian infantryman— led into a terraced courtyard and a series of galleries. One salon was "entirely ceiled and paneled with mirrors, ornamented with gilding and arabesque pattern-work, and furnished with couches, slightly raised from the floor," Mitford noted. In the domed reception hall, inlaid ivory and precious wood adorned the walls, and picture windows looked over the river. In every corner, servants, cooks, grooms, stable boys, coffee grinders, and pipe fillers stood ready to attend to the Resident and his guests.

The British Residency had become the center of Baghdad's small but vibrant social scene, drawing expatriate businessmen, European diplomats, explorer-adventurers in transit, and the city's Arab elite to multi-course meals in the spacious stateroom. A guest counted fourteen languages being spoken at one typical soiree hosted by Claudius James Rich, the amateur archaeologist and adventurer who had become the Resident at age twenty-one in 1808. Robert Taylor, who took the position in 1821, was an Arabic scholar and an "Asiatic prince," wrote another visitor, whose influence in Baghdad was said to rival that of the civilian governor of Mosul, or pasha. The qadi and the mufti of Baghdad, the city's two most important religious figures, often dropped by to consult with Taylor over obscure passages in Arabic manuscripts. "The [dining] service was performed by . . . Arabian and Indian servants in their native costumes," wrote Layard in 1840, "moving noiselessly about with naked feet, and attending promptly and well to the wants of the guests. . . . Evening was spent . . . either on the flat roof of the house if the heat was great, or in [the] beautiful domed chamber."

Outside the compound, life in Baghdad was harsh. Three waves of Ottoman conquest against the Safavid Empire, a Shia dynasty, had brought all of what is now Iraq under the authority of Constantinople in the seventeenth century. But the devastating war against Catherine the Great's Russia had emptied the Ottoman treasury. Bedouin tribes were in a state of low-level rebellion, trade had dried up, and corruption permeated the ranks of officialdom. Baghdad's lively grand bazaar was filled with "Arabs, Persians, Turks, Jews and all kinds of people and all kinds of costumes," Henry Ross noted, but "all is going to decay."

In 1831 the Tigris overflowed its banks, destroyed seven thousand homes, and left pools of stagnant water that became breeding grounds for mosquitoes. Malaria killed 12,000 of a population of 70,000, with mortality reaching 120 people a day. "The streets presented a shocking spectacle of misery," wrote an English observer. "The sick lay in every direction—at the doors of houses, in the bazaars, and open spaces." Layard visited the pasha in 1840 and was appalled by his apathy and self-indulgence. "Masses of fat hung upon him," he wrote. "Such was the type of many Turkish functionaries, who took no exercise, rarely left their divans and their long pipes, gorged themselves twice a day with the most fattening dishes, and thought of little but the delights of the harem."

The pasha appeared proactive only when it came to dealing with criminals, Layard noted, placing them alive on stakes as a warning at two ends of a "bridge of boats" crossing the Tigris. One Englishman Layard knew "had recently seen four culprits thus exposed, one of whom was said to have lived for several days in excruciating agonies."

In the 1830s Robert Taylor proposed that the East India Company place a fleet of armed steamboats on the Tigris and Euphrates, which, he believed, could pacify rebellious Bedouins and make the territory safe enough to bring prosperity to Baghdad. Taylor persuaded the pasha to grant a firman, or edict, authorizing the first boat: the *Nitocris*, named after a Babylonian queen, an iron steamer with six swivels and two large guns. In 1836 the steamer began trips between Baghdad and Basra. Astonished locals called the vessel *Al Dhukani*—"Smoke"—and regarded it, wrote Taylor, as "a new prophet . . . sent into the world." But Taylor fell afoul of the East India Company over accusations that he'd helped his brother and son-in-law gain a stake in the steamboat concession, suggesting that corruption was just as much a British problem as it was an Ottoman one. Twenty-two years after Taylor took on the post in Baghdad, the firm unceremoniously recalled him to London.

◄───────►►

After settling in as Taylor's replacement, Rawlinson threw himself into the pleasures of life in a diplomatic backwater. Footmen and armed sepoys accompanied Rawlinson every time he set foot outside the compound, saluting, beating drums, and making every excursion a spectacle. Rawlinson embarked on rafting trips down the Tigris and hunted lions and boars in the desert. He became one of the first Europeans to explore the mysterious mud-brick ruins of Nippur, later revealed to be a five-thousand-year-old Sumerian city that had served as the seat of worship of Enlil, the "Lord Wind" and ruler of the cosmos. "These ruins are supposed to be . . . the abode of hobgoblins & devils of all sorts, so that I had great difficulty in enlisting anybody to accompany me to such a haunted spot," he wrote years later in an illustrated memoir for his young sons. Hunting lions with a few servants in the wilderness beyond Nippur, Rawlinson lost the trail leading back to camp and wandered in total darkness for hours before his dog, Tiger, found the way to the dying embers of their campfire.

Henry Ross visited the Residency while Rawlinson was recuperating from a broken collarbone caused by a tumble from a horse during a "pig sticking" expedition outside Baghdad. Rawlinson's Portuguese-Indian chef served the men cheese, ale, and sweets, before a servant led them into the tearoom for chai and *kalians*, Persian water pipes. Rawlinson then retreated upstairs, blaming being "on the sick list" for cutting the meeting short. "He is excessively clever and bears a high reputation among the diplomats both at home and in India," Ross noted. Yet he "is rather haughty and keeps all around him at a certain distance."

Rawlinson had more on his mind than pomp and pig hunts. After being swept up for four years in the Great Game and the war in Afghanistan, he looked forward to a more intellectual pursuit: deciphering cuneiform. "The interest in the inscriptions . . . had never flagged," he wrote. "[I]t was sharpened perhaps by the . . . delay." Early in his posting Niels Ludvig Westergaard, a Danish linguist, had stopped by Residency bearing copies of Old Persian texts that Niebuhr had missed at Persepolis. He also presented a long inscription engraved on the sepulcher of Darius on the cliff at Naqsh-e Rustam, a few miles from Darius's ceremonial capital. Despite the abrasion of the rock and the difficulties that Westergaard had encountered tracing the letters through a telescope, Rawlinson called the copy "a gem."

Shortly afterward, he organized a return to Behistun. Joined by a support staff that included James Felix Jones, the *Nitocris* captain, Rawlinson camped again by the springs, scaled the wall with ropes, and reached the ledge where he had copied inscriptions by hand in 1836. He turned this time to a more efficient method, pioneered by the German archaeologist Karl Richard Lepsius, the leader of a Royal Prussia Expedition to Egypt in 1842. Rawlinson spread moist filter paper with a stiff, long-bristled brush across the wall and, dabbing to release the air bubbles beneath the surface, made papiermâché "squeezes" of the two hundred fifty remaining lines of Old Persian. The casts were allowed to dry and then peeled off the rock, providing precise, negative images of the characters.

But Rawlinson wasn't finished. Inscribed on the huge rock face to the left of the Old Persian were 593 lines of what scholars had come to recognize since Niebuhr's day as Elamite cuneiform. Often used during the Achaemenid era for bureaucratic records and diplomatic correspondence, Elamite was a much older and more complicated script than Old Persian, with four times as many unique characters and a number of signs consisting of eight, nine, even ten wedges. (Old Persian characters usually had no more than five.) If the Elamite could be deciphered, Rawlinson reasoned, then it, along with the Old Persian, could be used to unravel the third script: Akkadian. Rawlinson sensed more strongly than ever that the Behistun inscriptions could be his Rosetta Stone.

There was just one problem: the Elamite slab lay on the other side of a twenty-foot gap in the ledge, a natural aperture that the scribes had apparently surmounted using scaffolding. At first, Rawlinson tried laying the ladder across the abyss, but the wooden frame was too wide: "It would of course have tilted over if a person had attempted to cross it in that position." He flipped the ladder on its side, so that the upper rail rested on the ledge at its two ends and the lower rail hung over the precipice. Planting his feet on the lower rail and grasping the ladder's upper side, he began to traverse the gap.

Moments later, the bottom rail ripped away and went crashing over the precipice, leaving Rawlinson dangling from a wood plank. Watching in horror from the Old Persian side, Jones steadied what remained of the ladder and guided him back to safety. Later, Rawlinson brought up a sturdier ladder, crossed the gap, and made squeezes of the Elamite as well. As he worked, he had a clear view of further peril: the giant slab directly above his head, on which the Achaemenid scribes had engraved the Akkadian inscription, was deteriorating. Water trickling from above had "almost separated the overhanging mass from the rest of the rock," he wrote. Soon, he expected it to come "thundering down into the plain, dashed into a thousand fragments." Time was running out.

Back in Baghdad, Rawlinson settled down to continue his work—only to be interrupted by unforeseen violence. Relations between the Ottoman rulers, adherents of Sunni Islam, and their predominantly Shia subjects in Baghdad and Basra had been tense for generations. The Shias refused to recognize the Ottomans' claim to lands that had been part of the Islamic caliphate established by the Prophet Muhammad. Rawlinson had barely returned to the Residency when the new Ottoman pasha of Baghdad tried to garrison troops in the holy Shia city of Karbala, to strengthen control over the restive population. When Shias rioted, Ottoman forces massacred five thousand people and desecrated the Imam Husayn Shrine, one of Shia Islam's holiest sites.

When Arabs living in the nearby marshes rose up in solidarity, Rawlinson had to persuade the pasha not to seize the *Nitocris* and send it down the Euphrates to mow them down. In Persia, where he had strong ties from his days as a military trainer, he met with religious and government officials, trying to calm Shia outrage after the Karbala massacre. Later, he ventured north to Kurdistan and met with tribal leaders to quell another potential uprising. He also tried to settle a long-running border dispute between Turkey and Persia. Losing faith in the ability of the Ottomans to police their territory, he pushed the pasha to allow more steamships on the Tigris and Euphrates. He believed the armed vessels would give rebellious Bedouins a "wholesome dread of British authority."

At last, the violence settled down, somnolence returned to Baghdad, and Rawlinson retreated to a cottage overhanging the river, built at the end of the Residency garden. Sitting at his desk with the Old Persian texts of Behistun—414 lines—spread before him, he approached the decipherment with "unremitting assiduity," his brother wrote. Back in Europe, Rawlinson knew, his half dozen competitors were making advances as well. He worked through fevers, stomach bugs, a broken clavicle, and the scorching heat of the summer. During the worst of it, his office was cooled to about ninety degrees by, noted George Rawlinson, "the action of a waterwheel, turned by the Tigris, which poured a continuous stream of Tigris water over the roof."

Rawlinson could also turn for distraction to a few companions: the beasts that prowled the Baghdad Residency. An eccentric English physician in Baghdad, John Ross, had gotten Rawlinson interested in collecting exotic pets. In the early 1840s Ross had adopted a juvenile leopard that would lie in wait at Ross's home with his paws on a windowsill overlooking the street. "When a sheep or a donkey passe[d] he spr[ang] down upon them and br[oke] their necks, leaving the doctor to pay the damage," noted Henry Ross (no relation to the physician). Ross next adopted another big cat: a male lion that prowled alone through Baghdad's bazaars, terrifying shoppers and merchants, until the British governor-general in Bombay told Ross to keep the animal locked up at home. Rawlinson cared for the lion while Ross was out of town, and nearly touched off a diplomatic incident. When an Ottoman dignitary dropped by for tea at the Residency, the official suddenly "felt his right hand, which was hanging down, being licked by the very rough tongue of some animal," Henry Ross recounted. "Looking down he saw the lion. With one bound he cleared the room, darted out of the door and down the stairs."

Soon Rawlinson began building a menagerie of his own—a fitting avocation for a man who believed he could submit anything to his will. He purchased an orphaned lion cub found in rushes along the Tigris and "gave strict orders to the household that only he

Rawlinson's sketch of the British Residency courtyard
in Baghdad, with his pet leopard secured by a chain

should feed it," George Rawlinson wrote. "The lion would follow him about, all over his house and garden, like a dog." Next came a leopard, Faed, that dozed under a verandah or prowled around the Residency courtyard at the end of a chain. At night he slept in the Resident's bedroom or curled up beside him on the roof. "He certainly did now & then alarm the children who came into the courtyard by sniffing at them, or licking his lips," Rawlinson noted, "but his education & sense of right and wrong overcame his wilder & more savage propensities and he was perfectly obedient to my orders." A pet mongoose wandered freely, attacking the venomous snakes that sometimes crept into the Residency past the sepoys' watchful eye.

◂—————▸

Racing to the finish to beat his European rivals, who, he assumed, were making rapid progress as well, Rawlinson dispatched his 541-page magnum opus, *The Persian Cuneiform Inscriptions at Behistun, decyphered and translated, with a memoir on Persian cuneiform inscriptions in general, and on that of Behistun in particular,* to the Royal Asiatic Society in the summer of 1846. "These tablets have been a sealed letter to the world for at least twenty centuries," Rawlinson declared, adding with an imperialistic flourish that "[i]t has been reserved for civilized Europe to reveal their mysteries." Rawlinson devoted 250 pages to an analysis of every Old Persian character, with examples of its use, and its equivalent characters in other ancient languages. The Old Persian letter *kh* ◀𝖸, for instance, was the first character of Khurush, Cyrus the Great. Rawlinson provided the name of the king in ancient Greek **Κῦρος**, Hebrew **כורש**, Persian ‫خور‬, Sanskrit 𑀓𑀼, and Avestan 𐎤𐎢𐎼𐎢𐏁.

He had deciphered thousands of Old Persian words; mastered genders, tenses, cases, gerunds, and regular and irregular verbs;

and, by comparing it with the Avestan and Sanskrit, reconstructed the pronunciation of a language that was last spoken in the early third century BCE. This was the time that the North African republic of Carthage began to challenge Rome for dominance; and the Seleucid Empire and the Ptolemaic Empire, founded by Alexander the Great's successors, battled for control of the eastern Mediterranean.

Just as remarkable, Rawlinson had met the challenge of reading badly damaged inscriptions. In "Notes on the Text," Rawlinson explained how rock fissures that had opened by "the percolation of water from above" had obliterated hundreds of characters and destroyed sections of text. But Rawlinson filled in missing letters by studying the undamaged characters and words nearby ("The context fully supports the restoration of the letter 𒁹 both in *Mádamchá* and *Pársamchá*," he wrote), finding duplicate phrases elsewhere in the text ("As *hamatak'hshiya* occurs again in line 70, I have no hesitation in restoring 𒀼 𒁹 𒀀 at the end of this line"), or taking guesses based on faint outlines and partial mutilations. Sometimes, defeated, he admitted that "I have no clue" about the missing letters. But he believed his restorations had been "bold and felicitous."

There were other narratives against which the story told at Behistun could be compared. The rise of Darius had been chronicled by Herodotus in the *Histories* about sixty years after the monarch's death and by Ctesias in *Persica* thirty years later. According to Herodotus, the childless Achaemenid king Cambyses II, the son of Cyrus the Great, faced a rebellion led by his brother, Bardiya, in 522 BCE. Fighting Bardiya's insurgent army, the king suffered a thigh wound that turned gangrenous and died in what is modern-day Hama, Syria. Bardiya crowned himself ruler, and a cabal known as the Gang of Seven, including Darius, plotted his overthrow. The gang fought its way into his fortress near Isfahan and overwhelmed his bodyguards. "The seven … found the king in bed with a Babylonian concubine," Ctesias recounted. "When the king saw them, he jumped up. And when he found none of his weapons, he smashed a golden chair to pieces and fought using one of its legs." Darius and the other conspirators beat Persia's new ruler to death, then agreed that whichever plotter's horse neighed first when the sun rose would become king. Darius then secretly ordered his servant to rub his hands over the genitals of a mare in heat. At dawn, when the servant held his hands up to Darius's horse's nose, the animal whinnied excitedly, and Darius took the throne.

But the story carved by Darius's scribes at Behistun was, wrote Lloyd Llewellyn-Jones, a professor of ancient history and scholar of Persia at Cardiff University, "a rich mélange of untruths, spin, and pure bravado." (Not that Herodotus was any more reliable. He had a reputation for weaving his narratives from hearsay and legend; the fifth-century BCE Athenian historian Thucydides dismissed much of what he wrote as fiction.) In Darius's version there was no Gang of Seven, no nefarious plotting, no regicide. Instead, Darius described himself as going to war against a villainous Zoroastrian priest named Gomátes (Gaumata in Persian). The king "Cambyses, unable to endure his misfortunes, died," he declared, without specifying the cause. Darius then gathered an army of "well-wishers," attacked Gomátes, killed him and his followers, and seized the throne.

Darius then luridly recounted his military campaign to control the empire. He marched to Babylon and drove insurrectionists into the Euphrates, where the "water destroyed them." He slaughtered a rebel army in Armenia. (In ancient times, this was a highland kingdom between the Black and Caspian Seas that included eastern Turkey, modern-day Armenia, and Azerbaijan.) He defeated the Medes, capturing and then torturing to death a chieftain named Phraortes. "I cut off his nose and ears and his lips," Rawlinson translated. "He was held chained at my door; all the kingdom beheld him. Afterwards, at Ecbatana, I had him crucified." After describing the tortures of other rebels, Darius proclaimed, "I fought nineteen battles . . . By the grace of Ormazd, I smote them, and I made nine kings captive." (Ormazd was another name for the supreme Persian god Ahura Mazda.) Then he had likenesses of the prisoners—the "liar" kings—carved at Behistun, with Gomátes beneath his feet. Each, clad in his national costume, was identified by an epigraph above his head: "This Gomátes, the Magian, was an impostor . . . This Phraortes was an impostor . . . This Sitratchames was an impostor." Darius ended with a warning to those who might consider defacing the inscriptions: "If thou shalt dishonour them," he declared, "may Ormazd be thy enemy, and mayest thou be childless, and that which thou mayest do, may Ormazd spoil for thee."

Darius also conjured up a genealogy that strengthened his dubious claim to the Achaemenid throne: "From deep in the past has our dynasty been royal," he avowed. "[E]ight of my dynasty were kings before me; I am the ninth. Nine in succession we have been king." In fact, none of the eight ancestors he mentioned, with the exception of Teispes, who predated Cyrus, were kings. Darius was drawing phony links between his family and the line of Cyrus to bolster his legitimacy.

The Royal Asiatic Society published Rawlinson's memoir in its entirety in 1847. It was, he wrote, with only a bit of exaggeration, "all that remains of the ancient Persian language, and all that contemporary native evidence records of the glories of the Achaemenids." Scholars across Europe recognized it as a singular achievement. Amid political crises, illnesses, and debilitating heat, Rawlinson had deciphered the extinct writing of an empire that had vanished centuries before the rise of Rome and the crucifixion of Jesus. He had opened the way for an understanding of the two parallel texts inscribed at Behistun. His rivals in Europe, including both distinguished professors of philology and talented amateurs, hadn't come close. Rawlinson's memoir established him as one of the foremost Middle Eastern linguists on the planet, a resurrector of the dead. Now Rawlinson believed he was moving closer to making Behistun his own Rosetta Stone. Eager to focus on the Akkadian, the most difficult and significant of the three writing systems, he turned over his papier-mâché squeezes of the Elamite inscriptions to Edwin Norris at the Royal Asiatic Society. Norris, a formidable linguist known for keeping his own ego in check in the service of making other scholars look good, leapt at the opportunity to help Rawlinson. While Norris labored in London, the next step for Rawlinson would be transcribing the Akkadian version of Darius's texts and comparing it to the Elamite and Old Persian. And events were unfolding 250 miles north of Baghdad that would give Rawlinson's efforts greater urgency. "It is my firm belief," he wrote in his memoir, "that the discoveries that have been already made are but a prelude to others of far greater moment."

CHAPTER SEVEN

BOTTA'S FIND

A usten Layard landed at Constantinople's Golden Horn estuary on a sweltering morning in July 1842 and traveled by skiff up the Bosphorus for two hours to the summer residence of the British ambassador. He walked into Stratford Canning's reception hall in a disheveled, haggard state. He was badly sunburned and clad in an ill-fitting, borrowed suit; his jaw throbbed from an abscess contracted on the boat journey through the Black Sea. "I have applied a few leeches to my face and hope to be well in a day or two," he had written to his mother. After a long wait, a young attaché appeared, "asked me roughly for the despatches of which I was the bearer, informed me that the ambassador was too much occupied to see anyone, and, turning on his heel left the room without deigning to listen to what I had to say." Layard wrote an irate letter to Canning from his hotel room complaining about "this rude and uncourteous treatment." Then he booked passage on a ship to England.

And that might have been the end of it, had not Canning decided to invite him for a meeting the next day. The diplomat sized up the brash young courier with the swollen jaw. "His earnest gray eyes seemed to penetrate into one's very thoughts," Layard wrote of his first impression of the ambassador. A London merchant's son whose father had died when he was an infant, Canning had gone to Cambridge with tuition raised from relatives and had earned his diplomatic chops in Washington, D.C., and St. Petersburg. "A broad and massive overhanging brow gave an air of profound wisdom and sagacity," Layard went on. "He was altogether a very formidable looking personage." Canning questioned him about conditions along the Ottoman-Persian border, and then told him to cancel his ticket home and prepare a report. Soon Layard was going undercover to investigate unrest in Ottoman-ruled Serbia and Bosnia and an uprising in Albania. (Canning instructed him to look for the "extent and causes of the insurrection . . . the apparent policy of the . . . authorities [and] the strength of the respective parties.") When not snooping around the empire, Layard settled into life in Constantinople and grew close to the ambassador and his family. He held out hopes for a permanent position as a salaried attaché. But the mounds of Mesopotamia continued to beckon.

◄─────►

Nine hundred miles away, in Mosul, Paul-Émile Botta, the French consul-archaeologist, was losing patience with the whole business. He'd never been one to stay anywhere too long. Born in 1802 in Turin, the son of a noted Italian historian, Botta had become a naturalized French citizen in his early teens. He studied Arabic and botany in Rouen, sailed to the Hawaiian Islands as a shipboard naturalist, and in Cairo in 1830 befriended the travel writer, novelist, and nascent politician Benjamin Disraeli, who wrote that Botta had "the most philosophic mind that I ever came in contact with." Later he joined the pasha's army in Egypt and explored Yemen and the Red Sea before being dispatched to Mosul by the French government to search for the remains of Nineveh. He'd had high hopes of finding

something extraordinary. "The only information the secular authors have transmitted to us about [the Assyrians] is incomplete and
often contradictory or even mythical," he would write in *Monument
de Ninive* in 1849. "The holy books mention them only incidentally,
when circumstances bring them into contact with the Hebrew . . .
There could be no doubt, however, that . . . there existed a mighty
empire whose origins are lost in time, which had spread over the
majority of Asia." But after three months of finding nothing but
bricks and "worthless fragments" at Kuyunjik (the name, a diminu-
tive of *koyun*, or "sheep" in Turkish, possibly derives from the Qara
Qoyunlu, or "Black Sheep" dynasty, a Turkic monarchy that ruled
over the region in the fourteenth and fifteenth centuries), Botta had
begun to look around for other excavation sites.

Botta was still indulging his drug habit, which he'd picked up in
China and plunged deeper into during two years sharing barracks
with Ottoman troops in Sennar, a city on the Blue Nile in Sudan.
Rawlinson noted in a correspondence with the Royal Asiatic Society that Botta is "quite befuddled with opium." He apparently had
no difficulty securing a regular supply. As far back as 3400 BCE,
the Sumerians had produced what might have been the world's first
poppy crop, referring to the flower in tablets as *Hul Gil*, the "joy
plant." A winged spirit, or genie, holding a poppy flower, would
turn up in a bas-relief in an Assyrian palace built around 700 BCE.
By Botta's day, Mosul not only had a sizeable poppy production of
its own but also lay on the overland opium-trading route from India
to Europe. In 1793, the East India Company had secured a monop-
oly of opium commerce and shipped twenty thousand pounds a
year from the subcontinent and from Anatolia to England for both
medicinal and recreational use.

Rawlinson's colleague at the consulate, Henry Ross, was equally
conscious of Botta's habit. "We are great friends in spite of his vio-

lent denunciations of England which entirely depend on how much opium he has taken," Ross noted. And yet "between smokes, the Frenchman was a delightful companion, open-minded and generous." He was also in luck. In March 1843, a farmer from Khorsabad, a village thirteen miles northeast of Mosul on the bank of a Tigris tributary, the Khosr, brought Botta a piece of a bas-relief from the mound there and suggested there was much more to be found. Botta abandoned Kuyunjik and set up camp beside the Khosr, a muddy stream that in summer became a breeding ground for mosquitoes. A dun-colored tell rose dozens of feet above the plain, with the village perched on top, and the low mountains of Northern Mesopotamia rising directly behind it.

Botta was an avid practitioner of a young science. Renaissance scholars had taken an interest in the art and civilization of ancient Greece and Rome. But archaeology—defined by Cambridge professor Grahame Clark in 1939 as "the systematic study of antiquities as a means of reconstructing the past"—didn't begin in earnest until 1748, when Charles VII, the king of Naples, became intrigued by the recent discovery of ancient statuary at the base of Mount Vesuvius by amateur diggers. The king dispatched prisoners and engineers equipped with tools and explosive powder to hunt for more treasures there for his Saxon queen, Maria Amalia. Blasting and digging through sixty feet of hardened lava, they soon came to a staircase marked with an inscription: THEATRUM HERCULANENSE. They had discovered the ruins of Herculaneum, the fabled Roman city destroyed by the eruption of Vesuvius in 79 CE. The same year, engineers digging a canal beside the Bay of Naples stumbled upon a bigger find: the ruins of Pompeii. Beneath layers of softer pumice lay paved streets, frescoes, bread in bakers' ovens, and the remains of citizens lying where they had died, choked by volcanic fumes and buried by ash. "Stretched out full-length on the floor was a skeleton," C. W. Ceram wrote in *Gods, Graves and Scholars: The Story of Archaeology*, a definitive account of the excavations of Pompeii, "with gold and silver coins that had rolled out of bony hands still seeking, it seemed, to clutch them fast."

The recovery of Herculaneum and Pompeii stirred a fascination with the new science and created a powerful sense of connection to the ancient world. Over the next decades the methodology would become more systematic, with an emphasis on studying objects in situ, to establish a chronology of human progress. In 1818 archaeology received another boost thanks to Giovanni Belzoni, an Italian engineer and circus strongman from Padua. Belzoni cleared sand and rubble from the entrance to the great temple of Abu Simbel in Upper Egypt; discovered tombs in the Valley of the Kings at Thebes; and found a doorway leading to the pharaoh's burial chamber in the Second Pyramid on the Giza Plateau—discoveries that remained unrivaled in Egypt until Howard Carter entered Tutankhamen's tomb in 1923.

In Khorsabad, Botta hired local workmen and distributed picks, shovels, brooms, buckets, and ropes. He organized labor teams and ordered them to spread out across the dun-brown mound and cut trenches in the earth. Soon tunnels bathed in gloom snaked through the tell, strewn with broken bricks and crammed with sweating, singing, shirtless laborers. A pallor of yellow and ochre dust hung over the scene; the rhythmic *chink-chink-chink* of picks on rock and brick echoed through the labyrinth. Days after his arrival, the French consul watched, thrilled, as his workmen hoisted by ropes from a trench a large white alabaster frieze that had survived in near-perfect condition. It was a battle scene, the first significant relic (besides the one described by Claudius Rich that Islamist fanatics had smashed to pieces) to emerge from the remains of the Assyrian empire in 2,500 years.

The image was bursting with energy, violence, and emotion. An armor-clad warrior toppled over backward, mortally wounded by a lance. Behind him, two archers fired arrows at a tower atop a fortress. One figure in the tower raised his arms toward the heavens in despair, while another hurled a spear. Two more Assyrian archers in chain mail and pointed helmets aimed their arrows at the fort. A cuneiform inscription was emblazoned above the scene. "Unfortunately, it was so defaced that I despair of being able to transcribe much of it," Botta wrote to Julius von Mohl, a German Middle East scholar who had recommended him for the post and republished his letters in the *Journal Asiatique*, a Paris periodical. "I will copy all I can of this inscription, because one single historical name may suffice to explain the relief."

Botta descended into a deep trench that his workers had dug and followed it into a room lined with thick alabaster slabs. The palace chambers had been so solidly built that they had withstood the weight of accumulating debris and sand. He stared in amazement at perfectly preserved figures from a distant age: men with plaited hair and beards wearing garments still flecked with red and black paint. One appeared to be an Assyrian king, wearing a tiara ornamented with red bands. "His right hand grasps a long red staff, and the other is placed upon the hilt of a sword," Botta wrote to von Mohl. "His robe is adorned with rosettes, and under it, hangs a sort of scarf, beneath which his sword is passed." Botta noted evidence of the palace's destruction: heaps of charcoal covered the floor, along with remnants of burned beams. Botta now expressed his certainty that this, not the mound opposite Mosul, had been the Assyrian capital that had tantalized humanity since the era of the ancient Greeks. *"Nineveh,"* he wrote to his superiors in Paris, *"est retrouvé"*—Nineveh is found.

In fact, there was no way to know exactly what he'd found. Cuneiform characters covered the chamber walls, but he couldn't read them, or even say where one word started and the next began. He could make no judgment about whether the script was composed of a phonetic alphabet, logograms, or a mix of the two. "The more I look at the [characters] the less I understand this system of writing," he confessed to Layard. "I believe it cannot be alphabetical for the different groups [of wedges] are far too numerous to represent letters," he wrote. "It seems to me more likely that these groups are words or parts of words." He hoped that "some learned man" would one day reveal its secrets.

Layard formulated his own impressions about the mysterious script. Common sense and his understanding of geography told him that the language would likely be of Semitic origin, one of the three language families that, according to a popular philological theory of the era, had originated with the descendants of Noah's three sons. After the Flood, the philosopher, mathematician, and scientist Gottfried Wilhelm Leibniz believed, the family of Shem, known as the Semites, had dispersed across the Middle East and parts of Africa. There, their single language gradually divided into different branches of the Semitic family, including Aramaic, Amharic (spoken in Ethiopia), Arabic, Syriac, and Hebrew. And the complex cuneiform script suggested that it was a precursor to the writing found at Persepolis or Cyrus's earlier capital, Pasargadae. "I quite agree with you in believing this monument to be anterior to Cyrus," Botta wrote. "But they stump my imagination . . . and I do not believe that we can arrive to any certainty before the inscriptions are deciphered."

◄◄──────►►

Layard kept track of Botta's progress with intense interest—and envy. The sixty thousand francs (about $300,000 in today's money) that Botta had received from the French government had allowed him to hire three hundred workers to dig trenches in the mound. In May 1844 Eugène Flandin, the artist who had struggled up the cliff at Behistun, arrived at Khorsabad on an official mission to sketch Botta's discoveries. Hoping that the British ambassador would be inspired by the French example, Layard wrote to booksellers in England for dictionaries in Hebrew, Chaldean (a misnomer for Aramaic for 1,500 years), and Syriac, so that he could steep himself in other Semitic languages. When Flandin passed through Constantinople on the way back to Paris from Khorsabad, Layard made a point to meet the thirty-four-year-old artist and examine his sketches of Botta's bas-reliefs.

As it happened, Ambassador Canning had recently initiated a search for antiquities, hoping to give the British Museum an edge in a competition with the Louvre. Adolf Michaelis, a professor of classical archaeology in Strasbourg, noted around this time that the British government had "recommended its diplomatic representatives in classic lands to keep the interests of the British Museum ever before their eyes, and it has liberally supported their researches." Just before Layard came along, Canning had dispatched a team to the Turkish city of Bodrum, or Halicarnassus, the birthplace of Herodotus, to secure fragments of a grand mausoleum built between 353 and 350 BCE. Alexander the Great and other conquerors had picked apart most of the mausoleum, considered one of the Seven Wonders of the Ancient World. In the fifteenth century, what was left of its marble friezes—twelve slabs depicting Greeks battling Amazons, a single block showing centaurs wrestling a breed of men known as Lapiths, along with panels of standing lions and a running leopard—had ended up embedded in the walls of a castle built by the Knights Hospitaller of St. John, the order of Christian warriors that had formed during the Crusades. Canning pressed the sultan for a firman authorizing him to take the treasures to England. Despite the angry opposition of residents of the city (and some members of the Turkish government), Canning would obtain his consent in 1846.

In his memoir *Nineveh and Its Remains*, Layard would describe the "repugnance" of Ottoman officials at having to surrender to Canning's team the marbles from the castle, "which was more jealously guarded than any similar edifice in the Empire." Layard's observation belied a common assumption in Europe that Western archaeologists removed treasures from Asian palaces and tombs only with the consent of the local authorities. Canning triumphantly announced that he had shipped what became known as the Bodrum Marbles on "Her Majesty's vessel *Siren* to Malta with the intention of presenting them to the British Museum"—a still-controversial act of appropriation.

By then, Layard had persuaded Canning that much more beyond Khorsabad remained to be appropriated in Mesopotamia. "It was true that M. Botta had labored unsuccessfully for above three months in the great mound opposite Mosul," Layard explained in a memoir, "but that mound much exceeded in extent any other known ruin; and it was possible that in the part hitherto explored the traces of the buildings . . . were completely lost." The British Museum wasn't willing to finance an archaeological project that had already failed once, so Canning agreed to advance a modest £60 to Layard (the equivalent of about $9,600 today) out of his own pocket. If the results proved to be promising, Canning said, he was sure the museum would provide more money. Layard scraped together another £60 from his dwindling savings.

Layard and Canning knew that the Ottoman authorities would not make it easy for them. Botta had conducted his excavations with a firman from the Sublime Porte, a title used by Western diplomats to refer to the Ottoman government. (The expression originated as the French *La Sublime Porte*, a translation in turn of the Turkish *Bâbiâli*, referring to the gate providing access to the sultan's palace.) Yet even with that document in hand—which Canning and Layard lacked—the Frenchman had faced constant interference. Out of spite, suspicion, or (perfectly valid) resentment at the idea of a foreigner appropriating his country's treasures, the pasha of Mosul had thrown some of Botta's workmen in prison and threatened to torture them, according to Botta's letters to von Mohl. Playing on Ottoman fears that the "Franks"—a word the Turks applied to all Western Europeans—were conspiring to take over their territory, the pasha reported to the sultan that the consul was digging trenches to turn the mound into a "fortress." In response, the sultan forbade Botta to ship antiquities out of the country. Then the pasha demanded that Botta quit the site, though François-Adolphe de Bourqueney, the French ambassador in Constantinople, managed to get the order rescinded. In drafting his marching orders to Layard, Canning advised his protégé to be as discreet as possible.

An English surveyor gave Layard a quick mapping course in the hills around Constantinople. In October 1845, elated to be setting off once again, Layard caught a ferry back to the Black Sea port of Samsun. From there he headed with three horses and a "post boy" assistant through the forested mountains along the coast. The territory remained, he observed, "in a very disordered and dangerous state and overrun by brigands and plundering Kurds and Arabs." But, after traveling 740 miles in twelve days, he reached Mosul without incident on October 27. A nagging sense of being upstaged tempered his anticipation. "I have every reason to hope that I shall be to a certain degree successful," he wrote to his mother, "though M. Botta's great discovery makes one despair a little."

CHAPTER EIGHT

THE MOUND

Austen Layard paid a courtesy call on the pasha of Mosul to announce himself on his first day in the Northern Mesopotamian crossroads. But as he sat politely in a salon in the governorate, Layard would write, he could barely restrain his revulsion. The pasha "had one eye and one ear; he was short and fat, deeply marked by smallpox, uncouth in gestures and harsh in voice," Layard noted. His account of the meeting, published in his memoir, oozes disparagement: the pasha, he claimed, had driven Mosul and its environs to "a state of terror and despair" by extortion and turning his police on anyone he suspected of disloyalty. But the report probably should not be taken at face value. Layard was on a stealth mission, bent on stealing from Turkish Arabia as much treasure as he could, and it served his interests to portray the Ottoman governor as a corrupt autocrat. Still lacking a firman, Layard told the pasha nothing about his real intentions.

Ottoman vigilance forced Layard to change plans. Rather than begin his excavations at Kuyunjik, directly across the Tigris from Mosul, where he'd likely be spotted, he targeted a more obscure location: Nimrud. Twenty miles downriver from Mosul, the mound was believed by Greek historians to mark the site of the Assyrian city of Calah, or Kalhu, mentioned in the tenth chapter of the book of Genesis. ("Out of [the] land went Asshur," the passage declares, "and built Nineveh, and the city Rehoboth, and Calah . . .") In 879 BCE King Ashurnasirpal II, starting a tradition, established a new capital to mark his ascendancy. Relocating the royal seat upriver from the 1,500-year-old city of Ashur, Ashurnasirpal II constructed a great palace at Kalhu "with halls of cedar, cypress, juniper, box-wood, teak, terebinth, and tamarisk as my royal dwelling and for the enduring leisure life of my lordship," inscriptions would reveal. "Beasts of the mountains and the seas, which I had fashioned out of white limestone and alabaster, I had set up in its gates. I made the palace fittingly imposing." After his laborers finished the palace, Ashurnasirpal II threw a party for 69,574 citizens: "For ten days I feasted, wined, bathed, and honored them and sent them back to their home in peace and joy." Ashurnasirpal II filled the 940-acre city with a ziggurat for the warrior god Ninurta; six more temples; a zoo with ostriches, lions, and monkeys; and a "Canal of Abundance" that coursed through a park landscaped with exotic flora. "Streams of water as the stars of heaven flowed into the pleasure garden," an inscription proclaimed.

After Nineveh's destruction in 612 BCE, its downriver counterpart, which had remained an important Assyrian city, was besieged by "the King of the Persians," Xenophon claimed in the *Anabasis*, his 370 BCE account of the Greek mercenary army's retreat from Persia. But he "was unable by any means to take [it]." A cloud, it seemed, "having covered the sun, hid it from view, till the people deserted it, and so it was taken." Xenophon and his men marched past the ruined city, which he called "Larissa." "The breadth of its wall was five and twenty feet and the height of it a hundred," Xenophon observed. "It was built of bricks made of clay, but there was under it a foundation, the height of twenty feet."

Layard and Mitford had floated by the mound in the moonlight on their raft in 1840 on their way to Baghdad and Babylon. The next morning they had picked up, Layard wrote, "a few fragments of bricks, pottery, and alabaster, upon which might be traced the well-defined wedges of the cuneiform character." This time, Layard had a new traveling companion, Henry Ross, and a plan to avoid attracting the suspicions of Turkish authorities. Known in the region as a skilled hunter of lions and wild boars, Ross dispatched his greyhounds to the site "as though for one of my usual hunting expeditions," he wrote. Then he and Layard, having packed the bare essentials to disguise their intentions, boarded a two-paddle raft in Mosul. "We went down the Tigris . . . carrying food and a pickaxe," Ross wrote.

The companions docked after dark beside the village of Naifa, a short horseback ride from the mound. They found their way to a hovel belonging to a sheikh, the village chieftain, who offered them space on his dirt floor. Surrounded by the headman and his family, Layard found it impossible to sleep that night. "Hopes, long cherished were now to be realized, or were to end in disappointment," he recalled. "Visions of palaces under-ground, of gigantic monsters, of sculptured figures, and endless inscriptions floated before me."

The next morning, he and Ross hired for a pittance several men from the village, including the sheikh in whose house they'd spent the night. Then they saddled their horses and rode to the mound. One month before the winter rains, "[t]he eye wandered over a parched and barren waste, across which occasionally swept the whirlwind, dragging with it a small cloud of sand," Layard wrote. After pursuing some hares with Ross's hunting dog, they began hacking into the earth with their one pickaxe, "and soon blistered our hands and found the work very exhausting," Ross recalled. "But the sight of a small row of [carved] heads revived our energies."

The labor team from the village arrived. Near the spot where Layard and Ross had planted their axe, the sheikh spotted a white piece of alabaster protruding from the ground. Diggers cleared the surrounding earth and exposed the top of a huge slab. Soon twelve more slabs of the same size—white, unmovable, and forming a square with a single gap on one side—emerged. By sheer luck they had located a buried chamber within the vast heap of earth and debris; the gap in the square marked an entrance. Excitedly, Layard dug down the face of one of the stones, and that same day made a remarkable discovery: an intact room lined with smooth alabaster walls and filled with piles of charcoal. "The slabs, which had been nearly reduced to lime by exposure to intense heat," Layard wrote, "threatened to fall to pieces as soon as uncovered."

For days the crew dug trenches, climbed through portals into more rooms paneled with eight-foot-high alabaster slabs, and encountered hundreds of lines of cuneiform. In one bare room Layard recovered tiny fragments of ivory edged with gold. One displayed an image of a king holding an Egyptian cross, or ankh, the symbol of life, another a crouching sphinx. "These pieces no doubt formed part of a throne," Ross wrote, probably more out of excitement than certainty. But Layard desperately wanted rich pictorial representations of battles, sieges, and Assyrian gods and kings—the kind of bas-reliefs Botta was finding in abundance at Khorsabad. And after days of digging trenches, climbing through doorways, and entering chambers that had been remarkably preserved, he had turned up nothing.

He kept trying. In late November, workers cleared rubble from the mound's southwest corner and exposed a door carved with flowers and scrollwork. Suspecting he was getting close to something big, Layard ordered the men to open a trench from the ornate door into the mound's interior. Clearing charcoal, charred wood, and bricks, they exposed the top of the chamber wall and dug down. One side of the wall was blank.

The other was covered with bas-reliefs.

Two chariots, each pulled by a steed adorned with tassels and rosettes, raced across a plain. Each chariot carried three warriors, including a beardless man, perhaps a eunuch, clad in chain mail and a pointed helmet. The eunuch grasped a bow in his left hand and pulled an arrow taut. A sword adorned with two lions was sheathed at his side. The charioteer prodded his horses with reins and a whip; the shield bearer warded off arrows. Layard noted down every detail: the six-spoked wheels and molded edges of the chariots; the ornamental quivers filled with arrows and a hatchet. The vanquished, dead and dying on the ground, wore tunics descending to their knees, while "a simple fillet round the temples" held their hair in place.

Below this bas-relief, separated by several lines of cuneiform inscriptions, another frieze depicted the siege of a walled city. Assyrian archers wearing pointed helmets and carrying bows and quivers climbed ladders placed against a castle wall and prepared to launch a catapult, while defenders fired arrows from turrets and manned a sling. A female figure atop an arched gateway, her long hair falling in ringlets, begged for mercy.

◂———▸

Layard's correspondence with his mother in England captured his excitement. "I have been employed like the veriest mole in grubbing up the earth," he wrote to her in late November. "I have no doubt that the whole mound of Nimroud . . . contains the ruins of one great palace, and that, if I am able to continue my excavations, I shall be richly rewarded." Not that he expected to find treasures inside, apart from on the walls. "The whole building seems to have been pillaged and burnt, and nothing besides the slab remains, except a few copper nails." He admired the "spirit" of the bas-reliefs and pondered the enigma of the accompanying writing. "The inscriptions . . . are exceedingly numerous, amounting fully to one hundred, and I have been . . . fully occupied in copying these extraordinary specimens of penmanship." Soon, he hoped, "you will have the pleasure of seeing some of the fruits of my labour in the British Museum." He guessed in correspondence with Botta that the Assyrian works were much older than the bas-reliefs at Persepolis. It was likely, he felt, that the Assyrian sculptures had been created long after Egypt's golden age in the early second millennium BCE, and that Assyria's artists had observed the Egyptian work and improved on it. "The great gulf which separates barbarian from civilized art has been passed," he would later declare in the *Malta Times*. Layard praised Assyrian art as "immeasurably superior to the stiff and ill-proportioned figures of the monuments of the Pharaohs."

In Constantinople, Canning was ecstatic. "Layard is making very important discoveries in Mesopotamia," he wrote to his wife in January 1846. "He has sent me the outline of a most beautiful piece of sculpture representing warriors in active fight, and chariots and horses with splendid trappings. . . . The French are jealous to an extreme." He was thrilled at the prospect of learning how closely the narratives aligned with those of the Old Testament, and at the glory that awaited him when the relics reached England. "Major Rawlinson . . . offers to send up a steamer in the spring to secure whatever Layard may have succeeded in getting out," he wrote. "I am quite proud of my public spirit in the cause of antiquity and fine art." Yet after paying Layard's expenses out of his own pocket for many months, he was looking for official support. "I must not ruin either you or the children," he declared, "and I propose to call in the aid of Government—whether Whig or Tory—to accomplish

what may easily prove beyond my reach." He called Layard's excavations "the most astonishing and important series of discoveries"
since the days when Giovanni Belzoni "explored the Tombs of the
Kings in Thebes."

Layard readied himself for a long sojourn in the field. Arab
workers erected for him a three-room hut of "sun-dried bricks
made of clay and chopped straw from their threshing floor," wrote
Ross, who was dividing his time between Mosul and the mound. But
after a heavy rainfall, "the inside walls were quickly clothed with
sprouting barley which, for want of light, grew longer and whiter
every day and hung down the walls in fantastic festoons." The hut,
furnished with nothing more than "a few rude chairs, a table and
wooden bedstead," was the first of several primitive accommoda-
tions in which Layard lived near the mound. For a while he camped
in a tent, surrounded by Arabs who had either pitched tents as well
or, lacking the money to buy the black goat-hair cloth, had erected
small huts of reeds and dry grass. Conditions would deteriorate
during the Mesopotamian summer, when hot desert winds "burnt
up and carried away the shrubs; flights of locusts, darkening the
air . . . destroyed the few patches of cultivation and . . . completed
the havoc commenced by the heat of the sun." Dwelling in the tent
became unbearable and the huts swarmed with vermin; Layard ordered his men to cut a recess into the riverbank and screen the front
with reeds and branches. "I was much troubled, however, with
scorpions and other reptiles, which issued from the earth forming
the walls of my apartment," he wrote, "and later in the summer by
the gnats and sandflies, which hovered on a calm night over the
river."

Through the winter and spring of 1846, before the suffocating
heat set in and the insects came out, Layard and Ross worked at
a breakneck pace. They were still excavating without a firman,

however, and they knew that their status was precarious. One day a company of Ottoman soldiers galloped up to the dig site, following their greyhounds in pursuit of a gazelle. "They pulled their horses up sharp and threw their arms in the air with exclamations of astonishment at finding Europeans in such a place," Ross recounted, "and then demanded [to know] what we were doing and by whose orders we were digging." Ross and Layard claimed to be sightseers, but the pasha in Mosul was not fooled. He accused Layard of digging up Islamic graves and ordered him to cease work. "[T]he wicked Pasha of Mosul . . . is trying to counteract us," wrote Ross, who suspected that their French rivals somehow had a hand in the obstruction. In the end, Canning intervened in Constantinople. The one-eyed, one-eared pasha was replaced with a more sympathetic governor, and the digging resumed. The effort to impede Layard, wrote Ross, "was unsuccessful owing to the dread the Porte had of the . . . Great Ambassador. Indeed, the name of Canning was known throughout the length and breadth of Turkey and was a terror to evil-doers"—and to government functionaries trying to protect their cultural patrimony.

Canning never publicly discussed his sway over the sultan—but the empire was weakening and relied on Great Britain as its guarantor against collapse. Ottoman officials faced Russian expansionism, and rebellions in Montenegro, Serbia, and Bosnia. And conflict was building in Palestine between the Roman Catholics and the Greek Orthodox over control of the Church of the Nativity in Bethlehem and the Church of the Holy Sepulchre, the site of the tomb of Jesus, in Jerusalem. By tradition, the sultan enforced a "Status Quo" in which the Catholics and the Greek Orthodox shared access to the holy sites, though the Orthodox kept the keys to the main door of the Nativity Church. Brawls between Catholic and Orthodox priests broke out on a regular basis. By the 1840s, the French leadership was agitating for Catholic control, the tsar claimed the protection of the eleven million Orthodox in the Ottoman Empire as a casus belli, and the sultan was caught in the middle. The Turks regarded Canning as "the voice of England in the east," and took comfort in his presence, so they were apparently loath to stand in the way of his demands for the empire's antiquities.

In April, Canning informed Prime Minister Robert Peel about Layard's discoveries at Nimrud—presenting the project as his own idea. "Botta's success at Nineveh has induced me to adventure in the same lottery, and my ticket has turned up a prize," Canning boasted, referring to Layard only as his "agent" in the field. Botta had gotten the jump on Layard by three years, but the Englishman, the ambassador believed, was gaining ground. "If the excavation keeps its promise to the end there is much reason to hope that Montagu House"—the original, eighteenth-century name for the British Museum—"will beat the Louvre hollow."

◂─────▸

Freed of the ousted pasha's interference, Layard and his labor teams picked up the pace. "Every day brings fresh discoveries," Layard wrote jubilantly to his mother. Layard now concentrated his excavations in the northwest corner of the mound, in what he believed was the original palace of Nimrud. An account of his expenses from the period captures what a complex venture the dig had become in the course of a few months: Layard lists salaries for basket carriers, diggers, porters, carpenters, security guards, and overseers, cash outlays for "hiring skins for two rafts," nails and screws, tents, mending tools, half a dozen horses, potable water, "hiring of a donkey" to bring the water to the mound, postage for "papers and parcels," and "presents" for the pasha's representatives.

In a newly excavated chamber, a bas-relief displayed a figure wearing a "high conical tiara," with a prisoner lying prostrate at his feet. The image represented, Layard was sure, the first Nimrud king, who would later be identified as Ashurnasirpal II. Days later, he and his workers unearthed an unsettling find: a colossal human head, apparently detached from a winged lion that had guarded a palace gate. The decapitated visage stared blankly from a pile of rubble. Workmen recoiled from the apparition with terror and uttered prayers. Some cried out that Layard had unearthed the remains of Nimrod, the mythological figure who had given the mound its contemporary name. Mentioned in Genesis and Chronicles, he was an ancient hunter, great-grandson of Noah, and "infidel giant" regarded as an enemy of Islam. When workers fled to Mosul and reported the discovery, residents poured into the streets, demanding that Layard stop stirring up evil spirits. The new pasha convinced the population the figure was made of stone, which tempered their panic, but the fear and hostility aroused by the vestiges of ancient polytheists would linger—and would find a destructive echo nearly two centuries later when Islamic State militants invaded the area.

Layard uncovered other friezes that opened a window onto Assyria's superstitions, omens, sacred emblems, and fantastical deities. A half-man, half-bird, with a red-tipped tongue, feathery wings, and the head of an eagle adorned one huge alabaster slab; Layard suspected the bas-relief depicted the Assyrian god Nisroch, in whose temple, according to 2 Kings 19, King Sennacherib had been slain by his two sons in 681 BCE. "And it came to pass," the passage relates, "as he was worshiping in the house of Nisroch his god, that Adrammelech and Sharezer his sons smote him with the sword; and they escaped into the land of Armenia." He observed winged figures holding a square bucket and a pinecone—talismans used, he

speculated, in a purification ritual. A "sacred tree" depicted hon-
eysuckles or tulips springing from two tendrils, mysterious motifs
echoed in the later carvings of the Achaemenids and the ancient
Greeks.

Soon Layard made the most remarkable find so far: two intact
winged lions with human heads. Each one measured fourteen feet
long and seventeen feet high and each stood sculpted in high relief on a block of marble that formed a gateway to the palace. In
the throne room, workmen turned up two more winged guardian
spirits, "the most magnificent specimens of Assyrian sculpture that
could be well found," Layard exulted. Ingeniously endowed with
five legs, they appeared to be standing still when viewed from the
front but striding forward when observed from the side. "They
could find no better type of intellect and knowledge than the head
of a man; of strength, than the body of a lion; of ubiquity, than the
wings of a bird," Layard wrote in *Nineveh and Its Remains*. "These
winged human-headed lions were not idle creations . . . their meaning was written upon them."

In fact, the lamassus' origins, not yet understood by Layard,
were embedded deep in Mesopotamia's mythical past—a primor-
dial time before men and beasts became clearly differentiated. The
warrior god Ninurta defeated a legion of winged, human-headed
monsters, domesticated them, and then brought them home to
become benevolent protectors of humanity. Standing at the en-
trances to palaces and throne rooms, their stone likenesses were
meant to scare away the forces of chaos. "Nothing so beautiful as
these lions was discovered by the French," Layard gloated to his
mother. "They are admirably drawn, and the muscles, bones, and
veins quite true to nature." (Layard was getting early intimations of
the Assyrians' fascination with the human body, manifested by the
hundreds of medical texts that would be found later in royal librar-

ies at Nineveh.) "There is also a great *mouvement*—as the French well term it—in the attitude of the animal," he continued. Their presence in the palace was a mystery that captivated Layard. "How the Assyrians moved these immense blocks, I cannot conceive," he wrote. "There are no marble quarries, that I know of, within seven or eight miles, and they must have had good ropes to stand the actual brute-force necessary to move such weights."

But even as his finds grew more compelling, Layard's position was becoming more precarious. Word of Layard's excavations reached the qadi of Mosul, the powerful Muslim judge who delivered rulings based on Sharia law. The judge accused Layard of a host of crimes: stealing treasures from the mounds, unleashing demonic creatures from the pre-Islamic past, and digging up cuneiform inscriptions that exposed a nefarious plot. The writings, he claimed disingenuously, "proved the Franks once held the country, and . . . intended immediately to resume possession of it, exterminating all true Mussulmans." This manipulative weaving of fact and fiction riled up much of Mosul's population. Layard publicly castigated the qadi as a "fanatic" and a man of "infamous character." Then Layard made things worse.

In early spring 1846, the two adversaries found themselves on the same decrepit ferry across the Tigris. Layard stood beside the helmsman on a raised part of the deck. The qadi rode in steerage with the other passengers and their animals. Staring up at Layard, the qadi muttered contemptuously, loud enough for Layard to hear, "Shall the dogs occupy the high places, whilst the true believers have to stand below?"

In his memoir Layard bragged that he delivered to the qadi "a blow on his head with a short, hooked stick, such as the Bedouin Arabs use when riding their camels, and which I always carried with me." It was apparently meant as a mild rebuke. "As he wore a thick turban, I did not believe that the blow would have had much effect," Layard wrote. But he had miscalculated: "I was surprised to see the blood streaming down his face."

The qadi's attendants pulled out swords and pistols. Two Albanian "irregular" troops attached to the Ottoman army rushed to protect Layard. The Englishman grabbed the qadi by the throat and threatened to throw him overboard, forcing the attendants to retreat. When the boat docked, the qadi, with blood dripping down his face, rushed through the bazaars, exclaiming that he had been assaulted by an infidel. "The Prophet and his faith have been insulted," he cried.

Fortunately for Layard, who had to hide out while enraged crowds massed in the streets, the newly appointed pasha came to his defense. The Ottoman military had waged a war between 1811 and 1818 with Wahhabist guerrillas in the Arabian Desert just south of Mesopotamia, and the possibility of a surge of radical Islamist sentiment in Mosul must have alarmed Turkish officials. As Layard told the story, the pasha dismissed the qadi as a "notorious fanatic," and deployed police to prevent riots. Albanian irregulars guarded Layard for the next few weeks. "My life was, I believe for some time in danger, so much so that Rawlinson, at the suggestion of the Pasha of Baghdad, ordered me to leave Mosul and to live with him until the matter had blown over," he recalled. But Layard refused, and the issue eventually died down.

◄──────►

Layard had admired Rawlinson ever since reading, back in 1839 and 1840, his account of his Zagros Mountains adventures. Now Rawlinson was doing research into cuneiform in Baghdad, and Layard was now deeply engaged in helping him. He had first reached out to the diplomat while living in Constantinople in March 1845, dis-

patching sketches of a few Akkadian characters that Botta had sent
him from Khorsabad. But Rawlinson was still absorbed in the Old
Persian, and Edwin Norris was feeding him reports from London
about his own progress on Elamite. "I have paid but little attention
to the Babylonian character," Rawlinson admitted. As soon as he
was done with those two systems, he wrote, "I hope to attack the
Babylonian with some chance of success and these four inscriptions
will doubtless prove of infinite value."

Layard's dispatch from Constantinople helped to shift Rawlinson's focus. Soon Rawlinson obtained more sketches directly from
Botta, and began thinking deeply about the nature of the script and
the language. Although he dismissed much of what he read in the
Bible, he was inclined to accept the predominant theory that all the
world's languages had originated with Noah's three sons, and that
the descendants of Shem had likely disseminated their linguistic family across the Near East. "My own idea," he wrote, "is that one general Semitic alphabet prevailed from [Mount] Ararat to the Persian
Gulf—at Khorsabad and Nineveh, at Babylon, at Susa, and in the
third column of the trilingual tablets of Persepolis . . . and Bisitun."

During the Christmas season in 1845, two months after beginning his excavations on the mound and before his troubles with the
qadi, Layard had traveled by the *Nitocris* from Mosul to Baghdad to
meet Rawlinson for the first time. The British Museum was leaning
toward financing the excavations at Nimrud, and Layard needed
to discuss with Rawlinson how to ship the friezes and the winged
lions and bulls down the Tigris. They had other issues to talk about.
Layard had turned up exciting evidence, he believed, of a direct
connection between Hebrew and Akkadian: the half-bird, half-man
god in the Northwest Palace, he maintained, appeared to represent
the Assyrian deity Nisroch cited in the Old Testament. The name
must have derived from the word *nisr*, "eagle" in many Semitic lan-

guages. "Is [the language] Chaldaean?" he had mused in a letter to his mother, using the misnomer for Aramaic. "Or is it some dialect, long forgotten, of one of the existing family of languages . . . Or is it some unknown language, which will have to be reconstructed?" He had made some progress in understanding how the writing system worked. A decade earlier, Georg Grotefend had identified a single vertical stroke ⊤ before proper names in the Akkadian texts at Persepolis, and a three-wedge sign ⪦ that preceded the names of cities and countries. Layard had relied on these determinatives, he told Rawlinson, to identify sequences of characters that spelled proper names and the names of cities—but he was, he admitted, unsure where the words ended, stumped by the logograms, and clueless about how to pronounce them.

Rawlinson was swept up by Layard's enthusiasm as they sat in the reception hall overlooking the Tigris. The gray-green stream lay just beyond the picture windows, flowing past a row of flat-roofed, brick villas and palaces, some of them sagging on the muddy riverbank, housing foreign embassies and wealthy Baghdadi families. The two fell into a deep discussion about language groups, with Rawlinson now challenging Layard's certainty that Akkadian was closely related to Hebrew. He proposed that it was closer to Coptic, the ecclesiastical language derived from ancient Egyptian, that also bore a resemblance to Chadian, the Berber language of the Saharan Tuaregs, and other North African tongues. The men were thoroughly engaged with each other, George Rawlinson reported; they also complemented each other well. "Layard was a man excellently fitted for the work of an explorer and excavator, strong, robust, determined," wrote Rawlinson. He was "active, energetic, and inured to hardship by his previous travels in wild regions." Henry Rawlinson had had plenty of adventures of his own, yet, his brother opined, he was a more cerebral figure than Layard: "the classical scholar, the linguist, the diligent student of history, the man at once of wide reading and keen insight, the cool, dispassionate investigator and weigher of evidence."

Rawlinson was just finishing his translation of Old Persian for the Royal Asiatic Society journal, and after toiling on it since the mid 1830s, he was eager to leave that "drudgery" behind. With the two men working closely together on the initial "one hundred inscriptions" from the Nimrud palace, and presumably many more to follow, Rawlinson predicted that "the histories of the early Assyrians and Babylonians" will be "more thoroughly explored than those of Egypt."

That was a lot to hope for. Napoleon's 1798 conquest of Egypt had initiated an obsession with the civilization along the Nile. Europeans devoured accounts by French sketch artist and writer Vivant Denon, who accompanied Napoleon's army, creating mesmerizing images of wonders like the Sphinx of Giza: "Though its proportions are colossal, the outline is pure and graceful," he wrote, "the expression of the head is mild, gracious and tranquil." Waves of scientists and antiquarians soon followed. Edgar Allan Poe's short story "Some Words with a Mummy," about the reanimation of an embalmed—and garrulous— Egyptian corpse, lightly mocked the craze for Egyptology that spread to America after the publication of British travel writer John Gardner Wilkinson's bestselling *Manners and Customs of the Ancient Egyptians* in 1837.

Assyria would soon enough astonish the public in France, England, and other parts of Europe and the United States, but it would never have the same popular appeal as ancient Egypt. For one thing, the civilizations of Assyria and Babylon left behind few intact monumental structures like the pyramids, the Sphinx, or the colossal rock-cut temples of Abu Simbel. They lacked lurid curiosities like mummies and venomous asps. Having emerged from a

A nineteenth-century artist's rendering of
the Palace at Nineveh on the Tigris River

remote, unstable part of the world, they proved far less inviting and accessible for travelers than the temples and tombs along the Nile. And though the Pharaohs of Egypt had their military adventures, there was something disconcerting about Assyria's relentless focus on war, conquest, booty, and slaughter.

Still, in the eyes of Assyriologists, the achievements of the Mesopotamian civilizations matched if not exceeded those of Egypt. The Assyrians invented siege warfare, constructed grand palaces and temples, developed a sophisticated administrative system, standardized legal codes, recorded celestial phenomena such as planetary movements and eclipses, and amassed the greatest libraries of the ancient world.

Going back further in his book *History Begins at Sumer*, the famed University of Pennsylvania Assyriologist Samuel Noah Kramer lists thirty-nine "firsts" established by early Mesopotamians that would become essential parts of modern life. Among them: the first schools, the first "Farmer's Almanac," the first cosmogony and cosmology, the first proverbs and sayings, the first library catalogue, and the first love song. It's not difficult to imagine an alternate reality in which the names Sennacherib and Nebuchadnezzar II would evoke the same excitement as Rameses and Tutankhamen, and the palaces of Nimrud and Nineveh would inspire as much wonder as the Great Pyramid and the Valley of the Kings. It was pure bad luck that, except for Babylon's Ishtar Gate and a handful of monumental lamassus, no surviving traces of Assyro-Babylonian culture could compare with Egypt's grand remains—and almost nobody wanted to travel to Turkish Arabia, and its equally unstable successor, Iraq, to see what was left.

As Rawlinson and Layard went their separate ways, each man expressed admiration and affection for the other. "I had long wished to make the personal acquaintance of Major Rawlinson, with whom I had long kept up a constant & regular correspondence," Layard wrote to his mother, "and I received no disappointment on meeting him. You may suppose that we are already deep in discussion & researches on Assyrian, Persian, and Babylonian antiquities, languages, geography &c &c—for on these subjects, you know the Major is probably the first living authority." Layard was convinced that "before two or three years have expired we shall be able to get at the mysterious contents of the Assyrian cuneiform inscriptions—and then Nimroud will give us a rich historical collection." Rawlinson, too, was elated. With his relationship to the archaeologist now established, and the prospect of a steady supply of antiquities coming to him from the Nimrud palace, Rawlinson believed he was ideally positioned to grasp the Akkadian writing system before anyone else. He had no idea that competition was already coming from faraway Ulster—and a man who was his opposite in nearly every respect.

CHAPTER NINE

HINCKS

On June 9, 1846, an officer of the Royal Irish Academy in Dublin, a venerable learned society founded in 1785, read aloud to the other members a paper submitted by a fifty-three-year-old rector in the Church of Ireland. Edward Hincks was unknown outside of a tiny circle of Egyptologists, who admired his work deciphering religious inscriptions from Thebes and attempting to figure out how the pharaohs measured weeks, months, and years. Hincks had been studying Old Persian as well as hieroglyphs, and he believed he had picked up something that few, if any, other experts had noticed: cuneiform characters were a unique mix of vowels, consonants, *and* syllables. There were, for example, the characters *ja, ji,* and *ju; ta* and *tu; da, di,* and *du; ga* and *gu.* "[I]n the inscriptions of Darius" at Persepolis, he declared in his paper, the name of an ancient Persian civilization in present-day Uzbekistan and Turkmenistan is in "one place written *Shuguda,*" using individual consonants and vowels, "and in another *Sog[u]da;* where the secondary form of *g* preceding *u* must, I think, be read syllabically *gu.*" Hincks included a table in his article that contrasted his readings (on the right) with those of Danish decipherer Niels Ludvig

Westergaard, who, Hincks believed, had failed to recognize the vowel implicit in some Old Persian signs.

	gh	g(u)
	dh	d(u)
	q	k(u)

One institution taking notice was the Royal Asiatic Society, some of whose directors were accomplished linguists. Edwin Norris, then the assistant secretary of the society and Henry Rawlinson's main contact in London, prided himself on speaking forty-eight languages, including Sanskrit, Māori, Arabic, and Berber; he had recently translated a series of mystery plays written in Middle Cornish, a Celtic tongue that had gone extinct at the end of the eighteenth century. Norris had observed that Rawlinson, in a rough unfinished draft of the Behistun paper, presented to the secretary in the spring of 1846, had produced readings of Old Persian words that scrunched together consonants into vowel-free combinations, putting the writing system close to Hebrew and Arabic, though Norris, who was fluent in Sanskrit, had the sense that Persian belonged, like that ancient language, to the Indo-European, not the Semitic, family. Puzzlingly, Rawlinson had identified several signs that he claimed were all pronounced *m*, several that stood for *j*, several that stood for *l*, and so on. Thanks to Hincks, the reason for these odd readings was now clear: Rawlinson had mistaken syllables for consonants.

When the *Literary Gazette*, an influential weekly magazine that was then at its height of popularity, published a summary of Hincks's paper, Norris dispatched Rawlinson a copy. Two months later, Rawlinson submitted a "Supplementary Note" to his earlier paper. Without making mention of Hincks's findings, Rawlinson had switched many of the characters he'd interpreted as consonants to syllables. It was not unusual for philologists to draw on each other's published work, but the fact that Rawlinson failed to acknowledge Hincks's contributions raised eyebrows. "It is evident that Major R. caught the idea of simplifying his alphabet . . . from you," wrote George Cecil Renouard, a retired professor of Arabic at Cambridge University and frequent correspondent with Hincks. Still, Hincks accepted Rawlinson's assurance to the Royal Asiatic Society that he had sent his corrections to London long *before* Hincks's article had reached him in Baghdad, and the possibility of scandal faded.

But the Irish rector soon returned to Rawlinson's consciousness. In January 1847, the *Dublin University Magazine* featured Hincks's six-thousand-word review of Rawlinson's *The Persian Cuneiform Inscription at Behistun*, his translation of and commentary on the cliff narrative of Darius the Great. Hincks began his critique with an appreciation of Rawlinson's achievement, praising his "vast labour" and the "no trifling danger" the diplomat had faced. Then he displayed his own mastery of the subject. Hincks explained the relationships among Sanskrit, Avestan, and Old Persian and summarized the Zoroastrian religion. He compared the ancient Persian king to Henry VII, since both were not heirs to the throne but ascended through violence. He likened a rebel leader in the Achaemenid Empire to Perkin Warbeck, a fifteenth-century pretender to the English throne hanged by Henry VII in 1499.

Hincks eviscerated the work of fellow philologists. German scholar Christian Lassen, who had recently published a volume of Old Persian translations, "seems . . . to have been completely destitute of the peculiar talent of the decipherer," Hincks sniffed. Lassen had badly botched the values of a quarter of the twenty-four signs he claimed to have deciphered, Hincks said: "[T]he grossness of many of [his] mistakes are such as to create astonishment." (Lassen had also hit upon the unique mix of syllables, consonants, and

vowels in Old Persian, so perhaps Hincks was lashing out especially hard at a serious rival.) Hincks was far more complimentary
about Rawlinson's work: "We do not hesitate to say that a more
interesting—and, on many accounts, a more important—addition
to our library of ancient history has never been made." Yet Hincks
subjected Rawlinson to rigorous scrutiny. He challenged his interpretation of the winged creature that hovers above Darius at Behistun. "Major Rawlinson calls this figure in the air 'an angel,' but
surely it is intended for . . . the supreme deity to whose aid Darius
attributes all his success," Hincks wrote. He quibbled with him over
vocabulary choices: he should have used "state" instead of "army,"
and "people" rather than "government." He questioned Rawlinson's proper names: "We will not vouch for these combinations
of letters." Confronting Hincks's linguistic and historical expertise, says Kevin Cathcart, professor emeritus at University College
Dublin, the diplomat-scholar must "have been in shock."

◄◄———————►►

Edward Hincks was born in the southern Irish city of Cork in August 1792. His father, Thomas Dix Hincks, was a beloved Presbyterian minister who belonged to a "nonconformist" branch of the
Church that rejected the Holy Trinity and held that Jesus Christ was
only "semi-divine." (Known as the Arians, they distinguished themselves from their fellow nonconformists, the Unitarians, who went
even further against Presbyterian doctrine, maintaining that Jesus
was a human being.) The elder Hincks was also an agriculturalist,
philosopher, and scholar of classical Greek, Hebrew, and Arabic,
who encouraged his son's fascination for ancient languages. They
were a distinguished family. William, Edward's younger brother by
two years, would become a renowned Unitarian minister in Liverpool and a professor of natural history at Queen's College in Cork

and University College at the University of Toronto; the youngest, Francis, immigrated to Canada, where he earned distinction as a journalist and businessman and rose to become the province's premier. (Hincks's extended family didn't fare badly either: his second cousin was the famed Victorian novelist Elizabeth Gaskell, author of *North and South*.)

Like his siblings, Hincks got off to a precocious start. When Hincks was six or seven, his teacher at the Midleton School in Cork offered his students a prize if they could translate two lines of verse by the Roman satirist Juvenal above the classroom door. Hincks's classmates ignored the challenge. Hincks gave it a go. It was one of the few times that his deciphering effort, he wrote, "was in vain." (Decades later he figured out the prosaic answer: "Within this door let no foul sight appear / and no foul words be uttered. Boys are here.")

Hincks entered Trinity College Dublin in 1807 at fifteen. He won awards for Latin composition, studied Hebrew, and dabbled in Syriac, Etruscan, and Sanskrit. He mastered advanced mathematics, wrote a satirical essay about the Iroquois chief Hiawatha, and composed a flowery, thousand-line epic poem about Napoleon's defeat at Waterloo. To Hincks's dismay his classmates laughed at the composition. "It did me considerable injury," Hincks admitted. (Hincks's grandson and biographer, E. F. Davidson, passed judgment on the effort decades later: "The work . . . is not worth rescuing from oblivion.") Perhaps unsurprisingly, Hincks was not uniformly popular with his peers. He was proud, sometimes arrogant, grumpy, "not able to suffer fools gladly," says Kevin Cathcart, and quick to lash out if he felt he had been wronged. He quarreled with critics of his verse and carried on running feuds with the Trinity College provost and with a prominent Trinity graduate, Charles Wall. A fellow student suggested that Wall, twelve years older than Hincks, might have been jealous of the younger man's academic superiority. (Wall, a Hebrew professor at Trinity, would, years later, publicly question the validity of Hincks's and other linguists' cuneiform decipherments.) "Even in early life [Hincks] made enemies as well as friends," his grandson observed. His grandfather, Davidson wrote, took "a jaundiced view of things."

In 1819, after spending twelve years as a student, teaching fellow in theology and classical philosophy, and assistant librarian at the university, Hincks abandoned academics. In a career switch that caught some by surprise, he was ordained as a minister in the Church of Ireland, the Irish counterpart of the Church of England, founded by King Henry VIII and subsequently presided over by English monarchs. Hincks's decision sparked a family drama: his father was anything but pleased that his eldest son had signed on with the Anglicans, the Presbyterian Church's Protestant rival. In some parishes, "each church accused the other of coaxing people away," says Kevin Cathcart. It's unclear why Hincks chose to reject the Church of his father. It may have had to do with his long affiliation with Trinity College, founded in 1592 to consolidate the rule of the Tudors in Ireland. Perhaps he was also drawn to the reassurance of Anglican doctrine and the beauty of its traditions and aesthetics, not that different from those of Roman Catholicism.

Whatever the case, his decision to join the Church of Ireland led to a painful estrangement from his brother William, who wrote to their father in 1822 that "our correspondence appears to have entirely ceased . . . Though I can have but little sympathy for his opinions, I truly respect him and only want . . . to feel toward him all the warmth of fraternal love." Both Thomas and William Hincks would have regarded Edward's choice as a spurning of their nonconformist denominations, which are far less hierarchical, place a great emphasis on individual conscience in matters of faith, and vehemently reject state control of the church.

The Church of Ireland offered Hincks a position in the parish of Ardtrea, a market town of old stone houses and a few thousand inhabitants that straddles County Londonderry and County Tyrone, 105 miles north of Dublin and forty-six miles west of Belfast. The salary was £800 a year—worth about $95,000 today—a generous remuneration for a churchman in rural Ulster. Just to the east of the village lay Lough Neagh, the largest lake in the British Isles. Hincks's motive to leave Trinity may well have been that he felt "a genuine call to the work of a parish priest," his grandson wrote, or it may have been disillusionment with academe and the arguments with peers that seemed to consume much of his time. Whatever the case, while Rawlinson was adventuring and fighting wars in West Asia, Hincks was burrowed away in a parsonage, largely detached from the world.

Yet Hincks found ways of satisfying his intellectual passions. In the fall of 1821, he entered a contest in the *Quarterly Journal of Science, Literature and the Arts*, a London-based magazine. The Napoleonic Wars were still fresh in the public's mind, and with them a fascination for spycraft, cryptography, and coded messages dispatched between military commands and foreign embassies. The *Journal* prepared five versions of a two-hundred-character cipher and gave its readers three months to solve the puzzle. If the code "does not lend itself to detection, before the first of January," the editors declared, "the method must be allowed to be tolerably secure."

Hincks not only decoded the cipher and received the £100 prize (worth about $12,000 in today's money), but he also wrote back to the *Journal* using the same code, pleased with his intellectual accomplishment and eager to upstage the code's creator. But it was another achievement in decipherment, announced in Paris a few months later, that would capture Hincks's imagination and stoke his ambitions to play on a much bigger stage.

In 1798, Napoleon Bonaparte led an expeditionary force of forty thousand soldiers and ten thousand sailors in thirteen ships across the Mediterranean to Alexandria, the start of a military campaign to seize the Ottoman territories of Egypt and Syria. That July, after a punishing march without water across the desert, the French slaughtered a force of Mamluks—an Ottoman military caste descended from slaves taken primarily from the Caucasus and Central Asia at the Battle of the Pyramids. Then they seized Cairo, cementing their conquest of the territory. The following July, a company of Napoleonic soldiers rebuilding a fort in the town of Rashid, or Rosetta, on the Egyptian coast, stumbled across a 1.7-ton broken black stele embedded in a wall and covered with inscriptions. The French commander recognized the find as potentially extraordinary and alerted the Commission of the Sciences and the Arts, a team of French "savants" who had traveled with Napoleon's army and set up shop in Cairo.

They soon identified the writing as a trilingual proclamation composed by a group of priests for the coronation of the eleven-year-old Greek-Egyptian king Ptolemy V in 196 BCE. One copy of the decree was inscribed in ancient Greek, at the time the dominant language of Greek-governed Egypt; one was in Egyptian hieroglyphs (a word from the Greek meaning "sacred carving"), the script for official proclamations of the pharaohs; and the third was written in a cursive, or shorthand, version of hieroglyphs called Demotic, a more informal and messier script used for ordinary correspondence by literate Egyptians—perhaps seven percent of the population at its peak in the third century BCE.

In 1798, Admiral Horatio Nelson destroyed Napoleon's fleet in the Battle of the Nile, and in 1801 Lieutenant-General Ralph Abercromby defeated the French ground forces in the Battle of Alexandria. The Capitulation of Alexandria compelled the French to "hand over all antiquities found by them and to relinquish all rights to any seized at sea by the naval blockade." An English diplomat named William Richard Hamilton, escorted by British foot soldiers, confiscated the Rosetta Stone from a warehouse in Alexandria and delivered it to the British Museum, with the words "Captured in Egypt by the British Army 1801" painted on its side. General Sir Tomkyns Hilgrove Turner, who escorted the Rosetta Stone from Egypt to England, saluted the acquisition of this "proud trophy . . . not plundered from defenceless inhabitants, but honourably acquired by the fortune of war." A group called the Society of Antiquaries copied the inscriptions and sent plaster replicas to scholars at Oxford, Cambridge, Dublin, and Edinburgh, as well as abroad to Paris and Philadelphia.

At the time of the discovery, attempts to decipher the writing of the pharaohs had been mired for millennia in misconceptions. The first appearance of hieroglyphs dates to around 3200 BCE, some two hundred years after the first pictograms in Sumer; use of the writing system ceased three and a half millennia later, after the Roman emperor Theodosius I shut down all non-Christian temples in 391 CE. Understanding of the ancient writing and language faded, swept away completely after the seventh-century CE Islamic conquest. Unlike cuneiform, though, hieroglyphs never disappeared from view: locals and visitors to Egypt encountered the signs on tombs and temples along the Nile. "There is hardly the space of an awl or a needle-hole," a traveler from Baghdad had observed in 1183, "which does not have an . . . engraving of [this] script which is not understood." Eight obelisks inscribed with hieroglyphs had been brought to Rome while Egypt was an imperial province between 30 BCE and 641 CE, and most had been on public display ever since. And a pink-granite obelisk from Luxor, carved during the reign of Rameses II around 1290 BCE, would soon come to dominate the Place de la Concorde in Paris. Yet nobody had a clue what the writing on the obelisks meant.

Since classical times, scholars clung to the notion that hieroglyphs, with their captivating pictograms of birds, mammals, reptiles, human body parts, trees and plants, ropes, earthenware, and other recognizable objects, served as talismans and allegories. This gave rise to one improbable "translation" after another. "Rather than burrow into the ground in search of mundane meanings behind the cryptic symbols," Edward Dolnick wrote in *The Writing of the Gods*, scholars "sailed aloft into ever more far-fetched realms of hot air and learned silliness." In *Hieroglyphica*, a fifth-century treatise written in Greek, the Egyptian priest Horapollo maintained that the hieroglyphic symbol of a hawk stood for "a god" or "something sublime," because among birds, he wrote, "only the hawk flies straight upward." Alternate meanings, he went on, included "sight" because of the raptor's keen vision, "boundaries," because it was said to hover above an imminent battleground for seven days, and "mother," since, he claimed, "there is no male" in this genus of raptors. (Though his explanation was nonsensical, he improbably got the last meaning right.) The picture of a hare meant "open," because, he posited, the animals never close their eyes. English Egyptologist Thomas Young characterized Horapollo's conjectures as a "puerile collection of conceits and enigmas."

The seventeenth-century Jesuit priest Athanasius Kircher ventured further into absurdity. Kircher provided a fifty-four-word translation of the characters inside a cartouche—an oval-shaped ring containing a short string of hieroglyphs—on an obelisk in Rome's Piazza della Minerva. "The protection of Osiris against the violence of Typho," Kircher's "decipherment" began, "must be elicited according to proper rites and ceremonies by sacrifices and by appeal to the tutelary Genii of the triple world." The signs would turn out to stand for the single-word name of a pharaoh. It wasn't until the eighteenth century that Egypt scholars began to take a new look at the supposedly mystical characters. Abbé Jean-Jacques Barthélemy, a French philologist who had deciphered the Aramaic-like writing and language called Palmyrene in two days in 1754, asserted in the 1760s that the cartouches were used to cordon off the names of kings. After the Rosetta Stone's discovery, Antoine Isaac Silvestre de Sacy, a French Orientalist, posited that only foreign names appeared inside these enigmatic cartouches. One of de Sacy's Eastern-languages students had noticed that Chinese singled out the names of foreign missionaries and diplomats with special markings on the characters. Chinese is composed almost entirely of logograms, but the markings indicated that these altered signs were meant to be read phonetically. De Sacy believed that the Egyptian cartouches had served the same purpose as the Chinese markings.

These hypotheses paved the way in the 1810s for Thomas Young, a British polymath celebrated for his research and theories on capillary action, astigmatism, the perception of color, heart and artery function, and light waves. Young found the name PTOLEMAIOS—the Greek Egyptian king to whom the Rosetta Stone was dedicated—repeated a dozen times in the Greek inscriptions on the stele, then searched the fourteen surviving lines of hieroglyphs for cartouches appearing with the same frequency and containing a similar number of characters. By lining up the Greek letters and the hieroglyphs, he obtained the approximate phonetic values of seven ancient Egyptian characters.

P   O   L   E S
T   M

But Young's conviction that all the glyphs inscribed outside the cartouches had to be logograms stymied him. Once thought to be a sure bet to break open the language, he failed to advance beyond that initial eureka moment, creating an opening for Jean-François Champollion, a French philologist and Egyptophile, who demonstrated the original, flexible thinking that characterizes the greatest decipherers.

Soon after Young's breakthrough, Champollion found the names of two Greco-Roman rulers, KLEOPATRA and ALEKSANDRIS, on an obelisk from Philae, an island near Aswan on Egypt's Upper Nile, expanding knowledge of hieroglyphs to fourteen phonetic signs. But his key achievements came through his knowledge of Coptic, which had originated in Egypt in the fourth century CE and was still in use as an ecclesiastical language. Champollion believed that Coptic had developed from ancient Egyptian, and that it could be used to glean both the sounds and meanings of hieroglyphs. On an inscription from a temple at Abu Simbel, in 1822, he found a sign inside a cartouche that looked like the picture of the sun. On a hunch, Champollion assigned it the sound *ra*, or alternatively, *re*, the word for "sun" in Coptic. Then he combined *ra* with the three other signs inside the cartouche, the phonetic values of which he had picked up from the Rosetta Stone. He wound up with RAMESES, the nineteenth-dynasty pharaoh.

RA MES S S

The discovery had tremendous implications. Not only had Champollion confirmed that Egyptian names inside a cartouche (not just foreign ones) could be written at least partly with phonemes, he had also shown that a relationship existed between Coptic and the far older language.

In another cartouche, Champollion found the sign for an ibis

⟟, a representation, he knew, of the god Thoth. Using this logo-gram and the phonetic signs that followed, ⟟ 𓏠 𓈖 𓈖, Champollion worked out the name of the king THOTHMES. This led to a far bigger step forward. Phonetically, the last two characters of THOTHMES spelled the Coptic word *mise*, which means "to give birth." Acting on another hunch, Champollion searched the Rosetta Stone and found the same two characters buried in the phrase "the *birthday* of the king." Glyphs, he suddenly under-stood, could spell words phonetically not just inside cartouches but *anywhere* in the text. With one insight, Champollion swept away the old perception of hieroglyphs as a mystical language of high concepts and abstractions. According to a possibly apocry-phal story told by a nephew, Champollion cried out to his brother *"Je tiens l'affaire!"* (*"I've got it!"*), fainted, and didn't emerge from his bed for five days.

On Friday, September 27, 1822—nine months after Edward Hincks solved the cipher in the London magazine—Champollion presented his draft translation of the Rosetta Stone to the Académie des Inscriptions et Belles Lettres in Paris, closing the book on two thousand years of fallacious thinking.

Liberated from the preconceptions that had impeded would-be decipherers for two millennia, Champollion made a series of addi-tional discoveries: Hieroglyphs could function as both logograms *and* as the letters of an alphabet, with their phonetic values derived in often clever ways from the logographic meaning. In the case of *RA*, the object and the sound were interchangeable. (If English worked according to the same principles, you could write "Sun-day" as "☀Day.") In many cases, though, the logogram's first letter provided its sound when it was used as a phonetic character: thus, the sign for a horned owl 𓅓 could sometimes stand for the bird—*mutloch* in Coptic—but it also made the sound *m*. A sign might also function as a rebus—a puzzle in which words are represented using sound-alike pictures, numbers, or letters. The picture of a duck, *sa* 🦆, could refer to the waterfowl, but more often it was used to mean "son," which was also pronounced *sa*. (In the same way, an English-language rebus might combine and to represent the name of the famous philanthropist and Microsoft cofounder Bill Gates.)

With his expanding alphabet and his knowledge of Coptic, Champollion searched through inscriptions for words he could piece together. He realized that the *P* Young identified in PTOLEMY ☐ made both the phonetic sound *p* and the word *p*—Coptic and ancient Egyptian for "the." A horizontal zigzag that looked like flowing water 〰️ stood for the letter *N* and the word *of*. He found silent characters, known as determinatives, that served as guides to how to read the signs that followed. The system used more than forty of these silent characters to help single out trees and plants, foreign lands, fish, foreigners, men and women, reptiles, and many other categories. The writing system would turn out to be a hybrid script with about seven hundred signs, including an alphabet of thirty letters, the forty determinatives, and hundreds of logograms. Consonants were bunched together into groups, as in Hebrew, with vowels almost always unwritten and inferred from context.

The decipherment of hieroglyphs opened a world that had remained a mystery for two millennia. With the new understanding came insights into Egyptian history, culture, art, and science. Scholars could examine momentous events, such as the tumultuous reign of Thutmose III, who expunged all traces of his powerful stepmother, Queen Hatshepsut, from the obelisks, statues, and temples of Thebes. They could study the process of mummification, Egyptian views of the afterlife, folktales, medicine, and quotidian life along the Nile.

Two decades on, the work of Champollion and his rival Young would provide a road map for deciphering Akkadian cuneiform. But though the two writing systems had similarities, Akkadian would prove to be vastly more complex. Its confounding rules—or rather, its apparent lack of them—would cast a shadow over the entire enterprise and expose its would-be decipherers to years of skepticism and even ridicule.

◄———►

Tucked away in his Ulster backwater, Edward Hincks continued his studies of the ancient languages that had captivated him at Trinity. But he published little at first and went unnoticed. In 1823, he married thirty-one-year-old Jane Dorothea Boyd; the couple would have four daughters in rapid succession. It was "probably a grievous disappointment to him that he had no son," Davidson observed. "The [diary] entries recording the arrivals of successive daughters show diminishing enthusiasm." The birth of his fourth didn't rate so much as a mention, perhaps reflecting the chagrin of a man whose own father had five sons and who, unlike Edward Hincks, could be sure of perpetuating his last name and his legacy.

After seven years at Ardtrea, Hincks made the move that would be the final one of his life. He became the rector, or parish priest, of Killyleagh, in County Down, a prosperous town with a thriving textile industry, twenty-two miles south of Belfast, where he would remain for the next forty years. His father had been appointed a professor of Oriental languages at the Royal Belfast Academical Institution, so the move brought him closer to his parents and a few siblings. But the job involved a six percent pay cut—from £800 to £750 a year.

Killyleagh, with a population of about twelve thousand, rose along Strangford Lough, the largest inlet in the United Kingdom.

Its islets, bays, coves, and mudflats supported a rich array of water birds, including one of the world's largest populations of Light-Bellied Brent Geese, small, dark fowl that migrate to Ireland each winter from the Arctic Circle. Hincks's parish, the Church of St. John the Evangelist, constructed in 1640, a large stone edifice with a Gothic tower, stood atop a hill with a view of the lough in one direction and in the other, Killyleagh Castle, a fairy-tale structure marked by twin round towers topped by conical cupolas, built in 1567. Hincks lived in a stone rectory next to the church.

In this halcyon setting, Hincks delivered Sunday sermons that praised devotion to God, good works, and reverence for the Bible. He often quoted Psalm 37:37 to urge his flock to behave with fairness: "Mark the perfect man and behold the upright: for the end of that man is peace." One parishioner spoke of his "kindness, gentleness, and humility; his anxiety for others' good; his readiness to spend and be spent in his Master's service." During the week, he gave advice and consolation to his parishioners at the rectory.

But Hincks wasn't afraid to shake things up. He had been a small boy in County Cork, a predominantly Catholic part of Ireland, during the Irish Rebellion of 1798, when lightly armed Catholic insurgents, the Society of United Irishmen, rose against discriminatory British rule; thousands of fighters and civilians had died. The uprising hardened Irish Protestants against Catholics, especially in majority-Protestant parts of the island such as Killyleagh. Hincks had grown up with a liberal-minded patriarch who was rigorous about his faith, but who defended Catholics against mob violence and supported their "emancipation" from oppressive British statutes. He had inherited from Thomas Dix Hincks an independent-mindedness and a persistence in the face of skepticism that would serve him well in decipherment. In Killyleagh, Hincks supported repealing laws that restricted Catholics' voting rights, banned them from serving in Parliament, and prevented their holding prestigious jobs such as practicing law or teaching at a university. Hincks earned "the ill will of influential persons in church and state," he acknowledged—as well as of some ordinary Protestants, possibly including his parishioners.

During a public debate in Downpatrick in 1825 between three Protestant clergymen, including Hincks, and three Catholic priests, Hincks was nearly assaulted by a man "who had brought into the Court-house a bottle of whiskey and having emptied it, was about to throw it" at him, a newspaper reported. The police stopped the "cowardly ruffian" before he could let loose the projectile and dragged him to "the gaol." Robert W. Kyle, one of the ministers who shared the platform with Hincks, commended him for his moral courage in seeking to extend "to our Romish fellow-subjects the same privileges which Protestants enjoyed." But he later rebuked Hincks for supporting the 1829 Roman Catholic Relief Act, which allowed Catholics to sit in Parliament and rolled back other oppressive laws. Kyle called the act a "national sin . . . by which Great Britain surrendered . . . to the enemies of [the] Gospel."

Hincks regarded his great passion, deciphering long-dead languages, as a way of establishing a bridge between modern and ancient peoples and emphasizing their common humanity. He researched Egyptian astronomy and the development of the Egyptian calendar, following in the footsteps of Herodotus, Sir Isaac Newton, and Sir Walter Raleigh (who did his research during the thirteen years he spent locked up for treason inside the Tower of London, with the assistance of 515 books and a pair of servants). He published scholarly papers on both hieroglyphs and Demotic that gained notice in the recondite world of philology. In 1844 he delivered a lecture on "The Ancient Egyptian Language" at the Downpatrick Mechanics Institute, his first attempt to introduce the world of the pharaohs to the public. He had a knack for making the subject accessible: the crowd reacted enthusiastically to his stories about the decipherment and the interplay of letters and pictograms in the writing. Not everybody shared the enthusiasm: Hincks's nemesis, Charles Wall, refused to accept the validity of the decipherment and tried to block Hincks from publishing his papers at the Royal Irish Academy and Trinity College.

Then Hincks made a discovery that astonished his fellow Egyptologists and classicists. Studying lithographs of hieroglyphs from the temple of Karnak in Thebes, Hincks noticed that every cartouche containing the name Amenophis III ("the god Amun is content"), one of Egypt's great pharaohs, had been defaced. Even more curious, the vandals had targeted only the glyphs that spelled out "Amun," the principal god of Egypt. For Hincks, it was clear that a dramatic religious upheaval had taken place along the Nile. Another quarter century would have to pass before enough hieroglyphs could be read to confirm Hincks's hunch: after inheriting the throne from Amenophis III in 1353 BCE, his son Akhenaten outlawed Egyptian polytheism, eliminated Amun and the rest of the pantheon, drove the population out of Thebes, and built a new capital, Tell el-Amarna, dedicated to a single god he called Aton. (Four years after Akhenaten's death, the court returned to Thebes, and Tell el-Amarna was abandoned.) Hincks's early insights made him revered among linguists. The Oxford Assyriologist A. H. Sayce would praise Hincks's deep understanding of hieroglyphs, and the facility with which he moved to cuneiform. "No problem in decipherment ever seemed to baffle Hincks," Sayce said. The English Egyptologist John Ray asserted that in the field of hieroglyphs, Hincks played a role nearly as important as Champollion's a decade earlier, constructing "the scaffolding and framework for the building that was to come."

As his public profile grew, Hincks's own domestic scaffolding was coming undone. In the 1830s, British parliamentarians began attacking the "tithe" system in Ireland—a tax paid by all occupiers of landholdings one acre or larger to support the Church of Ireland. Critics of the Church contended, probably unfairly, that the Irish clergy was already overpaid; Catholics and Dissenters joined in, contending that they were being forced to pay to support a church to which they didn't belong. In 1836 Parliament passed the Tithe Commutation Act, removing the tax from everyone except big landowners. Now, after withstanding the £50 pay cut that came with the new job at Killyleagh, Hincks saw his salary drop by another twenty-seven percent, to £554 a year, or about $65,000 in today's money. (Income tax in Great Britain at the time took ten percent of that amount.) "I have for many years applied myself diligently to the study of Egyptian literature," he wrote to the British prime minister, Robert Peel, in October 1842. (It was not uncommon for ordinary citizens at the time to appeal directly to high-ranking government officials.) "I have had some success in the opinion of others, as well as in my own." But the new law "has swept away more than a third of the available income on which I had calculated as mine for life . . . With a wife and a large family of daughters dependent on me, I can no longer afford to continue my Egyptian pursuits." Hincks was considering "disposing of my printed books for what little they may bring me; and allowing the information . . . to be lost to the world." He was taking the "humiliating" step, he wrote, of asking Peel to restore his former salary. In addition to the upkeep of his large house and the costs of raising his daughters, Hincks was burdened by medical care for his wife, who was often confined to bed with an undefined but apparently worsening illness; under those circumstances, the equivalent of today's $58,500 did not go far. Yet the prime minister—or, perhaps, a private secretary—scribbled a draft reply on the back of Hincks's letter, informing him that the government was unable to assist him.

Another brush-off followed. Always looking for new linguistic challenges, the rector had turned to the study of cuneiform in the mid-1840s. Working from Niebuhr's sketches, he sent unsolicited in 1846 a compilation of more than one hundred characters in Elamite, the second language at Persepolis, to Richard Clarke, the secretary of the Royal Asiatic Society. He was hoping for publication in the society's journal. Instead, Clarke coolly replied that the society was already communicating with Henry Rawlinson in Baghdad. Rawlinson, claimed Clarke, was making great progress in his investigations into all three cuneiform scripts. The message was clear. But Hincks, who was never known to submit docilely to a perceived humiliation, became determined to give the Royal Asiatic Society reason to regret its snub.

CHAPTER TEN

THE AKKADIAN
CONUNDRUM

As Edward Hincks dove into the study of Mesopotamian cuneiform in the spring of 1846, he began with a few assumptions. Old Persian, the simplest of the scripts that employed the wedge-based system, he knew, contained 44 characters. (These included 36 phonetic signs, 2 word dividers, and 6 logograms. Four logograms were used sporadically, in place of phonetic signs, to represent king, god, country, and earth; 2 stood for the supreme Persian god Ahura Mazda.) Elamite had about 130 characters. Akkadian consisted of between 500 and 1,000. (Botta counted 642 signs, based on his study of the bas-reliefs from Khorsabad.) These were far too many characters for a predominantly phonetic script, like Old Persian. But they also seemed far too few to be purely logographic, like Chinese. Hincks speculated that the writing was a hybrid, like hieroglyphs. Another analogy, though unknown to Hincks at the time, would have been Japanese, with its thousands of logograms and its two syllabaries: katakana, for foreign words, and hiragana, used primarily to inflect verbs and adjectives.

Hincks could see at once that Akkadian presented bigger challenges than hieroglyphs. The Egyptian logograms—such as an
eagle 🦅, a duck 🦆, a beetle 🪲, a rope 🎋, or a pyramid △—often
looked exactly like the objects they were meant to stand for. Or they
conveyed an idea through an illustration that, in at least a vague
way, related to their meaning: a teetering wall represented "falling"
🪜. A lute-like musical instrument 𝄞 was meant to symbolize "joy"
or "pleasure," and the doorway to a meetinghouse where elders
gathered ⋒ signified "counsel." Akkadian, which was an entirely
abstract script, provided no such clues to signs' meanings. In addition, no punctuation existed in Akkadian—there was no way to
tell where one word ended and another began. (*Scriptio continua*,
or writing without punctuation marks, spaces, or other dividers,
characterized ancient Greek, classical Latin, and many other languages; the thinking was that because speech was continuous, there
was no need to add markers between written words or sentences,
either, and that the context would make everything clear. Over the
centuries, most languages adopted dividers, though *scriptio continua*
continues to exist in many Southeast Asian languages, including
Burmese, Khmer, and Javanese.) The two signposts identified by
Grotefend and other decipherers at Persepolis—the determinative
vertical stroke 𝈿 before proper names and the three-wedge sign
𝈾 that preceded or sometimes followed the names of cities and
countries—were helpful but hardly enough to clear up the writing
system's obscurity.

Still, with his grounding in hieroglyphs, Hincks felt confident
at the starting gate. By this point Rawlinson and other scholars had
already published partial decipherments of Old Persian cuneiform,
but Akkadian was still untouched. He began his attempted decipherment by looking for the names of Achaemenid kings in the parallel
inscriptions in Akkadian and Old Persian at Persepolis. He believed

that the names would have been pronounced approximately the same way in the two languages, mostly because of the two civilizations' geographical proximity and their many interactions. By lining up the Akkadian signs with the Old Persian, just as Thomas Young had matched ancient Greek letters with hieroglyphs, Hincks obtained the approximate phonetic values of dozens of Akkadian characters. Hincks also noticed that the seven-character phonetic spelling of the word *king* in Old Persian 《𒆠.𒀹.𒈬.𒅖.𒆠 . 𒀀.𒅅 became a single character ⟹ when it was written in Akkadian. That gave him, he believed, his first Akkadian logogram—though he had no clue yet how to pronounce it.

Next, he examined something closer to home: the East India House Inscription, a 21-inch-by-18-inch limestone slab, inscribed on back, front, and sides with ten columns and eight hundred lines of finely carved Akkadian. Found in Babylon by Sir Harford Jones Brydges, the British Resident in Baghdad, around 1800, the slab was currently on display at the East India Company's headquarters on Leadenhall Street in the City of London. Scholars considered it one of the finest examples of Akkadian monument writing. It began with two forbidding-looking lines of text:

𒀭𒈗𒁀𒁕𒉿𒈨𒋆𒅅𒄀

𒈾𒀀𒌉𒀭𒁀𒊏𒆠

Hincks believed he could say with confidence a few things about the inscription. It was carved into limestone—an expensive material that must have been imported from a quarry hundreds of miles from stoneless Babylon—indicating that the text had special significance. (Unlike their Babylonian counterparts, Assyrian scribes worked regularly with limestone and what Layard called "a coarse alabaster." Both are soft rocks abundant, he wrote, in "the plains of [Northern] Mesopotamia as well as the lowlands between the Tigris

and the 'hill country.'" The scribes carved cuneiform signs using a
copper or stone chisel and buffed the result with sandpaper.) It was
almost certainly a royal proclamation and thus would likely begin
with the name of a king.

From comparing the trilingual inscriptions at Persepolis, Hincks
thought he could recognize the first, star-like sign. It was, he believed, a silent determinative for a god. So, the sign immediately
after this determinative should represent a deity. Therefore, the
Babylonian king must have incorporated the name of a god into
his own name, just as Thothmes (Thutmose), Rameses, and other
Egyptian pharaohs had done. Next came six signs that Hincks had
analyzed in the Akkadian inscriptions at Persepolis: they were phonetic characters, he thought, and they appeared to spell out *ku-du-
ri-u-su-ur*.

Hincks plugged in the names of Babylonian divinities mentioned in the Old Testament to see which might make sense. After
much trial and error, Hincks landed upon Nebo, the god of literacy and learning described in the book of Jeremiah. That would
make the name *Nebo-ku-du-ri-u-su-ur*, which sounded a lot like
Nebuchadnezzar—the Babylonian king who had sacked Jerusalem
and built Babylon into the world's most powerful city-state in the
sixth century BCE.

The next line began with another character that Hincks recognized from his study of the trilingual inscriptions: it was, he believed, a logogram for the word *king*. Next came a jumble of signs,
including the star-shaped "god" again. Ancient kings usually identified themselves in their inscriptions with the city or territory from
which they ruled. This suggested to him that the characters referred
to a place of great importance: perhaps a holy city 𒃻𒀭. Taking
another leap, Hincks declared that the first two lines of the inscription read:

NEBUCHADNEZZAR
KING OF BABYLON

Hincks marched ahead, trusting his instincts. He scrutinized copies of ancient bricks that Claudius Rich had picked up around Babylon. He studied a lithograph of the Bellino Cylinder, a nine-inch-tall fired-clay prism that Rich had dug up near Kuyunjik. (Rich had named the relic in honor of his German secretary-translator, Karl Bellino, who had transcribed the minuscule characters shortly before dying of cholera in Mosul at age twenty-nine.) Small clay "barrel cylinders" like this one contained abridged versions of the inscriptions carved on the walls of Assyrian palaces and presented a special challenge. "The writing is so minute, and the letters are so close to one another, that it requires considerable expertise to separate and transcribe them," Layard wrote.

Comparing all these inscriptions from various parts of Mesopotamia and different time periods, Hincks thought he could recognize several Akkadian logograms for "king," but had no idea how to pronounce the word nor why there should be so many signs for the same concept. He also found what he believed to be the logogram for "son" ⊻⊻. But that same character repeatedly showed up as the phonetic sign *a* in the names of certain kings. The Akkadian character appeared to have a double function: it could serve as both a logogram *and* a phonetic character. How, Hincks wondered, could one determine in what way it was being used? Early in his studies, Hincks was running headlong into the writing system's ambiguities.

◄◄―――――――►►

In 1843, a Vienna-born linguist, Isidore Löwenstern, had become the first scholar to posit that Akkadian was a Semitic language, like Hebrew, Arabic, Syriac, and Aramaic. Semitic languages share many words, have similar sentence structures, and conjugate verbs using three "root" consonants and different vowel combinations. Austen Layard and Edwin Norris concurred with Löwenstern, and Hincks was moving in the same direction. "The Assyrian and Babylonian languages appear to have much in common with the Semitic languages," Hincks declared in the summer of 1846. (Assyrians and Babylonians wrote the same signs in the same language, though they spoke in different dialects.) If he could just find a few indisputably Semitic words in the inscriptions, he thought, he'd have all the proof he needed.

So he began scouring the East India House Inscription again, when one three-character word caught his eye. He spotted it in the twenty-second line, directly under another reference to the "king" of some country—most likely Babylon, he thought, only this time written in a different way.

He noted the word's reappearance six lines later. And two dozen more times throughout the inscription.

Hincks consulted his growing list of phonetic values of Akkadian characters. The first sign, the three-stroke character ⟨character⟩, he believed was *a*.

To the second sign, a fish-like character that consisted of nine strokes ⟨character⟩, he applied the value *na*, which he'd gleaned from comparing the proper names in the inscriptions at Persepolis.

Hincks had encountered the third character in the Akkadian inscriptions covering the tomb of Cyrus the Great at Pasargadae in southwest Persia. It was the first sign ⟨character⟩ in *Kurush*, the Akkadian name for Cyrus: *ku*.

A-NA-KU.

The word bore some resemblance to the Hebrew pronoun *anokhi*, which means "I" or, in certain contexts, "I am." Hincks translated the two-line phrase that he'd seen in line twenty-one and twenty-two of the East India House Inscription as:

THE KING OF BABYLON

AM I.

Anaku and *anokhi* weren't, in fact, particularly close. But Hincks had decided that they were close enough. He announced that he had positively identified Akkadian as a Semitic language and boldly avowed that its pronunciation, grammar, and vocabulary were all about to fall into his grasp. "As to my Babylonian and Assyrian deciphering," he bragged in a letter to the *Literary Gazette* in June 1846, "I am not aware that anything in the right direction has yet been done by others. I feel confident of having mastered the great difficulty of making a commencement in each of these."

◄───────►

While Hincks was brashly proclaiming Akkadian to be a Semitic language based on a single word, he was also trying to work out all the different ways a character could be used in the script. As he had seen in the case of Nebuchadnezzar, the sign for a god ✳, which later became ➤, could serve as a silent determinative at the beginning of a word to denote that the subsequent sign or set of signs was the name of a divinity. (The stripped-down version of the sign began to replace its older counterpart around 800 BCE.) But both could also be employed as logograms meaning "god," Hincks claimed. He believed that in that case they made the sound *ili*, as in this version of Babylon, *bab-ili* ("the gate of god"): 𒁁 ✳. And not only that:

the same character could also be used to spell words phonetically. Based on his comparisons with the Old Persian and Elamite texts, Hincks declared that ➤ could have the phonetic value *an*—as in *an-na*, for "me"—and possibly other values as well. Hincks was convinced he had discovered one of the essential characteristics of the Akkadian writing system: one character could pretty much do anything.

As if that weren't complicated enough, Hincks declared that the writing system was rife with variant spellings of the same word. He had identified, he said, no fewer than seven different characters that could all make the sound *ba*, as in *Babylon*. English has its share of these variants: *collectable* and *collectible*, *dialog* and *dialogue*, *axe* and *ax*, *archaeology* and *archeology*. During the sixteenth century, when spelling rules hadn't yet been codified, "where" could be alternatively spelled *wher*, *whear*, and *whair*. Robert Greene, an English pamphleteer, in his 1591 essay *A Notable Discovery of Coosnage* (also spelled *coʒenage* and defined as the art of trickery or fraud), came up with four variant spellings of *fellow*—*felow*, *felowe*, *fallow*, and *fallowe*—as well as *been*, *beene*, and *bin*, *neibor* and *neighbor*, and nine variations of coney (a kind of rabbit, in this case used in the term "coney-catchers," or swindlers), including *cony*, *conny*, *conye*, *conie*, *connie*, *coni*, *cuny*, *cunny*, and *cunnie*. Many Elizabethan Britons spelled even their own names in different ways: William Shakespeare's signature has several variations, including Shakespeare, Shakspere, Shakspeare, and Shaksper. But this was all when modern English was in its infancy, struggling to form spelling rules. In Akkadian, Hincks believed, the system of multiple variants had never disappeared.

Norris, then the deputy secretary at the Royal Asiatic Society, dispatched a note to Hincks that November. "I am delighted to learn you are reading phonetically the great Babylonian inscription," he wrote, swept up by the parson's self-confidence. One month later, Hincks presented another paper before the Royal Irish Academy in Dublin: "On the Third Persepolitan Writing," referring to Akkadian. He claimed he had identified the phonetic values of one hundred Akkadian characters—all gleaned from comparing proper names at Persepolis, at Darius's and Xerxes's tombs at Naqsh-e Rustam, and at Cyrus the Great's tomb at Pasargadae. He announced a new discovery: many characters could be written two ways, he claimed, depending on whether they were inscribed on stone monuments or etched into clay. There were at least two different signs for "king": ⟩ 𒈗. He claimed he had cracked Akkadian numerals: 𒁹 𒈫 𒐈 𒐘 𒐙 𒐚 𒐛 𒐜 𒐞. And he had begun searching the texts for character patterns that resembled words in other Semitic languages. He found *bitu*, which appeared to be Akkadian for "house," akin to the Hebrew *bayit* or *bêtu* and the Arabic *bait* or *beit*. He identified the Akkadian *reshu* as "head," since it was close to the Arabic *rais* and the Hebrew *rosh*. And he felt that he was on the trail of a solution to the mystery of the logograms as well.

Hincks and Norris began exchanging letters about republishing the paper in the *Journal of the Royal Asiatic Society*. "I am very much rejoiced to hear that you mean to send a paper on the Babylonian inscriptions to the RAS," wrote George Renouard, the English philologist and one of Hincks's biggest cheerleaders. Renouard added a note of warning: "[I] think you will do well to send it without further delay." Renouard was worried about Hincks's competitor in Baghdad, who by now had taken note of Hincks's arrival on the scene—and had just begun working his way through the greatest trove of Akkadian relics in the world.

CHAPTER ELEVEN

◄◄———————————————►►

THE BLACK OBELISK

In the early summer of 1846, Henry Rawlinson secluded himself in his detached office at the Baghdad Residency, cooled to a barely tolerable ninety degrees by the flow of tepid river water on the roof. "I am . . . working desultorily at the inscriptions," he wrote to Layard. "The weather is too hot to . . . produce any really satisfying results . . . and after a few hours [*sic*] labor I generally throw aside my papers in disgust." Rawlinson had initially assumed that, like Old Persian, Akkadian was a phonetic script. But he counted hundreds of different signs in the inscriptions, which could mean only that the system was rife with logograms.

Rawlinson had identified two determinative signposts—◣◢ and ⊤—to steer him toward the names of people and places. But Akkadian kings, cities, countries, and other proper nouns were often written with logograms, and he, like Hincks, was at a loss about how to read them.

The taxing work environment compounded his frustration. At summer's height in July and August, the temperature outside often climbed above 120 degrees. Fever, heartburn, and rheumatism, as well as chronic indigestion that he referred to as "dyspepsia," tormented him. He found a modicum of comfort inside the *sardaub*—a subterranean room at the Residency used to escape the worst of the summer heat—but the lighting was so poor that it was rarely possible to work. After three years in Turkish Arabia and nineteen in Asia, he was desperate for an escape to England and had applied for his first leave of absence. During his years away he had missed the weddings of siblings, the achievements of his younger brother, George (a star cricketer at Oxford and a Fellow at Exeter College), and older brother, Abram (another first-class cricketer as well as a successful solicitor), and—just the previous year—the death of his father, Abraham, at the age of sixty-eight. The East India Company's board of directors, however, set strict conditions that he couldn't accept. "I regret to say that my leave taking after all has been refused," he wrote to Layard. "The board of directors says the thing is an absolute impossibility unless I vacate the residency, which I cannot afford to do at present." After devoting more than a decade of his career to the cuneiform inscriptions, he was determined to finish what he'd started. Giving up his sinecure in Baghdad, with its proximity to the mounds near Mosul and to Behistun, would mean abandoning to unqualified upstarts the project of a lifetime.

When he felt physically up to it, Rawlinson plunged back into the inscriptions. But he had an extremely limited number of Akkadian texts to analyze—inscriptions on a few tombs, Niebuhr's Persepolis sketches. Layard was discovering a bounty of inscriptions on the palace walls at Nimrud, but it was all new, and Rawlinson hadn't found the time or the logistical support to travel the 250 miles through lawless territory to Mosul. And to really grasp the language, he knew he needed texts, grammar, and vocabulary. John Chadwick, an English linguist and classical scholar who in the mid-twentieth century helped decipher Linear B—a syllabic script used for writing Mycenaean Greek that appeared around 1400 BCE—

even drew up a formula. The number of characters required for a successful decipherment could be expressed as "n squared where the n is the number of different signs in the script." For Linear B, which has 87 basic signs, the minimum number of characters to study would have been 7,569; for Akkadian cuneiform, it would have to be tens of thousands more. Ironically, during the early days of the Akkadian decipherment, Hincks had far more texts available to him than Rawlinson, who lived just a four- or five-day horseback ride from the palaces of Nimrud, the greatest trove of Akkadian inscriptions in the world.

Then, in late July 1846, Layard sent downriver his first twelve wooden crates filled with bas-reliefs. "I have been about twenty days occupied in effecting this, continually exposed to the most powerful sun," he wrote to his aunt, Benjamin Austen's wife, in London. Layard and his work teams had been forced to move immense blocks of stone, some nine feet square and one foot thick, "of the most fragile material covered with delicate sculpture; without even a rope capable of sustaining an ordinary weight, and without any machinery."

Resorting to a method that would be unthinkable today, Layard had sawed 2,500-year-old friezes in half or in thirds to reduce them to transportable size. (He sometimes cut through the alabaster horizontally, thinning out the slabs but leaving intact the bas-reliefs carved on them.) Then he placed them in carts "which in England would scarcely be used for carrying a load of hay." Layard had arranged with Rawlinson to ship the material by raft to the British Residency in Baghdad. These sturdily constructed keleks were capable of carrying "a load of from thirty to forty tons," observed Henry Ross, and had a shallow draft that allowed them to glide easily downriver, although they were susceptible to changing currents, sudden winds, shoals, and rapids, and occasionally ran aground or capsized. At the Residency, Rawlinson could inspect and copy the inscriptions before re-crating the antiquities and sending everything down the Tigris to a beachfront just north of Basra, where the East India Company leased a riverside residence it used as a commercial depot. Suddenly, a great opportunity had landed in Rawlinson's lap. "We are anxiously looking out for the arrival of your raft and shall examine the first fruits . . . with no small interest," Rawlinson wrote to Layard at the end of July.

On August 5, 1846, the first raft arrived at the dock in front of the Residency. Rawlinson and James Felix Jones removed a trove of bas-reliefs: eagle-headed gods, siege and battle scenes, and kings and their courtiers hunting lions, apparently the favorite sport of the royal court. The friezes "are certainly very fine, particularly the God & the fellow with the beak," Rawlinson wrote to Layard. He admired a carving of an arrow-pierced lioness in her death throes. But he was most excited about the inscriptions that accompanied the art. Suddenly Rawlinson had thousands more signs to work with—a number inching closer to Chadwick's mid-twentieth-century magic formula. The inscriptions held the key, he wrote, to "unfolding the history, theology, language, arts . . . [and] political relations of one of the most illustrious nations of antiquity, and in thus filling up an enormous blank in our knowledge."

Layard, just as enthusiastic and observant, shared with Rawlinson his insights. The archaeologist had noticed the same short inscription written repeatedly across the bas-reliefs at Nimrud. These near-identical texts contained small variants—characters that, it seemed, could be switched for one another to make the same word. Hincks had detected the same principle when he observed what appeared to be half a dozen different signs for the *Ba* in *Babylon*:

Akkadian appeared to be riddled with variants; Layard compiled a list of them.

Using the determinative signs for places and people, 𝕏 and T, Layard also put together a roster of fifty proper names written in Akkadian, including those of the kings who built the palaces and carved their stories on the walls. He, like Hincks, identified the sign for "son"—𝕏—which allowed him to construct a genealogical chain of Assyrian kings over a dozen generations, based on the template "King A, son of B."

The problem was that all these discoveries were useless if neither he nor Rawlinson could read the logograms composing the names. How might an archaeologist two millennia from now deduce the meaning and sounds of signs like @ or $ or % or & or even viz. and e.g.? To compound their confusion, some characters in Akkadian—as Hincks had already discovered—could apparently serve as a logogram *and* a phoneme, but there was no sure way to tell how the character was employed. As Rawlinson confronted this impasse, the miserable working conditions further sapped his morale and stamina. In September, cholera swept Baghdad, forcing Rawlinson to head twenty miles downriver to Ctesiphon, a ruined capital in the semi-desert wilderness founded in 120 CE by the Parthians, who ruled Persia after Alexander the Great. In 637 CE, an Islamic army captured the city. And when the Abbasid caliph made nearby Baghdad his capital the following century, Ctesiphon became a ghost town. The only trace of its glory was the Taq Kasra arch, a 110-foot-high vault of unreinforced brickwork that had once been part of a palace and had kept standing for 1,500 years. Rawlinson admired this vestige of a long-defunct empire deep in the bush—"around & about among the crumbling walls are Lions & hyenas & other wild animals," he reported—but his mind kept returning to the unfolding calamity. "About 5000 souls"—nearly ten percent of Baghdad's population—"have been carried off in a fortnight and [conditions are] anything but favorable to study," he wrote to Norris from the ruin left behind by the Prophet Muhammad's desert warriors.

◄◄————►►

Just after his return from Ctesiphon to the Residency the next month, Rawlinson first heard from Edwin Norris that a Church of Ireland parson named Edward Hincks had turned his attention to Akkadian. (Hincks was about to become even more familiar to Rawlinson after the publication of his deeply informed review of the Behistun *Memoir* the following January.) Tucked in a remote corner of Ulster, Hincks claimed to have worked out the sounds of dozens of Akkadian characters, not to mention to have spotted "Nebuchadnezzar," "Babylon," "Nineveh," and the pronoun "I." And Norris, no slouch when it came to linguistic acuity, seemed to think that Hincks had correctly deciphered the signs. On October 14, Rawlinson mentioned the parson for the first time on record—misspelling his name in a letter to a colleague. "[A] certain dr. Hinkes, an Irishman, has got much further than I pretend to have reached," he wrote. "Dr. Hinkes is certainly on the right track & a long way before me." After years of work in Persia and Mesopotamia, Rawlinson now had to contend with the intrusion of a neophyte—who might be overtaking him. Two months later he brought Hincks up again. "How Dr. Hinkes succeeded in sinking his first shaft, I hardly understand, but sunk it he certainly has, and unless I look about me, he will anticipate all I have to say on the subject."

Rawlinson was desperate to examine more texts. "[S]end down to my care any number of cases that you have ready," he urged Layard in December 1846. "I will have them carefully taken off the rafts and stored away in our depot on the river—there would be no rush I think in getting them taken down to Bussorah [Basra] at present—for there is not likely to be a ship in the Gulf for some time that could carry them off." He shared with Layard his dismay at his lack of progress with the logograms. "Few things continue to puzzle me more than whether the initial ⷭ𒀸 𒈗 of the Assyrians is the word for 'king' or 'the great God,' " he wrote. There were, he said, "equally good arguments for either rendering." Years later it would turn out that neither of Rawlinson's guesses was right. The word was a pair of logograms that combined to form "house big" or "palace." It appeared at the start of many inscriptions at Nimrud—a sort of setting that preceded the main text.

Rawlinson had received from Layard a list of four hundred Assyrian proper names, which had also "fairly puzzled" him, he said. And he was still making little headway classifying the Akkadian language. Rawlinson tacked back and forth between asserting that the language was akin to Hebrew, Arabic, and Aramaic, and placing it squarely in the North African camp, along with Berber, Coptic, and ancient Egyptian. All of these would come to be classified as Semito-Hamitic languages, about eighty idioms found across West Asia and the northern third of Africa. Grouped together today as "Afro-Asiatic" languages, they all derive from a single proto-Afro-Asiatic language spoken around ten thousand years ago. Ancient Egyptian branched off in the Neolithic era, about 4000 BCE; Hebrew, Arabic, Aramaic, and Akkadian went in a different direction around this time. Some similarities between ancient Egyptian and Akkadian words, such as *an* and *an'nânu* (here); *sut* and *su* (he); *lis* and *lisanu* (tongue); and *pirq'it* and *piqtu* (thin), suggest a common ancestor. Rawlinson could also spot connections between Akkadian and other Semito-Hamitic languages, including Phoenician and "Ethiopic" (Amharic). But he couldn't make a persuasive case for any of them. "The language . . . has to be reconstructed from square one," he wrote to Layard, "and how are we to interpret it with anything like certainty I am at a loss to divine."

What Rawlinson now had that Hincks lacked was a continuous flow of new inscriptions. With abundance, he believed, clarity would come. Just before Christmas, Layard and his diggers uncovered—buried horizontally ten feet below the Northwest Palace of Nimrud—a six-foot-six-inch-tall black-limestone obelisk. Five small bas-reliefs, crowded with imagery, decorated each of its four sides. Two hundred ten lines of cuneiform, consisting of thousands of characters, covered much of the base and the three-step summit. The twenty carvings, portraying vassals lined up before an Assyrian monarch, provided richly detailed glimpses of the royal court after a military victory. "The king was twice represented followed by his attendants; a prisoner was at his feet, and his vizier and eunuchs were introducing captives and tributaries carrying vases, shawls, bundles of rare wood, elephant tusks, and other objects of tribute," Layard wrote. "It appears to have been erected to celebrate the conquest of some remote country, for among the animals represented as brought to the King are the elephant, rhinoceros, lion, Bactrian camel, wild mule, ibex, stag, several species of Baboon & monkey."

The Black Obelisk of Nimrud, as it became known, covered with epigraphs that described its twenty scenes, like an Iron Age version of a graphic novel, would prove of enormous value to the decipherers. But for now, it was a riddle. On Christmas Day 1846, Layard dispatched the Black Obelisk and twenty-two other cases of bas-reliefs on a raft to Baghdad. Rawlinson received the cache soon after the new year. "The monument is . . . the most noble trophy in the world," he wrote to Layard, "and would alone have

An engraving from *Le Tour du Monde* of
the Black Obelisk of Shalmaneser III

been well worth the expense of excavating Nimrud." But he could only gaze on the column, mystified.

++————→-

Even more imposing relics made their way downriver. At the Nimrud Palace, Layard set out to organize the transport to the Tigris of two thirty-ton winged lamassus, each colossus carved out of a ten-foot-high block of marble. Layard and his team constructed a mulberry wood cart with sturdy wooden wheels and iron axles and dug a trench connecting the mound to a road leading to the river a mile away. Then, with mounting exhilaration, the workers carefully brought down from its pedestal one giant statue with ropes and laid it on its side. "The drums and shrill pipes of the Kurdish musicians increased the din and confusion caused by the war cry of the Arabs, who were half frantic with excitement," he wrote. For the workers, the thrill of wresting an ancient colossus from its tomb apparently outweighed any reservations they had about evacuating treasures from their homeland. "They had thrown off nearly all their garments; their long hair floated in the wind," Layard went on, "and they indulged in the wildest postures and gesticulations as they clung to the ropes."

What followed was an even more extraordinary scene: The workmen maneuvered the bull through the trench on greased rollers and hoisted it onto the cart. Layard led the procession down the road, followed by drummers, fifers, and three hundred men dragging the wagon with ropes, "all screeching at the top of their voices," he recalled. A quarter mile from the river, the wheels became stuck in the sand. "It was night before we contrived, with the aid of planks and by increased exertions, to place the sculpture on the platform . . . and slide [it] down on the raft." The team repeated the procedure with the second lamassu, and with equal elation, the following day.

◂—————▸

That spring, Rawlinson wrote to Norris that he was planning a return trip to Behistun, a 258-mile, three-day horseback ride across Turkish Arabia and Persia. He would not concede that Hincks had gotten the jump on him or surrender to frustration and despair. In the back of his mind lurked the hope that Hincks had gone wildly off course. "I will get long ladders and copy every Babylonian scrap," he vowed. At last, he wrote, he would make Behistun live up to its promise: it would become his Rosetta Stone. But he couldn't do that until he had the full Akkadian inscriptions on paper.

In September, when the summer heat had dissipated, he arrived at the cliff, prepared, his brother wrote, with "ladders, planks, strong ropes, nails, hammers, and pegs." One quick survey of the rock wall, however, made him consider putting the equipment aside. "The mass of the rock in question is scarped, and it projects some feet over the [Elamite] recess, so that it cannot be approached by any of the ordinary means of climbing," he wrote. Even the local "cragsmen," accustomed to tracking goats over the face of the mountain, told him to abandon any thoughts of scaling the cliff. But that wasn't an option. During his last visit three years earlier, Rawlinson had noticed that the giant slab was loosening, and seemed to be about to detach itself from the rock face. He saw no signs that the slab had eroded further, but he still felt that he had no time to waste.

Rawlinson first tried copying down the inscription, using his telescope during a time of day when the rock wall was sharply illuminated. Then he had a serendipitous encounter. "A wild Kurdish boy," he wrote in a memoir published in the journal *Archaeologia*, volunteered to climb to the inscriptions for him, in exchange for "a considerable reward" if he succeeded. (It wasn't clear what the compensation would be if he failed.) Rawlinson equipped him with the rope and pegs, and then he was off.

Rawlinson watched through his telescope. The boy squeezed himself up a cleft to the left of the overhanging slab, drove a wooden peg into the debris-filled crevice just above it, and tied on a rope. Then, carrying the other end, he traversed the slab "by hanging on with his toes and fingers to the slight inequalities on the bare face of the precipice, passing over . . . twenty feet of almost smooth perpendicular rock." The boy drove a second peg into a crevice on the right side of the slab and tied the other end of the rope to it. "Here with a short ladder," Rawlinson reported, "he formed a swinging seat like a painter's cradle and, fixed upon this seat, he took under my direction the paper cast of the Babylonian translation." (Curiously, in a letter to Norris dated September 20, 1847, Rawlinson attributed the climb to two Kurdish boys, not one, "who went up the precipice like cats and executed the task . . . from a swinging scaffold.")

For all its acrobatics, the boy's (or boys') achievement was less fruitful than Rawlinson had hoped. Two millennia's worth of rain and sand had worn away many characters. "Unfortunately . . . the left half . . . of the tablet is entirely destroyed, and we have thus the mere endings of the lines," he wrote. Still, Rawlinson had already had success filling in the gaps in the Old Persian on the adjacent rock wall, and after ten days camping in the valley, he left the cliff sounding optimistic. His "Kurdish boy" had obtained "a decent paper" impression of what was left of the Akkadian text, he wrote to Norris. He had hundreds of characters to compare against the 131 Elamite signs, which Norris was deciphering, and Old Persian. He now saw "no reason to despair" of understanding the language and declared that "land was in sight." And he downplayed the threat posed by his Irish rival, who, he told Norris, seemed to think he was "infallible." Once alarmed by Hincks's apparent progress, he was now "quite easy" about it. Rawlinson returned to Baghdad hoping for an advance that would vault him past the parson—just as England was getting its first look at what Layard had uncovered in Nimrud.

CHAPTER TWELVE

THE MUSEUM

On June 26, 1847, the *Illustrated London News* reported that the first nine crates of Assyrian artifacts had arrived at St. Katharine Docks near the Tower of London after a months-long journey from Basra. The huge commercial wharf and warehouse complex had opened nineteen years earlier, sweeping away crime-infested warrens with names like Dark Entry, Cat's Hole, Shovel Alley, Rookery, and Pillory Lane. The *Illustrated London News*, founded in 1842 and one of England's most popular magazines, thanks in part to its fine engravings and lithographs of battle scenes, society balls, and other newsworthy events, followed the antiquities' journey from the banks of the Thames to the steps of the British Museum. "The accounts . . . of the recent excavations . . . have excited the curiosity not only of the antiquarian but of all scriptural students," the weekly declared. The *Liberator*, an American weekly, heralded the appearance of Layard's "extraordinary discoveries at Nineveh . . . the very existence of which had become little better than a vague historic dream."

As the Assyrian treasures were arriving on the London docks, Layard was beginning the long journey home from Mosul. In a sign of his rising stature, fifty Ottoman horsemen escorted him and his protégé, Hormuzd Rassam, a twenty-year-old Chaldean Christian and the brother of Christian Rassam, the deputy British consul in Mosul. (The East India Company and the British government sometimes hired locals in such sleepy outposts.) The younger Rassam spoke English, Arabic, and Aramaic, the language of Jesus that was heard in the Levant, Mesopotamia, Eastern Arabia, and the Sinai Peninsula in the days of the Roman Empire, and could still be heard in pockets of the region. Layard had hired him at Nimrud as a translator, paymaster, and overseer of the Arab workers, and was so impressed that he was now taking him to England—a rare privilege for a resident of nineteenth-century Mosul—to enroll him at Magdalen College at Oxford. There he hoped Rassam would improve his language skills, embrace "English principles and feelings," as Layard put it, and then work beside Layard as a field archaeologist. (The plan would work even better than Layard had imagined: Rassam would soon write a note to Layard pledging to "sacrifice myself for England and worship forever the pure religion of Great Britain . . . I would rather be a chimney sweeper in England than a Pasha in Turkey.") As he and Rassam set out on their trip north, Josiah Forshall, a librarian and department keeper at the British Museum, congratulated Layard on his "happy success" and said he was soon expecting the arrival of twenty-three cases of antiquities, including the Black Obelisk. "The Trustees feel a deep interest in the enterprise in your hands," Forshall wrote.

But Layard was in for a rude shock when he reached London. Short on exhibition space, the museum had stashed his first antiquities in a basement gallery, with no natural light. "The first batch of Nimroud things are . . . in so bad a position that they cannot be seen," he complained to Ross. For an American newspaper correspondent in London, however, the "the somber, sepulchral light . . .

added to their effect. I seemed at once to be let down amid the subterranean palaces of the kings of Assyria."

◂—————▸

The Victorians pouring into the British Museum discovered an institution that was already nearly a hundred years old. The museum had grown—as so many had—out of one man's personal collection. Hans Sloane, the son of Scotch-Irish Protestants, was born in 1660 in Killyleagh, Ireland (Edward Hincks's home for forty years), where, as a boy, he became "very much pleas'd with the study of plants, and other parts of nature," he recalled. But it was in Jamaica, where tens of thousands of West African slaves and their progeny toiled in hellish conditions on the British colony's sugar plantations, that Sloane had developed a passion for collecting. As the personal physician to the wine-guzzling, slave-owning governor, the second duke of Albemarle, in 1687 and 1688, Sloane gathered stringed instruments made by slaves from calabashes, including an early form of banjo called a "strum strum"; nooses and whips used to punish and execute runaways; and samples of skulls and skin. Steeped in brutal plantation culture, he reported on the torture and execution of slaves in a clinical, sometimes approving tone. The punishment for rebellion was "nailing them down on the ground with crooked sticks on every limb, and then applying the fire by degrees from the feet and hands, burning them gradually up to the head, whereby their pains are extravagant . . . For crimes of lesser nature gelding, or chopping off half of the foot with an ax." These punishments, Sloane made sure to point out, "are sometimes merited by the blacks, who are a very perverse generation of people, and . . . [the penalties] are scarce equal to some of their crimes."

When not recording the torments of slaves, Sloane ventured into the jungle on botanical expeditions and compiled pop-up books filled with thousands of dried fruits, leaves, and stalks glued to the pages. Sloane left Jamaica in March 1689, five months after the duke's death, bringing his herbarium and other objects back to England. In 1695, he married a widow named Elizabeth Langley Rose, who had inherited from her late husband a three-thousand-acre Jamaican sugar plantation, including an enslaved workforce imported from the Bight of Benin and the Gold Coast (now Ghana). Sloane channeled some of the profits from his wife's estate—£3 million a year in today's money—into dinosaur fossils, elephants' teeth, corals, Paleolithic axes, birds' eggs, and eighty thousand other "curiosities." He displayed his collection at his home, Chelsea Manor, the former residence of Henry VIII.

The idea of creating museums for public edification dated as far back as the early third century BCE, when Ptolemy I and his son built the Mouseion, a complex for scientific and literary research in Alexandria. But it was the Ashmolean Museum in Oxford, which had opened in 1683 to anyone who paid a modest entrance fee, that ushered in the modern era of the museum as an egalitarian institution aimed at public uplift. "Even the women are allowed up here for a sixpence," noted a German scholar named Zacharias Conrad von Uffenbach disapprovingly in 1710. In 1752, one year before Sloane's death at ninety-two, he offered his entire collection to the British Parliament, in return for £20,000, today worth a hardly insubstantial $6,950,000. A museum housing the items should be located "in and about the city of London, where I have acquired most of my estates, and where they may by the great confluence of people be the most use," his will declared. Though parliamentarian William Baker dismissed Sloane's bequeathment as "a collection of butterflies and trifles," the House of Commons accepted the terms, and turned a crumbling seventeenth-century mansion on Montague Street in Bloomsbury into the "Museum of Britain." It opened its doors in January 1759, "a lasting monument of glory to the nation," as Edmund Powlett put it in a guidebook two years later.

Visitors entered the often damp and cold mansion to find a sumptuous scene: French frescoes on the ceilings, stones from the Appian Way at their feet, and a grand staircase leading to chambers filled with corals, wasps' nests, animals in jars of formaldehyde, and other oddities. Just who would be permitted to see these objects remained a subject of debate for several years. In 1756, board of trustees member Lord Charles Cadogan had urged that entrance be denied to "very low & improper persons, even menial servants." At first visitors had to request an appointment in writing, which kept the numbers down, and were given only two hours, on Mondays and Thursdays, to tour the institution. By the early 1760s the museum was open five days a week and admitted visitors free of charge. "[I]t is the property of the nation, everyone has the same right . . . to see it," marveled the German author Karl Philipp Moritz.

As the British Museum grew in popularity, the Louvre first opened its doors to the public. Built as a fortress in 1190 and reconstituted as a palace in the sixteenth century, it became a museum at the height of the French Revolution in 1793, with an exhibition of 537 paintings, many seized from the Catholic Church. Napoleon stocked it with treasures stolen by his army from across Europe. "Take everything you can, lose no opportunity to loot everything which is lootable in Athens and its surroundings," the French ambassador Marie-Gabriel Florent-Auguste de Choiseul-Gouffier instructed his agent in the city. (The ambassador sent to France a piece of the Parthenon frieze, which still resides in the Louvre.) During the Peace of Amiens that paused the Napoleonic Wars in 1802–03, British politicians flocked to Paris to see the looted art, and soon began devising strategies, as one put it, "to extend military conflict to a war by cultural means."

Henry Salt, the British consul-general in Cairo, and his Piedmont-born French rival, Vice-Consul Bernardino Drovetti, engaged in a "collecting furor," as Salt described it. In Egypt and across the Near East British diplomats oversaw the removal of antiquities to ports, the Royal Navy provided sea transport and stashed the relics in its arsenals, and royal gunners helped install sculptures at the British Museum. After Jean-François Champollion, the decipherer of the Rosetta Stone, became the curator of the Egyptian galleries at the Louvre, he organized an expedition to Egypt and secured one of the relics that the English had coveted most: another trilingual stone, this one five feet long and thirteen feet wide, with twenty lines of hieroglyphs, twenty-seven lines of Demotic, and fifty-nine lines of Greek. The "Caristie Stone" became one of the Louvre's most treasured possessions. (The English had used the threat of force to seize the Rosetta Stone from Napoleon's army in Egypt in 1801; it took a prime place in the British Museum's "Egyptian Saloon," surrounded by other antiquities that the British army had compelled the French to hand over, including bas-reliefs, sarcophagi, sphinxes, statues, and sepulchral ornaments.)

French and British politicians and museum directors justified their appropriations by arguing that Western European nations had a duty to "rescue" antiquities from "barbaric natives," who couldn't be trusted to keep the treasures safe. Between 1803 and 1812, Thomas Bruce, Lord Elgin, lifted two hundred tons of sculpture from Athens, including large parts of the Parthenon frieze. He arranged for a British warship to appear off Athens to persuade "public opinion of our watchfulness & ability to protect them." (Elgin later contracted what many assumed to be syphilis and lost most of his nose, prompting Lord Byron, who was appalled by the theft, to write: "Noseless himself, he brings here noseless blocks / To show what time has done and what the pox.")

In the late 1830s, the archaeologist Charles Fellows traveled up the River Xanthos in southern Anatolia and discovered the ruins of Xanthos, the capital of Lycia, a state bordering the Mediterranean coast that had flourished in the fifteenth and fourteenth centuries BCE. Obtaining a firman from the sultan, Fellows loaded a British naval ship with ornamented tombs, friezes, and marble slabs from the ancient city walls, and returned two more times to finish the job. In 1833, with the collection rapidly expanding, the British Museum trustees emptied out Montagu House (it was demolished in the 1840s) and moved the collection to a Greek Revival–style hall designed by the neoclassical architect Sir Robert Smirke. Sir Richard Westmacott, the leading sculptor of the era, created an allegorical tableau in limestone above the colonnaded entrance that traced humankind's ascent from the Stone Age to what was regarded as its apogee: the heights of European civilization.

The *Illustrated London News* engraving of a winged, human-headed lion from the palace of King Ashurnasirpal II, wheeled backward up the steps of the British Museum in 1852

The museum's board of trustees, some of the most powerful and learned men of the British Isles, oversaw the looting of what most of them regarded as inferior nations. The Archbishop of Canterbury, the Lord Chancellor, and the Speaker of the House of Commons appointed the director, known as the Principal Librarian. But a "standing committee" of thirteen "persons of leisure and ability," according to the museum's charter, managed day-to-day operations. In the mid-nineteenth century, the committee's members included William Rowan Hamilton, an Irish mathematician who had developed quantum mechanics; Henry Hallam, author of doorstops such as *The Constitutional History of England*; and John Frederick Campbell, a British peer. These lofty personages took time away from academics and politics to huddle in the bowels of the museum, quibbling over budgets, salaries, purchases, and plunder. Minutes from June 1848 show the trustees debating whether to pay a collector £250 (the equivalent of about $30,000 today) for a pair of ancient Egyptian papyrus scrolls; discussing Phoenician antiquities dug up near Tunis; and reviewing the acquisition for £150 ($18,000 in 2024) of a bronze head of the Roman emperor Hadrian found on the bank of the Thames and a stash of iron weapons for £4 ($480 today) from Battle Edge, an Oxfordshire field where the West Saxon king Cuthred defeated King Æthelbald of Mercia in 752 CE.

Engaged in a near-frenzy of acquisitions from across the Middle East and Asia Minor, the trustees raced to expand their square footage to keep up with the flow. "We do not recall a time when building operations, of one kind or another, were not going on," the *Morning Post* declared, "and notwithstanding the additions of the last twenty years, the cry is still for room." Fifty thousand people visited the British Museum in 1818. In 1851, that number exceeded two and a half million. "The antiquary and the scholar

roam [the galleries] with inexpressible delight," declared the
Times. "In the field of Oriental antiquities, the British Museum
is unsurpassed," agreed the *Morning Post*. "The colossal relics . . .
which, with infinite labour and great cost, have been collected in
this spot, must command the wonder and admiration of every intelligent beholder."

The board of trustees proved to be less generous when it came
to supporting its collectors and archaeologists in the field. Layard
complained about the "small means at my disposal" to hire laborers; pay for equipment to move the huge, heavy, and fragile objects; and arrange their safe transport to Baghdad and beyond. The
trustees had fixed his salary at just £150 a year (about $18,000 in
2024 money), a pittance for a man who—unlike, say, Sir Charles
Fellows, the son of a wealthy silk merchant from Nottingham—
lacked the independent means to self-finance his missions. The
British media looked on with sympathy. "[T]he gentleman . . . receives from one of the greatest and most wealthy nations in the
world the munificent stipend of £250 a year [*sic*] as a requital for
his exertions!" one newspaper reported with sarcasm. "France had
expended upwards of £40,000 on similar researches undertaken in
Assyria by a Frenchman." The *Illustrated London News* reminded its
sixty thousand readers that Layard had, along with Botta, been the
first to indicate the possibility that the Assyrian ruins even existed,
"though his suggestions were so coldly received . . . that he was left
to pursue his research unaided, excepting by the private resources
of Sir Stratford Canning."

Nor was the museum conscientious about following up on
Layard's discoveries. On a muddy riverbank near Basra, a dozen
objects—including lamassus and the alabaster head of the "infidel
giant," the decapitated visage that had frightened Layard's work
crew when they uncovered it in 1846—lay unguarded in sand and

heat throughout 1847. "Trade was almost completely stagnant in the Gulf . . . and the visit of any European vessel to Basrah a rarity," noted British Assyriologist Cyril John Gadd. And the trustees apparently didn't want to spend the money to hire a commercial vessel for the sole purpose of rescuing art. Precarious transport was the standard in Turkish Arabia; a year later, a raft carrying bas-reliefs and a human-headed lion ran aground in a fierce current north of Basra after days of heavy rains. Many crates sank in the mud, and it was thanks only to the salvaging efforts of James Felix, the captain of the *Nitocris*, that most of the objects were recovered. Rawlinson dismissed the trustees to Layard as "lousy English commissioners."

Not all public opinion was favorable toward Layard. The *Athenaeum* called Layard's sawing bas-reliefs into pieces to make them easier to transport an act of vandalism unsurpassed in the nineteenth century—although he wasn't the only person to use the tactic. Botta had employed the same strategy, cutting one lamassu, according to Layard, into eight pieces, which were painstakingly reassembled upon their arrival in Paris. Miraculously, the damage was nearly impossible to detect.

The Assyria discoveries drove the French-English cultural competition to a new degree of intensity. In May 1847, King Louis-Philippe opened the Salle de Ninévé in the northeast corner of the Cour Carrée, one of the Louvre's four main courtyards. Crowds lined up for hours to admire Botta's two winged bulls and dozen bas-reliefs, the first concrete evidence of a world that had disappeared 2,500 years earlier and had now, like a dream, resurfaced. (In 1846 the French consul had left Khorsabad and returned to Paris, fatigued by the hardships of Mesopotamia and largely convinced—wrongly, it would become clear—that he had removed everything of value from the mound.) Layard pronounced the

Parisian exhibition "miserable" (apart from the two colossi) and gloated "[w]e shall beat them hollow." But he expressed sympathy for his old friend and rival when civil unrest over joblessness, corruption, and inflation erupted in Paris and other French cities in February 1848, leading to the abdication of King Louis-Philippe and the installation of a republican government. "I fear [Botta] will be amongst the sufferers," Layard wrote to Henry Ross. "All Europe is at this moment in a state of convulsion, and no one can guess how it will end."

Fortunately for Botta, the new government dispatched him to Jerusalem and the Levant as ambassador. He spent the rest of his career there, consuming prodigious quantities of hashish and opium, which continued to take a toll. Gustave Flaubert, who met Botta in Jerusalem in the summer of 1850, described him as "a man in ruins, a man of ruins, in the city of ruins."

◄────►

Though Layard had been disappointed to see his precious artifacts stashed in the windowless basement, the gloomy display didn't seem to bother the British public. Everyone, it seemed, was clamoring for more glimpses of Assyria. Fifteen friezes in fine condition—including a procession of prisoners, a king crossing a river, and the victorious Assyrian army returning home—arrived at the museum in mid-1848. The *Illustrated London News* predicted that the new antiquities would "excite more interest and admiration than the sculptures of either Greece or Egypt." The media speculated that British museumgoers had become jaded and were hungering for something utterly new. To accompany the piece, the *Illustrated London News* published twenty-two lines of cuneiform text from a wall of the Nimrud palace—the first detailed image of the writing presented to an English newspaper readership.

But even as the public flocked to the British Museum and avidly read the *Illustrated London News*, their attention turned to another drama: the fate of the Black Obelisk, the 2,700-year-old limestone monolith that Layard had excavated at Nimrud in 1846. Along with dozens of bas-reliefs from the mound, the monument arrived in Bombay from Basra on the *Elphinstone*, a British warship, in March 1848. While another ship was readied for the journey to England, the governor general uncrated the obelisk and left it exposed on a dock in the heat and damp for the public to admire. The *Bombay Times* described a masterpiece "in the most perfect state of preservation—the polish unaffected by three thousand years of inhumation, and the lustre hardly gone." Then the artifacts were loaded onto a newly commissioned Royal Navy brig, the HMS *Jumna*. The ship would round the tip of India, take on goods in Calcutta, and turn back south to Ceylon. Trade winds would carry the *Jumna* past Madagascar and around the Cape of Good Hope. In a couple of months, it would sail up the Thames to London.

That was the plan, anyway. Ten days into the journey the *Jumna* ran into bad weather off Ceylon. Heavy squalls, accompanied by thunder and lightning, roiled the sea in the pre-dawn hours of April 23. At daybreak, the *Jumna* officers' logs reported, "great numbers of birds [are] apparently much terrified, hanging about the ship, alighting on the deck and rigging, and allowing themselves to be caught without resistance." At 1 p.m., "[b]lue sky appeared around the horizon . . . but *there was also an indescribable feeling in the atmosphere*." Then, early the next morning, three cyclones "approximated and combined," wrote the British sea captain and meteorologist Henry Piddington, and "the fury of the wind became irresistible." The power of the gale was "higher than the figures can express." Just before 11 a.m. on April 24, with the three hurricanes simultaneously bearing down on her, the *Jumna* rolled onto her side and flipped upside down.

Back in London, word of the storm reached the museum trustees, Layard, and the public—but there was only silence about the Black Obelisk's fate. By early summer Layard had reluctantly accepted that his treasures had sunk to the bottom of the Indian Ocean. And then, miraculously, on October 13, the *Jumna* limped into London's Chatham Docks. Before she had turned upside down, the *Jumna*'s crew had cut away the collapsed mainmast, which helped them right the ship. Then they hammered together a "jury mast" from surviving pieces of wood—and managed to sail the battered vessel to the Ceylonese port of Trincomalee for repairs. "The long-expected marbles from Nimroud . . . reported to have been lost at sea, have, we are happy to say, at length arrived," the *Athenaeum* exulted. The monument was transported under guard to the British Museum, where Layard was waiting for it. But his jubilation quickly turned to anger. Some artifacts had been badly damaged in the tempest and shipwreck; thieves had made off with others either in Ceylon or in England. "The state of the contents of the thirty boxes," one colleague declared, "was such as to evoke the strongest expressions of indignation. Privately he used much more emphatic language." But the obelisk, to the relief of Layard and the British public, remained intact, almost as if it had been carved yesterday.

◄────────►

Layard had spent much of the spring of 1848 ensconced at the Dorsetshire country estate of his cousin Lady Charlotte Guest, the wife of a Welsh parliamentarian and industrialist. His goal was to finish his memoir of his time in Mesopotamia, but he faced distractions: the Guests' ten children followed him around the manor, demanding that "Uncle Henry" tell them tales of his Middle Eastern adventures. Layard hunkered down, and just after New Year's in 1849, *Nineveh and Its Remains: A Narrative of an Expedition to Assyria during the Years 1845, 1846 & 1847* appeared in print.

Published by John Murray Press—whose authors included Jane Austen, Lord Byron, and Johann Wolfgang von Goethe—Layard's narrative was packed with tales of exotic encounters in the mountains and valleys of the Ottoman Empire, astonishing finds in the mounds, and speculation about the writing on the walls. The *Times* called the book "the most extraordinary work of the present age" and exulted in the "wonderful discoveries it describes . . . [and] the talent, courage, and perseverance of its author." The reviewer compared Layard to Mungo Park, the Scottish explorer who had navigated the Niger River in West Africa, wrote a bestselling memoir, and drowned in a canoe accident in the rapids there in January 1806 at thirty-five. The Earl of Ellesmere, president of the Royal Asiatic Society, and a noted linguist—he was best known for translating Goethe's *Faust*—called *Nineveh and Its Remains* "the greatest achievement of our time." He lauded Layard's "bold and enterprising spirit . . . as well as the indomitable perseverance, intelligence, and tact with which he has pursued his object."

Even Benjamin Austen sang his once-scorned nephew's praises. Layard had dedicated the book to his uncle, hoping to repair a long-broken relationship. Now Austen returned the affection. "No one speaks of any other book than Nineveh & of its modesty," he wrote to his nephew. Not only was the public talking about his adventures, but they were also taking his side in the dispute over money with the museum's board of trustees. "They abuse the Government & the Museum & praise your lenient treatment of them," Austen declared. "Your course, my dear Henry, is now clear. Nothing can stop you." The British Museum finally leapt into action, dispatch-

ing a ship to Basra to retrieve the lions and bulls that had lain there
for more than one year.

The interest in Assyria "is even still increasing," the *Illustrated
London News* noted, "if we may judge from the eagerness with
which Mr. Layard's 'Narrative' has been devoured, and by the
learned speculations and discussions which have originated in various quarters." Nearly eight thousand copies of *Nineveh and Its Remains* would be sold in its first year in print, a substantial amount
for a nonfiction book by a first-time author. Charles Dickens's *A
Christmas Carol*, by contrast, sold six thousand in its first five days
after its publication by Chapman & Hall on December 19, 1843;
and twelve more editions went through their entire print runs by
the end of 1844. Layard's sales wouldn't come close to that per-
formance, but "Murray anticipate[s] a continual steady demand for
the book," Layard would write to Edward Mitford. The companion
he had last seen in Southern Mesopotamia had made it through Afghanistan and India and settled in Ceylon. He was leading the life
that Layard might have had if they'd stayed together: running a
coffee plantation in the island's jungled hills.

◄────────►

Layard wasn't around to gauge the public reaction. His home leave
had ended in late 1848, and, with the British Museum's trustees waf-
fling on whether to resume excavations, he was obliged to return
to his job as a low-level attaché at the embassy in Constantinople.
For Layard, it must have felt like a backward move. So when, in
the spring of 1849, the trustees offered him a £50 bump in salary, to
£200 a year (the equivalent today of $24,000), to start excavations
again at Mosul, it didn't take him long to make up his mind. He set
out for Turkish Arabia in August 1849, at the height of the suffocating Mesopotamian summer. "The Trustees . . . have sent me back

with a ridiculously miserable grant to satisfy the exalted hopes and demands of the British public," Layard wrote to Mitford.

Traveling with him was a sketch artist, Frederick Charles Cooper, hired by the British Museum, and Hormuzd Rassam, whom the trustees had agreed to put on the payroll as Layard's personal assistant. At Oxford, Rassam—who would soon play a vital role in the excavations—had been flourishing. "He now writes a very decent hand and is greatly improved in his English," Layard wrote to Henry Ross. Rassam had formed a father-son-like relationship with the Magdalen College president, Martin Joseph Routh, though he had a harder time gaining acceptance by the students. A letter written by James Mozley, a Fellow at Magdalen, suggests that they viewed him more as an exotic specimen than as a peer. Another Fellow "has a Chaldean visiting him here . . . and I should think quite a beau in his own country," Mozley wrote to a colleague. "He wears ordinarily our common dress, but will put on his Asiatic one if you want him. He dined with us in Hall yesterday in it, and really looked exceedingly handsome."

From Constantinople the trio traveled for three days up the Bosphorus by steamer to the Black Sea port of Trabzon and commenced a land journey to Mosul. They arrived in Erzurum, a trading post in northeastern Anatolia on the main road to Persia, and continued by camel caravan to Mesopotamia. In September 1849, toward the end of the dry season, they reached Kuyunjik, and found it, wrote Layard, "[y]ellow and bare, as it always is at this time of year." Henry Ross had departed Turkish Arabia and probably wasn't coming back, and the work teams had gone home. The wind had swept through the trenches and covered everything in sand and debris—a reminder of how fast vestiges of the ancient world could be swallowed up by the Mesopotamian desert. "Heaps of earth marked the site of former excavations," Layard wrote, "the chambers first discovered having been again completely buried with rubbish. Of the sculptured walls . . . no traces now remained." Layard was eager to start work again. Beyond Kuyunjik, however, the entire region was in chaos.

CHAPTER THIRTEEN

THE BATTLE OF LACHISH

After twenty-two years in the Middle East and West Asia, Henry Rawlinson returned to England in late 1849 and threw himself into European high society. He dined with Queen Victoria and Prince Albert, who had both taken an interest in Assyriology and enthusiastically followed accounts of the excavations and attempts at decipherment. He was welcomed into the Athenaeum Club, based in a neoclassical mansion overlooking St. James Park, whose members included Charles Darwin and the Scottish essayist and historian Thomas Carlyle. Egyptologist Samuel Birch (who would go on to translate the ancient funerary texts known as *The Book of the Dead*) gave him a personal tour of the British Museum—the first time Rawlinson had been there. He complained about the Assyrian antiquities' relegation to the basement, but admired the museum's collection and the neoclassical setting. The British Museum and Buckingham Palace were just the beginning. "Society received him with open arms," his brother George recalled. "Learned bodies [were] anxious to secure him . . . invitations poured in."

The invitations culminated with a lecture at the Royal Asiatic Society on January 17, 1850, presided over by the Earl of Ellesmere.

"All the Savans [savants] in turn are to attend," Rawlinson wrote to
Layard, who was now back in Mosul, "& I am to explain the obelisk and give a general sketch of my notions on Assyrian history."
The crowd listened rapt as Rawlinson showed sketches and spoke
about the meaning of the recently salvaged Black Obelisk, perhaps
the most talked-about artifact of Assyria. Rawlinson announced
that the monument had been built to honor "King Temen-bar" and
to record the delivering of gifts and tributes from defeated vassal
states across the Middle East. One abject figure, kneeling before
the king, had an identifiable name, Rawlinson declared: he was
"Yahua, son of Hubiri." Rawlinson had struggled to learn more
about this "prince" of an unknown country, he said, but there was
"no mention in the annals." He offered educated guesses about
wild-animal names, including a double-humped camel apparently
from a lake region in western Persia. The name was written with
what appeared to be a mix of logograms and phonemes and contained the Indo-Persian word *udru*, for a Bactrian camel, which led
Rawlinson to the translation the "beast of the desert with the double
back." Samuel Birch was enthralled by the revelations. "All London
was moved," Birch wrote to Layard. "I was highly delighted and
astonished . . . It is a most triumphant discovery—and will make
the French & Germans stare."

The society's officers invited Rawlinson back a month later.
This time he festooned the walls with the papier-mâché "squeezes"
obtained by his young Kurdish assistant at Behistun. Prince Albert,
the guest of honor, sat front and center. With the trilingual inscriptions at Behistun as his guide, Rawlinson announced, he'd figured
out the sounds of more than a hundred Akkadian characters. The
writing system contained "undoubted marks of an Egyptian origin"
and probably wasn't directly related to the Semitic tongues of the
Middle East. The writing system had consonants and vowels, just

like the Roman alphabet, he said. And he'd acquired the names of more Assyrian monarchs through a thorough analysis of the characters' phonetic values. The ruler of Khorsabad was Arko-tsena. His son, who ruled from the Southwest Palace at Kuyunjik, was Bel Adonim Shah. Next in line came this king's son, Assar-aden-assar. Birch, again in the audience, thought that Rawlinson's follow-up was even better than his debut. "Today [Rawlinson] has read a second paper at the Asiatic Society . . . giving a masterly précis of his interpretations," he wrote to Layard. Hincks and Rawlinson, he declared, "are running neck and neck" in the race to decipher cuneiform.

The *Economist* declared that the breakthroughs in Akkadian had removed "perfect and unmeaning darkness" from the script and "are worthy of the age of gaslighting, mule-spinning, railways, electric telegraphs and tubular bridges." The *Athenaeum* dedicated three pages to Rawlinson's talk, alongside shorter reports on Commander Charles Mitchell Mathison's pioneering journey to isolated Japan on the HMS *Mariner*, and Reverend David Livingstone's discovery of Lake Ngami, "a shimmering lake, some 80 miles long and 20 miles wide," north of the Kalahari Desert. There was only one problem: almost everything that Rawlinson had said was wrong.

◄———————►►

Around the same time that Rawlinson stood on the dais in Mayfair, Edward Hincks was hunkered down in Killyleagh, dealing with a calamity. Five years earlier, ships from North America had inadvertently imported to Ireland, in the stores of potatoes carried to feed their passengers, a fungus-like pathogen, *Phytophthora infestans*. The organism causes a disease called "late blight" that, in warm, wet weather, covers the leaves and edible roots of the potato plant with lesions that make it rot. The blight spread across the island. "The leaves of the potatoes on many fields I passed were quite withered, and a strange stench, such as I had never smelt before, but which became a well-known feature in 'the blight' for years after, filled the atmosphere adjoining each field of potatoes," William Trench, a County Kerry land agent, remembered. "The crop of all crops, on which the [Irish] depended for food, had suddenly melted away."

People began starving to death during the first winter, mostly in the poorer south and west; but Killyleagh wasn't immune. County Down was suffering "a very great distress," Hincks reported to a British official, urging that there be "no delay" in implementing the Temporary Relief Act, which authorized the local authorities to set up soup kitchens for famine victims. Soon the Killowen Cemetery at the foot of the Castle spilled over with victims of starvation and sickness from the countryside. "The potatoes have failed everywhere—I tremble for Ireland in the winter," Hincks wrote to his friend George Renouard in England in September 1848. One million people would starve to death or die from hunger-related diseases and 1.5 million would flee the country before the potato crop began to recover in 1852. The Great Famine cast the differing circumstances of Hincks and his English rival in sharp relief. While Rawlinson was being feted in London salons, Hincks was comforting lost souls fleeing the rotting potato fields.

Hincks helped organize a committee to distribute relief, presided over funerals, and consoled bereaved parishioners. But linguistic investigation still dominated his life, and he could become lost in personal grievances. He had always suffered from a feeling of being overlooked by other scholars, and the publication of *Nineveh and Its Remains* stirred up his insecurities. Layard lavished praise on Rawlinson—and attributed to him one of Hincks's first apparent achievements: identifying Nebuchadnezzar II on the Babylonian tablet. "It is only within the last few days that I was aware of this *injustice* with which I have been treated in this work," he wrote to the *Literary Gazette*, which published his letter in its May 21, 1849, issue. Hincks suspected that English prejudices against "unhappy Ireland" had played a role and demanded a correction in a subsequent edition of *Nineveh and Its Remains*. It was, he declared, "no more than I am entitled to." Layard apologized to Hincks for "ascribing to others" the discovery.

Hincks spent hours a day at his desk in the rectory, grappling with the silent determinatives. He believed he had identified a few of these signs, such as the asterisk-like character that appeared before the name of a god ✴. Another determinative for a god was turning up in the inscriptions as well, a stripped-down version of the asterisk: ➤. These signposts stood out amid the uninterrupted jumble of the characters (there were no diagonal wedges, as in the Old Persian, to separate words) and helped to set off proper names. Hincks noticed that the scribes had often spelled the names of kings and places using the same signs as logograms in some inscriptions, and substituting phonemes in others; sometimes a proper name could be spelled two or three different ways in the same inscription. These variant spellings could help a decipherer figure out the sounds of the logograms. In this way Hincks had concluded early on that the "god" logogram was pronounced *ili*, as in *bab-ili*. But this was barely a beginning; he needed to go further.

Hincks turned to the inscriptions in the palace of Khorsabad, excavated by Paul-Émile Botta between 1842 and 1846. Botta had made copies of the signs, and the lithographs had been distributed across Europe for would-be decipherers. Searching for clues to the name of the king who built the palace, Hincks spotted, in many inscriptions, the single wedge indicating a proper name ⊤ followed by the same two signs: ⟨⟨ ⊁. Hincks believed he was looking at the name of the ruler referred to up until now only as the "Khorsabad king."

Who was he? The first character that came after the determinative was one that Hincks recognized. It was another logogram for "king." (Hincks had now identified three of them.) But in this case it appeared to form part of the king's given name—the Akkadian equivalent of King Vidor or Nat King Cole. The most common Hebrew term for king is *melek*, which appears often in both the Bible and Hebrew prayers. But Hincks believed that *sar*, meaning "ruler" or "high official," was a better fit. The book of Isaiah mentions a king named Sargon II, who ruled the empire at the end of the eighth century BCE.

At this point the pastor might have thought back to Hebrew names from the Bible, such as Samuel ("God has heard") or Nathan ("gift of God"), and reasoned that *sar*, or "king," must form part of a phrase. One Hebrew word, *kinu*, meaning "legitimate" or "true," seemed to work for the second character. That gave him *sar* for "king" and *kinu* for "legitimate"—"the king who is legitimate." The two logograms together, he believed, made the Akkadian name Sharru-kinu, or Sharru-kin. Sharru-kin, he decided, had become the Hebrew "Sargon."`

Convinced that the key to the names of the Assyrian kings was the Old Testament, he set about trying to establish the identities of the king's successors. In the inscriptions of Khorsabad, Hincks often found "son" 𒉽 followed by five characters that began with the determinative for "god." Many Mesopotamian kings leading up to Nebuchadnezzar II had been named after deities, and so he assumed that he was looking at Sargon's heir: 𒀭 𒈗 𒀸 𒆠 𒅎.

Hincks could not read any of the logograms after the sign for a god. But 2 Kings names Sargon II's son and successor as Sennacherib, one of the most bloodthirsty rulers of Assyria. Sennacherib was a villain in the Old Testament, and when his own proclamations were deciphered, he would end up looking worse. "I cut their throats like lambs. I cut off their precious lives as one cuts a string," he declared after one round of slaughter. "I made the contents of their gullets and entrails run down upon the wide earth. The wheels of my war chariot, which brings low the wicked and the evil, were bespattered with blood and filth." He ended with a gruesome flourish: "Their testicles I cut off and tore out their privates like the seeds of cucumbers." According to 2 Kings, Sennacherib destroyed Babylon in 689 BCE and made off with the relics of its supreme god, Marduk. Rawlinson had given this seminal ruler a different name: Bel Adonim Shah. But Hincks was certain this was wrong.

The Bible gave Hincks the name of Sennacherib's son and successor, mentioned in 2 Kings, the book of Ezra, and the book of Isaiah. This king took power after his two elder brothers, known in Akkadian as Arda-Mulissu and Nabû-sarru-uçur, assassinated their father and fled into exile in the mountainous kingdom of Urartu, near the Black Sea. Sennacherib's heir rebuilt Babylon, restored the relics of the god Marduk to its temple, and led a successful military campaign in Egypt. Like the appellations of most kings, his name was written with different spellings, sometimes with logograms, sometimes with a mix of logograms and phonemes. It depended, it seemed, on the whims of the scribe: 𒀭𒀸𒋩 𒀭𒀸𒋩.

The first part of the name, Hincks believed, was "Ashur," written in the first example with a logogram 𒀸 and in the second with two phonetic characters: 𒀸𒋩. Ashur was the name of the supreme god of the Assyrians, and the name the Assyrians called their country.

In the Bible, the king is called Esarhaddon.

◄◄ ———— ►►

Now living in a town house just down the street from the Athenaeum Club, in Piccadilly, Rawlinson was, as Layard put it, reaping "the laurels of his well-earned fame." He hunted in Scotland and dined out with London's elite. The East India Company promoted him to lieutenant colonel. He signed a contract to write essays on Eastern antiquities and would soon accept another high-profile project, editing his brother George's four-volume translation of Herodotus's *Histories*. His lecture tour took him to the Society of Antiquaries, the Royal Institution, the Victoria Institute, and the Sheldonian Theatre at Oxford, where Max Müller, a famed professor of modern European languages, saluted him as the man who had made "the ancient Persian language" as accessible as Latin. "I am enjoying myself most amazingly," he wrote to Layard, "being quite overwhelmed with attention from all parties, that is from Princes & Dukes downward." He tried to downplay the adulation, but he wasn't particularly convincing. "[R]eally when one knows the value of these things and there is thus no danger of having one's head turned," he assured Layard, "the whole thing is very enjoyable." He was off to spend a month in the country, he wrote to Layard, "shooting, talking, flirting." (It was during this period that he apparently met his future wife, Louisa Caroline Harcourt Seymour, the daughter of a Tory parliamentarian from Wiltshire, though Rawlinson never wrote about the encounter.)

All the while, Hincks's boasts of progress perplexed him. Rawlinson had come up with different readings for the names of the rulers Hincks had identified as the biblical trio Sargon, Sennacherib, and Esarhaddon. "Rawlinson . . . is much puzzled and vacillates in his philological ideas," Birch observed. Rawlinson accepted the genealogy presented by Diodorus Siculus, whose source was a writer and surgeon named Ctesias of Cnidus. Ctesias had served as the royal physician in the court of the fifth-century BCE Achaemenid king Artaxerxes II, and supposedly had been rewarded with access to the secret annals of Assyria. In this version, widely dismissed in antiquity as fiction, Ninus and Semiramis were the first king and queen of Assyria, while the thirtieth and last ruler was Sardanapalus. Diodorus described him as an effeminate weakling with skin "even whiter than milk, and painted eyelids . . . [who] lived the life of a woman, spending his days in the company of his concubines and spinning purple garments." He "pursued the delights of love with men as well as with women; for he practiced sexual indulgence of all kinds with no restraints." Sardanapalus committed suicide, according to Diodorus, by setting himself on fire with his concubines and all his possessions in the palace at Nineveh as his enemies closed in on him.

The Greek historians made no mention of the biblical names that Hincks consulted when he drew up his genealogical list. The chronicle *Excerpta Latina Barbari* listed thirty-nine kings over 1,430 years, starting with Belus and ending with Ninus II, with no overlap at all with scriptural accounts. In part this reflected the fact that knowledge of the Bible was probably thin in ancient Greece: the first translation from the Aramaic wasn't made until around 250 BCE and was promptly shipped off to the Library in Alexandria. Diodorus Siculus's universal history, *Bibliotheca Historica*, deals with world events from the reigns of the pharaohs to the era of Julius Caesar, covering Mesopotamia, India, Scythia, Arabia, North Africa, Troy, Greece, and Western Europe. But he makes no mention of the ancient Jews.

And Rawlinson was a skeptic of religion and of biblical narratives. One figure he appears to have admired was David Hume, the eighteenth-century leader of the Scottish Enlightenment, dubbed by the Victorian biologist Thomas Huxley "that prince of agnostics." Hume wrote in his 1733 treatise *Natural History of Religion* that "doubt, uncertainty, suspence of judgment appear the only result of our most accurate scrutiny, concerning [the Bible]." Steeped in a reverence for the classics, Rawlinson was also prone to favor the Greeks and Romans. He was hardly the only man of his time to embrace Greek versions of Assyrian history. Lord Byron's *Sardanapalus*, an 1821 tragedy in blank verse, drew on Diodorus's account of a vainglorious monarch's fiery end. Eugène Delacroix's 1827 *Death of Sardanapalus*, on display at the Louvre, depicts the king, draped in a white gown, sprawled on a red-linen-covered bed surrounded by dying courtesans and murderous attackers. As early as 1846, Layard tried futilely to convince Rawlinson that he was on the wrong track. "This, I fear, is rather too good a joke," he wrote about Rawlinson's genealogy. But the Akkadian signs were still so obscure that it was difficult to tell who was right.

Rawlinson and Hincks had blazed through Old Persian, but Akkadian presented a thornier problem. There still seemed to be no way to know in many cases—especially with proper names—when a sign was being used as a logogram and when it was employed as a phonetic character. Then there was the other problem: if the sign was a logogram, how did one pronounce it? Two people could look at the same name and come up with wildly different readings. It seemed to be a guessing game. "I cannot refrain from noticing," the French-German scholar Jules Oppert observed around this time, "the extreme difficulty there is in reading the names of Assyrian kings."

One example of this ambiguity could be found on the Black Obelisk. Hincks and Rawlinson had confronted a six-character name repeatedly on the column. The tip-off that it was a king's name was the determinatives for "person" and "god" that started off the sequence. Four more signs followed: 𒁹 𒈦 𒉺 𒀭 𒌋 𒁇.

Read phonetically, the four characters could spell *Di-man-u-bar*, though Rawlinson preferred to transliterate this as *Temen-bar*. Hincks called the king *Di-van-u-bar*. Both, it would turn out years later, had gone astray. The name was written with logograms and was pronounced *Shulmānu-asharedu*: "The god Shulmanu is pre-eminent." The Hebrew version was Shalmaneser III, a military expansionist who went to war against Syria and is referred to several times in the Old Testament.

The multiple phonetic values of the characters weren't just a Mesopotamian phenomenon. English exhibits polyphony as well: Consider the values of *gh* as it appears in *ghost, delight, rough, hiccough,* and *Edinburgh,* or of *ch* in *yacht, chiaroscuro,* and *chaff.* But in Akkadian this property extended to hundreds of characters.

Hincks enumerated up to seven different sounds that some of these signs could make. This sign ◫ , he insisted, could be pronounced *is, ish, iẓ, es, esh,* and *eẓ,* and have different values altogether when used as a logogram meaning "wood" (*ishu*) or as a determinative for objects made of wood, in which case it was silent. ⬱ could be *ug, uk, weg,* or *wek.* Hincks had found one sign, he thought, that made sounds as varied as *bar* and *mas*; another could stand for *ub, up,* and *ar.* Others seemed to make both *kur* and *lat, man* and *nis,* and *bis* and *gir.* There was "no . . . means of distinguishing between various classes of cuneiform signs" and no clue to which of many "powers" of a character to use, Rawlinson wrote. Skeptics would seize on this and use it to undermine the decipherers' credibility, he feared—rightly, as it turned out. After years of research, he admitted to Norris that he'd only overcome the problem of the variants to a limited extent, and couldn't grasp why the Assyrians had chosen such a difficult and inconvenient system. "I have been tempted," he confessed to Layard, "to abandon the study altogether in utter despair."

◂◂———▸▸

In his paper "On the Khorsabad Inscriptions," presented at the Royal Irish Academy in Dublin in June 1849 and published the following spring, Hincks addressed the confusion inherent in Akkadian writing. Some characters were used exclusively as logograms, he wrote. Others could serve as both logograms *and* phonetic characters. The logogram for "house" ⟬ had the sound *bitu* or *bitum* when it meant house, and *bi* when it was used phonetically. (The *um* ending, also seen with *ili* and *ilum*, for "god," was used in certain grammatical cases to modify a noun and fell out of use at the end of the Old Babylonian Empire, which was brought down by Hittite invaders around 1600 BCE.)

That seemed straightforward; it resembled the attributes of Egyptian hieroglyphs. But other logograms, Hincks posited, took an altogether different value when used as phonetic characters. The cuneiform sign for "god," for instance, ⊢⊤, was *ili, ilu,* or *ilum* when it was used as a logogram but became *an* when used as a syllable. The Assyrians and Babylonians, he intuited, must have borrowed their cuneiform characters from an older language. Hincks theorized that the sign for a god in Akkadian must have had the *an* sound in the older tongue. When the Assyrians and Babylonians adopted the sign, they attached to it their own word for a god, *ili*. But, when used phonetically, it retained its original sound, *an*.

Hincks compared it to the way that the English language had borrowed from Latin. The sign £ for *libra* is now read "pound"; *e.g.*, for *exempli gratia*, became "for example"; *viz.*, *videre licet* ("it is permitted to see"), came to mean "namely." The ampersand, &, which originally was a sign in Latin that bound the letters *e* and *t*, to make *et*, the word for "and," came to mean simply "and." This system was complex, Hincks conceded, but by looking at the signs in context, sounds and meanings would often become clear.

Some were convinced. William Desborough Cooley, an Irish scholar-explorer and a fellow in the Royal Geographic Society, declared that Hincks had achieved "unquestioned priority" in the "discovery of the ideographic element." The *Literary Gazette* expressed long-winded wonder at "a comparatively recluse student, who, with the great disadvantage of possessing but a small supply of texts to study, has nevertheless laboured with signal success . . . in solving some of the most difficult literary problems which have ever claimed the attention of the learned." The *Athenaeum*, in what must have stung Rawlinson, averred that Hincks had claimed "the foremost place in cuneiform studies. In sound scientific method [and] boldness of conjecture without rashness . . . he is unrivalled." Yet Hincks's findings did not convince the perennial skeptic Charles Wall, who called all attempts to decipher Akkadian cuneiform "no better than moonshine." (Wall did, however, admire Hincks's mastery of Old Persian and wrote that, "I consider no author superior to him, and very few his equals, in ingenuity combined with learning.") Rawlinson, for his part, dismissed Hincks's work as "wild and unintelligible." And he belittled Hincks as a "strange country parson."

◄◄――――――►►

In July 1850, Edwin Norris of the Royal Asiatic Society brought Hincks and Rawlinson together for a brief face-to-face encounter in London. It's not clear where they met—possibly at the society's headquarters—or how they got along. One month later, the rival decipherers traveled north to Edinburgh to deliver back-to-back lectures at the annual conference of the British Association for the Advancement of Science, held in the main hall of the seventeenth-century Parliament House. Members mingled beneath an oak-trussed roof that soared sixty feet above the inlaid timber floor. Light filtered through stained glass and arched windows, illuminating niches filled with marble sculptures and oil paintings of Scottish statesmen. After a chat in a committee room, Hincks stood in the chamber and shared a discovery: Akkadian characters, except for the logograms and the silent determinatives, were *exclusively* syllables, a view he said he had formed "in opposition to all other writers." Every character fit into one of three patterns, he said: consonant-vowel, vowel-consonant, or consonant-vowel-consonant.

Rawlinson quickly dismissed Hincks's theory. He maintained that its words were written like those in Arabic, Syriac, Hebrew, and other tongues of the Middle East, using an alphabet of about two dozen consonants, with the vowels rarely marked. On that theory he had transliterated the Akkadian name of Darius the Great's first rebel foe, Gaumata, as *G-m-a-t*. Hincks held that the rebel leader's name in Akkadian was spelled with four syllabic signs, *Gu-ma-a-tu*. Such small things could spell the difference, in Hincks's view, between clarity and incomprehensibility—and he would soon be proved right.

Hincks made other bold propositions that summer. Marching ahead with his conviction that Akkadian belonged to the Semitic family of languages centered in the Middle East, he believed that Akkadian and Hebrew constructed verbs the same way, forming tenses, cases, and related nouns around three consonantal "roots." The Hebrew *katab*, which means "to write," had the roots *k*, *t*, and *b* and verb forms including *katabnu* (we wrote), *yiktob* (he will write), and *niktob* (we will write), and the noun *koteb* (author). Hincks put together grammatical charts that showed the parallels between Hebrew and Akkadian verb formations.

Hincks also relied on Hebrew to expand his Akkadian vocabulary. There seemed to be hundreds, if not thousands, of cognates in Akkadian and Hebrew, he avowed, ranging from "chair" (*kussû* in Akkadian; *kisse* in Hebrew) to "repeat" (*shanû* in Akkadian; *shanah* in Hebrew) to "land" (*ershetu* in Akkadian; *eretz* in Hebrew). Hincks pored confidently through the Akkadian texts, identifying Hebrew-like words. Rawlinson wavered. Sometimes he agreed with Hincks that they were dealing with a purely Semitic language closely resembling those of neighboring civilizations. Then, stumbling across an Akkadian noun or verb that bore no resemblance to the Hebrew or Arabic equivalent, he discounted the possibility. To cite one example, the word *if* in Akkadian is *shumma*; it's *een* or *lu* in Hebrew.

Bit by bit, however, Rawlinson was accepting Hincks's interpretations. In his *Memoir on the Babylonian Translation of the Great Inscription at Behistun*, published in 1851 in the *Journal of the Royal Asiatic Society*, Rawlinson finally embraced Hincks's long-held belief that Akkadian belonged to the Semitic family. (Contemporary philologists divide the Semitic language group into two branches: Eastern Semitic, which includes Akkadian, and Western Semitic, encompassing Hebrew, Arabic, and Aramaic.) Following Hincks, he also provided mostly syllabic transliterations of 242 characters:

A   ra   bi

(Arabáya in Persian; Arabia in English)

D   à   ri   y   á   vas

(Darayavaush in Persian; Darius in English)

Most critically, Rawlinson's resistance to Hincks's biblical names for the Assyrian kings was softening. From this point on, Rawlinson abandoned his readings of "Bel Adonim Shah" and "Arko-tsena" and began referring to the kings who built the palaces at Khorsabad and Kuyunjik by the biblical names Sargon II and Sennacherib. He would never acknowledge that Hincks had probably been correct all along.

In 1851 and 1852, Assyria fever swept London. The popular *Illustrated London News* emblazoned a page with an engraving of a human-headed lion, weighing more than ten tons, being rolled on a ramp up the steps of the British Museum. "The piece of sculpture . . . was brought from the Docks on a truck drawn by eleven horses," the caption declared. "[W]e believe it is the largest monolith which has reached England from the buried city of the East." Literary magazines chronicled every move and countermove in the Rawlinson-Hincks competition. And now that both scholars agreed that the excavated palaces belonged to Assyrian kings who were mentioned in the Old Testament, they could examine whether the narratives on the walls lined up with those of the Hebrew Prophets. The first they studied were those of the Assyrian king who had been the greatest bane of the Jews: Sennacherib.

After Sargon II's death in battle in 705 BCE, 2 Kings relates, Tyre, Ashdod, Ashkelon, and other vassal cities of the Mediterranean coast refused to keep paying the treasury-depleting tributes. Sennacherib's forces crushed the resistance in Syria, and then headed south toward the Kingdom of Judea. Centered in the arid highlands, the kingdom had probably been founded in the tenth or early ninth century BCE, growing from sparsely populated settlements into an urbanized state with its capital at Jerusalem. The Jewish kingdom had also taken advantage of the confusion in the royal court and stopped paying tributes to Assyria. Hezekiah, the King of Judea, was a pious reformer who had reconstructed the Temple and removed sacrilegious idols. He was also a military strategist. Certain that a siege and attack were coming, he strengthened Jerusalem's walls, built defensive towers, and constructed a tunnel to bring fresh water into the city from a nearby spring in case Sennacherib's forces sealed off other sources.

Two decades earlier, the Assyrians had destroyed the Kingdom of Israel, Judea's northern neighbor. Now the army cut a bloody swath through the last remaining territory of the people of Kings Saul and David. "The plague," lamented the Hebrew prophet Micah, "has reached the very gate of my people, even to Jerusalem itself." Thirty miles southwest of Jerusalem, Sennacherib laid siege to Lachish, a city set in the arid hills and surrounded by thick ramparts. The army smashed down the walls with battering rams, slaughtered indiscriminately, and impaled the leaders of the resistance. The Second Book of Kings relates that Hezekiah, assessing the implacable force coming his way, lost heart. He sent an urgent message to Sennacherib, who was then camped outside Lachish. Hezekiah offered "a payment of three hundred talents of silver and thirty talents of gold. . . . Hezekiah cut down the doors and the doorposts of the Temple, which [he] had overlaid [with gold] and gave them to the king of Assyria."

Sennacherib accepted Hezekiah's gifts—then, determined to crush the Jewish upstart anyway, he resumed his march to Jerusalem. But as the Assyrian army bivouacked outside the city walls a deus ex machina arrived: an angel of the Lord "went out and smote in the camp of the Assyrians a hundred fourscore and five thousand; and . . . early in the morning, behold, they were all dead corpses," declares 2 Kings. Isaiah 37:37 records that "Sennacherib king of Assyria departed, and went and returned, and dwelt at Nineveh." The last Jewish kingdom had been temporarily spared.

Some agnostics and rationalists regarded Sennacherib's march through the Kingdom of Judea as a fable like the Flood and the parting of the Red Sea. Now, suddenly, the proof seemed within the public's grasp. The annals of the Kingdom of Judea campaign were carved on a colossal bull guarding the main entrance of Sennacherib's Southwest Palace. Layard had copied the inscriptions from that bull and turned them over to the British Museum.

In the August 23, 1851, *Athenaeum*, Rawlinson presented his decipherment. The translation was incomplete, but each twist and turn in 2 Kings aligned with its Assyrian counterpart: Sennacherib's annals mentioned "an expedition against *Luliya*, King of Sidon, in which he was completely successful." While carrying out operations against other Syrian cities, "he learned of an insurrection in Palestine." Turning south to deal with the Jews, he "ravaged the open country," taking "all the fenced cities of Judah" and threatening Jerusalem. Most extraordinary, the description of Hezekiah's tribute matched the one in 2 Kings. "Hezekiah . . . tendered to the king of Assyria . . . 30 talents of gold, 300 talents of silver," as well as "the ornaments of the Temple, slaves, boys and girls, and men-servants and maid-servants for the use of the palace." Frustratingly, Rawlinson couldn't find Sennacherib's account of why his army had retreated from Jerusalem: "There is no sign of any disaster having befallen it," he wrote to Norris. Perhaps another inscription would reveal the Assyrians' version of their abrupt withdrawal.

Herodotus had provided a different story from that of the Old Testament: his version of the failed Assyrian campaign had played out in the Nile River Delta, where, instead of Hezekiah, an early-eighth-century pharaoh heard the god Hephaestus tell him in a dream that "he should suffer no ill" from the Assyrian army. "I will send you champions," the god promised. In the Bible, the Assyrian soldiers had died of a divinely delivered pestilence. In Herodotus's version, field mice swarmed over the Assyrian camp, chewed up the army's quivers and bowstrings, "and ate the thongs by which they managed their shields." The next morning, "they commenced their fight, and great multitudes fell, as they had no arms with which to defend themselves." Could something like this have truly happened, only outside Jerusalem?

The *Athenaeum* article enthralled its thousands of readers. If proved to be accurate, Rawlinson's translation would constitute some of the first solid evidence that Bible stories were grounded in history. Even before the Enlightenment, skepticism had been rising about the Hebrew Scriptures. Thomas Hobbes, the author of *Leviathan*, and the seventeenth-century Jewish philosopher Baruch Spinoza cast doubt on whether Moses, Joshua, and Samuel had really written the stories attributed to them, and by the 1700s most biblical scholars agreed that the Pentateuch, the first five books of the Old Testament (Genesis, Exodus, Leviticus, Numbers, and Deuteronomy), were composites of dubious historicity thrown together by numerous authors over half a millennium ending between 450 and 350 BCE.

Academics cast a skeptical eye as well on later works such as the book of Daniel, purportedly written by a Jewish prophet who was brought to Babylon in captivity after King Nebuchadnezzar II's conquest of Jerusalem in 597 BCE and lived to witness the city's fall. In the book, Daniel described Nebuchadnezzar II's descent into madness and a seven-year retreat in the wilderness, where he ate grass, roamed "like an ox," let his hair grow as long "as eagle feathers," and allowed his fingernails to turn into "bird claws." But biblical scholars would determine that the book of Daniel was a collaborative effort written four centuries after the fall of Babylon, and that the authors probably conflated Nebuchadnezzar II with his son Nabonidus, who had lived like a hermit for years. According to the Dead Sea Scrolls, the last king of Babylon retreated in isolation at an Arabian oasis called Tayma, undergoing treatment for a chronic ulcer by a Jewish exorcist. It was like this with the entire Old Testament: the uncertainty about authorship, about the date the account was written, and about the reliability of the narrator or narrators made it impossible to know what stories to trust.

Rawlinson's discovery proved that some narratives could indeed be trusted. But it didn't convince Charles Wall or the grandees of the French Academy. The French academics, motivated perhaps by a degree of hostility and jealousy toward the English, were particularly unmoved. And perhaps to some of the doubters, the exact correlations that Rawlinson found in the inscriptions on the bull— "30 talents of gold, 300 talents of silver"—were too perfect. They were seen as evidence that he was fixing the game.

◄━━━━━━━►

One of the most vivid depictions of Sennacherib's path of destruction paneled the walls of the royal chamber of the Southwest Palace of Nineveh. This tableau, inscribed across a thirty-six-by-fifteen-foot slab, showed the siege and annihilation of a fortified city "evidently of great extent and importance," Layard wrote in his second memoir, *Discoveries Among the Ruins of Nineveh and Babylon*. Hundreds of archers, charioteers, horsemen, and slingers surround the ramparts; soldiers wield battering rams and ramps to break through the fortifications. Desperate defenders crowd the walls and towers, dousing the enemy's flamethrowers, firing arrows, and hurling rocks and torches. Another part of the frieze jumped forward in time, showing the battle's aftermath: victorious Assyrian troops plunder the governor's palace, soldiers cut rebel leaders' throats and hurl others to their deaths off the ramparts, prisoners march through an arid landscape of fig trees and olive groves. "Amongst the spoil were furniture, arms, shields, chariots . . . camels, carts drawn by oxen, and laden with women and children," Layard wrote. The triumphant king regards a procession of captives while seated on a magnificent throne. Inscribed above and just to the left of the king's head were four lines of commentary:

Hincks's and Rawlinson's readings of cuneiform inscriptions had now moved into near alignment. Both claimed to recognize the first six characters in the first line as a common way of spelling *Sennacherib* (Assyrian: *Sin-ahhe-eriba*), although neither could understand the logograms that his name comprised. (Sennacherib would turn out to mean "the moon god Sîn has replaced the brothers," probably referring to the fact that Sargon II's other sons were dead by the time the future king, celebrated as the incarnation of the lunar deity, was born.) In the same line, they read a logogram for "king" ◀◀ followed by the logogram for "world" or "totality" **I**. They saw "king" again ◀◀, followed by the determinative for "country" that Grotefend had first recognized at Persepolis ◀◀, and then the phonetic spelling of the nation of "Ashur" ▶ ▶Ψ. That gave them a complete first line: "Sennacherib, king of the world, king of the country of Assyria."

They agreed as well about the next three lines, which, they maintained, consisted of phonetically spelled words as well as the logograms for "throne of judgment" and a determinative for "city." But there was one critical difference between Hincks's and Rawlinson's readings. In Rawlinson's version, the full inscription read:

Sennacherib, king of the world, king of the country of Assyria,
Sitting on the throne of judgment
Before the city of *Aliqqu*
I give permission for its slaughter.

◄◄———————►►

Hincks insisted that Rawlinson had misread the critical third line. The rector translated the three characters at the end of that line, after the determinative for a city ►𒂍 ⟨𒀀 𒂊𒈨, not as Aliqqu but as *Lachish*—the fortified hilltop town that Sennacherib, according to 2 Kings, sacked and destroyed before resuming his march to Jerusalem. The tableau on the wall of Sennacherib's palace, Hincks proclaimed, was nothing less than the only portrait known to exist of the bloodiest victory in Assyria's war against the Jews—the battle and subsequent slaughter described in the Old Testament.

Or was this reading, yet again, too perfect?

CHAPTER FOURTEEN

FRIENDSHIP IN
THE DESERT

In September 1849, eleven months before the Edinburgh face-off between Hincks and Rawlinson over the nature of the Ak-kadian script, Austen Layard had arrived back in Mosul from his long sojourn in England and Constantinople. The archaeologist quickly resumed the life of a colonial lord of the desert. "Old servants take their places as a matter of course, and, uninvited, pursue their regular occupations as if they had never been interrupted," he wrote of moving back into the house he maintained in Mosul. "Indeed it seemed as if we had but returned from a summer's ride; two years had passed away like a dream." Layard rarely mentioned his servants by name in his writings, but they remained ubiquitously in the background: cooking meals, tending animals, erecting tents, gathering river turtles and truffles on excursions into the countryside, even bearing a hawk for hunting game in the desert. Layard seemed to treat his staff kindly—making sure they were paid promptly, giving them adequate time off—but they knew their place both at home and on the road. When they traveled with Layard, they crowded onto a separate raft, slept segregated on rooftops or in their own tents, and were among the last to receive food at banquets with Arab and Ottoman dignitaries. "The servants succeeded to the dishes," Layard wrote about one lavish meal in which boiled sheep was the main course, "which afterward passed through the hands of the camel drivers and tent pitchers . . . the conditions of the bones by the time they were delivered to a crowd of hungry dogs may easily be imagined." One can also imagine Layard identifying with the royal banqueteers depicted on the Assyrian bas-reliefs, who were always surrounded by their own bevy of attendants. "A procession of servants carr[ied] fruit, flowers, games and supplies for a banquet, preceded by mace-bearers," he wrote of a scene at Nimrud. "The first servant following the guard bore an object which I should not hesitate to identify with the pineapple."

Layard enjoyed traveling with his staff through Mesopotamia, but he was shocked at how the region's security had deteriorated since he'd been away in England. The government had pulled troops back from much of the countryside, and Bedouins in a low-level rebellion against the empire had stepped up attacks on desert caravans. Robbers lurked just beyond the walls of Mosul, ready to ambush anyone who emerged from the city gates. Around the time of Layard's arrival, a band of marauders had looted a postal caravan bound for Constantinople. Henry Ross, Layard's frequent assistant on the mounds, described the ordeal of one British officer who had been intercepted by Bedouins while rafting down the Tigris. "[T]he over-confident individual was armed to the teeth and had hinted at a determination not to be taken alive, [but] he was stripped of everything he possessed, even to his nether garments," wrote Ross, who had heard the story from a Bedouin informant. "It was both ludicrous and amusing to witness the delight with which they imitated his piteous supplication to be allowed to retain only his shoes," he went on. "This was denied him, and he was compelled to walk barefooted through the prickly camel-thorn back to the raft."

The Wild East atmosphere extended all the way to Basra. The Ottoman government had established a system of fortified lodgings for Shia pilgrims, traders, and others who dared to cross central and Southern Mesopotamia. "Large *khans* [rest houses] occur at convenient intervals, to provide for the security of travelers against . . . roving Bedouins," wrote William Loftus, an English archaeologist who made the journey from Baghdad to Southern Mesopotamia in 1849. "It is a large and substantial square building, resembling a fortress, being surrounded with a lofty wall, and flanked by round towers to defend the inmates in case of attack." The Englishman described the "noxious" atmosphere inside these desert strongholds. Persian pilgrims and animals were shut inside together, along with decomposing bodies being transported for burial in the Shia holy cities of Najaf and Karbala. "It is estimated that [even] in healthy seasons, a fifth of the travellers, overcome with fever and other diseases, find their graves in the desert," he wrote.

The violence wasn't confined to pilgrims and other foreign travelers. Jebour Arabs, who made up almost all of Layard's archaeological labor force, had feuded with their rivals, the Tayy, for as long as anyone could remember. But with the Ottoman soldiers in retreat, a spate of camel and livestock raids threatened to escalate into full-scale war. "People in England little know the difficulties [Layard] has to overcome, the presence of mind he has to have, and the immense tact . . . it requires to manage tribes so jealous of one another," wrote an English visitor to Kuyunjik in the *Times.* "He requires no small nerve . . . for in an hour of heat and rage, it might cost him his life." Layard had a colonial Englishman's sense of superiority over the Arabs, but he paid workers well, often joined them in their excavations, and expressed curiosity about their lives. It had an effect. The writer described how, after the theft of hundreds of Jebour sheep and oxen by the Tayy, the Jebour had loaded

Layard supervises the procession of the bull beneath the mound of Nimrud

their rifles and prepared to attack their foes. Layard had calmly persuaded them to lay down their weapons. Then "by the esteem . . . he commands among the Arab tribes, [he] prevailed on the Sheikh of the Tai [*sic*] to restore the whole of their booty . . . A thing never before heard of "—-especially since the Jebour had stolen hundreds of Tayy camels weeks earlier. "The power he has over these wild sons of the Desert is perfectly astonishing," wrote the visitor in the *Times*.

Another friend who met Layard in Kuyunjik around this time called him, in a letter to the *Times*, "one of the cleverest and most enterprising men I have ever known . . . He is carrying on excavations for the British Museum, or rather attempting to do it, as the paltry sum they allow him is quite inadequate." Layard, the friend went on, "has to do all the work of superintending, directing, copying inscriptions . . . [and] keeping up his influence with the Arabs, who are in semi-rebellion against the Turks, and against each other." Layard attributed much of his success to Hormuzd Rassam's "inexhaustible good humour, combined with necessary firmness [and] his complete knowledge of the Arab character." Perhaps Rassam's greatest accomplishment, Layard wrote, was keeping the "wild spirits" of the Arab workmen in check when they arrived en masse and in an excited state in Mosul to collect their monthly salaries.

Most Western commentary about the tribes of Turkish Arabia had a similarly patronizing tone. One of the few writers who transcended that was Lady Anne Blunt, an expert horsewoman and scholar who spent months observing both the pastoral Jebours— "living with their cattle all the year round in the same district and making as good subjects as the Sultan need have"—and the nomadic Bedouins, who migrated seasonally with their camels through the Tigris and Euphrates valleys. In the 1870s Blunt and her husband, the poet Wilfrid Blunt, followed the Shammar, one of the largest Bedouin groups in the region, numbering, she estimated, "twelve thousand five hundred tents," or fifty thousand people. Blunt drew a vivid picture of Bedouin life, one of "hard training, eating once a day, [and] sleeping on the ground." Doctors, she wrote, "do not exist, nor is there any knowledge ... of herbs. The sick man is obliged, whatever his condition, to move with the tribe ... In his tent he lies surrounded by his friends, who ... talk to him till he dies." The desert took a grim toll on most: "As young men, the Bedouins are often good-looking, with bright eyes, a pleasant smile, and very white teeth," Blunt observed. But by thirty, insufficient food and illness "have pinched and withered their cheeks, and the sun has turned their skin to an almost Indian blackness. At forty their beard turns grey, and at fifty they are old men. I doubt if more than a very few of them reach ... sixty."

Attempting to counter stereotypes of the Bedouins as a brutal and ignorant band of thieves, Blunt described a culture of hospitality, civility, and compassion. Bedouins chose their leaders by popular vote and refrained from killing their rivals even in the livestock raids that broke out constantly between tribes. "The Bedouin is essentially humane, and never takes life needlessly," she insisted. "He feels no delight . . . in shedding blood." But highway robbery, she acknowledged, was part of the unwritten desert code, and travelers passing through Bedouin territory without an official escort or a proper introduction could expect to lose their animals, money, even their shoes and clothes down to their underwear. Conversely, to refuse shelter or food to a stranger who had permission to cross their territory was considered an offense against human and divine law and "the very essence of depravity." As for the rebellion that was roiling Mesopotamia, Blunt argued that the Turkish strategy to pacify the nomads—encouraging agriculture, providing security for the roads, forming alliances with Bedouin chiefs to get them to act as police—was destined to fail. "The peaceful shepherd tribes are plundered by the Government [and] it is hardly to be wondered at that the great camel-owning tribes, who being always on the move . . . should have refused all proposals made them of abandoning their wild life," she wrote. Eventually she saw a day when the tables would be turned, and "the Bedouins, having exchanged their lances for more modern weapons, shall reign again supreme in the valley."

◄◄──────►►

Layard and Rawlinson kept apart for most of the time they overlapped in the region, given their workloads and the dangers of Mesopotamian travel. But separated by 250 miles of bandit- and rebel-infested semi-desert, they kept a friendship going anyway. They wrote once or twice a week to each other through 1846 and part of 1847, and again in 1849. Though most of Layard's letters have been lost, the diplomat's side of their correspondence captures the bond of two expatriates in an outpost far from home, where the risk of fatal disease or violent death was always present. After a Christmas 1845 soiree at the Residency that Rawlinson and Layard attended together, Rawlinson commented coyly on his friend's interest in the opposite sex. "There are various stories afloat about Madame having come over to bid you adieu," he wrote. Rawlinson's friend James Felix Jones had been there as well. "She is said to have been closeted with you for at least ten minutes, and there has been the devil's own work to patch up Jones's broken zeal." By now, Rawlinson had replaced the formal "my dear sir" of their early correspondence and adopted a lighter tone with the younger man. Four months later, with Layard back in Mosul, Rawlinson was complaining about his various ailments. "I have been ill almost the whole of the last fortnight and can finally say what has been the matter with me—[my] liver," he wrote. "But the Dr. says it is all owing to truffles."

A few weeks later the focus was on Layard's poor health: "You have been I suspect [pushing] yourself too much at Nimrood . . . I should recommend you to come down and pass a quiet winter with me and to make a fresh start with the spring." But Layard found it impossible to break away from his excavations. Meanwhile, Rawlinson was struggling with his own medical troubles. "I have been ailing so much all this last fortnight that I have had serious thoughts of taking shelter somewhere in the mountains," he wrote to Layard in August 1846. "I think the heat has affected my liver but Ross says it is merely stomach and [recommends] castor oil & soda water and constitutional rides in the grey of the morning."

But Rawlinson had more on his mind than illnesses. He often expressed his pleasure about the antiquities that Layard was sending down to Baghdad. "Your crates arrived all right and we have been regaling our antiquarian appetites on the contents ever since," he wrote to him in 1846. Rawlinson, however, considered the bas-reliefs to be "crude and unrefined," and compared them unfavorably to the Elgin Marbles and other classical art. Layard disagreed and feared that Rawlinson might discourage the trustees from financing further digs. "Heaven forefend that I should do anything to impede the excavations," Rawlinson reassured him. The images had more historical—if not aesthetic—value "than Pompeii or Herculaneum." But he considered the real prize to be the inscriptions. "[I] view every new Inscription as equal to gaining one of the lost decades of Livy," he proclaimed, referring to the first-century CE Roman historian, only one quarter of whose works have survived.

The men discussed political themes as well. Layard had little affection for the Kurds, who were carrying out a campaign of ethnic cleansing against their neighbors, the Chaldeans, Catholics who trace their roots to ancient Babylon and who lived at the time mostly in the Zagros Mountains. (This was the sect to which his protégé Hormuzd Rassam belonged.) Rawlinson had little interest in the Chaldeans, but he admired Kurdish strength and self-reliance and saw the mountain people as superior in character "either to the Turks or Persians." Should the Ottoman Empire collapse, as many geopolitical observers had predicted it would, he told Layard, "We should be looking to support the Kurds."

Rawlinson also kept Layard informed about his frustrations and breakthroughs in Akkadian decipherment. He shared with him what he thought were references to Jerusalem and the ten lost tribes of Israel. Later, in a reversal, he averred that Ninus, the supposed founder of Assyria, had never existed: "I throw all Greek traditions regarding Assyria to the winds." Then Rawlinson second-guessed himself, avowing that the Greek genealogists were right after all.

When Layard expressed skepticism, Rawlinson became indignant. "You do not appear to appreciate the progress [I have] now made in reading or at any note in understanding the Inscriptions," he sulked.

In the summer of 1849 Rawlinson had news to share. After twenty-two years in Asia without a break, he had at last been granted a home leave from the East India Company and was preparing to set out for England to oversee the publication of his second memoir on Behistun for the *Journal of the Royal Asiatic Society*. The trip presented an opportunity to stop at Nimrud to visit Layard on the way to the Black Sea. There would be plenty to talk about. He had managed to "connect all the names . . . in one continuous line of 10 kings," Rawlinson wrote. "I hope to explain all this to you when we meet." Layard was delighted by the prospect of another face-to-face encounter. "The Major has made wonderful discoveries which he intends to publish when he reaches England," Layard told Ross.

The only question was whether Rawlinson would be well enough to make the journey. Malaria had broken out in Baghdad, Rawlinson wrote, "and I fear it will be worse before it is better . . . I am now not very strong and must [avoid] the fatigue as much as I can." Aside from a few observations about a Hungarian uprising against the "absolutist" Hapsburgs in Vienna (one of the revolutions sweeping Europe at the time), Rawlinson remained preoccupied with his health and the fetid urban environment: "I count the days I am still obliged to remain here," he told Layard.

No sooner had malaria been brought under control than a cholera epidemic swept Baghdad. That September Rawlinson gathered his embassy staff and, along with much of the population, fled to the refuge of the countryside. "I am pitching my camp" amid the hyenas and lions in the ruins of Ctesiphon, "to keep my people as clear of the Cholera as I can," he wrote Layard. "The city does not contain one half of its usual inhabitants and if the mortality continues, it will be entirely deserted by the end of the week." At last, on October 10, back in Baghdad, he announced that he would be leaving for the north in five days. But more Bedouin raids had taken place on the road to Mosul. "I can hardly be at Nimrud before Saturday the 20th," he wrote. "Indeed, if the country should be as much disturbed as is commonly reported it should be necessary to take [an armed escort] from stage to stage." He would move fast, because "I travel in the lightest manner possible. No tent, no bed, no anything but a few things for the road, and my Cuneiform papers."

As soon as he got Rawlinson's news, Layard traveled downriver from Kuyunjik to Nimrud. A melancholy scene awaited him: the

Rawlinson's sketch of the Arch of Ctesiphon

hundreds of Jebour workers who had once jubilantly hoisted bas-reliefs, lamassus, and other antiquities from the tell's subterranean chambers had long ago dispersed. All was silent; a few "colossal heads of winged figures" rose surreally "above the level of the soil," Layard wrote. Then, on the morning of October 19, he received a pleasant surprise. An Arab assistant grabbed Layard by the hand as he walked across the mound and led him excitedly into an excavated chamber. There in the gloom lay Rawlinson, having arrived one day earlier than expected. He was wrapped in a cloak, "deep in sleep, wearied by a long and harassing night's ride," Layard recalled. "Beside the greetings of old friendship there was much to be seen together, and much to be talked over."

Layard was exuberant, but Rawlinson was not in any shape for an extended conversation. Exhausted and feverish, he took refuge from the heat with Layard all afternoon in a mud hut beside the mound. In the cool of the evening, with his temperature rising, he rode with Layard the wearying twenty miles across the plains to Mosul. The comrades had some exchanges about the chronology of Assyrian kings and Rawlinson's progress with cuneiform, but the long-anticipated encounter proved to be a joyless experience. "October 21: ride into Mosul with Rawlinson who was suffering much from fever and weakness, and he remained during the day in bed," Layard's journal records of the reunion. "[October] 22: Rawlinson [is] still too weak to leave the house." On the twenty-third, Rawlinson finally got out of bed. "I [l]ooked over the ruins and excavations . . . in the afternoon, but did not enjoy it much," he wrote, "as I was suffering all day & Layard had no medicine to relieve me." After a desultory tour, Rawlinson continued his journey to Constantinople and to England.

◂────────▸

Rawlinson's visit had been a disappointment. But Layard had too much else on his mind to brood about it. He and Rassam now focused their attention on excavating the Southwest Palace of Sennacherib at Kuyunjik, which Henry Ross had started exploring during Layard's absence in England. For the first time, Layard was able to grasp the extent of the cataclysm that had brought down Nineveh in 612 BCE. Almost all the friezes in the labyrinthine structure had been damaged or destroyed, and in every room the archaeologists confronted evidence of a conflagration that had turned "the sculptured paneling to lime"—crumbling it to a white powder—"and reduc[ed] the edifice to heaps of ashes and rubbish." Yet enough of the bas-reliefs had survived to provide unprecedented glimpses of a vanished civilization's ingenuity and brutality. A dozen panels arranged in sequence revealed the answer to a question that had perplexed Layard since his early excavations at Nimrud: How had the Assyrians transported those huge blocks of alabaster from the rock quarries to the palace? The first panels showed laborers—"probably captives from different conquered nations," Layard speculated—supervised by men armed with maces and clubs, pulling a block through the river shallows on a flat-bottomed boat. A hundred slaves hauled it to the riverbank, where artisans carved the block into a winged bull. They dragged the finished statue on rollers to the palace, and raised it erect by "cables, ropes, rollers, and levers" as the king looked on. The procedure resembled in reverse the very method Layard had used—minus slaves and armed enforcers—to bring the bulls from the ruins to the river 2,500 years later.

Layard examined bas-reliefs discovered by Ross that depicted, in narrative style, a military campaign led by Sennacherib. In a chariot, surrounded by horsemen and foot soldiers, the monarch sets off from the plain to a mountainous, wooded country. Cavalry and infantry pursue their foes through valleys, streams, and vineyards. "The vanquished turn to ask for quarter; or, wounded, fall under the feet of advancing horses, raising their hands imploringly to ward off the . . . deathblow," Layard observed. Every chamber offered variations on Assyria's dominant theme: the subjugation by brute force of lesser, weaker nations, an empire-building method emulated by Assyria's successors, the Achaemenids. Outside the palace, Layard confronted ten colossal bulls and six giant human figures—only the lower parts preserved—standing guard along a 180-foot-long facade marking the grand entrance. "On the great bulls . . . was one continuous inscription, injured in parts, but still so far preserved as to be legible throughout," Layard recounted. This was the account of Sennacherib's Kingdom of Judea campaign that Rawlinson would decipher nearly two years later in the *Athenaeum*.

In another chamber of Sennacherib's palace he gazed at images that depicted the darkest side of Assyrian civilization. Two prisoners "were stretched naked at full length on the ground, and whilst their limbs were held apart by pegs and cords they were being flayed alive," he recorded. "Beneath them were other unfortunate victims undergoing abominable punishments." An executioner held one man fast by the beard while another beat out his brains with an iron mace; "a torturer was wrenching the tongue out of the mouth of a second wretch who had been pinioned to the ground." The blood-covered heads of the dead, he wrote, "were tied round the necks of the living, who seemed reserved for still more barbarous tortures." Aside from illuminating the depths of Sennacherib's cruelty, the bas-reliefs were valuable for another reason: they were a powerful aid in decipherment. Epigraphs above the images displayed the determinative T, followed by blank spaces that were apparently meant to record the names of the tortured and executed. Layard, who had been studying the Akkadian texts and making some progress in decipherment, could understand that the victims had been condemned for blasphemy against the supreme god Ashur, and read the "almost purely Hebrew" Akkadian words *Lishaneshnu eshlup*—"their tongues had been pulled out." "The inscription, therefore, corresponds with the sculpture beneath," he wrote. "It is by such confirmatory evidence that the accuracy of the translations of the cuneiform characters may be tested."

Moving through a long corridor in the palace that had been cleared out by his workmen, Layard climbed through a breach in a wall. He entered a narrow, descending passage that had remained unseen and intact for two and a half millennia. Cryptic bas-reliefs—a servant bearing a pineapple, another carrying "dried locusts on rods"—covered the walls. After running into several dead ends, he found his way into a "spacious apartment" with wall-to-wall friezes, and then walked through a wide doorway guarded by fragments of a fish-god bas-relief. Thousands of clay tablets covered with cuneiform lay strewn across the floor. "To the height of a foot or more from the floor they were entirely filled with them," Layard wrote. "Some entire, but the greater part broken into many fragments, probably [caused by] the falling in of the upper part of the building." He had, he soon realized, discovered Sennacherib's document depository.

The largest tablets were nine inches long by six inches wide; some were as tiny as stamps. The characters "were singularly sharp and well-defined, but so minute in some instances as to be almost illegible without a magnifying glass." Some tablets, bearing seals marked with the determinative for "king," might, Layard thought, be royal decrees. He recognized others as lists of gods, and a few possibly as calendars. Miraculously, the inferno that had destroyed the palace in 612 BCE had baked the clay tablets to the consistency of stone, ensuring that they would survive. "The characters appear to have been formed by a very delicate instrument before the clay was hardened by fire," Layard observed, "and the process of accurately making letters so minute and complicated must have required considerable ingenuity and experience." Like Layard's own saga of survival and endurance in the Middle East, the Assyrian inscriptions had been subjected to extreme conditions and had emerged bruised but largely intact.

◄─────────►

Layard sensed that his time in Mesopotamia was ending. After his discoveries in Kuyunjik at Nineveh, he embarked in October 1850, one year after his brief meeting with Rawlinson, on a valedictory journey south to the mounds of Babylon. They had exerted a powerful hold on him when he first visited them with Mitford ten years before. On that trip he had merely observed the landscape and refrained from any excavating; he had been impatient to explore the Zagros Mountains. "The desolation, the solitude, those shapeless heaps . . . are well calculated to impress and excite the imagination," he had written then. Near the purported site of the Tower of Babel, he and Mitford had encountered Arabs who were digging up small cylinders "covered with mystic figures and with arrow-headed inscriptions." Layard had vowed that one day he would return and "clear up the mystery."

There had been a handful of attempts to excavate the ruins over the last four decades: In 1811 Claudius James Rich dug up bricks inscribed in cuneiform as well as the so-called Stela of Nabonidus, a frieze depicting the last king of Babylon carrying a staff, wearing a conical headdress, and worshiping the moon. Robert Mignan, a captain in the East India Company, conducted two digs in the late 1820s, uncovering a trove of relics, including an 8¾-inch-long inscribed cylinder "of the finest furnace-based clay" in a ruined palace called the Kasr. But the hostile terrain, the difficult climate, and the lack of monumental finds had discouraged further exploration. Archaeologists remained focused on Northern Mesopotamia.

This time Layard traveled with Rassam, an India-bound British adventurer named Romaine, and forty heavily armed Jebours for security. The banks of the Tigris were teeming with Bedouin guerrillas, who had stopped almost all traffic on the river and the roads between Mosul and Baghdad. To shield the party from the burning sun during the day and shelter them at night, the Jebours had rigged the rafts with "a wooden framework covered with thick felt," Layard noted. "The servants and cooking apparatus were on the large raft, and we all kept close company for . . . mutual protection."

They passed Tikrit, the birthplace of Saladin, the Kurdish conqueror and foe of Richard the Lionheart during the Third Crusade, and the ancient city of Samarra, famed for the ninth-century, golden-domed mosque that contains the shrine to the eleventh and twelfth Shia Imams. In Baghdad, they checked in at the British Residency, now being run in Rawlinson's absence by an East India Company diplomat transferred from Persia. At last, in December, after a lengthy stopover due to a renewed Bedouin revolt in central Mesopotamia, they pushed on toward Babylon. From the raft on the Euphrates they observed undulating heaps of earth, sand-choked ancient canals, parched thickets, and prowling jackals. "On all sides, fragments of glass, marble, pottery, and inscribed brick are mingled with . . . nitrous and blanched soil, which . . . renders the site of Babylon a naked and hideous waste." Layard searched for traces of the great wall of earth described by Herodotus, and other remnants of ancient glories. But laid low by malaria attacks, he accomplished little.

The return journey, by land, was the last straw. Menaced by Bedouins, soaked from constant rains, and so weak and sick that he had to be carried through the desert, Layard arrived back in Mosul in early 1851. He despaired of accomplishing much more in the increasingly chaotic atmosphere. "I do not see the slightest chance of my being able to explore the country properly before the Turks have fitted out a suitable expedition against the Arabs and reduced them to subjection," he wrote to Ross, assuming quite a militaristic tone. "The first thing necessary is an adequate supply of troops and of troops of the right kind. I do not see much chance of the Porte being able to afford this." This province, he declared, "is utterly ruined." News that the British Museum trustees had approved only another "miserable grant" finally drove him to declare an end to his archaeological career. After packing a last raft full of antiquities bound for Basra, he departed Mosul for the final time on April 28, 1851. He was thirty-four years old.

But his passion for solving the mysteries of Assyria, even from afar, remained undiminished. He arrived back in London to find Hincks and Rawlinson embroiled in the disagreement about the siege of Lachish. After studying the matter, he threw his backing—perhaps to the surprise of his old friend—behind the parson. In a letter to colleagues he called Rawlinson's theory unsupportable. The frieze, he agreed, "was the actual picture of the taking of Lachish, the city as we know from the Bible." He praised Hincks's "profound learning and singular sagacity."

Hincks impressed Layard further with a significant discovery on the Black Obelisk, the intricately carved limestone column covered with scenes of vassals presenting tributes to the Assyrian king, which Layard had discovered at Nimrud in 1846. When Rawlinson had studied this carving two years earlier, he had described one prostrate vassal as "Yahua, son of Hubiri . . . a prince of whom there is no mention in the annals and of whose native country I am therefore ignorant." But Hincks had a slightly different read on the phonetic signs that the vassal's name comprised, one that changed everything. The characters, Hincks declared, spelled *Ya-u-a* ⸰⸰⸰⸰, son of *Hu-um-ri* ⸰⸰⸰⸰, found in the Bible as "Jehu, son of Omri." The Second Book of Kings tells the story of Jehu, commander of chariots in the Kingdom of Israel, who murdered King Jehoram, ordered underlings to defenestrate the queen mother, Jezebel, and seized the throne in 841 BCE. He exterminated followers of Baal, a false idol that many Israelites worshiped, faced down a threat from King Hazael of Syria, and then confronted the Assyrians, who had marched west to the Levant, conquering Damascus and other Syrian cities. To avoid attack, Jehu presented to King Shalmaneser III—misidentified up to this point by Rawlinson as "Temen-bar" and by Hincks as "Divanubar"—silver, gold goblets, javelins, and other treasures. That was the scene depicted on the Black Obelisk, now recognized as the only portrait in ancient Middle Eastern art of an Israelite or Judean monarch.

It was a momentous find. Besides providing another correlation between Assyrian and "Sacred" history, the Jehu inscription marked, by far, the earliest mention ever of a figure from Scripture. The Hebrew king had ruled nearly 150 years before the epic Battle of Lachish. "[I] [t]hought of an identification of one of the obelisk captives with Jehu, king of Israel, and satisfying myself on the point wrote a letter to Athenaeum announcing it," Hincks wrote in his diary at Christmas. The *Athenaeum* published the letter on December 27, 1851. A few months later, from Baghdad, Rawlinson would announce that he, too, had recognized "Jehu son of Omri" on the Black Obelisk. But Hincks, once again, had gotten there first.

CHAPTER FIFTEEN

KILLYLEAGH

When Austen Layard left England for Ceylon in 1839 at the age of twenty-two, he was an outsider who had struggled to find a place in British society. Tormented by his schoolmates for being too French, looked down on by his wealthy uncle for his apparent lack of seriousness, he had traveled to Asia with the hope of finding an identity and a mission. Now, back home twelve years later, he must have felt a degree of satisfaction at showing up those who had once scorned him. He was one of the most famous men in England. Everywhere he went, he was feted as a national hero. At a ceremony in 1852 at London's Guildhall, a fifteenth-century Gothic complex that served as the city's administrative headquarters, the city council presented him with an exquisite silver-and-gold box engraved with miniature scenes from an Assyrian lion hunt; the mayor praised his "zealous exertions in the discovery of the long-lost remains of Eastern antiquity." The artist Henry Wyndham Phillips painted his portrait, which would hang in the National Gallery on Trafalgar Square. It depicts Layard in a dark Bakhtiari-style vest and white gown with flowing sleeves, a string of worry beads dangling from his right hand. With wavy black hair, a handlebar mustache, and sideburns, he looks like a princeling out of the *Arabian Nights*. In the background, peeking out from behind a pulled-back curtain, an artist's rendering of the conical ziggurat of Ashur looms over a desert landscape.

Layard was one of the most sought-after guests at the Highgate soirees of Angela Georgina Burdett-Coutts, a philanthropist described in London newspapers as "the richest heiress in England." Charles Dickens, William Wordsworth, the Duke of Wellington, Italian soprano Fanny Tacchinardi Persiani, and other luminaries from the arts, sciences, and politics mingled in the landscaped gardens, meadows, and Georgian-era mansion of her Holly Lodge Estate near Hampstead Heath. Dickens and Layard met for the first time at a Burdett-Coutts party and quickly established a friendship. "Can you, and will you, be in town on Wednesday, the last day of this present Old Year?" Dickens wrote to Layard from his Bloomsbury town house in December 1851. At thirty-nine, he was then at the height of his creative powers and fame, having published *David Copperfield* one year earlier. "If yes, will you dine with us at a quarter after six, and see the New Year in with such extemporaneous follies of an exploded sort (in genteel society) as may occur to us?" Dickens and the author Wilkie Collins took an excursion to Italy the next year. "At Naples I found Layard, the Nineveh traveller," he wrote, "who is a friend of mine and an admirable fellow; so we fraternised and went up Vesuvius together, and ate . . . macaroni and drank . . . wine."

Politically Layard was on the rise as well. The Liberal government named Layard in early 1852 to a diplomatic post in Paris. After a government shakeup forced him out of the Foreign Service, he ran for Parliament in Aylesbury in central England. "My election is almost a certainty, and I come forward under very advantageous circumstances," he wrote to Henry Ross. "Once in the House I have a career open to me." Layard won the seat handily and on August 16 he delivered his maiden speech on the floor of the House of Commons, expressing indignation at the bellicosity of Tsar Nicholas I. The tsar was demanding the creation of a Russian protectorate over all eleven million Orthodox Christians in the Ottoman Empire, which the other European powers regarded as a pretext for pushing the Turks into a war they couldn't win. When Stratford Canning persuaded the Sublime Porte to reject Russia's demand, the tsar threatened to attack the Ottoman principalities of Moldavia and Wallachia—composing most of modern-day Romania. "We have on our hands a sick man—a very sick man; it will be, I tell you frankly, a great misfortune if one of these days he should slip away from us," the tsar, referring to the Ottoman Empire, menacingly told George Hamilton Seymour, the British ambassador to St. Petersburg. Russia seized the principalities in July 1853, almost a year after Layard's House of Commons speech, igniting the Crimean War. As allies of the Sublime Porte, British and French fleets would sail into the Black Sea and tens of thousands of troops would fight their way down the Crimean Peninsula to besiege the port of Sevastopol. The city would fall after nearly a year, in August 1855. Russia would sue for peace the following winter, ending one of the bloodiest conflicts up to that point in European history.

Layard seemed to anticipate the disaster that lay ahead if the tsar's aggression were to go unanswered. "As a speaker Mr. Layard is somewhat stiff, apt to hesitate, as if he had lost the thread of his discourse," *Reynolds's Weekly Newspaper* observed. Yet, "he has displayed a zeal, eloquence, and indignation which contrast most favourably with the apathy, subserviency, and indifference [of] his . . . colleagues." Layard quickly embraced his new role. "I found it, as you may suppose, somewhat different to the life I had been living in the East," he wrote to Ross, "but I soon fell into making speeches and talking politics with obstinate voters—and ended by turning out a far eno' hustings Orator." The *Lady's Newspaper & Pictorial Times* anointed him "among England's most promising statesmen."

⊷────────⊶

As Layard basked in his celebrity, Edward Hincks was following a more forlorn trajectory. Hincks turned sixty in 1852, and had grown more withdrawn and introspective in his Ulster backwater. The pastor "was something of a recluse," recalled Hariot Hamilton-Temple-Blackwood, a British socialite who married a peer, Lord Dufferin, at Killyleagh Castle in a ceremony presided over by Hincks. The parson absented himself from parties at the rectory that he ought to have been hosting, Hamilton-Temple-Blackwood noted, in which "tea cakes were provided for us and greatly appreciated." Hincks's wife was by this time an invalid, often confined to her room with an unspecified illness and, in the cruel observation

Portrait of Hincks in later years

of one member of the Hincks family, "no advantage at all . . . in society." Hamilton-Temple-Blackwood detected in Hincks a sense of dashed dreams and disappointment. It was only long after her wedding, she wrote, that she realized Hincks "was a celebrated man, and of course he should not have been confined to a little country parish." His proper place "should have been in the society of other learned men," and he should "have had complete leisure for his investigations, in the atmosphere of some great University."

Hincks did not seclude himself entirely from the wider world. In 1851, according to the pastor's diary, he visited "The Crystal Palace in Hyde Park" and, in Leicester Square, "Wyld's [Great] Globe and Panorama of Nineveh," a giant, hollow sphere representing Earth. Visitors climbed staircases and ramps to gaze at scale-model scenes of landscapes and man-made curiosities, including the Assyrian palaces. This amusement-park version of Nineveh was as close as Hincks would ever come to the palaces whose secrets he had devoted years to unraveling. On the visit to London to see the exhibitions, he was so preoccupied that thieves picked his pocket twice. "No doubt he was an easy victim," wrote his grandson E. F. Davidson, who described Hincks as the prototypical "absent-minded professor." It's unclear whether his distraction stemmed from his cuneiform studies, his money woes, or a combination of both, but it dominated people's impressions of him. Once, a coach in which Hincks was traveling to Belfast was involved in a collision, and several passengers riding outside were badly injured. When the door was opened, Davidson wrote, "Hincks was found sitting with his hands resting on his stick, quite unconscious of what had happened. He said only, 'I did not know that we had reached Belfast.'"

Hincks seemed to derive satisfaction from his duties as a parish priest: organizing a relief committee during the Great Famine, consoling those who had lost loved ones, delivering his sermons.

He enjoyed his morning constitutionals, a friend observed, when he would stroll the promenade that ran along the lake, or through the village square and the quiet streets of Killyleagh, greeting passersby. Still, parishioners picked up on his detachment. When two women from the church stopped by the rectory one day to seek advice about family problems, Hincks drifted off. He snapped to attention only to launch into a monologue about whether a large package of cuneiform squeezes from London could fit through his back door.

Then there was the time he appeared at his sermon wearing a red silk hood over his white sacramental gown. University graduates were permitted to wear these hoods during religious services as a symbol of their academic status. But the Irish and Anglican churches were being torn apart by a Catholicizing wing, led by Edward Bouverie Pusey, an Oxford University Hebrew professor who believed that the Church needed to include Latin liturgy in its Sunday services and elevate the importance of the Holy Eucharist. Pusey and his followers, known as the Puseyites, had adopted the red hood as a sign of their pro-Catholic sympathies. When Hincks appeared wearing the garment, in what he meant only as a nod to his Trinity College affiliation, some members of his congregation walked out in protest.

Later, a parishioner reported to a local paper, vandals broke into Hincks's vestry, "and left . . . the rector's hood a spectacle of shreds and patches." The *Belfast News Letter* was sympathetic to Hincks. "If it be true that the congregation of the Rector of Killyleagh . . . left the church for so silly a cause as this, we can only sincerely pity their blindness and want of Christian feeling," it opined. Hincks wrote to the *Downpatrick Recorder*, which had criticized his appearance in the hood, that it had never "occurred to me that the Protestant spirit of any of my parishioners could take alarm at . . . a mere badge of scholastic rank." He blamed "the Presbyterians of Killyleagh" for riling up his congregation, treating Church of Ireland "clergy, prayer-book [and] sacraments" with "ridicule and contempt," and mocking the hood as "a rag of popery." Hincks "could be naive and stubborn. He never thought people would make a big deal of this," says Cathcart. "He was flabbergasted, thinking 'this is what they do in England, what's the big deal?' And he put himself at the mercy of his enemies."

Rising hostility in the British Parliament toward the Irish clergy, and the threat of further slashing of their tithes, presented another source of anxiety for Hincks. "[M]y clerical income, which was above £800 a year when I began life, is now only £554 *net*; & in three years' time will be reduced to about £370," he complained to Layard, who had been distancing himself from Rawlinson and exchanging frequent correspondence with Hincks. The friendship was a regular source of consolation for the parson. "If I live three years more, I shall be one of the poorest men in the country," he lamented. Hincks had devoted his life to "the pursuit of knowledge, and [it] never brought me any pecuniary return." After twenty-five years in Killyleagh, Hincks had begun to think of leaving the town. In late 1851 he heard that the dean of nearby Armagh had died, opening a position that would give him authority over a dozen parishes and a higher salary, and "leave me enough to . . . spend some little time on books & traveling." Layard put in a good word, but Hincks was passed over for the job.

Hincks also began to cast his eye across the Irish Sea for employment, though he figured that his Irishness would work against him. Many Englishmen, Rawlinson included, looked down on the Irish as lazy, unintelligent, often physically unattractive, and prone to alcoholism and poverty. "The sole places that seemed to prosper amid the general blight . . . were the public-houses; and in them, the lowest orders of Irish were wrangling with might and main," wrote Dickens in *Oliver Twist* in 1838, describing the slums of Hockley-in-the-Hole, around central London's Clerkenwell Green. That prejudice often extended even to Protestants of English ancestry who lived in Ireland, such as Hincks, whose paternal grandparents had come from "the mainland" and whose mother had been born in England as well. A job in England would be best, he told Layard, "[B]ut, though of pure English descent, I have had the misfortune to be *born* in Ireland; and am consequently not to be provided for in England."

Hincks discussed with Layard the possibility of securing a professorship at Cambridge or King's College London, but that gained no traction. He had a more promising dialogue with Sir Henry Ellis, the principal librarian of the British Museum, about spending part of the year in London, deciphering Akkadian inscriptions. Though his responsibilities to his parishioners in Killyleagh would compel him to work remotely for parts of the stint, "I would place myself my whole time at the disposal of the Trustees," he assured Ellis. Layard wrote a letter of support to Ellis, praising Hincks's "extraordinary sagacity and learning." But for many months, Hincks heard nothing.

Despite their vastly different stations in life, Layard and Hincks had circled around each other since New Year's Day 1848, when Samuel Birch, the Egyptologist at the British Museum, dispatched to Layard several of Hincks's papers on cuneiform. Intrigued, Layard had shared with Hincks his discoveries in the Northwest Palace of Nimrud, including his observation that the name of "the earliest . . . of my Nimroud kings" could be written in at least two different ways, 𒁹 ⊢𒀖 𒌋 or 𒁹 ⊢𒈲 𒀖 𒌋. Neither man could read the whole name at that point. But Hincks recognized that the first inscription contained the logogram for *Ashur*, the supreme Assyrian god and the Assyrian nation, and the second showed the same name but written with two phonetic characters. (The king would turn out to be Ashurnasirpal II, the builder of the Northwest Palace at Nimrud, or *Ash-shur-nāṣir-apli*, "Ashur is guardian of the heir.") In a foreshadowing of the strife and accusations of betrayal to come, Rawlinson had reacted with alarm to the initial contact between his Mesopotamian partner and his principal rival. "All I beg of you is not to supply Dr. Hincks with materials before I can also have access to them, otherwise I fear he might give me the go-by," he wrote plaintively to Layard from Baghdad, worried about losing his privileged relationship with the archaeologist and, with it, his preeminence in the cuneiform competition.

Four years and a dozen letters later, Layard and Hincks began exchanging correspondence about arranging a face-to-face meeting. "I am anxious to know whether you are contemplating a journey to London," Layard wrote to Hincks in early 1852, making the first overture, "or, should you not, could I by any means spend a day or two in your neighborhood?" Layard had accumulated hundreds of inscriptions from his most recent excavations and was eager for the parson's help making sense of them. Hincks replied that he was "a prisoner" to his pastoral obligations but would welcome a visit from Layard. In July, Layard wrote another letter to Hincks, suggesting they spend some time together at the Dorsetshire estate of Lady Charlotte Guest. Layard had been encamped there during the summer, helping her install a chapel-like structure with stained glass windows to exhibit two winged, human-headed bulls that he had, with great logistical effort and string-pulling, procured for her at Kuyunjik—the only lamassus in private hands. Guest called the pavilion "the Nineveh Porch." Hincks again cited his obligations at church and politely declined. (Hincks lacked a reliable prelate to fill in for him when he was out of town, which left his movements particularly restricted. Even when a daughter got married in the south of England, he complained that he couldn't find a substitute and thus had been unable to attend the wedding.)

In September—after several false starts, including a planned visit to Killyleagh that Layard abruptly aborted because it conflicted with an invitation to a party in London—the Englishman finally cleared his schedule for a trip to see Hincks on his home ground. Carrying lithographs and papier-mâché squeezes, he caught a steamship from Liverpool across the Irish Sea to Dublin and boarded a locomotive north along the Irish coast. For some time now—possibly beginning with their meeting in Nimrud in October 1849—he had been pulling away from Rawlinson. Layard admired Rawlinson's energy and monomaniacal dedication to solving the Akkadian riddle, but he regarded Hincks as the diplomat's intellectual superior and a more reliable decipherer. Now Rawlinson was back in Baghdad doing double duty: representing the East India Company and serving as Layard's replacement as chief archaeologist for the British Museum, in charge of all excavations in Mesopotamia. Reports had been reaching Layard from his protégés that Rawlinson was treating them shabbily, even bullying them. By the time he set out for his meeting with Hincks, Layard seemed to have switched allegiances. "I have no doubt that we shall make some curious discoveries," he had written to Hincks before boarding the boat for Ireland. "Rawlinson has not the material and cannot forestall you."

A horse-drawn coach took him the last twelve miles from Comber through the verdant countryside to Hincks's rectory beside the old stone church in Killyleagh. "The small town stands on Lough Strangford, a very picturesque sheet of water in the midst of hills," Layard wrote to his uncle, Benjamin Austen. "The Doctor received me very hospitably and the neighbourhood has been gay with festivities in my honour." Word spread rapidly about Layard's visit, and female admirers competed for his attention. "The town swarms with young ladies, who at our dinners here have a proportion of three to one of the ruder sex," he wrote to his uncle, "speaking a rich brogue and having very free and . . . affectionate manners, which render their society peculiarly agreeable."

Day after day for two weeks, the thirty-five-year-old adventurer and the sixty-year-old churchman sat together in the rectory, united by their passion for decipherment and yearning to recover every detail of a lost civilization. They examined a copy of the Bellino Cylinder—the clay "barrel cylinder" discovered by Claudius Rich at Kuyunjik, which contained the record of the first two years of Sennacherib's reign. Hincks identified two clay fragments from the depository at Sennacherib's palace as a twelve-month, 360-day lunisolar calendar, which used mathematical calculations to set the beginning of each month by the appearance of the new moon crescent and added an extra month every three years to keep in line with the seasons. By the first millennium BCE, Babylonian calendars also included the solstices and eqinoxes, which were placed on the fifteenth day of the first, sixth, seventh, and tenth months of the year. Perhaps most significant, Hincks recognized a tablet, apparently created for aspiring Assyrian scribes, as a chart that showed the phonetic readings of some of the logograms. This was the first in a series of "lexical lists" or "syllabaries" that he hoped would make Akkadian largely comprehensible. At last, he could sound out the names of some Assyrian kings, cities, and territories, as well as common nouns written logographically. "The Doctor is an original and spends his whole time in his study," Layard wrote to Benjamin Austen. "He is wonderfully acute and logical and has already made greater progress than I anticipated." He praised Hincks's "ingenuity, acuteness, sagacity" and "singularly retentive memory, which peculiarly fitted him for a decipherer."

While Layard and Hincks worked their way through the inscriptions in Killyleagh, Rawlinson was brooding alone in the Residency in Baghdad. He had been embroiled in a dispute with Hincks that had gone on since late 1851 about another significant event in Assyrian-Jewish history: the conquest of the Kingdom of Israel and its capital, Samaria, and the dispersal of its ten tribes in 721 BCE. The Assyrian ruler Tiglath-Pileser III died in 727 BCE, and his son Shalmaneser V became king. Two years later, Tyre, Sidon, Akko, and Israel rose in revolt, stirred up by the promised support of some minor Nile Delta kings who had gained power as pharaonic Egypt fragmented in the ninth century. Then Hoshea, the king of Israel, had second thoughts, and came to the Assyrian camp at Tyre to make good on the tribute he had withheld. Shalmaneser V threw Hoshea in prison and laid siege to the Jewish kingdom for three years, finally destroying the resistance.

But in his inscriptions at the Khorsabad palace, Sargon II claimed credit for the conquest of the Kingdom of Israel, the deportation of 27,290 inhabitants, and the drafting of fifty prisoners into his chariot corps. The king then repopulated the territory with subjects from across his empire. "I again settled Samaria, more than [it had] previously been settled," he wrote. "I set my eunuch as governor upon them. I counted them among the people of the land of Assyria." A burning question had plagued the two decipherers: Which monarch was the real conqueror of the Jewish kingdom? In late 1851 Rawlinson had found an ingenious way of reconciling the stories: Sargon II, he argued, was simply an alternate name for Shalmaneser V.

Hincks disagreed. Based on references at Khorsabad, he believed that Sargon II was Shalmaneser V's brother. Sargon II had taken the throne by force and probably murdered his sibling. (Some

Assyriologists would later argue that Sargon had no connection to the dynastic line.) It was then, at the start of his reign, that he completed Shalmaneser V's half-finished conquest of Israel.

Rawlinson retorted that a figure with the distinctive name "Tartan" had been the Assyrian commander in the Samaria-Israel campaign and had turned up repeatedly in the annals of both Sargon II and Shalmaneser V, as well as in Isaiah 20:1. (Sargon II, according to the Old Testament verse, sent his general, Tartan, into battle against Ashdod rebels.) All this constituted evidence, Rawlinson argued, that the kings were one and the same person. If you'd had your brother murdered and usurped the throne, wouldn't you be suspicious of the military commanders who'd been loyal to him?

Hincks had an answer for that. "Tartan," he replied, was merely a generic term in Hebrew and Akkadian that meant "Field Marshall." Therefore the name proved nothing, and Rawlinson was mistaken. On this matter, too, Layard threw his backing behind Hincks. Rawlinson, he declared in a letter to the parson, "is wrong on many points." Layard also thrashed Rawlinson for the way he had gained access to the annals of Sennacherib, the translation of which had thrilled the public when it appeared in the *Athenaeum*. "Had not Col. Rawlinson *by an accident* obtained possession of my papers, he would not have been able to publish his last discovery," he told Hincks. The implication seemed to be that Rawlinson had obtained copies from the British Museum without first securing Layard's approval.

Rawlinson's physical ailments probably made the situation worse. Right after his return to Baghdad in October 1851, he suffered from a headache, abdominal pain, and constipation that he attributed to the abrupt change "to a sedentary existence after being on horseback for days on end." He was also contending with "a very rebellious liver . . . and a most detestable climate." It was getting harder to recover from these troubles, he admitted; "I have no longer the energy of youth." Still, determined to impress Layard, Rawlinson traveled north to do some first-hand research on the mound at Kuyunjik. "I shall soon have [the Akkadian] . . . at my fingers' ends as I once had the Persian," he vowed to Norris. In March 1852, he examined the annals of Sennacherib on the giant bulls in front of the palace, and "by dint of fingers as well as eyes, recovered, I believe, every word and almost every letter."

He claimed to be making progress. He recognized the cuneiform signs that spelled, in several ways, Esarhaddon, the king who had conquered Egypt and rebuilt Babylon after his father's destruction of the city. He declared that he had also worked out the name of the powerful eighth-century BCE king who had fathered Shalmaneser V and, possibly, Sargon II: Tiglath-Pileser III, 𒌫 𒉿 𒀲 𒀀 or *Tukulti-api l-Esharra*, meaning "my trust belongs to the son of Esharra." The discovery filled in another piece of the genealogical puzzle that Rawlinson had been working on for years. "We shall [soon] have a very fair idea of Assyrian history from about 950 BC to 600 BC," he wrote excitedly to Norris. Scholars would refer to that period as the Neo-Assyrian era, when the empire was at its height.

There were more discoveries to announce. Layard had arranged for the transport to England of some clay tablets that he had found in Sennacherib's palace. But thousands remained in situ, and Rawlinson, his energy restored, spent hours sifting through them. He found tablets for professional scribes that contained what he believed were the "names of countries, rivers, cities, mountains, weights and measures, divisions of time, points of the compass . . . stones, metals & trees." He examined "treatises on geology, metallurgy, and botany—also astronomical & astrological formulae . . . It gives us a most curious insight into the state of Assyrian science."

Rawlinson didn't go into specifics, and it's hard to know

whether he was far enough along to grasp the complicated texts. It would be some years before scholars would comprehend the mix of superstitions and scientific observation that marked the Assyrians' approach to the natural world. They prescribed both homeopathic therapies and magical incantations for ailments ranging from skin ulcers to infected eyes. "Dried figs and apricots" were recommended for a toothache, which the Assyrians, like the Egyptians, attributed to a "worm " that "dwells in the gums." For "scabies and itch" of the head, one tablet advised, "thou shalt bray"—grind into small pellets—"sulphur, mix it in cedar oil, and anoint him." (Sulfur springs and mines were plentiful along the Tigris near Nineveh.) Headache sufferers were advised to grind together "meerschaum, sulphur, kelp, and muza-stone," mix it with cedar oil, enclose it in "scarlet wool," and bind their temples. To "cure" prematurely gray hair, "a stork in the fire thou shalt boil, their dung thou shalt take, in oil thou shalt mix," and recite an ancient Sumerian charm. Another tablet offered a remedy for pinkeye: "Pure palm-fiber thou shalt chew, twist with thy hand, bind the man or maid on their temples," and recite another incantation: "The eye of the man is sick, the eye of the maid is sick, the eye of the man and the maid who shall heal? . . . The eye of the man or maid will recover."

Assyrians scrutinized stars and other celestial bodies, both to divine the future and understand natural phenomena. One tablet records the earliest description of a solar storm: a red cloud that covered the sky in 660 BCE. (Looking for corroboration, modern astronomers studied carbon-14 levels in tree rings. They revealed that solar energetic particles, or SEPs—visible in the night sky as a red aurora—did indeed hit Earth's atmosphere in unusually large numbers that year.) Babylonian astronomers used spherical geometry and arithmetical trigonometry to calculate the 23.5-degree tilt of Earth's axis away from the perpendicular plane of its orbit, which causes the length of daylight and the height of the sun at midday to vary throughout the year.

Assyrian prognosticators studied the liver of a sacrificial lamb, a practice known as extispicy. Usually in the presence of the king, the soothsayer would ask the gods a question—whispering it into the slaughtered animal's ear—then examine anomalies, discolorations, and protrusions on the organ to determine whether the answer was positive or negative. (All of this was explained in a text, "If the Liver is a Mirror of Heaven," which Ashurbanipal—not to be confused with Ashurnasirpal II, who had ruled Assyria two and a half centuries earlier—read avidly in his youth.)

Astrologers of the Neo-Assyrian court observed planetary and lunar phenomena almost daily and presented their interpretations to the king. An astrologer named Balasi gave Ashurbanipal a compendium of omens on March 15, 669 BCE: "If the moon is unexpectedly late and is not seen: there will be an uprising in a ruling city," he predicted. "If Mars keeps going around a planet, barley will become expensive . . . If the moon is seen on the sixteenth day: the king will be strong and have no equal . . . If the moon is surrounded by a halo and a planet stands in it: robbers will go on a rampage." Astrologers observed the relationships between the planets and fixed stars, identifying bad omens and looking for counterbalancing signs. A total lunar eclipse could signify a calamity for the king, who was advised to stay indoors while it was unfolding, but its negative effects could be canceled if Jupiter appeared at the same time. Court exorcists performed elaborate rituals to reduce the dangers—installing, for instance, a substitute king and queen who "ruled" during the eclipse while the real king tilled crops in the fields. When the phenomenon was over, the substitutes were put to death.

◄―――――――►

None of Rawlinson's discoveries in the library, however, seemed to loosen the bond between Layard and Hincks, or to ease Rawlinson's hurt over his fallout with his onetime friend. And Rawlinson reacted in a way that would become customary for him. The archaeologist belonged to a tribe of "riflers," Rawlinson wrote to Norris from Baghdad, indiscriminately carrying treasures out of Assyria's palaces. (Norris, a man of seemingly infinite patience, kept a diplomatic silence about the growing rift between two men he admired.) He had developed "a very mean opinion of [Layard's] learning and a still meaner opinion of his fair dealing." He brooded jealously over the news that "Layard has been fraternizing with Hincks at Killyleagh." The Irishman, he wrote, was "an unscrupulous and really shrewd antagonist." He feared that academics would now embrace Hincks and dismiss him, Rawlinson, as a "pirate, having never yet made a discovery or broached an original idea." When a second volume of Layard's memoirs, *Discoveries in the Ruins of Assyria and Babylon*, appeared in Great Britain in 1853, filled with praise for Hincks and ignoring Rawlinson almost completely, Rawlinson exploded. "It is written in a tone of systematic disparagement of my labors and exaggerated laudation of Hincks," he declared. "It is unfair from beginning to end and I . . . will carry the war straight into the enemy's camp." Layard and Rawlinson's mutual acquaintance, the prominent architect James Fergusson, who had codesigned, with Layard, the "Nineveh Court" at the Crystal Palace, chimed in with effusive praise for Layard's book, which enraged Rawlinson further. "If Fergusson calls all this 'fair and impartial,' " he wrote, "all I can say is God deliver me from my friends."

◂——————▸

In April 1853, after months of back-and-forth discussions and Layard's prodding, more news came that was bound to disturb Rawlinson: Henry Ellis and the trustees of the British Museum offered Hincks a one-year contract translating the museum's trove of Assyrian inscriptions. Hincks was to start with the Black Obelisk and then move to the annals of Sennacherib, providing transliterations and English translations. The salary was a mere £120, the equivalent of about $15,000 in 2024, but it barely mattered. Hincks had the imprimatur of Great Britain's most illustrious cultural institution, and the opportunity to inspect hundreds of relics.

After two short trips to London to introduce himself to the staff and familiarize himself with the materials, the parson in June began the job he had been dreaming of for years. In a workroom in the museum, with a magnifying glass and spiral notebooks on his desk, Hincks spent his days trying to unravel the 2,500-year-old secrets of the Neo-Assyrian Empire. "Up at 6, working at my inscriptions," he wrote in his diary on June 13, in his modest lodgings on Great Russell Street in Bloomsbury, a short walk from the museum. "At Museum from 10 to 4. In the evening at inscriptions till bed at 9¾." Days later, his recognition of an Assyrian calendar stimulated him so much that he could barely sleep. "Awake several hours in the night," he wrote. "Thought over a paper on the Assyrian month, which was lunar."

Hincks gazed with admiration on the black-limestone obelisk. After its fraught journey from the palace of Nimrud to London, he now had the pillar to himself. With the help of the lexical lists for Assyrian scribes, Hincks had progressed far enough to make sense of much of what he was seeing, though he still mistakenly read the name of the king as "Divanubar," instead of "Shalmaneser III." He inspected a stone slab from the Northwest Palace of Nimrud, excavated by Layard in 1845–46. It was, as Hincks read it, an account of Ashurnasirpal II's conquests of the Aramaeans and Neo-Hittites in what is now Syria in 880 BCE. The inscription described the king crushing a rebellion in a city called Tela after a two-day battle. Hincks wrote to Layard that he had never encountered a more lurid account of an Assyrian monarch's cruelty:

> I built a pillar over against the city gate and I flayed all the chiefs who had revolted, and I covered the pillar with their skins. . . . I cut the limbs off the officers who had rebelled. Many captives I burned with fire and many I took as living captives. From some I cut off their noses, their ears, and their fingers, of many I put out their eyes. I made one pillar of the living and another of heads and I bound their heads to tree trunks round about the city. Their young men and maidens I consumed with fire. The rest of their warriors I consumed with thirst in the desert of the Euphrates.

He scrutinized three cylinders of the son of Esarhaddon, now known to be Ashurbanipal, the most learned and perhaps most homicidal ruler of the Neo-Assyrian Empire ➤⟊⟊⊿ ⇌ ⟊. Ashurbanipal had led a life of drama and violence from the day, in 669 BCE, that he ascended the throne as his father's chosen successor— instead of his less able older brother, Shamash-shum-ukin. One cylinder recounted Ashurbanipal's attack on the Persian kingdom of Elam in 653 BCE following provocations and a lunar eclipse that foretold the downfall of its king, Teumman. Ashurbanipal's soldiers captured and beheaded Teumman and his son Tammaritu at the Battle of Til-Tuba. Ashurbanipal had the Elamite king's head preserved and hung it as a trophy from a tree in his secluded garden. In his inscriptions, the king presented himself as an intellectual and an athlete as well as a slaughterer. "I cantered on thoroughbreds . . . I made arrows fly as befits a warrior . . . I took the reins of a chariot like a charioteer and made the rims of its wheels spin," the king declared. "I learned the . . . secret lore of all of the scribal arts . . . I can resolve complicated divisions and multiplications that do not have an easy solution. I have read . . . texts in obscure Sumerian and Akkadian that are difficult to interpret." (Assyrian kings often left it to their palace scribes to come up with the language for these boasts.)

Hincks worked his way through the tiny characters on the Bellino Cylinder, chronicling the first two years of Sennacherib's reign, and prisms from the era of Nebuchadnezzar II. He examined terra-cotta tablets inscribed with prayers, astrological commentary, and maps of the heavens filled with the logogram for "star." A typical prayer from Ashurbanipal to Marduk, the supreme god of Babylon, asked him to "guide [me] on the right path," make "the house which I have built stand forever," and grant the monarch "old age . . . numerous offspring [and] the heavy tribute of the kings of the world and mankind." Inspecting Taylor's Cylinder, a nine-inch-tall prism inscribed with more annals from Sennacherib's siege of Jerusalem, he found the king had tried to put a positive spin on the abruptly curtailed attack. Hezekiah "had not been obedient to my yoke," the ruler declared. "Himself I confined within Jerusalem, his royal city . . . And I made his territory small." To Hincks, it appeared likely that the king, unable to penetrate the city's walls, had been forced to abandon his campaign.

After the museum staff turned over the annals of Sennacherib and Ashurbanipal, something odd happened: they rebuffed Hincks's requests to examine other cylinders and tablets, insisting that the materials could not be found. Hincks suspected there was more to it than that. Beneath the cordiality, the curators seemed suddenly to be following a hidden agenda. Why wouldn't a place of learning want this millennia-old knowledge brought into the modern world?

One possible clue to what was going on lay with Rawlinson, who made no secret of his displeasure over Hincks's appointment.

Since most of the relics that Hincks was deciphering had passed through the diplomat's hands as they made their way down the Tigris toward the Persian Gulf, Rawlinson had become fiercely proprietary about them. In his view, Hincks—who had barely left his Irish rectory while Rawlinson toiled for over a decade in the heat and squalor of Mesopotamia—hadn't earned the right to examine them. Layard tried to soothe his old friend's injured feelings. Rawlinson still had access to inscriptions in situ at Nimrud and Nineveh, he said, and Hincks desperately needed to supplement his income as a churchman. Rawlinson was unmoved. "You talk a great deal of Hincks's difficulties but is Baghdad 'a bed of roses'?" he replied. "My constitution is marred by this infernal climate and after 18 years laborious study on the Cuneiform inscriptions I should like to know what single reward or encouragement I have personally received from the British Govt." Later, looking back on his Baghdad exile, he would amplify this sentiment: "For twelve weary years—broken only by one brief visit to England—I resided in an exhausting climate, cut off from all society, sparingly supplied with the comforts of civilization, and in fact, doing penance in order to attain a great literary object." The material at the British Museum was Rawlinson's personal "game reserve," he claimed, and Hincks was an "unscrupulous poacher."

Rawlinson reminded the British Museum that he had been traveling between Baghdad and Northern Mesopotamia, supervising fieldwork, and laboring on decipherment. "I certainly thought that my recent exertions in the service of the Trustees had given me a special claim on their consideration," he wrote. Hincks's hiring "must give rise . . . to an impression that I have not been considered competent to undertake the task." Perhaps the way to convince the doubters, he was coming around to thinking, would be to have multiple independent translators compare notes. In a fair fight, he was certain to best the parson, once and for all.

CHAPTER SIXTEEN

◄◄─────────────────────────────►►

TALBOT

By the early 1850s William Henry Fox Talbot—the wealthy polymath who shared credit for the invention of photography and who would soon initiate the cuneiform contest—had become one of England's most celebrated men. Born in a Dorset manor house that belonged to the family of his mother, Lady Elisabeth Theresa Fox Strangways Talbot, in February 1800, Talbot had lost his father, a debt-ridden army officer named William Davenport Talbot, when he was five months old. Four years later his mother remarried a naval officer, Charles Fielding, and soon had two daughters with him. But she doted on her firstborn child, encouraging his love of languages, mathematics, and other intellectual pursuits.

William grew into a scientific prodigy "of a very superior capacity," his schoolmaster, the Reverend Thomas R. Hooker, remembered. He dabbled in experiments with volatile chemicals and, at twelve, nearly blew up his dormitory at his boarding school, Harrow, while trying to gild steel with a solution of gold diffused in nitric and hydrochloric acid. "It exploded with the noise of a pistol and attacked the olfactory nerves of the whole household," recalled one instructor. When Talbot announced his intention to study mathematics at

Cambridge, Lady Elisabeth, who warmly supported her son in all his endeavors, reacted with mock alarm. "You seem so mathematically inclined that I ought to send you to Oxford to counteract it," she wrote, "that you may not grow into a rhomboidal shape, walk elliptically, or go off on a tangent." At seventeen, Talbot enrolled in Trinity College at Cambridge, where he won a prestigious award for classical Greek and studied—and critiqued—Newton's system of infinitesimal calculus, a vital tool for the analysis of the laws of motion.

Soon he was spinning off in new directions. In the 1820s, he moved to the family estate, Lacock Abbey, a Gothic onetime ruin that his mother had devoted much of her time and energy to restoring. There Talbot conducted experiments using a camera obscura, Latin for "dark chamber," a room with a small hole in a wall through which the light that passes projects an inverted image—"fairy pictures, creations of the moment," he wrote—onto the opposite wall. During his 1833 honeymoon in Italy, Talbot thought back to those ephemeral images while attempting to sketch Lake Como with the aid of a camera lucida, a four-sided prism held over a drawing surface. The device presented a reflected view of a scene, so that the artist could simply trace it onto his sketchpad without looking up. Talbot realized, he wrote in his memoir, *The Pencil of Nature*, "how charming it would be if it were possible to cause these natural images to imprint themselves durably and remain fixed upon the paper."

At Lacock Abbey in 1834, Talbot discovered that fine writing paper treated with a precise mixture of salt, silver chloride, mercury, and potassium iodide and then covered by a glass plate turned dark when left in sunlight—and stayed dark after being sprinkled with a second layer of a salt compound. When he covered the paper with a leaf or a plant, and exposed it to the sun for ten minutes or longer, the uncovered areas darkened, while the part hidden beneath the flora remained white—producing a perfect "negative" image of the object. He called these productions "sciagraphs," or drawings of shadows, and referred to the new craft as "the art of photogenic drawing." Five years passed in which Talbot devoted himself to other intellectual pursuits. Then, in 1839, Louis-Jacques-Mandé Daguerre announced triumphantly that he had found a way to capture images from a camera obscura onto a metal plate—shocking Talbot back into focus. He began experimenting with miniature box cameras scattered around the Lacock Abbey grounds and produced, he wrote, "very perfect but extremely small pictures such as might be supposed to be the work of some Lilliputian artist."

Talbot tried different chemical mixtures and shortened exposure times. In 1840, one year after the appearance of the first daguerrotypes, he presented his own breakthrough: a $2\frac{7}{16}$-inch-by-$1\frac{3}{4}$-inch portrait in profile of his bonnet-wearing wife, produced after an exposure of around one minute. Then he captured a series of pictures in and around the Gothic halls of Lacock Abbey, which became perhaps the most photographed building of the early 1840s. He called the images calotypes, from the Greek *kalos*, meaning "beautiful," or talbotypes. (Talbot quickly grew bored shooting the same scenes over and over. "I must now really transport my apparatus to some locality where picturesque objects are to be met with," he wrote to his friend the mathematician John Herschel, "such as a cathedral or a seaport town.")

Talbot and a Dutch assistant, Nicolaas Henneman, opened a photography studio on London's Regent Street, received a commission to photograph the Great Exhibition in the Crystal Palace at Hyde Park in 1851 (the original fair that preceded the exhibit featuring the "Nineveh Court" by three years), and equipped photographers with cameras on French expeditions to Mesopotamia in the early 1850s. By then, Talbot's restless mind had gravitated to other enthusiasms: the observation of comet tails, aurorae, and solar eclipses;

the development of industrial coating, an electrolytic engine, a solar microscope, and long-lasting batteries (a medium named Joseph Jennings used one in the 1850s in an unsuccessful attempt to resuscitate a corpse); and the study of Latin, Greek, Icelandic, Hindustani, Breton, and Celtic. He had a longtime interest in horticulture, meticulously recording events in his garden and conservatory: "Two large Box trees planted at the angles of the terrace," he wrote in a notebook in 1829. "*Orobus vernus* in flower. A *ranunculus* in the shrubbery now in bud . . . Wild violets blue & white have been in flower some time." And he was increasingly consumed by his most difficult project: the decipherment of Akkadian cuneiform.

Talbot's interest in Middle Eastern studies had begun in the 1830s, at a time when Rawlinson, Hincks, and Layard were all being

Portrait of William Henry Fox Talbot taken in 1864

drawn into the same discipline. Fascination with "the Orient"—a broad-brush term that referred to the Ottoman Empire, the Levant, Persia, India, Japan, and China—was sweeping Europe, though it was an ambivalent obsession. Ancient Greek and Roman portrayals of Persia as an autocratic and decadent civilization, a land of tyrannical kings and castrated courtiers, had been passed down to the modern age. Edward Gibbon's *The History of the Decline and Fall of the Roman Empire* attributed the downfall of Rome in part to its "infection" by vices of the East: "The simplicity of Roman manners was insensibly corrupted by the stately affectation of the courts of Asia," he wrote. John Stuart Mill regarded the Battle of Marathon, in which a Greek army defeated the forces of Darius the Great, as a watershed cultural moment, a victory of the forces of democracy and reason over the barbarous Asians. And the French man of letters Charles-Louis de Secondat (Baron de Montesquieu) in 1721 wrote that "Liberty was intended for the genius of European races, and slavery for that of the Asiatics."

But scholars also began to talk about "the Oriental Renaissance." Historians at the university in Göttingen were entranced by Niebuhr's accounts of Persia and engaged in vigorous debates over whether King Jamshid or Darius the Great had built Persepolis. (During a stroll through the medieval town of Göttingen in July 1802, Georg Grotefend bet a colleague that Persepolis's builder was Darius; the wager led him to try to decipher the Old Persian inscriptions to ascertain the truth.) The French Orientalist Antoine Isaac Silvestre de Sacy translated Arabic, Persian, and Turkish, trained a generation of students in Eastern languages, and served as the first president of the Société Asiatique, founded in 1821. The Orient, one French writer put it in 1841, bears "an antiquity more profound, more philosophical, and more poetical than that of Greece and Rome."

Talbot's initial inquiries focused on connections among ancient languages and the shared mythology of Near Eastern civilizations. In *The Antiquity of the Book of Genesis*, written in 1839, he posited that the "sacred narrations" from the Old Testament "had spread abroad far beyond the narrow limits of Judea." Because the people of neighboring nations probably spoke Aramaic and other Semitic tongues, he wrote, "Jewish records were written in an idiom that could have cost the wise men of Chaldea but little difficulty" in understanding. Recent archaeological finds in Phrygia, a kingdom in western Anatolia that had lasted from around 1200 to 700 BCE, appeared, he noted, to depict scenes from Genesis. "The coins of the city exhibit an ark on the waters," he wrote, "a raven . . . a dove . . . an olive-branch . . . a woman in the ark . . . [and] another man and woman on the shore, with uplifted hands, as if returning thanks."

Talbot's work on the Phrygians kindled his curiosity about the language and writing of another "idolatrous" nation contemporaneous with the Hebrews: Assyria. Enthralled by Layard's finds at Nineveh and Nimrud, he procured in 1853 a copy of the archaeologist's *Inscriptions in the Cuneiform Character from Assyrian Monuments*. Relying in part on the spadework of Hincks and Rawlinson, Talbot mastered the phonetic values of hundreds of characters, identified logograms and determinatives, and used his familiarity with Hebrew to expand his Akkadian vocabulary. Talbot expected to be embraced by the philological community, but Assyriologists and other academics were less than welcoming to a novice who had come late to decipherment. The British Association for the Advancement of Science, the organization that Hincks and Rawlinson had addressed in Edinburgh in 1850, turned down Talbot's offer to talk to them about his progress. In May 1854, he wrote to Edward Hawkins at the British Museum requesting talbotypes of the newly arrived Kuyunjik tablets. "As I take great interest in the

Assyrian inscriptions, and have made considerable progress in the study . . . and as the Museum is now photographing a series of clay tablets . . . for distribution," he wrote, "I should be much gratified if you would give me a copy of the work at the time of its completion." Talbot sent ten letters to Hawkins and other curators over several months, but all went unanswered. Ironically, the "father of photography" couldn't get his hands on the fruits of the technology he had co-invented.

Talbot kept plugging away, relying on material that he found in bookstores and libraries. Sitting in his Lacock Abbey study at a desk crafted for King George IV and gifted to him by his friend Queen Victoria, surrounded by a telescope, a box camera, and a spherical astrolabe designating the annual path of the sun, Talbot worked through long and complex passages inscribed on the Bellino Cylinder and the Cylinder of Esarhaddon. He left some parts of his translations blank and italicized sections he wasn't sure about, a mark of how much doubt still surrounded the Akkadian writing system. "In that battle, of all his army," one section of his translation of the Bellino Cylinder began, "he alone . . . fled to the city of Gurumann, and *from thence he escaped to the islands at the mouth of the river Euphrates?*" He struggled as well with a description of the Assyrian conquest of Sidon that he found on the Cylinder of Esarhaddon: "From that island I *drove* (?) him, and I destroyed his . . . His *coined money* (?), His goods, gold, silver carbuncle stones that were . . . And *beautiful* (?); precious woods of two kinds, precious vestments *belonging to his queen* (?), and the treasures of his palace, to a vast amount I carried away." The multiplicity of character values and the unfamiliar vocabulary opened "the door to all manner of uncertainty," he admitted.

Much of the academic community shared Talbot's concerns. English literary magazines, the British Association for the Advancement of Science, and many European scholars had applauded Hincks's and Rawlinson's apparent advances in the field, but officers of the Royal Asiatic Society, Rawlinson's patron, and many others remained skeptical about their methodology. It didn't help that Hincks and Rawlinson continued to quarrel about the names of Assyrian kings, having come up with a variety of readings, for instance, for the builder of Nimrud, Ashurnasirpal II—including Ashurakhbal, Asshur-idanni-pal, Asshur-izzirpal, and Asshur-yuzhur-bal. For his part, the German-French scholar Jules Oppert had weighed in with another variation: Assur-iddannapalla.

In 1856, Talbot began looking for a way to demonstrate the soundness of the system. Polyphony was a stumbling block to decipherment, he acknowledged in letters to colleagues, but phonetic values and meanings could often be gleaned by examining surrounding characters and words, and some signs had only one or two values. "The object at present," he wrote to Edward Hincks, with whom he'd begun a regular correspondence, "is to carry a conviction of the truth of these discoveries to the minds of scholars . . . who are hesitating whether to admit them or not." Nothing, he wrote to Hincks, would be as persuasive as "the agreement between two independent translators."

That September, Talbot sent his famous letter to Norris of the Royal Asiatic Society, asking for membership to boost his credentials as an Assyriologist ("You cannot do us a greater honor," Norris replied) and proposing that the society sponsor a public comparison of the results of a pair of decipherers. As far as Talbot was concerned, however, Hincks would not be one of them. Talbot imagined that a face-off between Rawlinson and himself—back from Baghdad and ensconced in a private workroom at the museum—would change the minds of skeptics. Norris replied enthusiastically. The only question was whether Rawlinson would play along.

It didn't look promising at first. Rawlinson had been eyeing Talbot suspiciously since his return from Mesopotamia in late 1855. He regarded the polymath as another interloper intent on stealing his glory and denied him access to lithographs and talbotypes of newly arrived tablets from Kuyunjik. Still, Rawlinson understood the need to establish the decipherers' credibility. Grudgingly, he laid out the terms by which he'd be willing to grant Talbot's request: he would provide him with the museum's private materials, so long as Talbot promised not to publish his translations. Talbot refused and, after Norris conducted shuttle diplomacy between the men, Rawlinson dropped that demand. Talbot then proposed that the scholars work on translations of the annals of Sennacherib. Norris wrote back to Talbot that Rawlinson "thinks it would be a more satisfactory proof of the truth of decipherment, if you should take up something which is quite new." The obvious choice, both Talbot and Rawlinson agreed, was the three-thousand-year-old cylinder from the mound at Qal'at Sherqat forty miles south of Mosul. Now known as the Inscription of Tiglath-Pileser I, it had recently arrived in London from Mesopotamia.

Even then, obtaining a copy of the prism for Talbot wasn't easy. Bureaucratic protocols, poor communication and rivalries between museum departments, and an aversion to allowing an outsider, even one as accomplished as Talbot, access to proprietary material all slowed down the process. Norris prodded his contacts at the museum half a dozen times in late 1856 and early 1857 on Talbot's behalf, finally declaring in mid-January 1857 that "the red tape [metaphorical] is all unwound."

The inscription, at last, was ready.

CHAPTER SEVENTEEN

THE END OF AN ERA

On a humid spring morning in 1852, Hormuzd Rassam, the twenty-five-year-old protégé of Austen Layard, led a team of workers on foot through the bush toward the mound at Qal'at Sherqat, the site of the original Assyrian capital, Ashur, and of its most sacred temple. At that moment, another crew organized by Victor Place, Paul-Émile Botta's successor as the French consul in Mosul, approached the tell from a different direction. Gone were the days when Layard had the run of Mesopotamian territory, extracting Assyrian treasures and shipping them down the Tigris to Rawlinson without having to worry about competition. Place had already conducted extensive excavations at Khorsabad, and, besides Qal'at Sherqat, he had in his sights the northern half of the mound of Kuyunjik, where the British had been digging near-continuously for five years.

On this fateful morning, Rassam sent ahead several teams of Jebour workers to claim "certain good spots" on the mound, a one-hundred-foot-high "stupendous structure," wrote Rassam, that, viewed from the south, soared upward like an Egyptian pyramid. Rassam followed with backup support. But as Rassam and his men approached Qal'at Sherqat, "we heard the sound of the war-cry and a great hubbub coming from the mound, which convinced us that our men had come into collision with those of the French," Rassam remembered. "The Arabs who were with me at once took to their heels to help their comrades in the struggle." As men raced ahead to confront the interlopers, threading around trees and bushes, their "rapid march drove in utter confusion from their haunts the wild boars, hares, hyenas, jackals, foxes, and the other wild animals inhabiting that thicket," Rassam recalled, "and disturbed the roosting of the francolins, partridges, and quails; and if the statement of the Arabs who flew to the rescue is to be believed, they actually saw a lion turn tail as they rushed through the wood." Rassam arrived at the archaeological site to find the scene in chaos: the Bedouin guide of the French team was spread-eagle on the ground, with a man from Rassam's crew sitting on top of him, warning that he would kill him if he made a move. Another member of Rassam's team was keeping the French overseer at bay, preventing him from even reaching the mound. Only a last-minute agreement between the teams prevented the encounter from escalating into violence. "[I]t is a known fact that, whenever the British and French interests clash in foreign lands," Rassam observed, "there is sure to be jealousy and ill-feeling created."

◂────▸

After two years of adulation and comfort in England, Rawlinson, now forty-two, had returned to Baghdad, reluctantly, at the end of 1851. Driven by an ex-soldier's sense of duty and a feeling that much was left to be discovered in the mounds, he was supervising all British archaeological excavations in Mesopotamia, as well as running the Residency. But the burdens of the two jobs, the competition for antiquities, the rivalry with Hincks, the estrangement from Layard, concerns about his legacy, and worry about his physical safety weighed on him. Journeying down the Tigris from Qal'at Sherqat in 1852 on a covered raft that he had converted into a floating writer's studio, Rawlinson came under attack from brigands hiding on the riverbank. "I was quietly seated, pen in hand writing my papers, when I was aroused by a sharp short sound & found [my] inkstand shattered to bits under my nose, my face covered with ink," he recounted. The attackers shot dead his river guide and "[t]he firing did not cease till he . . . landed with a few men," George Rawlinson wrote, "while the assailants took to their heels, and no more was seen or heard of them." Soon after that, Rawlinson dispatched by Ottoman post a trove of his cuneiform notes and translations, bound for Constantinople and then London, to be read at the annual meeting of the Royal Asiatic Society. Attackers on the road to Mosul ambushed the convoy and made off with everything. "The whole of the foreign correspondence [was] distributed among these marauders," the society reported, "who are said to be now wearing the unknown Babylonian characters as amulets."

And the successes of the rival archaeological teams were putting pressure on Rawlinson to make some notable finds of his own. At Khorsabad—now known, thanks to Hincks's discovery of the king's name, as Dur-Sharrukin, the city of Sargon II—Place's team was coming up with discoveries that equaled those of the British at Kuyunjik, excavating seventy-eight rooms, 131 doorways, four large corridors, and eight inner courtyards, for a total of nine thousand square meters. Gabriel Tranchand, the French expedition's photographer, had captured with his talbotype camera work teams posed before giant bull guardians at the palace entrance, and dispatched them home to an enthralled French public.

A second French expedition led by Fulgence Fresnel—a diplomat, philologist, and knight of the Légion d'honneur—arrived in Mosul from Constantinople in the spring of 1852. The team had an even more ambitious agenda than Place, announcing plans to spend several years exploring both the northern mounds and the ruins of Babylonia. That put them on a collision course with Rawlinson, who was expanding his focus to Southern Mesopotamia, four to five hundred miles south of Mosul, in search of the birthplace of civilization. In 1849 he had dispatched a visiting British archaeologist named William Loftus to Warka, the contemporary name of Uruk, to excavate the mounds there. Loftus had sent back a clay cylinder bearing a cuneiform inscription that contained the name *Húr*. Rawlinson, exhilarated by the find, believed that Warka must be the biblical Ur, from which Abraham had set out for a territory called Canaan around 2100 BCE, following the command of God to found a new nation. (In fact, Uruk, older and larger than Ur, lies fifty-eight miles northwest of Abraham's supposed birthplace.)

When Rawlinson met the French team at the foot of the Kuyunjik mound in the winter of 1852, he was initially welcoming. Fresnel's deputy was Jules Oppert, the Hamburg-born scholar, adventurer, and man-about-town. In spite of his severe appearance—a colleague described the twenty-six-year-old as "a dark, short, thinnish gent—wears spectacles—steel—dressed in black"—Oppert had a bonhomie that would make him a favorite of everyone from the French royal family to scholars across Europe. Oppert had published in Germany a book about the Old Persian language and writing, *Das Lautsystem des Altpersischen*, in 1847, a few months after Rawlinson's magisterial translation of the inscriptions at Behistun appeared in print. The work, in which Oppert displayed a deep understanding of Avestan and Sanskrit, had caught Rawlinson's eye. "Oppert," he now wrote to Norris from Mosul, "is a young laborious German and will be a great Orientalist." They were, he avowed, "thick as thieves."

But Rawlinson's warmth faded. Weeks later, the diplomat read

an article that Oppert had written for the *Journal Asiatique* in Paris
that questioned the accuracy of some of Rawlinson's Behistun translations. And he turned on him with a vengeance. Oppert, Rawlinson
complained to Norris in London, had written a "flippant, offensive
[and] . . . untrue" paper and was "animated by anti-English feeling."
It was a charge for which Rawlinson provided no evidence, and it
conflicts with many descriptions of Oppert. "His kindly thought for
others, his exact and ready memory [and] his power of conversation in German . . . French and English render[ed] him a delightful
companion," wrote a correspondent in the *Hebrew Standard*. "His
worldliness remained one of his most engaging and surprising characteristics," agreed the *Times*. Rawlinson's portrait of Oppert as an
Anglophobe also doesn't jibe with Oppert's praise of "British hospitality toward strangers" in his lecture "On Babylon: And on the
Discovery of the Cuneiform Characters and the Mode of Interpreting Them," which he would deliver in London in March 1856. He
had come to know Britons well, he said, "during a long residence in
the East and afterwards at their domestic hearths." Oppert, who was
inclined to think the best of people, was taken aback by Rawlinson's
sudden animus. "He reproached me . . . to the point of going beyond
the measure worthy of such a scholar," he wrote to a colleague.

When the Fresnel-Oppert expedition turned its attention to Babylon in the summer of 1852, Rawlinson watched their movements
closely. As the team sat stranded in Baghdad because of a flare-up
of Arab unrest in the central hinterlands, Rawlinson could barely
restrain his glee. "He and Fresnel are vegetating here in inglorious
idleness," Rawlinson wrote to Norris. The Frenchman deserved, he
wrote, "a slap . . . as he is insufferably vain and anti-English." The
French team finally left Baghdad for Hillah, a sultry town of domed
white mosques and palm groves on the Euphrates River near Babylon. Rawlinson received reports of their progress while encamped

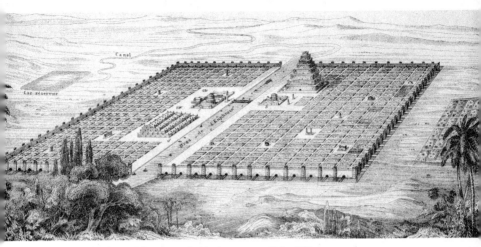

Plan of the city of Babylon around the fifth century
BCE according to Herodotus's description

at Ctesiphon, where he had retreated for the second time to recover
from his "inveterate enemy dyspepsia."

Soon he gloated that "[t]he French have found nothing at Babylon . . . Fresnel and Oppert are fighting like cat & dog and the excavations make little progress in consequence." In fact, the mission
would ultimately be considered a success: Oppert measured remnants of the ancient city walls, discovered a stone colossus that he
called the "Lion of Babylon," and identified the mud-brick ruins of
one of Nebuchadnezzar II's palaces. In October 1853, having finished their excavations in Babylon the French team headed back
north, and Oppert wrote a letter of gratitude to Rawlinson, thank-
ing him for treating him with kindness and for sharing information
during a stopover in Baghdad. It leaves one to wonder whether the
British diplomat had saved his ill feelings for his private correspondence, while maintaining a facade of friendship.

◄◄─────────►►

It wasn't only the French rivalry that rattled Rawlinson. Thanks to Layard, the white British males who once dominated archaeology no longer had exclusive rights to the domain. One symbol of the more equitable era was Matilda Badger Rassam, the sister of an English missionary and the wife of the British vice-consul in Mosul, Christian Rassam. Recruited by Layard to help organize shipments to Baghdad and supervise digs in his absence, Rassam, apparently the only woman with a hands-on role in the excavations, had proved herself as intrepid as Rawlinson had been in his prime. In April 1850, while attempting to transport two giant half-human, half-lion colossi to the Tigris, she'd nearly been swept away following days of heavy rain. Huge volumes of water spilled over the Tigris banks and inundated the village of Nimrud, drowning inhabitants, submerging the lamassus, and forcing her to take refuge on the mound. "The rain began to fall in torrents, and there were we, servants, workmen etc. huddled together in a miserable black tent which admitted a greater part of the rain," she wrote to Layard. At daybreak, "we went to the edge of the Tel to take a view of the village, but there was little or nothing of it to be seen, the whole plain had the appearance of a rolling sea dashing itself against the foot of the mound." She later spotted villagers' decomposing bodies floating in the river. But "the morrow was worse than the preceding day," she wrote. "During that night we were literally swimming & the servants were engaged bailing the water out of the tent."

Rassam and Rawlinson didn't get along. "I am rather astonished that Col. Rawlinson does not write to you occasionally about the excavations, knowing that you must take great interest in everything connected with the mound," she wrote to Layard, then in London, in July 1852. "You were the means of bringing to light so many things which otherwise might have lain buried in the bowels of the earth for 3 or 4000 years longer." She also didn't like Rawlinson's aloofness and his air of superiority, the result, she believed, of spending most of his lifetime surrounded by subordinates. "I will tell you, confidentially, that whatever we do, and however much interest we may take in the excavations, it does not seem to please him," she wrote. "When he passed through Moossul [*sic*] on his return from England, he saw me pushing 3 large cases of Tablets with my own hands . . . he never said, 'thank you.'" Since Rawlinson's return, she went on, "I usually send him from one or two cases of Tablets & other small objects every month, but they are received with such bad grace . . . that I feel determined not to take any more interest in the excavations if I can help it."

Matilda's brother-in-law, Hormuzd Rassam, was another newcomer changing the look of Mesopotamian archaeology. In 1853, under Rawlinson's direction, Rassam uncovered the find that would reshape understanding of the ancient world: a fired-clay cylinder containing the annals of an Assyrian king whom Rawlinson could now identify as Tiglath-Pileser I 𒀭 𒀭 𒀭 𒀭 𒀭, the contemporary of the Trojan and Greek warriors and the prophet Samuel. The discovery took place in a temple at Qal'at Sherqat, where Layard had dug up an identical prism during his last months in the country. Rassam's relic was badly shattered, but Rawlinson "succeeded in uniting the fragments with a composition of gum-water and powdered chalk and obtained a copy of the entire inscription . . . [a]bout 800 lines in length," his brother recounted. The minuscule text, which Rawlinson began to translate during his downtime, offered a window into Assyria's early years as an aggressor nation in the twelfth century BCE. Oppert, Talbot, Rawlinson, and Hincks would attempt to decipher its eight hundred lines in the Royal Asiatic Society challenge.

A few months after that collaboration, though, the two men found themselves at odds. Rassam was unhappy about a deal that

Rawlinson had struck with Victor Place that ceded the French access to the northern half of Kuyunjik. The arrangement was, Rassam thought, outside the bounds of archaeological etiquette. "It was understood . . . that no agent of any museum was to intrude in the sites chosen by the other," he would write in his memoir. But Place was still focused on Khorsabad, thirteen miles away, and, on the evening of December 20, 1853, Rassam gathered a team and invaded Kuyunjik. Moving stealthily, in case any French excavators were on-site, Rassam found nothing then or on the next two nights. Then, on the fourth evening, his persistence produced a remarkable discovery. At the top of a ramp-like subterranean hallway stood "a beautiful bas relief in a perfect state of preservation." The sculpture was a depiction of Ashurbanipal—the last great king of the Neo-Assyrian Empire—and marked the entrance to the king's North Palace, paneled with fine bas-reliefs. Rassam gazed at rooms covered with alabaster carvings of "men leading dogs for the hunt; dead lions; others in the agony of dying, of which several are shown bristling with arrows and vomiting blood," he wrote. "The suffering of one lioness . . . is beautifully portrayed; resting on her forepaws, with outstretched head, she vainly endeavours to gather together her wounded limbs." It all would have been claimed by the French had not Rassam made his preemptive strike.

Near the lion hunt tableaus, Rassam made an even more momentous find: piles of "inscribed terra-cotta tablets of all shapes and sizes," he wrote, that Ashurbanipal had apparently collected from across his vassal states and kingdoms. "The largest of these . . . were stamped with seals, and some inscribed with hieroglyphic and Phoenician characters." Rassam had found what would become known as the Library of Ashurbanipal, a trove that exceeded what Layard had come across in a damaged chamber at Sennacherib's nearby palace in 1849. The thirty thousand tablets in Ashurbanipal's archive included bureaucratic records; texts on magic and veterinary medicine; works of poetry and fiction; and more. The tablets would provide a picture of life in the royal court of Nineveh, the construction of its temples, and the superstitions and brutality of its rulers, as well as the belief systems, customs, and art of Assyrian vassals from Babylon to the south to Urartu in the north. They included seventy works on astrology and one hundred that dealt with extispicy, incantations to ward off ghosts, and a compendium of anti-witchcraft rituals that provided instructions for exfoliation to cleanse the body of a hex or of moral failings. Medical texts detailed treatment for kidney diseases and psychological illnesses. Not all the texts were literary or therapeutic: other tablets documented in chilling detail Ashurbanipal's pleasure in bringing suffering on his enemies. "I placed him in a neck stock, bound him up with a bear and a dog, and made him guard the Citadel Gate of Nineveh," he wrote of one disobedient vassal. The rebel was then "slaughtered like a lamb."

One key piece of information was—by necessity—absent from the texts in the Library of Ashurbanipal, the last of which had been gathered before the monarch's death in 631 BCE: an account of Nineveh's final days. In the book of Jonah, God commanded the prophet to deliver a warning to the ruler of Assyria: "Arise, go to Nineveh, that great city, and cry against it; for their wickedness is come up before me." Jonah, after dodging God for some time (and ending up in the belly of a whale), made his way to "an exceedingly great city of three days' journey" with a population of "more than 120,000." When the king learned that God had ordered Nineveh to be destroyed in forty days, the distraught monarch "rose from his throne, took off his royal robes, covered himself with sackcloth and sat down in the dust," earning his subjects a temporary reprieve. Not long after Jonah's warning, though, other Hebrew Prophets were again predicting Nineveh's imminent destruction. "There shall the fire devour thee; the sword shall cut thee off; it shall eat thee up like the canker worm," declared Nahum, probably writing in Jerusalem in the mid-seventh century BCE, a few decades after Sennacherib's rampage through Judea and siege of the holy city. Nineveh would not recover, Nahum went on, because its "injury has no healing."

The Babylonian Chronicles, a series of forty-five tablets written in Akkadian cuneiform, recounting the history of the region beginning in the eighth century BCE, and deciphered in the 1920s, contains a partial account of the city's fall. Seventy lines about Nineveh recount the chaotic rule of Ashurbanipal's son, Sîn-sharru-ishkun, in the late seventh century BCE. During his reign, an official named Nabopolassar established himself as king of Babylon and declared the city-state's independence. In 615 BCE the Medes of Persia, united by a ruler named Cyaxares, attacked the Assyrians' religious capital, Ashur, and inflicted "a terrible defeat upon a great people." The Medes pillaged the city and reduced its divine sanctuary, the holiest place in Assyria, to rubble. That victory demoralized the population, and fueled an alliance between Nabopolassar and Cyaxares to seize Nineveh and finish off the Assyrian Empire.

Ctesias of Cnidus described how, in 612 BCE, a huge army of Assyria's former vassals—Medes and Babylonians—carried out a "great siege" of Nineveh that dragged on for two years. The defenders fought from "one hundred fifty guard towers," he wrote, each two hundred feet high. But when the Tigris flooded its banks and swept away part of the city walls, the attackers stormed through the gaps. In Ctesias's denouement, the last Assyrian king was Sardanapalus, whose downfall would inspire Lord Byron and Eugène

Delacroix in the 1820s. Sardanapalus, wrote Ctesias, "built an enormous pyre in the palace and heaped all the gold and silver on it, as
well as his royal clothing." Then he gathered his concubines and
eunuchs, lit the pyre, and "burnt himself and all the others to death
and razed the palace to the ground." A more reliable account in
The Babylonian Chronicles says that the siege lasted three months,
and that the king, whom it names as Sîn-Sharru-ishkun, was struck
down by Babylonian assailants while defending the city. Babylonian
and Medean troops, seeking vengeance for years of cruelty and conquest, swarmed Nineveh and set it ablaze.

In 1990, archaeologists from the University of California,
Berkeley, excavated the central passageway of the Halzi Gate, the
largest of the capital's fifteen entrance points. They discovered the
skeletons of eight men, four adolescents, and four children, along
with a dagger handle, pieces of armor, and other weaponry and
military equipment, which had lain undisturbed for 2,600 years.
Embedded in the leg bone of one man was a triple-bladed bronze arrowhead, shaped to inflict maximum tissue damage. Just outside the
fifty-foot-thick walls lay the skeletons of a stallion and its rider. All
the individuals found at the scene, the archaeologists determined,
had died either defending or fleeing a city on fire. "Nineveh is laid
waste!" declares the book of Nahum. "Who will bemoan her?"

Dur-Sharrukin, north of Mosul, and Kalhu, today called Nimrud, twenty miles downriver from Mosul, were the next to burn,
probably within months of Nineveh's destruction. After the dev-
astation of its four main cities, including Ashur, the state disinte-
grated. The royal line ended. Canals silted up and irrigation systems
ceased to function. The rural population fled. Cuneiform, already
giving way to Aramaic script, disappeared from Northern Mesopotamia. An "empire without a mission," as the German Assyriologist
Eckart Frahm called it, dedicated to nothing but "the forceable ac-

cumulation of wealth," collapsed on itself, and disappeared beneath the sands.

The demise of Assyria left Babylon, long Assyria's vassal state, as the last vestige of the Semitic language–speaking civilizations that had dominated Mesopotamia for a millennium. But its days as a thriving and independent kingdom, too, were numbered. The book of Daniel relates the story of Belshazzar, the crown prince of Babylon. Seventy-three years after the torching of Nineveh, Belshazzar, described by Xenophon as a "riotous, indulgent, cruel and godless" man, held a drunken banquet at the palace. Revelers sipped wine from the golden and silver goblets that his grandfather, Nebuchadnezzar II, had seized from the Temple of Jerusalem. A disembodied human hand suddenly appeared and scrawled four Hebrew words on the wall: MENE, MENE, TEKEL, UPHARSIN. Daniel, who arrived with the first Jews captured by Nebuchadnezzar II's army in Jerusalem and remained as a royal adviser throughout the Babylonian captivity, interpreted the message for the prince: He had been found wanting. His life would soon be over. Babylon was about to fall. The army of Persians and Medes marched into the city immediately after the prophecy, in October 539 BCE. As the holy messenger had foretold, the invaders murdered Belshazzar, a few days before Cyrus the Great rode into Babylon, probably through the Ishtar Gate, in triumph.

Rawlinson would never properly acknowledge Hormuzd Rassam's discovery of the Library of Ashurbanipal. Nor would he easily accept another young archaeologist from a different background than he was used to, who strode noisily onto the scene just as Rawlinson was winding down his archaeological career. William Loftus— who would memorably describe the fortress-like inns filled with

Shia pilgrims, domestic animals, and corpses on the road to Najaf and Karbala—was the son of an innkeeper in Newcastle upon Tyne, a gritty port city at the edge of Northumberland in northern England. Without money or contacts, he attended Cambridge, became a fellow at the Royal Geological Society, and then landed a coveted job as a naturalist on the Baghdad-based Turco-Persian Frontier Commission. The group examined the long-running dispute over territory in the Zagros Mountains and conducted scientific research on the side. A three-day tour of Nineveh and Nimrud in 1849 "inspired him with the wish to find for himself an untouched site in this antique land," wrote his biographer, "where . . . discoveries of a brilliance equal to those of Layard were waiting to be made."

Loftus conducted excavations for the British Museum, with Rawlinson's initial blessing, at Warka and Susa, the ancient capital of the Elamites, which was destroyed by Ashurbanipal between 648 and 647 BCE but rebuilt by the Achaemenid kings and turned into the empire's administrative capital. Before returning to London, he made several important finds at Warka: three glazed coffins filled with dust, along with "numerous written bricks, gold earrings, nose rings, and studs," reported the *Nitocris* captain James Felix Jones. Rassam found him to be "active, intelligent, and thoroughly in earnest." Loftus then reappeared in Baghdad in August 1853, as the representative of the Assyria Excavation Fund, a private venture that claimed to have the backing of Prince Albert. This time, Rawlinson was less welcoming. Irked that the new company had used his name without permission in fundraising materials, and that Loftus wanted to excavate on Rawlinson's turf at Kuyunjik, Rawlinson threatened to block him from the mounds. "He will embarrass the operations which I am now conducting on behalf of the Museum," he wrote to Henry Ellis.

The dispute that followed threatened to bring Rawlinson's career in the Near East to a sour end. In early 1854 the British Museum's board of trustees, citing a budget crunch, abruptly cut off funding to Rawlinson's Assyria excavations. Worried that French or American archaeologists would rush to the mounds in the vacuum, Rawlinson grudgingly invited Loftus to dig at Kuyunjik under the banner of the Assyrian Excavation Fund. Months later, however, when the trustees came up with £1,500 (worth about $300,000 today) to restart the dig, Rawlinson reversed himself. Loftus, he wrote, would have to leave the mound. Loftus refused. "After all that has passed, I am not a little surprised that the Museum should again wish to resume the excavations," he wrote to Rawlinson in June 1854. He decried the "species of indignity" to which "I have been subjected." Irritated, Rawlinson replied, "I think your indignation has run away with your judgment."

The men sent heated letters back and forth throughout the summer. The confrontation was little more than "a storm in a slop bucket," Rawlinson admitted to Norris, but pride, and, perhaps, a vague disdain for Loftus's humble background, made him unable to back down. In September, in an echo of the near-violent encounter between French and English labor teams at Qal'at Sherqat, Rassam's and Loftus's crews almost came to blows inside Ashurbanipal's palace on the Kuyunjik mound. The affair ended a month later, when Rawlinson agreed that Loftus could stay—so long as he agreed to serve under the authority of the British Museum. Loftus accepted the terms—by now the Assyria Excavation Fund was losing money and on the verge of collapse—but he didn't stay long. In early 1857 he became the assistant to the superintendent of the Geological Survey of India, based in Calcutta. A few months later he contracted amoebic dysentery, which developed into an abscess of the liver. He died at sea on November 27, two weeks after his thirty-eighth birthday, a promising archaeological career cut short, and a rift with Rawlinson never fully healed.

◄◄─────►►

It often went like that in this part of the world. More than two hundred years after the aristocratic Italian traveler Pietro della Valle had mourned the death at Persepolis of his bride during childbirth, grievous injury and illness could strike down anyone in his or her prime. Rawlinson, too, almost became a victim. In late 1854, he fractured his collarbone in a riding accident, a serious injury that was compounded by the fact that the "bone had been broken before," noted his brother George, "and this . . . inducing much suffering, and rendering the cure long and tedious." Heavily bandaged and with one usable hand, the diplomat began making plans, his brother wrote, "on taking the furlough so long looked forward to" and opened discussions with the East India Company about terminating his career in Mesopotamia.

He had one final job to attend to: arranging for the transport home of the Assyrian and Babylonian treasures gathered under his watch. But the British Museum trustees, who had received many boatloads of antiquities from Mesopotamia in the last seven years, balked at taking more material. Their interest, Rawlinson understood, had waned from its peak five years earlier. So, he reached out to Victor Place, the French consul, who was preparing a large shipment of antiquities bound for the Louvre. Putting aside the ill feelings between them over digging rights, Place agreed to transport fifty-two crates filled with Loftus's and Rassam's bas-reliefs and other relics from Warka and the North Palace of Ashurbanipal. By now, though, the Ottoman Empire had all but ceded control of the countryside, and the river, to rebellious Bedouins. Ten officials in Baghdad advised the French government in an urgent letter "that we cannot consent to [the antiquities'] transportation during such disorder." Moving the treasures down the Tigris by raft had once been a romantic enterprise. But that era, too, was coming to an end.

Place ignored the warning. That April (1855), a flotilla of keleks and a three-mast cargo ship massed on the Tigris in Baghdad. Workers loaded 235 crates filled with basalt and alabaster statues, bas-reliefs, and iron, bronze, gold, and silver relics excavated by French teams from the mounds of Khorsabad, Nimrud, and Kuyunjik. Two human-headed lamassus, weighing thirty-two tons apiece, each went on a separate kelek. Two other rafts each bore a fourteen-ton "genie" (a bearded male figure sprouting birds' wings). Days before Place was to accompany the flotilla on its journey downriver, the French government ordered him to report for a new consular posting in Moldavia. He hurriedly appointed as his substitute on the river journey a Swiss-French former aristocrat known to history only as A. Clément, who had fled the 1848 Revolution and was teaching French to a Kurdish chieftain in Baghdad.

The first seven days on the river passed without incident, though Clément repeatedly had to hand over gifts and large sums of money to armed men in exchange for the right of passage. Then, on May 21, three miles north of Qurnah, where the Tigris and Euphrates come together, the expedition fell apart. A dozen Arab rebels emerged from the reeds, "where they had hidden, no doubt awaiting a favorable moment to attack us," Clément recounted in a memoir eleven years later. "Then the general pillage began." Armed with spears, swords, and shields, the attackers waded through the shallows, boarded the ship, looted it, and sank it in three fathoms of water. Canoe-born bandits swarmed over the keleks, intending to strip the lumber—a scarce and valuable commodity in the southern semi-desert. They ripped off "the strong pieces of wood and pierc[ed] the inflated skins with their lances," Clément wrote. A kelek carrying a lamassu and several crates sank to the river bottom; a companion raft, bearing one of the two genies, drifted ashore, where the winged giant toppled over and was lost in the murk. The other rafts, stripped of their frames, floated downstream toward Qurnah, where they would be salvaged from the muddy riverbank. Then the attackers stripped Clément naked and forced the French tutor to walk barefoot through bramble in 120-degree heat to the safety of an Ottoman armed barge on the river. It took him many weeks to recover.

The loss to Western museums was incalculable. British naval forces managed to rescue twenty-eight of the 235 crates, which they shipped to the Louvre. But one winged bull, one winged genie, forty-one crates of antiquities belonging to Fresnel, eighty-four crates belonging to Place, and eighty crates bound for a Berlin museum through a deal the French had with the Prussian government either were stolen or sank to the bottom of the river. (The British cargo, which had traveled at the last minute in a separate flotilla, made it through intact.) It was the greatest material loss in the history of archaeology.

After a grueling sea journey to Bombay with a shattered clavicle, and then a slog to England via Aden, Suez, Trieste, and Vienna, Rawlinson arrived at his residence on Savile Row in Mayfair in late 1855. It was only then that he learned the full story about the disaster. But it was no longer his concern. He submitted his resignation to the East India Company, guaranteed a sizeable pension, and then left the Foreign Service as well. Turkish Arabia, with its heat, disease, violence, and strife on the archaeological mounds, was finally behind him.

CHAPTER EIGHTEEN

THE UNRAVELED
MYSTERY

In late March 1857, Edwin Norris, the secretary of the Royal Asiatic Society in Mayfair, set in motion the challenge that Norris hoped would prove, once and for all, the validity of the cuneiform decipherment. Four of Europe's most esteemed scholars and linguists would now attempt, independently, to transliterate and translate eight hundred lines of Akkadian text inscribed on the three-thousand-year-old prism found by Hormuzd Rassam beneath a temple in the ancient capital on the Tigris. About the height of a bowling pin, the prism was known to contain the annals of Tiglath-Pileser I, who had expanded the empire to Syria and the Mediterranean Sea around 1100 BCE. From what Rawlinson claimed to have gleaned in Baghdad, the text chronicled his military campaigns, building projects, temple consecrations, hunting expeditions, and tributes paid by vassals from far-flung corners of the empire. All were described with tiny characters pressed together on a sixteen-inch-high fired-clay column held together by gum-water and chalk. The selection of the cylinder, the Washington-based newspaper the *National Era* declared, had been "calculated to tax to the utmost the powers of independent decipherers."

Over the next three weeks, Norris assembled a six-man panel of judges, including some of the most renowned historians and linguists in England. They were William Whewell, master of Trinity College at Cambridge; George Grote, a classicist known for his voluminous *History of Greece*; William Cureton, a canon of Westminster Abbey and British Museum trustee; John Gardner Wilkinson, called England's "Father of Egyptology"; Horace Hayman Wilson, the first Boden professor of Sanskrit at Oxford and the director of the Royal Asiatic Society, whose Sanskrit-English dictionary had proved valuable to Rawlinson in Persia; and Henry Hart Milman, dean of St. Paul's Cathedral in London. None considered himself an expert in Semitic tongues, but that didn't matter. Their job would simply be to compare the four participants' English translations, note similarities and discrepancies, and confirm "that the versions sent in were made independently, the seals of the translators having been broken in their presence." The deadline for the submissions was set for May 15.

At Norris's direction, a lithographed copy of the cylinder arrived at Edward Hincks's rectory in Killyleagh on April 26. William Henry Fox Talbot had apparently never even suggested that Hincks should be included in the cuneiform challenge, although Talbot owed much of what he knew about Akkadian to the Irishman's pioneering efforts. It had been left to Norris to bring up his name, almost as an afterthought, at the March meeting of the Royal Asiatic Society. Then, the British Museum had inexplicably taken more than a month to prepare a copy of the cylinder for Hincks, leaving the parson with just eighteen days to submit his translation to the society. "I will translate as much as I can; but the time allowed is so short that I shall probably not go through much more than half of the inscription," he wrote to Talbot. Oppert, the gregarious German-French explorer and scholar, worked from a lithographed copy as well. Talbot and Rawlinson had already completed their translations in late winter. Norris wrote that he had confidence in the decipherers and expected that the four versions would closely resemble one another. Whether Hincks's and Oppert's decipherments were any good seemed almost—to this corner of the British establishment—of little importance. Hincks, after all, was an outsider who had been brought in only at the last minute, and Oppert's inclusion stemmed from the fact that he'd happened to be a guest of the society in March, when Talbot's challenge was announced. Neither man was a member of the English elite.

◂———▸

In the period leading up to the great test, the antipathy between Hincks and Rawlinson had grown even more toxic. The churchman had spent several fruitful months at the British Museum in 1853 and 1854, inching closer, it appeared, to escaping from the obscurity of a rector's life in rural Ireland. (Unable to find a prelate to fill in for him at the church, Hincks had been forced to commute back and forth from Killyleagh and do much of the decipherment remotely.) Ensconced in solitude in a workroom in the bowels of the museum, Hincks had pored for many hours at a stretch over some of the museum's prizes: the Bellino Cylinder; the Black Obelisk of Shalmaneser III; a hexagonal prism describing Esarhaddon's conquests; and tablets from the Library of Ashurbanipal, filling notebooks with an unparalleled outpouring of translations and annotations. His one-year employment agreement ended on June 6, 1854. Hincks anticipated the accolades of the museum's curators and the promise of more work. Instead, the trustees delivered dismaying news: they were not renewing his contract.

Bewildered and humiliated, Hincks returned to Killyleagh and reached out to Layard, who had become a confidant, complaining bitterly about being "cast-off" by the trustees without explanation. Had Rawlinson, he wondered, played a surreptitious role in his ouster? Then there was the matter of his two black spiral notebooks, which, in his hasty exit, he had been obliged to leave behind in his workroom. They contained "a mass of information which is (I flatter myself—indeed I have no doubt) *of very great value*," he told Layard, and he feared they would fall into Rawlinson's hands. When he learned, in mid-1855, that the diplomat was on his way back to London from Baghdad, he sensed that his trepidations would soon be borne out. "I have no doubt," he wrote to Layard, "that *he* will be allowed free access to all that the Museum possesses. I am thus *disheartened*."

Hincks had other grievances against Rawlinson: he'd become convinced the diplomat had been trying to steal credit for Hincks's insights into Akkadian. The pattern dated as far back as 1849, when Hincks had claimed that he had recognized "compound logograms," or the juxtaposition of two logographic characters to make an entirely new word: thus "son" and "woman" made "daughter" 𒂷 𒊩, while "house" and "great" made "palace" 𒂍𒃲. More recently, Hincks considered himself the first to identify the "syllabaries"—tablets intended for aspiring scribes that listed logograms with their phonetic values. Hincks had spotted them in the trove that Layard brought to Killyleagh in 1852, hastening an end to years of struggle to make the names of kings and other logograms comprehensible. But Rawlinson insisted that he'd found the compound logograms before Hincks had—and that he had discovered a trove of lexical lists before Hincks, too, while poring through the clay tablets in the Library of Sennacherib at Nineveh.

Hincks didn't think much of some of Rawlinson's "translations" either. Recently, Rawlinson claimed to have turned up new parallels between the annals of Assyrian and Babylonian kings and the Bible.

An inscription at Birs Nimrud, near Babylon, he said, recorded the raising of the Tower of Babel—largely regarded by biblical scholars as a myth—on that spot precisely 2,940 years before the reign of Nebuchadnezzar II. A passage in the East India House Inscription, he declared, confirmed the biblical story about Nebuchadnezzar II's "madness" found in the book of Daniel. Both of Rawlinson's readings, Hincks insisted, were fantasies. Having initially discounted the veracity of biblical history, Rawlinson now, in Hincks's opinion, was claiming to find confirmation of its truth everywhere he looked. The British public seemed to be accepting Rawlinson's purported discoveries, Hincks wrote to Layard. If they wished to be deceived, he added, it was their own business.

Rawlinson had the backing of much of the public and the British elite, but some of Hincks's fellow Assyriologists gathered around the pastor in support. Oppert, back from his expedition to Babylon, expressed in the mid-1850s his desire "to enter into scientific intercourse with a man whose first-rate sagacity I esteem." And though William Henry Fox Talbot had overlooked Hincks in the months leading to the cuneiform challenge, he remained an admirer. Letters passed frequently between Killyleagh and Lacock Abbey, filled with new insights into Akkadian etymology, Hebrew cognates, the phonetic values of logograms, and verb conjugations. Hincks shared with Talbot his long-held dream of becoming the first professor of Akkadian at Oxford or Cambridge. "I have often felt that it is discreditable to the English universities that there is not any professor of the newly discovered ancient Oriental languages," he wrote in February 1857. Soon he was nudging the inventor-linguist-scientist to use his connections with the Cambridge administration to get him a job: "I should hope . . . that the knowledge of what I have already done . . . . would inspire confidence," he wrote. Talbot claimed to be willing, but nothing ever came of Hincks's entreaties.

Hincks also asked Talbot for help obtaining information from the British Museum about the fate of his missing notebooks. This request would soon produce a disturbing answer.

◂┼───────┼▸

On Wednesday, May 20, 1857, the judges gathered at the Royal Asiatic Society's town house on New Burlington Street. London's newspapers were filled that day with stories of the waning Parliamentary support for Lord Palmerston's government (it would collapse the following year); the society wedding of the daughter of the banker and philanthropist Baron Lionel de Rothschild; and the ratification of the Treaty of Paris, which ended a five-month-long conflict between the United Kingdom and Persia over control of Afghanistan—the latest episode of the Great Game. But in the quiet corridors of the Mayfair headquarters, the focus was on the Iron Age. The judges filed into the ground-floor ballroom, filled with mementos from members' Asian travels. Indian javelins, daggers from Yemen, and a samurai sword hung on the walls. A large cabinet held Chinese amulets designed to ward off demons and bring good fortune. There were kits for smoking opium, Sanskrit scrolls, the skin of a thirteen-foot boa constrictor, and a giant coconut from the South Seas. A brass globe of the zodiac, crafted by the chief astronomer of Mosul in 1275 CE, displayed forty-eight constellations. An Egyptian mummy had once been on exhibit, dissected by a physician for fellow members, until complaints about the "unpleasant smell" had obliged him to donate the three-thousand-year-old corpse to the King's College Museum.

Dean Henry Hart Milman of St. Paul's Cathedral, the chairman of the committee, unsealed the envelopes in front of his colleagues. "The four translations have been made in different and distant places," without the four parties having "any communication with each other," the Egyptologist John Gardner Wilkinson attested. Hincks, he noted, had completed only twenty-eight of the fifty-four sections in the abbreviated time he'd been given. Oppert, working at French government expense in London, had finished just twenty-one. Talbot, having started the work in February, had completed his in six weeks. "[Only] those of Mr. Fox Talbot and Sir Henry Rawlinson are entire," Wilkinson noted.

Then the judges began to read and compare the translations.

The results initially looked less than promising. Oppert, Talbot, Rawlinson, and Hincks had all struggled with a wealth of unfamiliar vocabulary and a multiplicity of potential character readings. The decipherers disagreed over the names of wild animals, cities, countries, and vassal kings. In one account of a royal hunt, Rawlinson identified the prey as "wild buffaloes." Hincks called them "wild elephants." Talbot, at a loss, used the Akkadian word *amsi* ("elephant"). Oppert didn't answer at all. What Rawlinson called "300 fugitive heretics," Hincks referred to as "300 fugitive female slaves." Even with the new lexical lists, many Akkadian logograms confounded them.

Yet as the judges dove deeper into the translations, they found themselves struck by the extent to which the four decipherers *did* agree with one another. In one paragraph, the participants named thirty-nine countries "in the same manner exactly," the judges noted with admiration. Later in the annals, the four translated an account of one of Tiglath-Pileser I's military campaigns with striking similarity:

Rawlinson: "Then I went to the country of Comukha, which was disobedient and withheld the tribute and offering due to Ashur my lord."

Hincks: "At the time I went to a disaffected part of Qummukh, which had withheld the tribute by weight and tale belonging to Ashur, my lord."

Talbot: "I then advanced against Kummikhi, a land of the unbelievers who had refused to pay taxes and tribute unto Ashur, my lord."

Oppert: "In these days I went to the people of Dummukh, the enemy who owed tributes and gifts to the god Assur, my lord."

Rawlinson: "I plundered their movables, their wealth, and their valuables. Their cities I burned with fire, I destroyed and ruined."

Hincks: "I brought out their women, their slaves, and their cattle; their towns I burned with fire, threw down, and dug up."

Talbot: "Their women . . . I carried off. Their cities I burned with fire, destroyed and overthrew."

Oppert: "I took away their captives, their herds, and their treasures; their cities I burnt in fire; I destroyed, I undermined them."

The judges also examined the king's warning to miscreants who would dare damage or desecrate his cylinders. Here, too, except for curious variations of one god's name, the translations produced by three of the four participants were impressively close:

Rawlinson: "He who shall injure my tablets and cylinders, or shall moisten them with water, or scorch them with fire, or expose them to the air . . . Anu and Vul, the great gods, my lord, let them consign his name to perdition."

Talbot: "He who my stone tablets and my memorial records shall injure or shall destroy them; with water shall efface them; or with fire shall consume them; or shall deface the writings . . . May Anu and Yen, the great gods, my lord, utterly confound him."

Hincks: "He who shall hide or obliterate my tablets and my floors shall *wander* on the waters, shall be *suspended* in the fire, shall be besmeared with earth . . . May Anu and Iv, the great gods, my lords, *energetically* punish him."

◄───────►

The judges critiqued the work of each decipherer. Oppert's translation of the cylinder, with tortured English prose and wide divergences from the work of the others, was deemed the weakest. "It is to be regretted," the panel wrote, "that Dr. Oppert did not translate into French, in which language his version would have been clearer and more precise." The judges looked favorably on Talbot, who had taken an interest in Assyriology just a few years earlier. But they bestowed their highest accolades on Hincks and Rawlinson, "who are understood to have prosecuted the study for the longest time and with the greatest assiduity." Their submissions displayed "the closest coincidences." In hundreds of cases the two had arrived "at the same conclusions."

The panel's verdict was unanimous. "Both as to the general sense and verbal rendering, [the results] were . . . remarkable," it declared. "There was a strong correspondence in the meaning assigned, and occasionally a curious identity of expression as to particular words."

Norris, however, was uncertain whether the challenge would put matters to rest. He rued the fact that, in retrospect, none of the judges he'd selected knew much about Semitic languages, a lack of expertise that he thought might undermine their credibility—even though the panel's only task was to examine how closely the English translations resembled one another, not to study the original writing. "Now that it is done, nothing seems likely to come of it," Norris wrote dismissively to a colleague. "To me, and I may say, to Sir G[ardner] Wilkinson, the result was perfectly satisfactory . . ." But would doubters really be convinced? As he perused the judges' assessment, he also noted with regret that "many lines . . . of difficult construction, or uncertain meaning, had been left untranslated."

These shortcomings turned out not to matter. When Norris made the verdict public in early June, British literary journals along with general-interest newspapers and magazines endorsed the judgment. Under the headline "A Literary Inquest," the *Athenaeum*, with perhaps ten thousand readers, many of them highly educated and influential, declared that the test "has been now carried out in a manner which . . . ought to set the question definitively to rest." The Assyro-Babylonian language, *Chambers's Journal*, a popular weekly magazine of literature, science, and the arts with a circulation of more than eighty thousand, concluded, "with its . . . arrow-headed character, so inexplicable but a few years past, is [now] an unraveled mystery."

The result was "a complete triumph for the Assyriologists," declared Paul Haupt of Johns Hopkins University, one of the leading philologists and ancient writing scholars of the late nineteenth century. "Henceforth there could be no doubt as to the soundness of the principles laid down by [Assyriology's] expositors." Talbot sent a note of congratulations to Hincks a few days after the verdict was announced. "I have no doubt that our experiment will convert a large number of candid and learned persons who have hitherto been skeptical," he wrote. Charles Wall, who had demeaned the decipherment in a letter to Hincks as "moonshine," was silent.

With the emergence of the four similar translations, it became instantly clear that the secrets of the ancient world would be secret no longer. Perhaps the greatest legacy of the Royal Asiatic Society face-off was that it inspired others to join this grand quest to understand humanity's past. In the early 1860s, a young, working-class Londoner named George Smith, who worked as a money engraver for the printing firm Bradbury & Evans, spent his lunch breaks hovering over boxes and wooden planks in a dimly lit room at the British Museum, deciphering fragmentary tablets retrieved by Layard and Rassam from the Libraries of Sennacherib and Ashurbanipal at Kuyunjik. Smith so dazzled Henry Rawlinson with his self-taught Akkadian that the older man provided him access to some of his most valuable possessions: the papier-mâché casts that he kept in his workroom at the British Museum.

One day, Smith, then thirty-two, made what remains the most momentous find in the history of Assyrian scholarship. He was reading a fragmentary, six-inch-by-five-inch tablet found in the Kuyunjik mound that told a story of a god-fearing king named Uta-napshti. Upon hearing the voice of a deity informing him that a flood will sweep over the world and "destroy the seed of mankind," he builds a large boat and climbs inside it as the rain begins to fall.

> After, for seven days and seven nights
> The flood had swept over the land
> And the huge boat had been tossed about by the windstorms and
>   the great waters,
> [The sun god] Utu came forth, who sheds light on heaven and
>   earth,
> [Uta-napshti] opened a window on the huge boat,
> The hero Utu brought his rays into the giant boat.

"On looking down the third column my eye caught the statement that the ship rested on the mountains of Nizir," Smith recalled. The reference apparently was to an 8,500-foot peak known today as Pir Omar Gudrun located near Sulaymaniyah in Iraqi Kurdistan. The description of the mountain landing, Smith wrote, was "followed by the account of sending forth of the dove, and its finding a resting place and returning. I saw at once that I had here discovered a portion . . . of the [Babylonian] account of the Deluge." The fragment of the "Great Flood" tablet that Smith translated was a copy of an original text written during the Old Babylonian period, probably a few hundred years before the account of Noah and the ark in Genesis, which most scholars think dates to around 1400 BCE. One of the foundational myths of Western civilization, it appeared, had originated on the Mesopotamian floodplain.

The discovery shocked and outraged many men of faith. It seemed to contest the belief that the Old Testament was a divinely inspired account, possibly a literal truth, passed down by the Hebrew patriarchs. Instead of God saving Noah as a sign of his favor, the tablet described a pagan divinity rescuing a Sumerian king. Some Western theologians tried to argue that the story had reached Mesopotamia only after coming directly from Noah himself. But others embraced the idea that the Great Flood story was a myth that reflected the shared experiences, memories, and yearnings of a whole host of ancient peoples. "We can now see that this greatest of literary classics did not come upon the scene full-blown, like an artificial flower in a vacuum," wrote Samuel Noah Kramer, the University of Pennsylvania Assyriologist. "Its roots reach deep into the distant past and spread wide across the surrounding lands. To say this is not to detract . . . from the significance of the Biblical writings, or from the genius of the Hebrew men of letters who composed them," he went on. Rather, "the Hebrew miracle," he wrote, "transformed

the static motifs and conventionalized patterns of their predecessors into what is perhaps the most vibrant and dynamic literary creation known to man." Irving Finkel, assistant keeper of ancient Mesopotamian script, languages, and cultures at the British Museum, described the way the story may have emerged: "There must have been a heritage memory of the destructive power of flood water, based on various terrible floods," he said. "And the people who survived would have been people in boats. You can imagine someone sunbathing in a canoe, half asleep, and waking up however long later and they're in the middle of the Persian Gulf, and that's the beginning of the flood story."

The find turned Smith into the most celebrated archaeological scholar in the world. The *Daily Telegraph* financed his travel to Kuyunjik in January 1873 to hunt for another lost fragment of the Deluge story, which he found after only one week of searching through the remnants of Ashurbanipal's Library. On a return trip that November sponsored by the British Museum, Smith determined that the Great Flood tablet was the eleventh in a series presenting the history of a hero whom Henry Rawlinson identified as "Izdubar." The name, written with three logograms, turned out to be a misreading of Gilgamesh, the legendary demigod-king who ruled Uruk in Southern Mesopotamia around 2700 BCE. Smith published a partial account of Gilgamesh's adventures under the title *The Chaldaean Account of Genesis* in 1872; the *Epic of Gilgamesh*, as it became known in the early twentieth century in translations done by Peter Jensen, R. Campbell Thompson, and Samuel Noah Kramer, tells the story of a hero who sets out to wander in the wild after the jealous goddess Ishtar murders his friend and possibly lover, Enkidu, "a man all muscle / the mightiest in the land." Searching for the secret to eternal life, Gilgamesh survives a battle with lions, a plunge to the bottom of the sea, and a journey through

a mountain before he encounters Uta-napshti, the only survivor of the Great Flood. Told that he will never achieve immortality, Gilgamesh returns to Uruk, humbled and accepting his human frailty. "Gilgamesh is fascinatingly complex," wrote Robert Macfarlane in the *New York Review of Books* in a 2022 review of a new translation by a young Danish scholar named Sophus Helle. "At times (priapic, solipsistic, childishly delinquent), he resembles Boris Johnson; at others (tired, wiser, sadder), he's more late Franklin Roosevelt." Literary scholars posited that *Gilgamesh*, with its picaresque tales of adventure, encounters with supernatural beings, god-man hero (like Achilles), and search for wisdom and immortality, influenced Homer's *Iliad* and *Odyssey*. The epic would be translated into dozens of languages. Sigmund Freud would regard the relationship between Gilgamesh and Enkidu as symbolic of the noble and bestial dual nature of man. In 1998 the *Columbia Anthology of Gay Literature* would include it as a major early contribution to the genre.

In 1876, the British Museum dispatched Smith on his third expedition to Kuyunjik, but an outbreak of civil unrest, a cholera epidemic, and mounting desert heat forced him to quit the mound before making any substantial new discoveries. On the journey home, he fell ill with dysentery and, after a few days sprawled on the floor of a filthy hut, he was carried by his assistant forty miles to Aleppo in a mule-drawn sedan chair. He died there shortly after his arrival; he was thirty-six years old.

◄━━━━━━►

The *Epic of Gilgamesh* was not conjured up entirely from the imaginations of Old Babylonian scribes. Some years after Smith's death, scholars traced the work to five epic poems written in the early third millennium BCE, when Uruk was the most powerful city-state in the Near East. The *Sumerian King List*, clay tablets inscribed with the names of the rulers of Ur, Kish, and other Mesopotamian city-states, identifies Gilgamesh as an early hero-king of Uruk, responsible for reconstructing the city's crumbling ramparts, and Sumerian poems about a hero named Bilgamesh contain narrative elements that also appear in the much later Gilgamesh epic. Bilgamesh sets off, like his counterpart, on an expedition into a cedar forest, climbs mountains to approach the gods, descends into the underworld, and expresses his fear and sorrow about the inevitable prospect of death. ("In my city a man dies, and the heart is stricken / a man perishes, and the heart feels pain.") The Gilgamesh epic is now regarded as the world's oldest narrative and its themes of courage, the lust for adventure, the brevity of life, and the joy of companionship have defined the human experience from the era of Sumer to the present, a span of five thousand years.

Long before Gilgamesh's origins were ascertained, Assyriologists had already caught glimpses of a Mesopotamian civilization that predated Assyria and Babylon by two millennia. In 1855, Rawlinson had published an article in the *Journal of the Royal Asiatic Society* reporting his discovery of non-Semitic inscriptions in cuneiform on bricks and tablets from Warka, the modern name of Uruk, and other ancient sites in Southern Mesopotamia. Writing in the *Athenaeum*, Rawlinson had declared that these people had "built all the primitive temples of Babylonia, worshipped the same gods, and inhabited the same seats as their Semitic successors." Rawlinson conjectured that the Assyrians and Babylonians had adopted the ancient cuneiform characters invented by this civilization for their own writing. From his examination of Sumerian inscriptions, Hincks declared that the earlier people spoke an agglutinative language, like Turkish and Finnish, that "glued" prefixes, infixes, and suffixes onto root words to change tenses and cases, specify genders, and otherwise modify the stem. (The Turkish root word *korkmak*, meaning "fear," for example, can take on forms such as *korkusuzlas-mak* for "to become fearless" and *korkusuzlastirilabilmek* for "to be able to be made fearless." Similarly, Sumerian has *angar*, for "It is placed," *ang-gar-re-en*, "you are placed," and *ba-ab-gar-re-en*, for "I am caused to be placed.") In 1869 Jules Oppert suggested calling the language "Sumerian," based on inscriptions he had found that used the title "King of Sumer and Akkad." (Akkad, a civilization that flourished after Sumer, had already given the Assyro-Babylonian language its name.) The name took hold in 1889, after archaeologists discovered a Babylonian tablet referring to the language as *li-sha-an shu-mi-ri*, "the language of Sumer."

The discovery that a non-Semitic people were the original inhabitants of Mesopotamia sparked furious pushback within the philological world. "It seemed impossible that so revolutionary a doctrine could be true," wrote Oxford Assyriologist A. H. Sayce. Many philologists insisted that the descendants of Adam and Eve had populated the land around Ur from the era of Genesis, beginning in the sixth millennium BCE. These philo-Semitic scholars could not accept, wrote Sayce, that "the first civilized occupants of the alluvial plain of Babylonia"—the fertile crescent that saw the birth of agriculture, architecture, writing, urban settlement—"were neither Semites nor Aryans," but a people with no link to modern Europe. "It was they who first drained the marshes . . . founded the great cities of the country, and invented . . . cuneiform." (Twentieth-century archaeologists would come to designate five other geographical areas as cradles of civilization, including the Nile River Valley, the Indo-Gangetic plain, the North China plain, the Andean coast, and the Mesoamerican Gulf Coast.) The backlash to the discovery was fierce. Joseph Halévy, the editor of *Le Revue Sémitique*, an influential Parisian journal, maintained as late as 1874 that, as Christopher Johnston puts it, "the so-called . . . Sumerian people

are a pure myth; no such people ever existed." Sumerian was simply a "priestly code" invented by the Semitic-language-speaking
Babylonians for religious incantations. But in 1877, French excavations at Lagash near Babylon uncovered thousands of Sumerian
texts, "about the most mundane subjects, not priests and religion,"
says Peter T. Daniels, an American linguist and scholar of writing
systems. Assyriologists came to accept what Hincks and Rawlinson
had suspected in the mid-1850s: the Sumerians had been the first
scribes of Mesopotamia, and left ghostlike vestiges of their language
in a writing system that the Assyrians and Babylonians had adopted
as their own. Akkadian's debt to Sumerian explained much of the
later language's bewildering complexities: the confusing mashups
of logograms and syllables, the multiple values of phonetic characters, the dozen or more signs that could all make the same sound.

Other insights into Sumerian culture, customs, daily life, and
literature lay in the thousands of inscriptions excavated in Southern Mesopotamia and held by the British Museum, now decipher-
able thanks largely to the lexical lists discovered at the Libraries of
Ashurbanipal and Sennacherib that displayed equivalents in Akkadian and the earlier language. Here was laid out the entire Sumerian cosmology, beginning with Enki, the god of water and wisdom,
who appointed the lesser deities responsible for agriculture—such
as Ishkur, the bringer of rain—and who ensured the fertility of
Sumer: "He opened up the holy furrows, and made the barley
grow on the cultivated fields . . . [He] made chickpeas [and] lentils grow . . . Enki multiplied the stockpiles and stacks, and with
[the god of wind and storm] Enlil's help he enhanced the people's
prosperity." Scholars found land-acquisition contracts between two
priestesses in the city of Sippar from 1800 BCE, and a marriage contract from ancient Kish in which a patriarch gives his daughter to a
man named Ipiq-Ishtar, in exchange for eighty grams or ten shekels

of silver, as a *terkhatum*, or bride price. The same contract contained a list of witnesses who had rolled their seals over the left-hand margin of the clay envelope that enclosed the contract and had given an oath in the name of Zababa, the war god and tutelary deity of Kish. A tablet from ancient Uruk described the twelve signs of the zodiac recognized by the ancient Mesopotamians, beginning with Virgo, the month of Elûlu, which ran from mid-August to mid-September. There were books filled with proverbs such as "Friendship lasts a day, kinship endures forever." A prism from the city of Larsam from 1740 BCE, dedicated to Nisaba, the patron deity of scribes, showed eight mathematical problems, including quadratic equations used to determine the dimensions of a rectangle. There were narrative poems about the creation of man. In the simplest one, the god Enki fashions a human being out of clay, and binds "upon it the image of the gods."

In the late spring of 1857, as he enjoyed the attention paid to the "great experiment" by the *Athenaeum* and other London newspapers, Edward Hincks received confirmation from Talbot of what he had suspected: Rawlinson's friends at the British Museum had been conspiring against him all along. On June 7, 1854, the day after the trustees paid Hincks the remainder of his £120 salary and terminated the relationship, Henry Ellis, principal librarian of the museum, had written to Rawlinson, who was still in Baghdad, inviting him to inspect Hincks's black notebooks and offering to send him copies. After that, for unclear reasons, they sat for half a year unattended. Then, in December 1854, William Sandys Wright Vaux, a curator of antiquities and author of the critically praised *Nineveh and Persepolis: An Historical Sketch of Ancient Assyria and Persia*, went looking for them. "From behind a pile of dusty old books were dragged out two copybooks containing Hincks's memoir and marked EH outside," he wrote to Rawlinson. "I have . . . now got his MSS from the secretariat den and proceed to send you as much detail about it as I can cram into this letter." Vaux delivered to Rawlinson a twelve-page excerpt—translations, notes about Hincks's methodology, and commentaries on the texts. It is not known what use, if any, Rawlinson made of the material, but the sharing of Hincks's notebooks by Vaux without his permission—and with his archrival—was a shocking breach of trust.

For the next three years the notebooks languished again, unpublished, on Vaux's desk, until in late 1857 the trustees placed them in the British Museum's Manuscripts Department, finally making them accessible to the public. Years later, a letter surfaced in the museum archives that Vaux had sent to Rawlinson in 1854, in which he addressed the museum's shoddy treatment of Hincks. "What would our friend Hincks say if he knew all this?" Vaux had written. "I shan't tell him, because I own I like the fellow, he is a queer cantankerous old chap . . . but his bark is worse than his bite. Much of his crabbedness," he went on, "arises from his having lived such a mere student's life, and from his coming from the Black North of Ireland." It is easy to imagine the two men, pillars of the English establishment, sharing a laugh at Hincks's expense. But it was the humble churchman from Ulster, long derided by men like Vaux and Rawlinson, whose work had surpassed that of the fiercely ambitious diplomat. And a time would come when this would be recognized.

◀──────▶

The Royal Asiatic Society basked in the afterglow of the decipherment challenge for about a month. Then all hell broke loose. Tensions had been building for years between the East India Company—the society's main benefactor—and the hundreds of thousands of Indian troops that the firm kept under its command. In early 1857, rumors spread through the ranks that the company was using cow and pig fat to grease the cartridges manufactured for its new generation of Enfield rifle-muskets. Indian soldiers had been trained to bite open the cartridge packets and place the enclosed gunpowder and the lead ball in the barrel of their rifles. If the cow and pig fat rumor were true, the procedure would be a sacrilege for both Muslims and Hindus. Tens of thousands of soldiers refused to load their weapons. "The idea quickly gained acceptance that the mistake was far from accidental," wrote William Dalrymple in *The Last Mughal*, "and was part of a wider Company conspiracy to break the sepoys' caste and ritual purity before embarking on a project of mass conversion." On May 10, British officers led eighty-five sepoys through the streets of Meerut, a city forty-five miles northeast of Delhi, in a "punishment parade" to prison, making an example of them. Third Bengal Light Cavalry troops stormed the jail and freed them. Then they went on a rampage. Sepoys looted a railway station, killed Europeans, marched to Delhi, and seized control of the Mughals' imperial capital. Battles between British officers and Indian soldiers broke out in Lucknow, Kanpur, Jhansi, Indore, and Arrah. The mutiny brought to the surface, in a bloody denouement, decades' worth of resentment at institutionalized racism and mistreatment by East India Company officers.

Word of the uprising didn't reach England until June 13, when a short article appeared in the *Illustrated London News*. Secretary Edwin Norris and the board of directors of the Royal Asiatic Society reacted with consternation. Most society members had been true believers in the East India Company's mission until the very moment of the mutiny. Three months earlier, at the same Saturday meeting in which Norris had announced the cuneiform challenge, George Buist, the editor of the *Bombay Times*, had enthralled attendees with an account of the company's latest technological achievement: engineers had completed twenty miles of railway tunnels through the Ghat Mountains between Bombay and Poonah (Pune), utilizing six thousand bullocks to drag tracks up mountainsides and forty thousand men to burrow and blast with black powder through "trap rock, greenstone, and siennate of the hardest description," Buist had said.

Despite an ability to mount such marquee events, the society had been financially struggling: "A reprehensible apathy" about Indian political affairs and culture, and competition with the Royal Geographic Society, one board member lamented, had driven membership down by nearly two-thirds, from 324 in the 1830s to just 140 in 1857. Now the future of the society's main benefactor, which provided the £400 annual donation that covered their lease on the New Burlington Street town house and other operating costs, had been thrown into doubt.

The mutiny dragged on for thirteen months, causing the deaths of thirteen thousand British troops and their Indian allies, forty thousand Indian mutineers, and thousands of civilians. British troops suppressed the rebellion in June 1858. In August Parliament passed the Government of India Act, which stripped the company of its administrative powers and placed its private army under the control of the Crown. "We shall respect the rights, dignity, and honour of the Indian princes as our own," declared Queen Victoria in a proclamation read at Allahabad that November, "and we desire that they as well as our own subjects shall enjoy that prosperity and that social advancement which can only be secured by internal peace and good government." The firm's power waned, and another parliamentary measure formally dissolved it in 1874. The Royal Asiatic Society continued to exist, but the mutiny had forced Britons to confront the most violent, corrupt aspects of colonial rule in India. "[T]here was a strong sense of embarrassment about the shady mercantile way the British had founded the Raj," William Dalrymple would write in the *Guardian*. "[T]hey liked to think of the empire as a *mission civilisatrice*: a benign national transfer of knowledge, railways and the art of civilisation from west to east, and there was a calculated and deliberate amnesia about the corporate looting that opened British rule in India."

◂—————▸

By the time the Indian Mutiny turned British public opinion decisively against the East India Company, Rawlinson had ceased to have any connection to the firm that had launched his professional trajectory. But other controversies, including his decade-long rivalry with Hincks, shadowed his career. "He has omitted all mention of my priority in asserting the truth which he has so recently embraced," Hincks had complained in 1852, referring to Rawlinson's acceptance of the biblical names of Assyrian kings and the Semitic origins of Akkadian. He never changed that view, writing to Norris a few years later that Rawlinson simply could not understand how anyone else was capable of making advances in cuneiform. Hincks remained convinced that Rawlinson had plagiarized his work and sabotaged him at the British Museum. He resisted the efforts of friends and family members to establish a détente.

Hincks's grandson, E. F. Davidson, believed that his accusations went too far: his "bilious" nature, Davidson thought, had made him prone to see plots against him. "One gets the impression that there was ... no active hostile feeling toward Hincks on [Rawlinson's] part, though probably some brusqueness and lack of fine consideration," he insisted. In 1863, Edwin Norris attempted to reconcile the adversaries. "I wish I could destroy the impression you have received of Rawlinson," he wrote to Hincks. "I know that his manner, contracted by long command of inferior Turks, Arabs, Persians, etc. may be deceptive, but I know also *that he has not* the feeling toward you which you suppose." Hincks was not persuaded.

Rawlinson's imperious personality and tendency to hog credit had left others feeling resentful. In letters and other writings, Rawlinson dismissed his field archaeologists, Loftus and Rassam, as his "subordinate" agents—the same language the British ambassador to Constantinople, Stratford Canning, had used to minimize Layard's role at Nimrud. "Hormuzd . . . writes me that the papers are full of the discoveries, but giving all the credit . . . to Col. Rawlinson, whereas he had nothing to do with it," Matilda Rassam had complained to Layard in the mid-1850s. In a reflection of Rawlinson's ability to influence the academic elite—even after his death—E. A. Wallis Budge, a distinguished Assyriologist at the British Museum, declared in his 1925 book, *The Rise & Progress of Assyriology*, that the Tiglath-Pileser I cylinder had been "discovered by Rawlinson at Kal'ah Sharkat [*sic*] in 1853," though Rawlinson had been 174 miles away in Baghdad at the time; Rassam had made the find. Rawlinson's ungenerous behavior is particularly hard to fathom given how much the Mosul-born archaeologist had helped to burnish Rawlinson's reputation. In their three-year collaboration, Rawlinson oversaw the transport of four hundred crates of antiquities down the Tigris to Baghdad, much of it dug up by Rassam. These treasures doubled the size of the British Museum's Assyrian collection. Rawlinson eventually did write a note to Rassam in which he acknowledged his debt to him. But it was too little, too late.

In time, the bad feelings faded into the background as Rawlinson continued to rise through the British diplomatic and political establishment. He died in 1895 at eighty-five, receiving a hero's send-off at a packed memorial service at St. George's Church in Mayfair's

Hanover Square. His death "brings to a close the long and eventful career of one of our most brilliant Oriental scholars and most distinguished Anglo-Indian statesmen," the *Times* pronounced. "His name will be permanently associated . . . with remarkable discoveries which opened a dead language." (His oldest son, General Sir Henry Rawlinson, would follow his father into military service, though his record was more controversial. As a commander of the Fourth Army during the Great War, he, along with General Douglas Haig, would send tens of thousands of soldiers to their deaths in a disastrous offensive at the Battle of the Somme in 1916.)

Austen Layard lost his Aylesbury seat in the House of Commons in 1857 and ended his career as British ambassador to Constantinople. After the rupture of his relationship with Rawlinson, he appears to have had no further contact with the man who had shared insights and excitement about Assyria with him throughout the 1840s. In 1869, he married Mary Enid Evelyn Guest, one of the ten children of his cousin Lady Charlotte Guest, who had been fourteen years old when Layard stayed for months at the family's Dorsetshire estate to write his memoir. Layard retired with his wife to a sixteenth-century palazzo in Venice, having come full circle from his days as a young dreamer reading *The Arabian Nights* in his family's Florentine villa. There he spent his last years amassing an art collection that included masterpieces by Titian and Tintoretto, which his widow donated to the National Gallery after his death, one year before Rawlinson's, at the age of seventy-seven. The *Illustrated London News* called his excavations "more startling and exciting than . . . any later discoveries, such as those of Dr. [Heinrich] Schliemann, in [Troy], or at Mycenae."

Jules Oppert produced nearly five hundred scholarly articles and books between 1846 and 1902 on everything from Assyrian law to the chronology of lunar and solar eclipses in antiquity to the topography of ancient Babylon. Oppert chaired the Assyriology Department at the Collège de France in Paris and founded *Revue d'Assyriologie*. He died in August 1905, just weeks before his eightieth birthday. "Never was a man of erudition so little of a recluse," wrote a *Times* correspondent in his obituary. Hormuzd Rassam kept up a prodigious pace of excavations across Mesopotamia for the British Museum. But after the publication of the *Epic of Gilgamesh*, looters descended on the mounds in search of Akkadian tablets to sell on the black market. Wallis Budge traveled to the excavation sites to investigate the crime wave and accused Rassam of collaborating with some of the black marketeers. In 1893 Rassam sued Budge for libel and slander and won a favorable decision by the judge at his civil trial (though the jury found for Budge), but the negative publicity damaged his reputation. He retired to Brighton, where he wrote his memoir, *Asshur and the Land of Nimrod: Being an Account of the Discoveries Made in the Ancient Ruins of Nineveh, Asshur, Sepharvaim, Calah, Babylon, Borsippa, Cuthah, and Van*. He died in 1910.

William Henry Fox Talbot produced dozens of translations of Akkadian annals after the Royal Asiatic Society challenge. Yet his greatest mission, to prove that Akkadian, for all its complexities and ambiguities, could be deciphered, remained under challenge to the end of his life. In 1862 Talbot reported to Hincks that the leading French philologists remained "fully convinced . . . of the entire futility of the pretended cuneiform discoveries." The multiple phonetic values of the Akkadian characters—polyphony—"must have been a source of embarrassment to the Assyrians themselves," he wrote to Hincks. "I am not surprised that modern literati are reluctant to admit the fact of their existence." Talbot died from heart disease at Lacock Abbey in September 1877. His "quarter century love affair with Assyriology [was] the ultimate intellectual challenge that he had been seeking all his life," wrote Mirjam Brusius, of the German Historical Institute London. "One could even argue that photography was just a phase he went through on the way to finding his true vocation."

Hincks, though plagued by jaundice and other maladies as he aged, kept working until his last hours. He was sorting through ideas about the acceleration of the moon's rate of revolution, and had just sent off an article about an ancient lunar eclipse to a journal in Berlin when he died suddenly at home at the age of seventy-four. His passing merited just a few short notices in the British press, several of which talked about his thwarted ambitions. The portrait of a frustrated loner lingered for decades. "Edward Hincks died . . . a scholar of the first rank, a country parson, a disappointed man," declared the *Times Literary Supplement* in a review of his grandson's compilation of his letters in the 1930s. "The church gave him no deanery, in which he might have had leisure and means to pursue his studies . . . The Government bestowed none of its ecclesiastic appointments on him, and gave him no assistance, other than a small pension," Davidson would write, summarizing his struggles. "No university offered him a chair. The British Museum employed him for one year but didn't publish his work."

For decades afterward, it was Rawlinson who was almost universally regarded as the genius who had deciphered both Old Persian and Akkadian cuneiform. The war hero, diplomat, and aristocrat enjoyed the support of the British establishment, from the British Museum's board of trustees to Assyriologists at its elite universities. One scholar coined the phrase "the Rawlinson Method" to describe the decipherment process, omitting any mention of Hincks. In 1901 Robert Francis Harper, a leading Assyriologist at the University of Chicago, pronounced Rawlinson "the Father of Assyriology," stating that Rawlinson "was the first to make the discovery of an inscription of any length and importance," and, dubiously, "the first to translate an Assyrian inscription." The view, repeated by Wallis Budge in *The Rise & Progress of Assyriology*, became orthodoxy in the academic world. Hincks had made contributions, Budge allowed, but this "in no way detracts from the value of Rawlinson's independent decipherment or robs Rawlinson of his priority."

In recent years, though, growing numbers of Assyriologists have challenged that view. Irving Finkel, of the British Museum, calls Rawlinson "a bully" who stomped over Hincks and tried to deny him credit for his accomplishments. "It is Hincks, and he nearly alone, who made it possible to read, once again, the memorials of the world's first civilization," declared Peter T. Daniels in a lecture occasioned by the bicentennial of the Irishman's birth.

Neither the Royal Asiatic Society nor the *Athenaeum* chose sides in the Hincks-Rawlinson dispute, but some closest to the rivalry made it clear where they stood on the issue. William Henry Fox Talbot never wavered from his support for Hincks. Rawlinson had made a monumental leap with his decipherment of Old Persian in the 1840s, but Hincks, Talbot declared, was the "first discoverer" of Akkadian. At almost every step, Talbot believed, Hincks had been first in identifying key aspects of the writing system. Hincks saw early that Akkadian was a Semitic language. He trusted the Bible as a guide to Akkadian history. Already steeped in ancient Egyptian, he wasn't long thrown off by the writing system's ambiguities. For Rawlinson, Hincks's recognition by those closest to the rivalry— first Layard, then Talbot—must have been both irritating and humbling.

The debate over who was first has sometimes distracted from the grandeur of what A. H. Sayce called "the archaeological romance of the nineteenth century," and what Samuel Noah Kramer termed one of the most "eloquent and magnificent achievements of nineteenth-century scholarship and humanism." In 1905, Sayce ranked the cracking of cuneiform above even Champollion's and Young's decipherment of hieroglyphs. "[T]he very names of the Assyrian Kings and of the gods they worshipped had been lost and forgotten; and the characters themselves were but conventional groups of wedges, not pictures of objects and ideas like the hieroglyphics of Egypt," Sayce declared. Thanks to Rawlinson and Hincks, and to a lesser extent Oppert and Talbot, "the ancient East has risen from the dead, with its politics and its wars, its law and its trade, its art, its industries, and its science." Sayce ended with an homage to Georg Grotefend, the German scholar who had begun the entire process by speculating that Sassanian inscriptions below Darius's tomb at Naqsh-e Rustam matched Old Persian texts at nearby Persepolis. "And this revelation of a new world, this resurrection of a dead past," Sayce wrote, "had started from a successful guess."

EPILOGUE

The thuds of helicopter-fired missiles sounded in the distance as we drove south along the Tigris River in northern Iraq. It was mid-March 2017, and the last three thousand fighters of the Islamic State were entrenched in the medieval warrens of Mosul, apparently determined to fight to the death. We passed checkpoints manned by the Hashd-al-Shaabi, or Popular Mobilization Forces, the Shia militia fighting the radical Islamists alongside Kurdish troops and the Iraqi Army. Huge, colorful banners depicting Imam Ali, the martyred son-in-law of the Prophet Muhammad, and Ali's murdered son, Imam Husayn, fluttered in the wind. After an hour's drive across treeless plains, we reached a police hut marking the entrance to the archaeological mound of Nimrud.

Two years earlier, in the spring of 2015, militants bearing sledgehammers had arrived in trucks, a policeman told us, intent on destroying all traces of the pre-Islamic culture that had thrived in Northern Mesopotamia for more than a thousand years. "Since Allah commanded us to shatter and destroy these statues, idols, and remains, it is easy for us to obey," one Islamic State leader had explained in a propaganda video. The officer escorted me and my guide, Layla Salih, a young government archaeologist on a fact-finding mission, across the mound to the Northwest Palace, built around 850 BCE. Tarpaulins on the ground covered shards of bas-reliefs that the Islamists had smashed. Many Iraqis had aptly come to refer to the group as Da'ish—"the ones who crush something underfoot." A few fragments—including a bearded Assyrian god carrying a pinecone, a symbol of spiritual enlightenment—still clung to the palace walls. In the distance loomed the remains of Nimrud's 2,900-year-old Great Ziggurat, or supreme temple, dedicated to the war god Ninurta, the patron deity of the city. The militants had bulldozed it from a 140-foot-high stepped pyramid into a thirty-foot stump.

It was a terrible reminder of the fragility of human knowledge, and of the myriad destructive forces—decay, natural disasters, and especially human intolerance—that threaten to extinguish it. Between 2012 and 2019, Islamic State fanatics carried out attacks on Sufi tombs and shrines in Libya and Mali; burned seven-hundred-year-old manuscripts about art and science in Timbuktu; torched a library in Tripoli; smashed winged bulls and other treasures at the Mosul Cultural Museum here in Iraq; and destroyed ancient Roman monuments and a theater at Palmyra in the Syrian Desert. Ironically, though, the radicals' efforts to wipe out knowledge from eras before our own had inadvertently led to a new discovery.

Salih and I continued north to Nineveh, across the Tigris from the Old City of Mosul. The riverfront skyline was enveloped in smoke. Soon all of the city's landmarks—the thirteenth-century leaning al-Hadba' minaret, the domed Umayyad Mosque, built during the reign of the Caliph Umar bin Al-Khattab in 642 CE—would be obliterated. When we reached the archaeological mound, Iraqi soldiers led us through a tunnel that Islamic State fighters had burrowed in search of antiquities to sell to unscrupulous dealers on the international black market. United Nations experts estimated that the group had earned tens of millions of dollars from the illegal commerce, trading everything from fragments of marble friezes to ancient mosaic *mihrab*, mosque niches indicating the direction of Mecca. We squeezed through passages illuminated only by Salih's iPhone flash-light, sometimes crouching painfully on the earthen floor.

Then, barely visible in the shadows from the pale stream of her light, a gypsum wall inscribed with thousands of tiny characters appeared. Salih had stumbled upon them the previous week while probing the tunnel for statuary. Unseen for two and a half millennia, until the fighters had exposed this secret corridor, the writing—just translated by an Iraqi Assyriologist—confirmed that the palace had been the royal seat of Esarhaddon, who had ascended the throne in 681 BCE after the assassination of his father, Sennacherib. "The palace of Esarhaddon, strong king, king of the world, king of As-syria, governor of Babylon, king of Sumer and Akkad," it began. Additional lines identified him for the first time as the ruler of Kush—a Nile Valley kingdom in what is now northern Sudan and southern Egypt.

I contemplated the signs that emerged from the darkness, rem-nants of the knowledge that the militants had tried to extinguish. Across the river, attack helicopters continued to hover above the Old City, firing missiles into the crowded warrens where the Islamic State was making its last stand. In the bowels of the palace, how-ever, I had no sense of the violence outside. I studied the wedges by the glow of the flashlight, trying to imagine the world in which they had been created. I pictured ornamented chariots and royal lion hunts; worshipers praying at the Temple of Ishtar; women leading cattle through the Gate of Shamash, the sun god, to the banks of the Tigris; and scribes recording for posterity the triumphs of a great Assyrian king. The Islamists had tried to obliterate all traces of that world that remained in Iraq—and had come terrifyingly close to succeeding.

◄─────►

In August 2023, I visited the British Museum to view the treasures that Austen Layard had brought home from the Mesopotamian mounds nearly two centuries ago. The controversy over the appropriation of national patrimony had gathered force over the past several years, and the museum seemed to stand at the center of nearly every recrimination and negotiation. Most prominently, the Nigerian government was agitating for the return of thousands of pieces of statuary—including sculpted heads and cast plaques—made by artisans in the Kingdom of Benin, now Edo State, beginning in the sixteenth century. British troops destroyed the traditional ruler's palace and stole the "Benin Bronzes" during a violent dispute over trading rights in 1897, at the height of colonial expansion in Africa. The Smithsonian Institution, the Metropolitan Museum of Art, six museums in Germany, and several in France and England had agreed to turn over most of their collections to Nigeria, which planned to install them in the still-unfinished Edo Museum of West Africa Art in Benin City. But Oba Ewuare I, the Kingdom of Benin's hereditary monarch, demanded that he take possession of the statues, paralyzing the hand-over process. The British Museum, which has nine hundred Benin Bronzes in its collection, the world's largest, remained vague about what it planned to return to Nigeria. The British Museum Act of 1963 prohibits the institution from giving away any of its holdings, but pressure has been building on the museum to begin making exceptions as a gesture of goodwill.

The museum and the Greek prime minister, meanwhile, were holding secret talks in luxury hotels, the *New York Times* reported, to bring home to Athens the Elgin Marbles that Thomas Bruce had absconded with in 1812. The two sides were still far apart, with Greece demanding a "loan," effectively in perpetuity, of a 250-foot-long marble frieze that once wrapped around the Parthenon in exchange for a handful of less valuable antiquities. Turkey had gone to the European Court of Human Rights a decade ago demanding the return of the Bodrum Marbles (the litigation was unsuccessful), and Egypt was hankering for the return of the Rosetta Stone, which the dictatorship of Abdel Fattah el-Sisi hoped to display alongside the treasures of Tutankhamen's tomb in a new national museum in Giza. The Iraqi government had begun a similar campaign to repatriate the objects that Layard had taken in the 1840s. An Iraqi-American artist named Michael Rakowitz had proposed in a letter to the British Museum to swap one of his experimental works— a contemporary interpretation of a winged bull made out of tins of date syrup—for a lamassu that had guarded the Nergal Gate at Nineveh. The British Museum ignored the proposal, though it did repatriate Sumerian clay tablets looted from Baghdad during the 2003 US invasion and obtained—inadvertently, the museum claimed—on the black market.

There were strong arguments to be made for returning antiquities to the countries where they had been created. Egypt, Nigeria, and Turkey had hired acclaimed architects and constructed or were building facilities as sophisticated as their Western counterparts, undercutting the claim that poorer countries were incapable of giving masterworks the kind of display and attention they merited. Maintaining that European and American museums were the only safe venues to "protect" these artifacts echoed the patronizing words of Lord Elgin and other colonial archaeologists and diplomats. Still, returning art to places with a history of corruption or violence did bear risks—as the rampage by ISIS in Mosul, Nineveh, and Nimrud had made horrifyingly clear.

◄————►

I locked my bicycle near the British Museum and walked down Great Russell Street, crowded with tourists from around the world on this warm summer day. Weaving around protesters from the Falun Gong religious movement (denounced as an "evil cult" and banned by the Chinese Communist government in 1999), a glazed-almond seller, and selfie portraitists, I crossed the courtyard, pausing for a glance at Sir Richard Westmacott's frieze above the portico celebrating the progress of humanity from the Stone Age. As I passed between Ionic columns and entered the museum, I flashed back to the sketch in the *Illustrated London News* in February 1852 that showed workmen wheeling one of Layard's winged bulls up a ramp on these steps. Depending on perspective, its delivery to the British Museum from the muddy banks of the Tigris had been an incredible feat of logistics, a naked act of thievery, or both.

The Queen Elizabeth II Great Court was abuzz with visitors. At least thirty people clustered around the Rosetta Stone in the main Middle Eastern gallery, drawn by the eternal allure of ancient Egypt. Behind the stele, galleries to the left and right contained what I had come to see: the bas-reliefs and statuary of Nimrud and Nineveh, rescued from their basement purgatory 170 years ago.

A winged lion and a winged bull flanked the doorway leading to the bas-reliefs from Nimrud's Northwest Palace, the first ruin excavated by Layard in the autumn of 1845. Each colossus stood about fifteen feet high. I imagined all the laborers, euphoric as they dragged the massive lamassus down to the Tigris. Scrutinizing the claws, hooves, tails, braided beards, and eyeballess human heads, I contemplated the origin myth that had driven Assyria's kings to re-cast these creatures of chaos as benevolent protectors of their empire. The walls inside the gallery were covered with friezes from the court of the ninth-century BCE king Ashurnasirpal II, who had ushered in the Neo-Assyrian age: beardless eunuchs fanned the monarch on his throne. Cuneiform snaked around rosetted tunics and squeezed between the feathers of an eagle-headed god. Familiar signs jumped out: the determinative for a person ⊤, the three-wedge character that connoted a city or a country ⊀⊀, the name of the king spelled with logograms ⊤ ⊢⊀⊤⊦. I wondered if the thrill of recognition I felt was anything like the excitement Layard and Rawlinson had experienced when the sounds and meanings of the characters suddenly burst forth after 2,500 years of incomprehension.

The next chamber displayed "the siege of Lachish," the giant bas-relief from Sennacherib's Southwest Palace at Nineveh. Helmeted soldiers slung stones, fired arrows, climbed ramps, battered down the walls. Victims lay crushed under horses or tumbled off ramparts to their deaths. Captive men, women, and children trooped dejectedly across the Judean Hills, accompanied by oxcarts piled with their belongings, the heartache of these displaced people, heading toward an unknown fate, reaching across 2,700 years. Lording over the scenes of subjugation and murder was Sennacherib on a magnificent throne. The Babylonian and Medean invaders who had sacked Nineveh in 612 BCE had left their calling card, violently chiseling away the head of the king.

Rawlinson had considered the Lachish bas-relief and other Assyrian sculptures more valuable as historical documents than as works of art. The largely undifferentiated faces, stiff bodies, and two-dimensionality could not compare, he argued, to the elasticity and animation of the Elgin and Lycian marbles. But the lion-hunt bas-reliefs of Ashurbanipal in the adjoining gallery belied Rawlinson's generalization. There, sculptors had captured the physicality of the hunt and the suffering of the animals with a brutal realism and compassion. They had also, it turned out, taken liberties with the truth: Ashurbanipal had slaughtered lions in an arena sealed off by soldiers, but had himself portrayed galloping in a chariot across the plain. This was in keeping with royal tradition. Though some monarchs such as Sargon II met their deaths on the battlefield, his son and many other kings kept a safe distance from danger. Sennacherib claimed in inscriptions at Kuyunjik that he "put on armor," "blew like the onset of a severe storm against the enemy," and "filled the plains with their corpses." In reality, he rarely got near the fighting, showing up only when everything was over to observe the bodies and deportees. The great Assyrian monarchs were as attentive to their image as modern-day politicians. Esarhaddon wrote that his enemies "trembled like reeds in a storm," and that he would sprinkle "the venom of death" over all of them. It was left to an aide-de-camp to bring him down to earth. The assistant wrote the king a gentle reminder not to get too close to the front: "Just as your royal fathers have done, stay in the hills and let your magnates do the fighting."

Layard, Botta, Rassam, and other archaeologist-adventurers had braved the dust and disease of Mesopotamia to retrieve these relics, driven by a hunger to understand the world and to grasp the immensity and longevity of human experience. Then, in a feat of analysis, intuition, and stamina, Rawlinson and Hincks had extracted meaning from the 2,500-year-old signs gouged in clay and carved in stone. Like the Assyrians whom they had devoted their lives to studying, the explorers and scholars had displayed both imperialistic hubris and insatiable curiosity. Their obsessive quest had reached across three millennia, revealing glimpses of a common humanity—the vanity and insecurity of the powerful, the universal thirst for knowledge, the yearning to transcend death. They had conferred onto those distant people a measure of immortality, as well as achieving it for themselves. I cast a final look at the collection and stepped back into the bustle of the Great Court.

ACKNOWLEDGMENTS

Sometimes old books spark new ideas. In my case, it was a passing reference to Austen Henry Layard that I'd made in *The Falcon Thief: A True Tale of Adventure, Treachery, and the Hunt for the Perfect Bird*, published in 2020, that served as the genesis for *The Mesopotamian Riddle*. In the spring of 2022, looking for inspiration, I began reading Layard's memoir, *Nineveh and Its Remains*, and became swept up in his story of archaeological discovery and adventure in the badlands of Northern Mesopotamia. As it happened, I had visited Nimrud and Nineveh five years earlier for *Smithsonian* magazine and immediately felt a visceral connection to his experiences. Further research led me to the decipherment rivalry that dovetailed with Layard's adventures, and the path ahead was laid out: I would write a book about two simultaneous quests, the search for a lost civilization that had been buried in the desert sands for 2,500 years, and the competition to understand the writing that it left behind.

My initial hunt for guidance, though, drew a rebuff from a curator at the British Museum. Scowling at me in his office, he advised me to come back "after you've earned your PhD in Assyriology." He called the decipherment story impenetrable, assured me that I wouldn't be able to find much information about the principal characters' lives, and threatened that he would write a negative critique of my work in the *London Review of Books*. I left his office and reeled down the front steps of the museum feeling demoralized. I almost gave up the project on the spot. Months later, when I emailed him with a couple of cuneiform-related questions, he shot me down again. "Not keen thank you," he answered back. "Had enough."

One good thing did come out of that encounter, however: his recommendation that I speak to Kevin Cathcart, an emeritus professor of Near Eastern languages at University College Dublin and an expert on the life of Edward Hincks. Cathcart invited me to see him in Dublin. We met on the Trinity College campus in September 2022 and spent three hours in conversation at a nearby café. He led me through the principles of Akkadian cuneiform and the ups and downs of Hincks's life, and invited me to stay in touch. For two years, via dozens of emails and Zoom calls, Cathcart demystified Akkadian, put me inside Hincks's head, sketched out the rivalry with Henry Rawlinson, directed me to vital research materials, and vetted my manuscript for errors. Through Cathcart I found my way to Peter T. Daniels, a New Jersey–based independent philologist and contributor to a 1994 collection of essays that Cathcart edited to commemorate the bicentennial of Hincks's birth. The enthusiasm, knowledgeability, and patience of both scholars helped me conquer doubts sowed in that British Museum encounter. I could never have written the book without their guidance.

I spent months researching this book at the British Library between 2022 and 2024. During my first month-long stint in London in August and September 2022, Philip Stoltzfus and Terrie Alafat, close friends for many decades, allowed me to base myself at their home just off Parson's Green while they were in the United States. Each morning I pedaled my Santander bike from their place through Fulham, Hyde Park, and Mayfair, past the British Museum in Bloomsbury, and finally to the British Library at King's Cross. A long dinner at Phil and Terrie's place was a requisite part of my subsequent visits to London, and their enthusiasm for the project convinced me that I was on the right track. Jonathan Clayton, an erstwhile *Times of London* Africa hand whom I've known since my years in Nairobi in the mid-1990s, introduced me to his friend Harry Stourton, who lodged me during further research trips in his town house in Notting Hill. He was always a warm and receptive host.

Others were a great help to me during my stays in London. Nancy Charley and Edward Weech, archivists at the Royal Asiatic Society, helped me sort through the trove of manuscripts, letters, diaries, and other material in the Henry Creswicke Rawlinson collection. I benefited from the work of Dr. Roger Parsons, a long-standing RAS volunteer, whose typed summaries and excerpts of Rawlinson's letters over the decades spared me the pain of having to decipher Rawlinson's often impenetrable scrawl. The staff at the Rare Book Room at the British Library, where I parked myself for many months over those two years, were unfailingly polite and helpful, as were their counterparts at the Royal Geographic Society.

Martin Worthington, associate professor in Middle Eastern studies at Trinity College Dublin, explained the fundamentals of the Sumerian language and writing and how that evolved into Akkadian. Moudhy Al Rashid, a research fellow at University of Oxford's Wolfson College, gave me a crash course in decipherment and the key players before I made my first research trip. Sophus Helle, the Berlin-based translator of the most recent edition of the *Epic of Gilgamesh*, shared his insights with me about Sumerian and Akkadian, and provided me with the introduction to Professor Worthington.

On the home front in Berlin, nobody was more important as a morale booster than Kevin Cote, my Philadelphia-born-and-raised colleague, friend, and bike-riding partner. For two years, during our hourslong rides along Berlin's Havelchaussée and long excursions to Potsdam, he provided advice on everything from book structure to art design, read and critiqued drafts, provided breaks from long days alone in front of the laptop, and stayed the project's number one enthusiast. In the United States, Edward Dolnick, a prolific author who has written authoritative and enjoyable books on everything from Newtonian physics to art forgery to the decipherment of Egyptian hieroglyphs, helped to kick-start this book in early 2022. Dolnick assured me that the big, popular book on Assyrian and Babylonian decipherment was yet to be written and urged me to plunge into the project. Andy McWilliam, one of the protagonists of *The Falcon Thief*, carried out a poll of twenty friends, family members, and booksellers in his hometown of Liverpool, England, and helped me decide on a book cover.

My *Smithsonian* magazine editors, Arik Gabbai and Debra Rosenberg, kept me gainfully employed and connected me to the world as I struggled to bring this book to fruition. My erstwhile *Smithsonian* editor and close friend Kathleen Burke was—as she has been for my last three books—a cheerleader and a bestower of valuable advice on structure and language. I also benefited from the friendship of Viv Walt, Jeff Schaeffer, Scott Johnson, Janet Reitman, Lee Smith, David Van Biema, Geoffrey Gagnon, Alex Laskaris, Alex Woolf, Bob Drogin, Frankie Drogin, Kate Feiffer, Aric Press, Steve Shalowitz, Bobby Worth, Simon Wilson, Nina Winquist, Sonya Laurence Green, Samantha Bolton, Sam Loewenberg, Diane Penneys Edelman, Peter Maass, Alissa Quart, Carl Hoffman, Alex Perry, Todd Anderson, and James Romm. I'm grateful to my mother, Nina Hammer; my stepmother, Arlene Nadel Hammer; and my sister, Emily Hammer, for their love and enthusiasm, and their fine company whenever I passed through New York.

Priscilla Painton, my editor on *The Bad-Ass Librarians of Timbuktu* and *The Falcon Thief*, believed in this book from the start and provided superb big-picture thinking that helped me shape the narrative. The hands-on editor this time was Megan Hogan, whom I first got to know while writing *The Bad-Ass Librarians of Timbuktu* in 2015. From the moment I handed in my thin first draft in mid-2023, she knew exactly what to do to make it work. She helped me deepen characters, raise the stakes, heighten the suspense, and expand the narrative into a story not only of Victorian Age rivalry, but also the rise and collapse of three ancient civilizations. Megan's assistant, Isabel Casares, helped me pull together images to give the book some extra panache; production editor Jonathan Evans oversaw the critical stages once the draft was in; and Jonathan Karp provided sage advice on everything from the title and subtitle to the cover art. I'm indebted as always to my agent, Flip Brophy, and her assistant, Jessica Friedman, who read an early draft and offered some valuable thoughts about how to speed up the pace.

One of the benefits of researching *The Mesopotamian Riddle* was being able to see my eldest son, Max, regularly in London, and our outings in Shoreditch, Peckham, and Covent Garden provided delightful breaks from the claustrophobia of the Rare Book Room. My second son, Nico, began university in Delft in 2023, and our stroll along the canals of Vermeer's city was a much-needed salve when I found myself in a book-writing cul-de-sac. My youngest, Tom, a twelve-year soccer player and die-hard fan of Bayern München, the Yankees, and Jimmy Kimmel, happily provides me with welcome distraction from the grind of the book-writing life. Finally, there's my partner, Cordula Krämer, who has now been through three of these projects. Between a demanding job in early-childhood education and raising a preadolescent son, she has a lot on her plate. But she's been a voice of encouragement and solidarity from the beginning, and my expressions of gratitude and love, I hope, need no decipherment.

NOTES

PROLOGUE: A CONTEST ON NEW BURLINGTON STREET

4 *"surpasses in splendor any city"*: Fahim Ahmed, "The Hanging Gardens of Babylon: One of Seven Wonders of the Ancient World," *The Crown*, Medium, August 10, 2020, https://medium.com/the-crown-writer/the-hanging-gardens-of-babylon-c096be79ac36.

4 *"Today the greatest world city of antiquity"*: Bruce R. McConkie, *The Millennial Messiah: The Second Coming of the Son of Man* (Salt Lake City, UT: Deseret Book, 1982), 423–24.

5 *"The monuments [Layard] has sent home"*: "A Late Letter from an American in London Has the Following Very Interesting Notes in Reference to the British Museum, One of the Most Remarkable Institutions in Existence," *Natchez Courier* 15, no. 71, August 30, 1850.

5 *"what you might get"*: Edward Dolnick, *The Writing of the Gods: The Race to Decode the Rosetta Stone* (New York: Scribner, 2021), 121.

8 *"with shouts of incredulity"*: A. H. Sayce, *The Archaeology of the Cuneiform Inscriptions* (London: Society for Promoting Christian Knowledge, 1908), 22.

8 *"[a] modern decipherer could"*: Charles Wall, quoted in *Dublin University Magazine*, vol. XXXIII, no. CXCVI (April 1849): 427.

8 *"[The] various values capable of being assigned"*: *Dublin University Magazine*, vol. XXXIII, no. CXCVI (April 1849): 426.

8 *"[I]t has now come to a question"*: "Miscellaneous," *The National Era*, July 18, 1857, 113.

9 *"the agent of the registrar of timber"*: Andrew Robinson, *Lost Languages: The Enigma of the World's Undeciphered Scripts* (New York: McGraw-Hill, 2002), 273.

10 *"it must indicate that"*: William Henry Fox Talbot, letter to Edwin Norris, March 17, 1857.

10 "before *the appearance of*": William Henry Fox Talbot in *Journal of the Royal Asiatic Society of Great Britain and Ireland*, Volume 18, 1861.

10 "*Our next meeting is on the 21st*": Edwin Norris, letter to Talbot, March 13, 1857, *The Correspondence of William Henry Fox Talbot*, Fox Talbot Collection, British Library, Document 7374.

11 "*His spontaneous wit*": *The Times*, excerpted in "Death of Dr. Jules Oppert," *Hebrew Standard*, September 8, 1905, 8.

11 "*By affording three independent versions of the same document*": Robert Wagner and Andrew Briggs, *The Penultimate Curiosity: How Science Swims in the Slipstream of Ultimate Questions* (Oxford: Oxford University Press, 2016).

12 "*whose names it was thought*": Norris, letter to Talbot.

CHAPTER ONE: RAWLINSON

14 "*the eye ranged ... across fields*": George Rawlinson, *A Memoir of Major-General Sir Henry Creswicke Rawlinson* (London, Longmans, Green, and Co., 1898), 6.

15 "*grew to be six feet high*": Ibid., 15.

15 "*happy, happy, happy circle*": Henry Rawlinson, "Journey of an Exile," July 6, 1827, Royal Asiatic Society Collection, archival file number IV/03/02.

15 "*the General*": George Rawlinson, *A Memoir of Major-General Sir Henry Creswicke Rawlinson*, 12.

15 "*The riches include hookahs*": William Dalrymple, "The East India Company: The Original Corporate Raiders," *The Guardian*, March 4, 2015, https://www.theguardian.com/world/2015/mar/04/east-india-company-original-corporate-raiders.

15 "*when the EIC captured*": William Dalrymple, *The Anarchy: The East India Company, Corporate Violence, and the Pillage of an Empire* (London: Bloomsbury, 2019), xxxv.

16 "*an intensity of grief*": Rawlinson, "Journey of an Exile."

16 "*laughing and joking*": Ibid.

16 "*When I sit by myself*": Ibid.

17 "*We ... found the man-ropes thrown down for us*": Henry Rawlinson, "Shark & Turtle Story," Personal Adventures, written January 1870–71, Sketches of life from 1833 to 1840, adventures told to boys, bound volume, diary 15 Royal Geographic Society, London. RGS Reference number HCR/15.

17 "*pleasant, good-natured old gentleman*": Rawlinson, "Journey of an Exile."

17 "*He lent them books*": John William Kaye, *The Life and Correspondence of Major-General Sir John Malcolm* (London: Smith, Elder, and Co., 1856), 496.

18 *"Parade at sunrise . . . play billiards"*: Henry Rawlinson quoted in Edmund Richardson, "The Riddle of the Mountain," *Inference* 7, no. 1, May 2022, https://inference-review.com/article/the-riddle-of-the-mountain.

18 *"the most momentous change"*: George Rawlinson, *A Memoir of Major-General Sir Henry Creswicke Rawlinson* (London: Longmans, Green, and Co., 1898), 36.

18 *"A crystal bath . . . occupies the center"*: Rawlinson, *A Memoir of Major-General Sir Henry Creswicke Rawlinson*, 51.

18 *"[all] that he knew was"*: Ibid., 308.

20 *"thrill of satisfaction"*: Ibid., 55.

21 *"[F]ew of these early cities contain signs"*: David Graeber and David Wengrow, *The Dawn of Everything: A New History of Humanity* (New York: Macmillan, 2021).

22 *"leader of law . . . leader of the plow"*: Ira Spar, "The Origins of Writing," in *Heilbrunn Timeline of Art History* (New York: Metropolitan Museum of Art, 2000), https://www.metmuseum.org/toah/hd/wrtg/hd_wrtg.htm.

23 *"Men separated by hundreds of miles"*: H. G. Wells, *The Outline of History: Being a Plain History of Life and Mankind* (New York: The Macmillan Company, 1921), 175.

23 *"I recited my tablet"*: Samuel Noah Kramer, *History Begins at Sumer: Thirty-Nine Firsts in Recorded History* (London: Thames & Hudson, 1956), 43.

CHAPTER TWO: PERSEPOLIS

26 *"I surrendered myself completely"*: Thorkild Hansen, *Arabia Felix: The Danish Expedition 1761–1767* (New York: New York Review of Books, 2017).

27 *"affected with a severe rheum"*: Carsten Niebuhr, *Travels Through Arabia and Other Countries in the East*, trans. Robert Heron, Volume I (Perth, Australia: R. Morison Junior, 1799), 353.

27 *"[his] fever was become doubly violent"*: Ibid., 326.

29 *"Look! A great army is coming"*: Jeremiah 50:41.

29 *"The most famous . . . was built"*: Herodotus, *The Histories*, Book I, Chapter 178, 221–23 Loeb Classical Library (Cambridge, MA: Harvard University Press, 1963).

30 *"second Exodus"*: Lloyd Llewellyn-Jones, *Persians: The Age of the Great Kings* (London: Headline Publishing Group, 2022).

30 *"king of the universe"*: Ibid.

31 *"The wealth of this city eclipsed everything"*: Herodotus quoted in Curtis and Tallis, *Forgotten Empire*, 104.

34 *"second Achilles"*: Ibid.

34 *"All had been mutilated"*: Diodorus Siculus, *Library of History*, Vol. VIII, section 69, trans. C. Bradford Welles, Loeb Classical Library (Cambridge, MA: Harvard University Press, 1963), 317.

34 *"A quantity of torches was collected"*: Diodorus Siculus, *The History of the World*, excerpt in M.M. Austin, *The Hellenistic World from Alexander to the Roman Conquest: A Selection of Ancient Sources in Translation* (Cambridge: Cambridge University Press: 2006), 38.

35 *"In a mountain cleft"*: Mahmud Harvai quoted in Curtis and Tallis, *Forgotten Empire*.

35 *"could not rest until he reached Persepolis"*: Barthold Georg Niebuhr quoted in Lawrence J. Baack, *Undying Curiosity: Carsten Niebuhr and the Royal Danish Expedition to Arabia 1761–1767* (Stuttgart: Franz Steiner Verlag, 2014), 221.

36 *"These Aethiopians wore on their heads"*: Herodotus, *Histories*, Book I: Chapters 178–216, Loeb Classical Library (Cambridge, MA: Harvard University Press, 1920), 45.

36 *"The image of these ruins"*: Barthold Georg Niebuhr quoted in Baack, *Undying Curiosity*, 221.

37 *"This place, without any doubt"*: García de Silva y Figueroa quoted in Maurice Pope, *The Story of Decipherment: From Egyptian Hieroglyphic to Linear B* (London: Thames & Hudson, 1975), 45.

37 *"occupies the entire height of the wall"*: Pietro della Valle quoted in Arthur John Booth, *The Discovery and Decipherment of the Trilingual Cuneiform Inscriptions* (London: Longmans, Green, and Co., 1902), 28.

38 *"the land of infidels"*: Cristelle Baskins, "Writing the Dead: Pietro Della Valle and the Tombs of Shirazi Poets," *Muqamas* 34, no. 1 (October 2017): 197–221.

38 *"In part of this great roome"*: Thomas Herbert quoted in Pope, *The Story of Decipherment*, 46.

38 *"The King, the Sovereign, Prince of all Princes"*: Ibid.

39 *"graffiti"*: Thomas Hyde quoted in Pope, *The Story of Decipherment*, 97.

40 *"These are all broken lines"*: Carsten Niebuhr, *Reisebeschreibung nach Arabien*, 158.

40 *"Those inscriptions on the higher parts"*: Barthold Georg Niebuhr quoted in Baack, *Undying Curiosity*, 221.

41 *"If my servant had stayed fit and well"*: Thorkild Hansen, *Arabia Felix: The Danish Expedition*.

CHAPTER THREE: BEHISTUN

43 *"a species of Asiatic writing"*: G. F. Grotefend, "On the Cuneiform Characters and Particularly the Inscriptions at Persepolis," appendix in A. H. L. Heeren, *Historical Researches into the Politics, Intercourse, and Trade of the Principal Nations of Antiquity*, Volume 2 (Oxford: David Alphonso Talboys, 1833), 313–60.

43 *"the patience, the persistence, the power of combination"*: Robert William Rogers, *A History of Assyria and Babylonia*, Volume 1 (New York: Abingdon Press, 1915), 61.

44 *"It was only reasonable to suppose"*: Henry Rawlinson, *Memoir on the Persian Cuneiform Inscriptions at Behistun*, in *Journal of the Royal Asiatic Society of Great Britain and Ireland*, vol. 10 (London: John W. Parker, West Strand, 1847), 5.

45 *"were not careful to reproduce exactly"*: Rogers, *A History of Assyria and Babylonia*, 67.

46 *"a few Zend [manuscripts] obtained in Persia"*: Rawlinson, *Memoir on the Persian Cuneiform Inscriptions at Behistun*, 8.

48 *"the place of the gods"*: Leo Deuel, ed., *The Treasures of Time: Firsthand Accounts by Famous Archaeologists of Their Work in the Near East* (London: Pan Books, 1964).

49 *"one hundred lance-bearers"*: Diodorus Siculus, cited in A. V. Williams Jackson, "The Great Behistun Rock and Some Results of a Re-Examination of the Old Persian Inscriptions on It," *Journal of the American Oriental Society*, vol. 24 (1903): 77–95.

49 *"the floating intelligence in his circle"*: John Macdonald Kinneir quoted in Booth, *The Discovery and Decipherment of the Trilingual Cuneiform Inscriptions*, 105.

49 *"At no time can [the climb] ever be attempted without great personal risk"*: Ker Porter quoted Ibid., 105.

49 *"the polished and perpendicular rocks"*: Eugène Flandin, *Voyage en Perse* (Paris: Gide et Jules Baudry, Éditeurs, 1851), 451.

50 *"The height of the inscriptions"*: Ibid.

50 *"lizard gymnastics"*: Ibid.

50 *"lump sugar, tea, milk, charcoal and wood"*: Henry Rawlinson papers, Royal Asiatic Society Archive, III/02, Miscellaneous documents.

51 *"The rock was bare, slippery, in places almost precipitous"*: George Rawlinson, *A Memoir of Major-General Sir Henry Creswicke Rawlinson*, 58.

51 *"had been washed down"*: Rawlinson, *A Memoir of Major-General Sir Henry Creswicke Rawlinson*, 146.

51 *"unless there were secret staircases"*: Ibid.

51 *"The interest of the occupation"*: Henry Rawlinson, *Memoir on the Persian Cuneiform Inscription at Behistun*, 14–15.

52 *"immense advantage . . . is obtained"*: Andrew Robinson, *The Last Man Who Knew Everything: Thomas Young, the Anonymous Polymath Who Proved Newton Wrong, Explained How We See, Cured the Sick, and Deciphered the Rosetta Stone, Among Other Feats of Genius* (London: Oneworld Publications, 2006), 155.

53 *"considerable progress"*: Edmund Richardson, "The Riddle of the Mountain," *Interference* 7, no. 1, May 2022.

53 *"I aspire to do for the cuneiform alphabet"*: Richardson, "The Riddle of the Mountain."

54 *"remarkable aptitude for the solution of riddles"*: Obituary of Georg Grotefend, *Journal of the Royal Asiatic Society*, 1853.

54 *"I felt convinced"*: Grotefend, "On the Cuneiform Characters and Particularly the Inscriptions at Persepolis," appendix in Heeren, *Historical Researches into the Politics, Intercourse, and Trade of the Principal Nations of Antiquity*.

54 *"a gem of brilliant simplicity"*: Cyrus H. Gordon, *Forgotten Scripts: Their Ongoing Discovery and Decipherment* (New York: Basic Books, 1982), 54.

54 *"leap of the imagination"*: Author interview with Kevin J. Cathcart, Dublin, September 17, 2022.

56 *"great parent of Indian languages"*: William Jones, quoted in Haruko Momma, *From Philology to English Studies: Language and Culture in the Nineteenth Century* (Cambridge: Cambridge University Press, 2013), 48.

58 *"On my arrival in Persia"*: Rawlinson letter to Henry Harkness, 1838, Royal Asiatic Society Collection, III/02/1.

59 *"If I keep my health"*: Ibid.

59 *"You remember laughing at me"*: Rawlinson letter to his sister, Maria Rawlinson, Royal Asiatic Society Collection, III/02/4.

CHAPTER FOUR: KANDAHAR

61 *"Indian army officers, political agents"*: Peter Hopkirk, *The Great Game: On Secret Service in High Asia* (London: The Folio Society, 2010), 107.

61 *"might be garrisoned there for years"*: Arthur Connolly quoted in Hopkirk, *The Great Game*, 117.

61 *"100,000 disciplined troops"*: George Rawlinson, *A Memoir of Major-General Sir Henry Creswicke Rawlinson.*

62 *"a young man of light make"*: Henry Rawlinson, letter to British officials, November 1, 1837, quoted ibid., 67.

63 *"In the state of public affairs in Persia"*: Henry Rawlinson, letter to Major-General Briggs, Secretary to the Royal Asiatic Society, October 7, 1838, Royal Asiatic Society Collection III/02.

64 *"Away I went on my black Arab [steed]"*: Henry Rawlinson, Personal Adventures, written January 1870-71, Sketches of life from 1833 to 1840, adventures told to boys, bound volume, diary 15 Royal Geographic Society, London. RGS Reference number HCR/15.

65 *"Army destroyed on Retreat from Cabul"*: Henry Rawlinson, diary, Royal Asiatic Society Collection, archive file number IV/07 (04).

65 *"a severe attack of brain fever"*: Henry Rawlinson quoted in Chaim Bermant and Michael Weitzman, *Ebla: An Archaeological Enigma* (London: Weidenfeld & Nicolson, 1979), 84.

65 *"Nothing remained of the papers"*: Unsigned biographical memoir of Henry Rawlinson from an unidentified periodical written in 1877; Royal Asiatic Society Collection, IV/16.

66 *"lamentable accident"*: Unsigned biographical memoir of Henry Rawlinson.

66 *"He was somewhat weary of governing"*: Rawlinson, *A Memoir of Major-General Sir Henry Creswicke Rawlinson*, 139.

CHAPTER FIVE: ON THE MESOPOTAMIAN PLAIN

68 *"From the top of the houses"*: Edward Ledwich Mitford, *A Land March from England to Ceylon Forty Years Ago*, Vol. I (London: W. H. Allen & Co., 1884).

69 *"Desolation meets desolation"*: Austen Henry Layard, *Nineveh and Its Remains: A Narrative of an Expedition to Assyria During the Years 1845, 1846, & 1847* (London: John Murray, 1867), 5.

69 *"made a deeper impression upon me"*: Layard, *Nineveh and Its Remains*, 5.

69 *"My imagination became so much excited"*: Austen Henry Layard, *Autobiography and Letters from His Childhood Until His Appointment as H.M. Ambassador at Madrid*, Vol. I (London: John Murray, 1903), 16.

70 *"hatred and contempt"*: Layard, *Autobiography and Letters from His Childhood*, 15.

70 *"having unsettled my mind"*: Ibid., 56.

71 *"that I . . . should make a very bad lawyer"*: Ibid., 98.

71 *"to realise the dreams that had haunted me"*: Ibid., 102.

71 *"the cupidity of the wild tribes"*: Ibid., 107.

72 *"Narratives of voyages and travels"*: Nandini Das and Tim Young, eds., *Cambridge History of Travel Writing* (Cambridge: Cambridge University Press, 2019), 110.

72 *"Keep moving!"*: Samuel Taylor Coleridge quoted in *Cambridge History of Travel Writing*, 105.

72 *"the stale civilization of Europe"*: Nandini Das and Tim Young, eds., *Cambridge History of Travel Writing*, 111.

73 *"I was now independent"*: Layard, *Autobiography and Letters from His Childhood*, 108–109.

73 *"marchlord of the horizons"*: Charles Swallow, *The Sick Man of Europe: Ottoman Empire to Turkish Republic, 1789–1923* (London & Tonbridge: Ernest Benn, 1973), 10.

74 *"ferocious conqueror has degenerated into"*: Swallow, *The Sick Man of Europe*, 5.

74 *"On a low round tower"*: Mitford, *A Land March from England to Ceylon*, 4.

74 *"long tufts of hair"*: Layard, *Autobiography and Letters from His Childhood*, 128.

75 *"a mean and poverty-stricken appearance"*: Ibid., 309.

75 *"[It] is enough to breed a pestilence"*: Mitford, *A Land March from England to Ceylon*, 280.

76 *"is alive with bats"*: Ibid., 281.

76 *"one of the most remarkable facts"*: Layard, *Nineveh and Its Remains*, xix.

76 *"A deep mystery hangs over Assyria"*: Ibid., 2.

77 *"the most renowned of all women"*: Diodorus Siculus quoted in Eckart Frahm, *Assyria: The Rise and Fall of the World's First Empire* (New York: Basic Books, 2023), 399.

77 *"The king . . . carried the Israelites"*: 2 Kings 17:6.

78 *"scrapings from the pot"*: *The Epic of Gilgamesh* quoted in Frahm, *Assyria: The Rise and Fall of the World's First Empire*.

79 *"They ate dogs and mongooses"*: Ashurbanipal quoted in Frahm, *Assyria*.

80 *"must surely have among the worst"*: Paul Kriwaczek quoted in Joshua Mark, "Assyria," *World History Encyclopedia*, April 10, 2018, https://www.worldhistory.org/assyria/.

80 *"made a point of lining their roads"*: Simon Anglim quoted ibid.

81 *"utterly uncouth royal fortresses"*: Jacob Burckhardt, *Reflections on History*, cited in Eckart Frahm, ed., *A Companion to Assyria* (Hoboken, NJ: Wiley & Sons, 2017), 3.

81 *"the bloody city, all full of lies"*: Nahum 3:1.

NOTES 329

81 "*will stretch out his hand against the north*": Zephaniah 2:13.

81 "*large unoccupied fortress*": Xenophon, *The Anabasis, or Expedition of Cyrus, and the Memorabilia of Socrates*, translated by the Reverend J. S. Watson with a geographical commentary by W. F. Ainsworth (New York: Harper and Brothers, 1863), Book III, 96.

82 "*is so completely destroyed*": William Tookes, *Lucian of Samosta: from the Greek, with Comments and illustrations of Wieland and others, in two volumes (Volume I)* (London: Longman Hurst, Reese, Orme, and Brown, 1820).

82 "*irregular oval*": James Felix Jones, *Memoirs of Baghdad, Kurdistan, and Turkish Arabia, 1857: Selections from the Records of the Bombay Government*, No. XLIII, Archive Editions 1998.

82 "*an immense bas-relief, representing men*": Claudius James Rich, *Narrative of a Residence in Koordistan, and on the Site of Ancient Nineveh; with Journal of a Voyage Down the Tigris to Bagdad, and an Account of a Visit to Shirauz and Persepolis*, Vol. 2 (London: James Duncan, 1836), 39.

83 "*sculpted upon the face of the rock*": Henry Rawlinson, "Notes on a March from Zohab, at the Foot of Zagros, along the Mountains to Khuzistan (Susiana), and from Thence Through the Province of Luristan to Kirmanshah, in the Year 1836," *Journal of the Royal Geographic Society of London*, Vol. 9 (1839), 31.

84 "*potent magician*": Henry Rawlinson, "Notes on a Journey from Tabriz, Through Persian Kurdistan to the Ruins of Takhti-Soleiman, and from Thence by Zenjan and Tarom, to Gilan, in October and November 1838," *Journal of the Royal Geographic Society of London*, Vol. 10 (1840), 21.

84 "*The view from the summit of the pass*": Ibid., 22.

84 "*treachery and murder*": Austen Henry Layard, *Early Adventures in Persia, Susiana, and Babylonia, Including a Residence among the Bakhtiyari and Other Wild Tribes before the Discovery of Nineveh*, Volume II (London: John Murray, 1887), 81.

85 "*That man! Why, if I could catch him*": Roger Sandall, "Layard of Nineveh: The Amazing Dumb Luck of a Victorian Romantic Gone Native," *The American Interest* 5, no. 6 (July 1, 2010), https://www.the-american-interest.com/2010/07/01/layard-of-nineveh/.

85 "*happier under a black Bakhtiari tent*": Layard, letter to Benjamin Austen, ibid.

85 "*I scarcely know which way to turn*": Austen Layard, letter quoted in Gordon Waterfield, *Layard of Nineveh* (London: John Murray, 1963), 86.

86 "*a sober citizen*": Benjamin Austen, letter quoted in Gordon Waterfield, *Layard of Nineveh*, 86.

86 "*M. Botta was a delightful companion*": Layard, *Early Adventures in Persia, Susiana, and Babylonia*, 369.

87 "*ruined his health*": Ibid.

CHAPTER SIX: THE PALACE ON THE TIGRIS

88 "*The pendant branches of the graceful date tree*": William Kennett Loftus, *Travels and Researches in Chaldea and Susiana: With an Account of Excavations at Warka, the "Erech" of Nimrod, and Shush, "Sushan the Palace" of Esther, in 1849–52* (London: James Nisbet and Co., 1857), 5.

88 "*to just 220 yards across*": Mitford, *A Land March from England to Ceylon*, 360.

88 "*He must be . . . void of poetry and sentiment*": William Kennett Loftus, *Travels and Researches in Chaldea and Susiana*, 5.

89 "*The Residency is a magnificent house*": Henry James Ross, letter to his sister Mary Ross, *Letters from the East 1837–1857*, ed. Janet Ross (London: J. M. Dent & Co., 1902), 34.

89 "*Asiatic prince*": Madame Helfer quoted in J. P. Parry, "Steam Power and British Influence in Baghdad, 1820–1860," *The Historical Journal* 56, no. 1 (2013): 145–73.

89 "*The [dining] service was performed*": Austen Henry Layard, *Autobiography and Letters from His Childhood Until His Appointment as H.M. Ambassador at Madrid*, Volume II (London: John Murray, 1903), 331.

90 "*Arabs, Persians, Turks, Jews*": Ross, letter to his sister Mary from January 26, 1845, *Letters from the East*, 32.

90 "*The streets presented a shocking spectacle*": William Kennett Loftus, *Travels and Researches in Chaldea and Susiana*, 8.

90 "*Masses of fat hung upon him*": Layard, *Autobiography and Letters from His Childhood*, Volume 1 (London: John Murray, 1903), 348.

90 "*bridge of boats*": Layard, *Autobiography and Letters from His Childhood*, Volume II, 343.

91 "*a new prophet*": Parry, "Steam Power and British Influence in Baghdad," 158.

91 "*These ruins are supposed to be*": Henry Rawlinson, *Personal Adventures*, written January 1870–71, "Sketches of life from 1833 to 1840, adventures told to boys," bound volume, diary 15 Royal Geographic Society, London. RGS Reference number HCR/15.

92 "*pig sticking*": Ross, *Letters from the East*, 34.

92 "*on the sick list*": Ibid., 37.

92 "*The interest in the inscriptions*": Henry Rawlinson, *The Persian Cuneiform Inscriptions at Behistun, decyphered and translated, with a memoir on Persian*

cuneiform inscriptions in general, and on that of Behistun in particular, Journal of the Royal Asiatic Society, 4.

92 *"a gem"*: Ibid., 15.

93 *"It would of course have tilted over"*: Rawlinson quoted in *The Treasures of Time*, ed. Leo Deuel, 126.

94 *"almost separated the overhanging mass"*: Ibid., 126–30.

95 *"wholesome dread of British authority"*: Parry, "Steam Power and British Influence," 167.

95 *"the action of a water-wheel"*: George Rawlinson, *A Memoir of Major-General Sir Henry Creswicke Rawlinson*, 148.

95 *"When a sheep or a donkey passe[d]"*: Ross, letter from January 26, 1845, *Letters from the East*, 37.

96 *"felt his right hand"*: Ibid., 38.

96 *"gave strict orders to the household"*: George Rawlinson, *A Memoir of Major-General Sir Henry Creswicke Rawlinson*, 149.

97 *"He certainly did now & then"*: Henry Rawlinson, *Personal Adventures*, written January 1870–71, "Sketches of life from 1833 to 1840, adventures told to boys," bound volume, diary 15 Royal Geographic Society, London. RGS Reference number HCR/15.

97 *"These tablets have been a sealed letter"*: Henry Rawlinson, *The Persian Cuneiform Inscriptions at Behistun, decyphered and translated, with a memoir on Persian cuneiform inscriptions in general, and on that of Behistun in particular*, 52.

98 *"The context fully supports"*: Henry Rawlinson, "Notes on the Text," ibid., xliii.

98 *"The seven . . . found the king"*: Lloyd Llewellyn-Jones and James Robson, *Ctesias's "History of Persia": Tales of the Orient* (New York: Routledge Classical Translations, 2010), 180.

99 *"a rich mélange of untruths"*: Lloyd Llewellyn-Jones, *Persians: The Age of Great Kings*.

99 *"Cambyses, unable to endure his misfortunes"*: Rawlinson, *The Persian Cuneiform Inscriptions at Behistun, decyphered and translated, with a memoir on Persian cuneiform inscriptions in general, and on that of Behistun in particular*, Royal Asiatic Society, xxviii.

99 *"water destroyed them"*: Rawlinson, *Memoir on the Persian Cuneiform Inscriptions at Behistun*, 30.

99 *"I cut off his nose and ears"*: Ibid., xxxii.

100 *"This Gomátes, the Magian, was an impostor"*: Ibid., xxxvii.

100 *"If thou shalt dishonor them"*: Ibid.

100 *"all that remains of"*: Ibid., 18.

101 *"It is my firm belief"*: Ibid., 52.

CHAPTER SEVEN: BOTTA'S FIND

102 *"I have applied a few leeches"*: Austen Layard, letter quoted in Waterfield, *Layard of Nineveh*, 91.

102 *"asked me roughly for the despatches"*: Layard, *Autobiography and Letters from His Childhood*, Volume II, 16.

102 *"His earnest gray eyes"*: Ibid., 19.

103 *"extent and causes of the insurrection"*: Austen Layard, letter of April 30, 1844, Papers, vol. XLVI, Correspondence 1844–June 1846, British Library Manuscript Collection.

103 *"the most philosophic mind"*: William Flavelle Monypenny, *The Life of Benjamin Disraeli, Earl of Beaconsfield*, Vol. I, 1804–1837 (London: John Murray, 1910), 235.

104 *"The only information"*: Paul-Émile Botta, *Monuments de Ninive: Ouvrage publié par ordre de gouvernement sous les auspices de M. Le Ministre de L'Intérieur, Tome II [Monuments of Nineveh: Public works by the order of the government under the authority of the Minister of the Interior, Volume II]* (Paris: Imprimerie Nationale, 1849).

104 *"quite befuddled with opium"*: Henry Rawlinson, letter to Edwin Norris, July 13, 1852, Royal Asiatic Society Collection III/07/14.

104 *"We are great friends"*: Henry Ross quoted in Nora Kubie, *Road to Nineveh: The Adventures and Excavations of Sir Austen Henry Layard* (London: Cassell, 1965), 20.

105 *"the systematic study of antiquities"*: Grahame Clarke quoted in John Romer, *The History of Archaeology* (New York: Checkmark Books, 2001), 110.

105 *"Stretched out full-length on the floor was a skeleton"*: C. W. Ceram, *Gods, Graves, and Scholars: The Story of Archaeology* (New York: Random House, 1994), 5.

107 *"Unfortunately, it was so defaced"*: Paul-Émile Botta to Julius von Mohl, *Le Journal Asiatic, 1843–44*, 6–7.

107 *"His right hand grasps"*: Ibid., 32–33.

107 "Nineveh . . . est retrouvé": Paul-Émile Botta quoted in Karl Moore and David Charles Lewis, *The Origins of Globalization* (New York: Routledge, 2009), 13.

108 *"The more I look"*: Correspondence of Austen Henry Layard with Paul-Émile Botta, French archaeologist, traveller, and decipherer, September 20, 1843,

Supplementary Layard Papers, Volume XII (ff. 170) 1. ff.1–64 v., British Library Manuscript Collection, British Museum Ad MS 58161, 1838–1901.

108 "*I quite agree with you*": Ibid., letter dated February 18, 1845.

109 "*recommended its diplomatic representatives*": Adolf Theodor F. Michaelis, *Ancient Marbles in Great Britain*, translated from the German by C. A. M. Fennell (Cambridge: Cambridge University Press, 1882), 183.

110 "*which was more jealously guarded*": Austen Layard, *Nineveh and Its Remains*, 11.

110 "*Her Majesty's vessel* Siren *to Malta*": Stanley Lane-Poole, *The Life of the Right Honourable Stratford Canning, Viscount Stratford de Redcliffe, from His Memoirs and Private and Official Papers*, Volume II (London: Longmans, Green, and Co., 1888), 151.

110 "*It was true that M. Botta*": Layard, *Nineveh and Its Remains*, 9.

111 "*fortress*": Paul-Émile Botta, *Letters on the Discoveries at Nineveh*, trans. C. Tobin (London: Longman, Brown, Green, and Longmans, 1850).

111 "*in a very disordered and dangerous state*": Austen Henry Layard, *Autobiography and Letters from His Childhood*, Volume I, 153.

111 "*I have every reason to hope*": Ibid., 157.

CHAPTER EIGHT: THE MOUND

112 "*had one eye and one ear*": Layard, *Nineveh and Its Remains*, 12.

112 "*a state of terror and despair*": Ibid., 13.

113 "*Out of [the] land went Asshur*": Genesis 10:11.

113 "*with halls of cedar, cypress*": "Stones of Assyria: Ancient Spirits from the Palace of Ashurnasirpal II," brochure accompanying the 75th anniversary exhibition at Williams College, March 17, 2001, 2.

113 "*For ten days I feasted*": Ashurnasirpal II quoted in the Metropolitan Museum of Art online catalogue, "Human-headed winged lion (lamassu), Assyrian, ca. 883–859 BCE."

113 "*Streams of water as the stars*": Ashurnasirpal II quoted in Diodorus Siculus quoted in Eckart Frahm, *The Rise and Fall of the World's First Empire*.

113 "*the King of the Persians*": Xenophon, *The Anabasis, or Expedition of Cyrus, and the Memorabilia of Socrates*, translated by the Reverend J. S. Watson with a geographical commentary by W. F. Ainsworth (New York: Harper and Brothers, 1863), Book III, 96.

113 "*The breadth of its wall was five and twenty feet*": Ibid., 95.

114 "*as though for one of my usual*": Henry James Ross, *Letters from the East*, x.

114 "*Hopes, long cherished*": Layard, *Nineveh and Its Remains*, 15.

114 "*[t]he eye wandered over a parched*": Ibid., 15–16.

114 *"After pursuing some hares"*: Ross, *Letters from the East*, xi.

115 *"The slabs, which had been nearly reduced"*: Layard, *Nineveh and Its Remains*, 16–17.

115 *"These pieces no doubt formed"*: Ross, *Letters from the East*, xi.

116 *"a simple fillet round the temples"*: Layard, *Nineveh and Its Remains*, 29.

116 *"I have been employed"*: Layard, *Autobiography and Letters from His Childhood*, Volume I, 160.

117 *"The inscriptions . . . are exceedingly numerous"*: Layard to his mother, ibid., 162.

117 *"The great gulf which separates"*: Layard to *Malta Times* quoted in Mogens Trolle Larsen, *The Conquest of Assyria: Excavations in an Antique Land* (New York and London: Routledge, 1996), 176.

117 *"Layard is making very important discoveries"*: Stratford Canning letter, January 3, 1846, quoted in Stanley Lane-Poole, *The Life of Stratford Canning*, Volume 2 (London: Longmans, Green, & Co. 1888), 148.

117 *"Major Rawlinson . . . offers to send"*: Stratford Canning, letter, ibid., 149.

118 *"sun-dried bricks made of clay"*: Henry Ross, *Letters from the East*, xi.

118 *"a few rude chairs"*: Ibid.

118 *"I was much troubled"*: Austen Layard, *Nineveh and Its Remains*, 84.

119 *"They pulled their horses up sharp"*: Ross, *Letters from the East*, xi.

119 *"[T]he wicked Pasha of Mosul"*: Ibid., xii.

119 *"was unsuccessful owing to the dread"*: Ibid.

120 *"Botta's success at Nineveh"*: Stratford Canning letter, April 18, 1846, quoted in Stanley Lane-Poole, *The Life of Stratford Canning*.

120 *"If the excavation keeps its promise"*: Ibid.

120 *"Every day brings fresh discoveries"*: Austen Henry Layard, *Autobiography and Letters from His Childhood*, Volume I, 162.

120 *"hiring skins for two rafts"*: Austen Layard, "Excavation Accompts," Layard Papers, Volume CXXVIII, British Library Manuscript Collection, British Museum Ad MS 39058.

121 *"high conical tiara"*: Austen Layard, *Nineveh and Its Remains: With an Account of a Visit to the Chaldean Christians of Kurdistan, and the Yesidis, or Devil Worshippers; and an Enquiry into the Manners and Arts of the Ancient Assyrians* (Paris: A. & W. Gagliani and Co., 1850), 25.

121 *"infidel giant"*: Ibid., 30.

121 *"And it came to pass"*: 2 Kings 19:37, King James Version.

122 *"sacred tree"*: Layard, *Nineveh and Its Remains*, 43.

122 *"the most magnificent specimens"*: Ibid., 28.

122 *"They could find no better type"*: Ibid.

122 *"Nothing so beautiful as these lions"*: Layard, *Autobiography and Letters from His Childhood*, 166.

123 *"There is also a great* mouvement*"*: Ibid., 167.

123 *"Shall the dogs occupy"*: Ibid., 169.

124 *"The Prophet and his faith"*: Ibid.

124 *"notorious fanatic"*: Ibid., 170.

125 *"I have paid but little attention"*: Henry Rawlinson to Austen Layard, May 28, 1845, Layard correspondence, 1844–June 1846, British Library Manuscript Collection, 38976.

125 *"My own idea . . . is that"*: Ibid.

126 *"Is [the language] Chaldaean?"*: Layard, *Autobiography and Letters from His Childhood*, 167.

126 *"Layard was a man excellently fitted"*: George Rawlinson, *A Memoir of Major-General Sir Henry Creswicke Rawlinson*, 151.

127 *"drudgery"*: Henry Rawlinson to Edwin Norris, May 28, 1847, Royal Asiatic Society Collection III/04/13.

127 *"the histories of the early Assyrians"*: Henry Rawlinson, letter to Royal Asiatic Society, November 27, 1845, Royal Asiatic Society archive III/04.1.

127 *"Though its proportions are colossal"*: Vivant Denon, *Travels in Upper and Lower Egypt: In Company with Several Divisions of the French Army, During the Campaigns of General Bonaparte in that Country, and Published Under His Immediate Patronage*, Volume 1 (London: T. N. Longman and O. Rees, 1803), 270.

129 *"firsts"*: Samuel Noah Kramer, *History Begins at Sumer: Thirty-Nine Firsts in Man's Recorded History*, xx.

129 *"I had long wished"*: Austen Layard to his mother in Layard, *Autobiography and Letters from His Childhood*; Mogens Trolle Larsen, *The Conquest of Assyria*, 86.

CHAPTER NINE: HINCKS

131 *"[I]n the inscriptions of Darius"*: Edward Hincks, "Some Passages of the Life of King Darius, the Son of Hystaspes, by Himself," review of H. C. Rawlinson, *The Persian Cuneiform Inscription at Behistun, Deciphered and Translated, with a Memoir* (London, 1846), *Dublin University Magazine* 29, no. 169 (January 1847): 14–27.

133 *"It is evident that Major R."*: George Cecil Renouard to Hincks, December 18, 1846, in E. F. Davidson, *Edward Hincks: A Selection from His Correspondence, with a Memoir* (London: Oxford University Press, Humphrey Milford, 1933), 139.

133 *"vast labour"*: Edward Hincks, "Some Passages of the Life of King Darius, the Son of Hystaspes, by Himself," 14.

133 *"[T]he grossness of many of [his] mistakes"*: Hincks, "Some Passages of the Life of King Darius," 14.

134 *"Major Rawlinson calls this figure"*: Ibid.

135 *"Within this door let no foul sight"*: E. F. Davidson, *Edward Hincks: A Selection from His Correspondence*, 6.

135 *"It did me considerable injury"*: Davidson, *Edward Hincks*, 8.

135 *"The work . . . is not worth rescuing"*: Ibid.

135 *"not able to suffer fools gladly"*: Author interview with Kevin J. Cathcart in Dublin, September 17, 2022.

136 *"Even in early life"*: Davidson, *Edward Hincks: A Selection from His Correspondence*, 18.

136 *"each church accused the other"*: Author interview with Kevin J. Cathcart.

136 *"our correspondence appears to have"*: William Hincks to Thomas Dix Hincks, April 22, 1822, courtesy of Kevin J. Cathcart.

137 *"a genuine call to the work"*: Davidson, *Edward Hincks: A Selection from His Correspondence*, 8.

137 *"does not lend itself to detection"*: "Mr. Chenevix on a New Method, " *Quarterly Journal of Science, Literature and the Arts*, (1821), Volume 10, 96.

139 *"proud trophy . . . not plundered"*: General Sir Tomkyns Hilgrove Turner, "An Account of the Rosetta Stone," Read June 8, 1810, *Archaeologia, or Miscellaneous Tracts Relating to Antiquity*, Society of Antiquaries of London, Volume 16 (1812): 214.

139 *"There is hardly the space of an awl"*: Edward Dolnick, *The Writing of the Gods: The Race to Decode the Rosetta Stone* (New York: Scribner, 2021), 4.

140 *"Rather than burrow into the ground"*: Dolnick, *The Writing of the Gods*, 133.

140 *because among birds*: Andrew Robinson, *The Last Man Who Knew Everything*, 145.

140 *"puerile collection of conceits"*: Ibid., 144.

140 *"The protection of Osiris"*: Ibid., 146.

143 *"Je tiens l'affaire!"*: Edmund Richardson, "The Riddle of the Mountain," *Interference* 7, no. 1, May 2022.

145 *"probably a grievous disappointment"*: Davidson, *Edward Hincks: A Selection from His Correspondence*, 12.

146 *"Mark the perfect man"*: Extract from "Remembrance of a Faithful Pastor: A Sermon Preached in the Parish Church of Killyleagh, Co. Down on Sunday, the 9th December, 1866, being the 2nd Sunday of Advent, after the Decease of Edward Hincks, DD, Ex FTCD, Rector of Killyleagh, by the Venerable Thomas Hincks" (Dublin, 1866), courtesy of Kevin J. Cathcart.

146 *"kindness, gentleness, and humility"*: Ibid.

147 *"the ill will of influential persons"*: Kevin J. Cathcart, "Edward Hincks (1792–1866): A Biographical Essay," in *The Edward Hincks Bicentenary Lectures*, ed. Kevin J. Cathcart (Dublin: Department of Near Eastern Languages, University College Dublin, 1994), 5.

147 *"who had brought into the Court-house"*: Davidson, *Edward Hincks: A Selection from His Correspondence with a Memoir*, 31.

147 *"to our Romish fellow-subjects"*: Robert W. Kyle quoted ibid., 31.

148 *"No problem in decipherment"*: A. H. Sayce, *The Archaeology of the Cuneiform Inscriptions* (London: Society for Promoting Christian Knowledge, 1908), 31.

148 *"the scaffolding and framework"*: John Ray, "Edward Hincks and the Progress of Egyptology," in *The Edward Hincks Bicentenary Lectures*, ed. Cathcart, 59.

149 *"I have for many years applied"*: Edward Hincks in Davidson, *Edward Hincks*, 130.

CHAPTER TEN: THE AKKADIAN CONUNDRUM

153 *"a coarse alabaster"*: Layard, *Nineveh and Its Remains, volume 2 of 2, With an Account of a Visit to the Chaldaean Christians Kurdistan, and the Yezidis, or Devil-Worshipers, And . . . of the Ancient Assyrians*, 254.

155 *"The writing is so minute"*: Austen Layard, *Discoveries among the Ruins of Nineveh and Babylon, with Travels in Armenia, Kurdistan and the Desert* (London: G. P. Putnam, 1853), 296.

157 *"As to my Babylonian and Assyrian deciphering"*: Hincks, letter to *Literary Gazette*, June 15, 1846, in *The Correspondence of Edward Hincks*, Volume I (1818–1849), ed. Kevin J. Cathcart (Chicago: University of Chicago Press, 2007), 139.

158 *"I am delighted to learn"*: Edwin Norris, letter to Hincks, in *The Correspondence of Edward Hincks*, 144.

159 *"I am very much rejoiced"*: George Renouard, letter to Hincks, December 18, 1846, in Davidson, *Edward Hincks: A Selection from His Correspondence*, 139.

CHAPTER ELEVEN: THE BLACK OBELISK

160 *"I am ... working desultorily"*: Henry Rawlinson to Austen Layard, July 22, 1846, Layard papers, Volume XLVII, correspondence July 1846–47, British Library Manuscript Collection, British Museum Additional Manuscripts 38977.

161 *"I regret to say that my leave"*: Henry Rawlinson to Austen Layard, July 8, 1846, ibid.

162 *"n squared where the n is the number"*: Andrew Robinson, *The Last Man Who Knew Everything: Thomas Young*, 55.

162 *"I have been about twenty days occupied"*: Austen Layard to Mrs. Benjamin Austen, July 27, 1846, in Layard, *Autobiography and Letters from His Childhood*, 173.

162 *"which in England would scarcely be used"*: Ibid.

162 *"a load of from thirty to forty tons"*: Henry James Ross, letter to his sister Mary, *Letters from the East*, 86.

163 *"We are anxiously looking out"*: Rawlinson to Layard, July 22, 1846, Layard papers.

163 *"are certainly very fine"*: Henry Rawlinson to Austen Layard, August 5, 1846, ibid.

163 *"unfolding the history, theology"*: Henry Rawlinson to Layard, August 19, 1846, ibid.

164 *"around & about among the crumbling walls"*: Henry Rawlinson, *Personal Adventures*, written January 1870–71, "Sketches of life from 1833 to 1840, adventures told to boys," bound volume, diary 15 Royal Geographic Society, London. RGS Reference number HCR/15.

164 *"About 5000 souls ... have been carried off"*: Henry Rawlinson to Edwin Norris, November 27, 1845, Royal Asiatic Society collection file III/04/6.

165 *"[A] certain dr. Hinkes"*: Rawlinson, letter to Edwin Norris, Royal Asiatic Society collection file III/04/6.

165 *"How Dr. Hinkes succeeded"*: Mogens Trolle Larsen, *The Conquest of Assyria: Excavations in an Antique Land* (London and New York: Routledge, 1996), 201.

165 *"[S]end down to my care"*: Rawlinson to Layard, December 23, 1846, Layard papers, Volume XLVII, Correspondence July 1846–47.

166 *"Few things continue to puzzle me"*: Rawlinson to Layard, December 23, 1846, ibid.

166 *"fairly puzzled"*: Ibid.

167   *"The language . . . has to be reconstructed"*: Henry Rawlinson to Austen Layard, June 23, 1846, British Library Manuscript Collection, ADD MS 38976, 395–400.

167   *"The king was twice represented"*: Austen Layard, *Nineveh and Its Remains*, Volume I, 245.

167   *"The monument . . . is the most noble trophy"*: Rawlinson quoted in Robert Wagner and Andrew Briggs, *The Penultimate Curiosity: How Science Swims in the Slipstream of Ultimate Questions* (Oxford: Oxford University Press, 2016).

170   *"I will get long ladders"*: Henry Rawlinson to Edwin Norris, Royal Asiatic Society Collection, December 7, 1846, III/03/8.

170   *"ladders, planks, strong ropes, nails"*: George Rawlinson, *A Memoir of Major-General Sir Henry Creswicke Rawlinson*, 155.

170   *"The mass of the rock in question"*: Henry Rawlinson, "Notes on Some Paper Casts of Cuneiform Inscriptions Upon the Sculptured Rock at Behistun Exhibited to the Society of Antiquaries," *Archaeologia* 34, no. 1 (1851): 73–76, https://www.cambridge.org/core/journals/archaeologia/article /abs/xnotes-on-some-paper-casts-of-cuneiform-inscriptions-upon-the -sculptured-rock-at-behistun-exhibited-to-the-society-of-antiquaries -by-lieutcol-h-rawlinson-cb-frs-and-dcl/BFBB86659323FAA12133E 3601A15FF71.

170   *"A wild Kurdish boy"*: Henry Rawlinson memoir in *Archaeologia* magazine, 1850, excerpted in George Rawlinson, *A Memoir of Major-General Sir Henry Creswicke Rawlinson*, 156.

171   *"by hanging on with his toes"*: Ibid.

171   *"who went up the precipice"*: Henry Rawlinson, letter to Edwin Norris, Behistun, September 20, 1847, Royal Asiatic Society Collection, III/03/X.

171   *"Unfortunately . . . the left half"*: Ibid.

171   *"Kurdish boy"*: Henry Rawlinson quoted in *The Treasures of Time*, ed. Leo Deuel (London: Pan Books, 1964), 130.

171   *"no reason to despair"*: Henry Rawlinson, letter to Edwin Norris, Behistun, September 20, 1847, Royal Asiatic Society Collection, III/04/17.

171   *"land was in sight"*: Ibid.

CHAPTER TWELVE: THE MUSEUM

173   *"The accounts . . . of the recent excavations"*: "The Nimroud Sculptures," *Illustrated London News* 10, no. 269, June 26, 1847.

173   *"extraordinary discoveries at Nineveh"*: *The Liberator*, January 8, 1847, 8.

174 *"English principles and feelings"*: Layard on Rassam, quoted in Mogens Trolle Larsen, *The Conquest of Assyria*, 132.

174 *"sacrifice myself for England"*: Rassam to Layard, quoted ibid., 195.

174 *"happy success"*: Josiah Forshall, letter to Layard, January 22, 1847, Layard Papers, British Library Manuscript Collection.

174 *"The first batch of Nimroud things"*: Austen Layard, letter to Henry Ross, December 31, Letters to Henry Ross 1847–1857, in Layard Papers, Volume XI, British Library Manuscript Collection Additional MS 38941.

174 *"the somber, sepulchral light"*: "A Late Letter from an American in London Has the Following Very Interesting Notes in Reference to the British Museum, One of the Most Remarkable Institutions in Existence," *Natchez Courier* 15, no. 71, August 30, 1850.

175 *"very much pleas'd with the study"*: James Delbourgo, *Collecting the World: The Life and Curiosity of Hans Sloane* (London: Allen Lane, 2017), 3.

175 *"nailing them down on the ground"*: Ibid., 78.

176 *"Even the women are allowed"*: Ibid., 306.

176 *"in and about the city of London"*: Ibid., 311.

176 *"a collection of butterflies and trifles"*: Ibid., 314.

177 *"a lasting monument of glory"*: Ibid., 328.

177 *"very low & improper persons"*: Ibid., 319.

177 *"[I]t is the property of the nation"*: Ibid., 331.

177 *"Take everything you can"*: Marie-Gabriel-Florent-Auguste de Choiseul-Gouffier quoted in Holger Hoock, "The British State and the Anglo-French Wars over Antiquities 1798–1858," *The Historical Journal* 50, 1 (March 2007): 55.

177 *"to extend military conflict"*: Hoock, "The British State and the Anglo-French Wars over Antiquities 1798–1858," 55.

178 *"collecting furor"*: Ibid., 57.

178 *"public opinion of our watchfulness"*: Ibid., 60.

178 *"Noseless himself"*: George Gordon, Lord Byron, quoted in Maya Jasanoff, "Review: Empires of the Imagination: Politics, War, and the Arts in the British World, 1750–1780 by Holger Hoock," *The Guardian*, March 5, 2010, https://www.theguardian.com/books/2010/mar/06/empires-imagination-politics-holger-hook.

180 *"We do not recall a time"*: "The Nineveh Inscriptions," *Morning Post*, August 13, 1850, 2.

180 *"The antiquary and the scholar roam"*: *The Times*, March 29, 1850, "The Report on the British Museum," 7.

181   *"The colossal relics"*: "The Nineveh Inscriptions," *Morning Post*, 2.

181   *"small means at my disposal"*: Austen Layard to his mother, March 22, 1847, *Autobiography and Letters from His Childhood*, 173.

181   *"though his suggestions were so coldly received"*: "The Nimroud Sculptures," *Illustrated London News*, June 26, 1847, 409.

182   *"Trade was almost completely stagnant"*: Cyril John Gadd, *The Stones of Assyria: The Surviving Remains of Assyrian Sculpture, Their Recovery, and Their Original Positions* (London: Chatto & Windus, 1936), 42.

182   *"lousy English commissioners"*: Rawlinson to Layard quoted in Larsen, *The Conquest of Assyria*, 111.

183   *"[w]e shall beat them hollow"*: Layard to Stratford Canning, December 31, 1847, Layard Papers, Volume XI, British Library Additional MS 38941.

183   *"I fear [Botta] will be amongst the sufferers"*: Layard to Ross, May 19, 1848, Letters to Henry Ross 1847–1857, Layard Papers, Volume XI, British Library Additional MS 38941.

183   *"a man in ruins"*: Gustave Flaubert, letter 264, August 10, 1850, *Correspondance, Nouvelle Edition Augmentée, Deuxième Série (1847–1862)* (Paris: Louis Conard, 1926), 25.

183   *"excite more interest and admiration"*: "The Nimroud Sculptures Lately Received at the British Museum," *Illustrated London News*, December 16, 1848.

184   *"in the most perfect state"*: *Bombay Times* quoted in "Fine-Art Gossip," *The Athenaeum*, No. 1078 (June 24, 1848): 635.

184   *"great numbers of birds"*: Henry Piddington, "A Nineteenth Memoir on the Law of Storms in the Indian Ocean and China Seas, being the Cyclones of the Sir Howard Douglas and of H.M. Brig Jumna in the Southern Indian Ocean, January to April 1848," 10.

184   *"approximated and combined"*: Ibid., 32.

185   *"The long-expected marbles from Nimroud"*: "Fine-Art Gossip," *The Athenaeum*, No. 1095, (October 21, 1848): 1057.

185   *"The state of the contents of the thirty boxes"*: Layard colleague quoted in Gadd, *The Stones of Assyria*, 48.

186   *"the most extraordinary work of the present age"*: "Nineveh and Its Remains," *The Times*, February 9, 1849, 5.

186   *"the greatest achievement of our time"*: Earl of Ellesmere quoted in Gordon Waterfield, *Layard of Nineveh*, 190.

186   *"No one speaks of any other book"*: Gordon Waterfield, *Layard of Nineveh*, 192.

187 *"is even still increasing"*: "The Nimrud Sculptures, Just Received at the British Museum," *Illustrated London News* 14, no. 364 (March 31, 1849).

187 *"Murray anticipate[s] a continual steady demand"*: Layard to Mitford, March 22, 1850, in Layard, *Autobiography and Letters from His Childhood*, 191–92.

187 *"The Trustees . . . have sent me back"*: Ibid.

188 *"He now writes a very decent hand"*: Austen Layard to Henry Ross, July 23, 1848, Letters of AH Layard to Henry Ross 1847–1857, Layard Papers, Volume XI, British Library Additional MS 38941.

188 *"has a Chaldean visiting him"*: George Goodhart, "Unburying an Archaeologist: The Forgotten Story of Hormuzd Rassam," *Uncomfortable Oxford*, November 6, 2022, https://www.uncomfortableoxford.com/unburying-an-archaeologist-the-forgotten-story-of-hormuzd-rassam.

188 *"[y]ellow and bare, as it always is"*: Austen Layard, *Discoveries among the Ruins of Nineveh and Babylon; with Travels in Armenia, Kurdistan, and the Desert* (New York: Harper & Brothers, 1859), 56.

188 *"Heaps of earth marked the site"*: Ibid.

CHAPTER THIRTEEN: THE BATTLE OF LACHISH

190 *"Society received him with open arms"*: George Rawlinson, *A Memoir of Major-General Sir Henry Creswicke Rawlinson*, 161.

191 *"All the Savans [savants] in turn are to attend"*: Rawlinson to Layard, in Mogens Trolle Larsen, *The Conquest of Assyria: Excavations in an Antique Land*, 217.

191 *"prince . . . no mention in the annals"*: Henry Rawlinson, "On the Inscriptions of Assyria and Babylonia," *Journal of the Royal Asiatic Society* 12 (1850): 447.

191 *"beast of the desert"*: Samuel Birch, letter to Layard, March 2, 1850, Layard Papers, Volume XLIX, British Library Manuscript Collection.

191 *"All London was moved"*: Birch quoted in Larsen, *The Conquest of Assyria*, 217.

191 *"undoubted marks of an Egyptian origin"*: Rawlinson quoted in *Paul Émile Botta's Letters on the Discoveries at Nineveh*, trans. C. Tobin (London: Longman, Brown, Green, and Longmans, 1850).

192 *"Today [Rawlinson] has read a second paper"*: Samuel Birch, letter to Layard, March 2, 1850, Layard Papers, Volume XLIX, British Library Manuscript Collection.

192 *"perfect and unmeaning darkness"*: "Nineveh and Persepolis," *Economist*, June 15, 1850, 658.

192 *"The leaves of the potatoes on many fields"*: William Trench quoted in "The Irish Potato Famine 1846–1850," DoChara: Insider Guide to Ireland, Septem-

ber 17, 2008, https://www.dochara.com/the-irish/food-history/the-irish
-potato-famine-1846-1850/.

193 *"a very great distress"*: Edward Hincks to Renouard, September 7, 1848, in
"Edward Hincks (1792–1866): A Biographical Essay," in *The Edward Hincks Bicentenary Lectures*, ed. Cathcart, 5.

193 *"The potatoes have failed everywhere"*: Edward Hincks to Renouard, September 7, 1848.

193 *"It is only within the last few days"*: Hincks in *Literary Gazette*, May 21, 1849.

194 *"ascribing to others"*: Austen Layard, letter to *Literary Gazette*, August 1849.

195 *"I cut their throat like lambs"*: Erika Bleibtreu, "Grisly Assyrian Record of Torture and Death," *Biblical Archaeology Review* (January–February 1991): 52–62.

197 *"the laurels of his well-earned fame"*: Austen Layard, *Discoveries among the Ruins of Nineveh and Babylon*, 100.

197 *"the ancient Persian language"*: Max Müller quoted in Mogens Trolle Larsen, *The Conquest of Assyria*, 179.

197 *"I am enjoying myself most amazingly"*: Mogens Trolle Larsen, *The Conquest of Assyria*, 224.

197 *"Rawlinson . . . is much puzzled"*: Samuel Birch quoted in Larsen, *The Conquest of Assyria*, 225.

198 *"even whiter than milk"*: Diodorus Siculus quoted in Eckart Frahm, *Assyria: The Rise and Fall of the World's First Empire* (New York: Basic Books, 2023). 577.

198 *"that prince of agnostics"*: Christopher Lane, *The Age of Doubt: Tracing the Roots of Our Religious Uncertainty* (New Haven: Yale University Press, 2011), 22.

198 *"doubt, uncertainty, suspence of judgment"*: Christopher Lane, *The Age of Doubt*.

199 *"This, I fear, is rather too good a joke"*: Larsen, *The Conquest of Assyria*, 120.

199 *"I cannot refrain from noticing"*: Jules Oppert, "On Babylon; and on the Discovery of the Cuneiform Characters, and the Mode of Interpreting Them," read March 13, 1856, at the Historic Society of Lancashire and Cheshire, 1–17, https://www.hslc.org.uk/wp-content/uploads/2017/10/8-7-Oppert.pdf.

200 *"no . . . means of distinguishing between"*: Larsen, *The Conquest of Assyria*, 289.

200 *"I have been tempted . . . to abandon"*: Henry Rawlinson quoted in Chaim Bermant and Michael Weitzman, *Ebla: An Archaeological Enigma* (London: Weidenfeld & Nicolson, 1979), 101.

201 *"unquestioned priority"*: William Desborough Cooley, letter to *The Athenaeum*, May 1850.

202 *"a comparatively recluse student"*: *The Literary Gazette*, 1850.

202 *"the foremost place in cuneiform studies"*: *The Athenaeum*, quoted in Larsen, *The Conquest of Assyria*, 226.

202 *"no better than moonshine"*: Charles Wall, letter to Hincks, August 29, 1850, in E. F. Davidson, *Edward Hincks: A Selection from His Correspondence* (Oxford: Oxford University Press, 1933), 161.

202 *"I consider no author superior"*: *The Correspondence of Edward Hincks*, Volume II, 1850–1856, ed. Kevin Cathcart (Dublin: University of Dublin Press, 2008), 5.

202 *"wild and unintelligible"*: Mogens Trolle Larsen, *The Conquest of Assyria*, 225.

203 *"in opposition to all other writers"*: Peter Daniels, "Edward Hincks's Decipherment of Mesopotamian Cuneiform," in *The Edward Hincks Bicentenary Lectures*, ed. Cathcart, 43.

205 *"The piece of sculpture . . . was brought"*: *Illustrated London News*, February 25, 1852, 184.

206 *"The plague . . . has reached the very gate"*: Micah 1:9, King James Version.

206 *"a payment of three hundred talents"*: 2 Kings 18:14, King James Version.

206 *"went out and smote"*: 2 Kings 19:35, King James Version.

206 *"Sennacherib king of Assyria departed"*: Isaiah 37:37, King James Version.

207 *"an expedition against Luliya"*: Henry Rawlinson, "Assyrian Antiquities," *The Athenaeum*, August 23, 1851, 902–3.

207 *"There is no sign of any disaster"*: Henry Rawlinson, letter to Norris, January 28, 1852, Royal Asiatic Society Collection III/07/2.

207 *"he should suffer no ill"*: Herodotus, *The Histories*, Book II, Chapters 99–182, Loeb Classical Library (Cambridge, MA: Harvard University Press, 1963), 449.

208 *"like an ox"*: Daniel 4:32, King James Version.

209 *"evidently of great extent and importance"*: Austen Henry Layard, *Discoveries among the Ruins of Nineveh and Babylon*, 126.

209 *"Amongst the spoil were furniture"*: Ibid.

CHAPTER FOURTEEN: FRIENDSHIP IN THE DESERT

212 *"Old servants take their places"*: Austen Henry Layard, *Discoveries among the Ruins of Nineveh and Babylon*, 49.

213 "*The servants succeeded to the dishes*": Austen Layard, *Nineveh and Its Remains*, Volume I, 64.

213 "*A procession of servants*": Layard, *Discoveries among the Ruins of Nineveh and Babylon*, 289.

213 "*[T]he over-confident individual was armed*": Henry James Ross, *Letters from the East 1837–1857*, ed. Janet Ross (London: J. M. Dent & Co., 1902).

214 "*Large khans [rest houses] occur at convenient intervals*": William Kennett Loftus, *Travels and Researches in Chaldea and Susiana: With an Account of Excavations at Warka, the "Erech" of Nimrod, and Shush, "Sushan the Palace" of Esther, in 1849–52* (New York: Robert Carter & Brothers: 1857), 14.

214 "*People in England little know*": Letter dated "Christmas Day, 1849," excerpted in Austen Henry Layard, *Autobiography and Letters from His Childhood*, 193.

215 "*The power he has over these wild sons*": Layard, *Autobiography and Letters from His Childhood*, 149.

215 "*one of the cleverest and most enterprising men*": Extract from a letter by an unnamed writer, dated January 22, 1850, *The Times* (British Library Collection), 135.

216 "*inexhaustible good humor*": Austen Layard quoted in Jane Waldron Grutz, "Iraq's First Archeologist," AramcoWorld, May/June 2018, https://www.aramcoworld.com/Articles/May-2018/Iraq-s-First-Archeologist.

216 "*living with their cattle*": Lady Anne Blunt, *Bedouin Tribes of the Euphrates* (London: John Murray, 1879), 185.

216 "*As young men, the Bedouins*": Ibid., 199.

217 "*The Bedouin is essentially humane*": Ibid, 203.

217 "*The peaceful shepherd tribes*": Ibid., 282.

217 "*the Bedouins, having exchanged*": Ibid., 283.

218 "*I have been ill*": Henry Rawlinson to Austen Layard, Layard Papers, April 1846, Layard Correspondence 1844–46, British Library Manuscript Collection 38976.

218 "*There are various stories afloat*": Henry Rawlinson to Austen Layard, January 2, 1846, Layard Papers, British Library Manuscript Collection 38976, 294–95; 38977.

218 "*You have been I suspect*": Henry Rawlinson to Austen Layard, Layard Papers, Volume 47, correspondence 1846–47, bequeathed by Lady Layard, British Library Manuscript Collection, Additional Manuscripts 38977.

218 "*I have been ailing so much*": Henry Rawlinson to Austen Layard, August 5,

1846, Layard Papers, Volume XLVII, Correspondence July 1846–47, British Library Manuscript Collection, Additional Manuscripts 38977.

218 *"I think the heat has affected"*: Rawlinson to Layard, Layard Papers, Letters 1849–50.

219 *"Your crates arrived all right"*: Rawlinson to Layard, August 5, 1846, Volume XLVII, Correspondence July 1846–47, British Library Manuscripts Collection, Additional Manuscripts 38977.

219 *"Heaven forefend that I should do anything"*: Rawlinson to Layard, August 1846, Volume XLVII, Correspondence July 1846–47, British Library Manuscripts Collection 38977.

219 *"[I] view every new Inscription"*: Ibid., August 1846.

219 *"either to the Turks or Persians"*: Ibid., September 1846.

219 *"I throw all Greek traditions"*: Mogens Trolle Larsen, *The Conquest of Assyria: Excavations in an Antique Land* (London and New York: Routledge, 1996), 209.

220 *"You do not appear"*: Ibid., 211.

220 *"connect all the names"*: Ibid.

220 *"The Major has made wonderful discoveries"*: Layard, letter to Ross, August 25, 1849, Letters to Henry Ross 1847–1857, Layard Papers, Volume XI, British Library Additional Manuscripts 38941.

220 *"and I fear it will be worse"*: Henry Rawlinson to Austen Layard, Layard Papers, Letters 1849–50, British Library Manuscript Collection 389789.

220 *"I count the days"*: Rawlinson to Layard, Layard Papers, Letters 1849–50.

220 *"I am pitching my camp"*: Ibid.

221 *"I can hardly be at Nimrud"*: Henry Rawlinson to Austen Layard, October 10, 1849, Layard Papers, Letters 1849–50, British Library Manuscript Collection 389789.

222 *"colossal heads of winged figures"*: Austen Layard, *Discoveries among the Ruins of Nineveh and Babylon*, 82.

222 *"deep in sleep, wearied"*: Ibid., 83.

222 *"October 21: ride into Mosul"*: Layard Papers, Journal, August 1849–May 1850.

222 *"[I] looked over the ruins"*: Quoted in Mogens Trolle Larsen, *The Conquest of Assyria*, 208.

222 *"Rawlinson continued his journey"*: Austen Layard, *Discoveries among the Ruins of Nineveh and Babylon*, 83.

223 *"the sculptured paneling to lime"*: Ibid., 56.

223 *"probably captives from different conquered nations"*: Ibid., 58.

224   "*The vanquished turn*": Ibid.

224   "*On the great bulls*": Ibid., 117.

224   "*were stretched naked at full length*": Ibid., 390.

224   "*a torturer was wrenching the tongue*": Ibid.

225   "*their tongues had been pulled out*": Ibid., 392.

225   "*spacious apartment*": Ibid., 290.

225   "*To the height of a foot or more*": Ibid.

225   "*were singularly sharp and well-defined*": Ibid., 296.

225   "*The characters appear to have been formed*": Ibid., 298.

226   "*The desolation, the solitude*": Layard, *Autobiography and Letters from His Childhood*, 349–50.

226   "*of the finest furnace-based clay*": Oxford, Bodleian Library, Phillipps-Robinson Manuscripts, d 291, f. 12, cited in Toby Burrows, "Reconstructing the Phillipps Collection," online post on Wordpress.com, April 18, 2015.

227   "*a wooden framework covered with thick felt*": Layard, *Discoveries among the Ruins of Nineveh and Babylon*, 398.

227   "*On all sides, fragments of glass*": Ibid., 413.

228   "*I do not see the slightest chance*": Layard, letter to Ross, February 12, 1851, Letters to Henry Ross 1847–1857, Layard Papers, Volume XI, British Library Additional Manuscript 38941.

229   "*[I] [t]hought of an identification*": Edward Hincks, diary entry December 21, 1851, *The Correspondence of Edward Hincks*, Volume II: 1850–1856, ed. Kevin J. Cathcart, 73.

CHAPTER FIFTEEN: KILLYLEAGH

230   "*zealous exertions in the discovery*": "The Layard Box" in *The Times*, 1847.

231   "*the richest heiress in England*": John Parker Anderson, "Burdett-Coutts, Angela Georgina," in *Dictionary of National Biography* (2nd Supplement), ed. Sidney Lee (London: Smith, Elder & Co.), 259–66.

231   "*Can you, and will you, be in town*": Charles Dickens to Layard, letter dated December 16, 1851, Tavistock House, Tavistock Square. Letters from Charles Dickens to Sir Henry Layard, 1851–1859, Layard Papers, Volume XVII, bequeathed by Lady Layard, British Library Manuscript Collection, Additional MS 38947.

231   "*At Naples I found Layard*": Charles Dickens, letter from 1854, Letters from Charles Dickens to Sir Henry Layard, 1851–1859, Layard Papers, Volume XVII.

231   "*My election is almost a certainty*": Layard to Ross, April 10, 1852, Letters to

Henry Ross 1847–1857, Layard Papers, Volume XI, British Library Manuscript Collection, Additional MS 38941.

232 *"We have on our hands a sick man"*: Tsar Nicholas I quoted in Christopher de Bellaigue, "The Sick Man of Europe," *New York Review of Books*, July 5, 2001, https://www.nybooks.com/articles/2001/07/05/the-sick-man-of-europe/.

232 *"As a speaker Mr. Layard is somewhat stiff"*: "Parliamentary Sketches," *Reynolds's Weekly Newspaper*, July 2, 1854.

232 *"I found it, as you may suppose"*: Layard to Ross, September 19, 1852, Letters to Henry Ross 1847–1857, Layard Papers, Volume XI, British Library Manuscript Collection.

233 *"among England's most promising statesmen"*: "Henry Austen Layard, M.P. for Aylesbury," *The Lady's Newspaper & Pictorial Times* no. 476, February 9, 1856, 92.

233 *"tea cakes were provided for us"*: Hariot Hamilton-Temple-Blackwood quoted in E. F. Davidson, *Edward Hincks: A Selection from His Correspondence with a Memoir*, 22.

234 *"no advantage at all . . . in society"*: Davidson, *Edward Hincks: A Selection from His Correspondence*, 18.

234 *"was a celebrated man"*: Hamilton-Temple-Blackwood quoted in Davidson, *Edward Hincks*, 22.

234 *"No doubt he was an easy victim"*: Ibid., 21.

234 *"'I did not know that we had reached Belfast'"*: Ibid.

235 *"and left . . . the rector's hood"*: Letter from "A Puritan" to the editor of the *Banner of Ulster*, November 1853, courtesy of Kevin Cathcart.

235 *"If it be true that the congregation"*: "Alleged Puseyism in Killyleagh" from the editor of the *Belfast News Letter*, December 2, 1853.

235 *"occurred to me that the Protestant spirit"*: Letter from Edward Hincks to the editor of the *Downpatrick Recorder*, December 14, 1853.

236 *"He was flabbergasted"*: Author interview by phone with Kevin Cathcart, October 2023.

236 *"[M]y clerical income"*: Kevin J. Cathcart, "Edward Hincks (1792–1866): A Biographical Essay," in *The Edward Hincks Bicentenary Lectures*, ed. Cathcart, 11.

236 *"leave me enough to . . . spend some little time"*: Ibid., 12.

236 *"The sole places that seemed to prosper"*: Charles Dickens, *The Adventures of Oliver Twist, and a Child's History of England* (London: Gresham Publishing Company Ltd., 1912), 44.

237 *"[B]ut, though of pure English descent"*: Cathcart, "Edward Hincks (1792–1866): A Biographical Essay," 12.

237 *"I would place myself my whole time"*: Ibid., 15.

237 *"extraordinary sagacity and learning"*: The Correspondence of Edward Hincks, Volume II: 1850–1856, ed. Kevin J. Cathcart (Dublin: University College Dublin Press, 2007), 150.

237 *"the earliest . . . of my Nimroud kings"*: Layard to Hincks, January 20, 1848, in Davidson, *Edward Hincks: A Selection from His Correspondence* (Oxford: Oxford University Press, 1933), 145.

238 *"All I beg of you"*: Rawlinson to Layard, Layard Papers, Letters 1851–52, British Library Manuscript Collection 38978, 23–26.

238 *"I am anxious to know"*: Layard to Hincks, January 8, 1852, in Davidson, *Edward Hincks*, 168.

239 *"I have no doubt"*: Layard to Hincks, July 28, 1848, in Davidson, *Edward Hincks*, 174.

239 *"The small town stands on Lough Strangford"*: Austen Layard to Benjamin Austen, October 3, 1852, The Correspondence of Edward Hincks, Volume II: 1850–1856, 140–41.

240 *"The Doctor is an original"*: Ibid.

241 *"I again settled Samaria"*: Shawn Zelig Auster, "Sargon in Samaria—Unusual Formulations in the Royal Inscriptions and Their Value for Historical Reconstruction" (*Journal of the American Oriental Society*, Volume 139, No. 3, July–September 2019), 595.

242 *"is wrong on many points"*: Austen Layard to Hincks, July 10, 1852, The Correspondence of Edward Hincks, Volume II: 1850–1856.

242 *"Had not Col. Rawlinson by an accident"*: Layard to Hincks, January 8, 1852, in Davidson, *Edward Hincks: A Selection from His Correspondence*, 168.

242 *"a very rebellious liver"*: Rawlinson, letter to Edwin Norris, August 22, 1852.

243 *"I have no longer the energy of youth"*: Henry Rawlinson, letter to Edwin Norris, June 1, 1852, Royal Asiatic Society Collection, III/07/11.

243 *"I shall soon have [the Akkadian]"*: Henry Rawlinson, letter to Edwin Norris, March 14, 1852, Royal Asiatic Society Collection, III/07/6.

243 *"by dint of fingers as well as eyes"*: Henry Rawlinson, letter to Edwin Norris, March 14, 1852.

243 *"We shall [soon] have a very fair idea"*: Henry Rawlinson to Edwin Norris, February 29, 1852, Royal Asiatic Society Collection, III/07/5.

243 *"names of countries, rivers"*: Henry Rawlinson to Edwin Norris, April 15, 1853, Royal Asiatic Society Collection, III/09/5.

244   *"worm . . . dwells in the gums"*: Warren R. Dawson, *The Beginnings: Egypt & Assyria* (New York: Hafner Publishing Company, 1964), 65.

244   *"thou shalt bray"*: R. Campbell Thompson, *Assyrian Medical Texts from the Cuneiform Tablets at Koyunjik* (Oxford: John Bale, Sons & Danielson Ltd., 1924), 2.

244   *"Pure palm-fiber thou shalt chew"*: Thompson, *Assyrian Medical Texts from the Cuneiform Tablets at Koyunjik*, 31.

245   *"If the moon is unexpectedly late"*: Karen Radner and Eleanor Robson, eds., *The Oxford Handbook of Cuneiform Culture* (Oxford: Oxford University Press, 2011), 449.

246   *"riflers"*: Henry Rawlinson to Edwin Norris, July 22, 1852, Royal Asiatic Society Collection, III/7/15.

246   *"a very mean opinion"*: Henry Rawlinson to Edwin Norris, July 22, 1852, Royal Asiatic Society Collection, III/7/15.

246   *"Layard has been fraternizing"*: Henry Rawlinson to Edwin Norris, November 25, 1852, Royal Asiatic Society Collection, III/7/23.

246   *"pirate, having never yet made"*: Henry Rawlinson to Edwin Norris, July 2, 1852, Royal Asiatic Society Collection, III/7/13.

246   *"It is written in a tone"*: Henry Rawlinson to Edwin Norris, July 2, 1852, Henry Rawlinson papers, Royal Asiatic Society Collection, file III/7.

246   *"If Fergusson calls all this"*: Henry Rawlinson to Edwin Norris, May 24, 1853, Royal Asiatic Society Collection, III/09/8.

247   *"Up at 6, working"*: Edward Hincks diary entry, in E. F. Davidson, *Edward Hincks: A Selection from His Correspondence*, 183.

249   *"had not been obedient to my yoke"*: 2 Kings 19:35–36.

250   *"You talk a great deal"*: Henry Rawlinson to Austen Layard, August 1853, British Library Manuscript Collection BL38981.

250   *"For twelve weary years"*: Henry Rawlinson, *The Athenaeum*, no. 2976 (November 8, 1884): 593.

250   *"game reserve"*: Henry Rawlinson to Edwin Norris, April 20, 1853, British Library Manuscript Collection BL 38981, 286–88.

250   *"I certainly thought that my recent exertions"*: Henry Rawlinson, May 24, 1853, Western Asiatic Department Manuscript Collection, British Museum.

CHAPTER SIXTEEN: TALBOT

251   *"of a very superior capacity"*: H. J. P. Arnold, *William Henry Fox Talbot: Pioneer of Photography and Man of Science* (London: Hutchinson Benham, 1977), 32.

251 *"It exploded with the noise"*: Arnold, *William Henry Fox Talbot: Pioneer of Photography and Man of Science*, 34.

252 *"You seem so mathematically inclined"*: Arnold, *William Henry Fox Talbot: Pioneer of Photography and Man of Science*, 38.

252 *"fairy pictures, creations of the moment"*: William Henry Fox Talbot, *The Pencil of Nature* (ebook published by DigiCat, originally published 1844), page number not available.

252 *"how charming it would be"*: Ibid.

253 *"the art of photogenic drawing"*: William Henry Fox Talbot, "Some Account of the Art of Photogenic Drawing, or the Process by which Natural Objects May Be Made to Delineate Themselves Without the Aid of the Artist's Pencil," *Philosophical Transactions of the Royal Society of London* 4, no 4 (December 1843): 120.

253 *"very perfect but extremely small"*: William Henry Fox Talbot, "Some Account of the Art of Photogenic Drawing," *Philosophical Magazine* 14, no. 6 (March 1839): 205–6.

253 *"I must now really transport my apparatus"*: Arnold, *William Henry Fox Talbot*, 95.

254 *"Two large Box trees planted"*: Ibid., 260.

255 *"The simplicity of Roman manners"*: Edward Gibbon, *The History of the Decline and Fall of the Roman Empire*, quoted in Zachary Lockman, *Contending Visions of the Middle East: The History and Politics of Orientalism* (Cambridge: Cambridge University Press, 2010), 15.

255 *"Liberty was intended for the genius"*: Charles-Louis de Secondat, Baron de Montesquieu, quoted in Lloyd Llewellyn-Jones, *Persians: The Age of Great Kings* (London: Wildfire, 2022).

256 *"sacred narrations . . . had spread abroad"*: William Henry Fox Talbot, "The Antiquity of the Book of Genesis," in *Hear the Church! A World for All by a Doctor of Divinity but Not of Oxford* (London: Thomas Ward & Co., 1839), 14.

256 *"The coins of the city"*: Ibid.

256 *"As I take great interest"*: William Henry Fox Talbot, letter to Edward Hawkins, British Museum; Mirjam Brusius, "From Photographic Science to Scientific Photography: Talbot and Decipherment at the British Museum around 1850," in *William Henry Talbot: Beyond Photography*, eds. Mirjam Brusius, Katrina Dean, and Chitra Ramalingam (New Haven: Yale University Press, 2013).

257 *"In that battle, of all his army"*: W. H. F. Talbot, *Assyrian Texts Translated* (London: Harrison & Sons, 1856), 1.

257 *"From that island I drove (?) him"*: Ibid., 10.

258 *"The object at present"*: William Henry Fox Talbot to Edward Hincks, December 24, 1856, *The Correspondence of Edward Hincks*, Volume II: 1850–1856, edited by Kevin Cathcart.

258 *"You cannot do us a greater"*: Edwin Norris to William Henry Fox Talbot, October 3, 1856, *The Correspondence of William Henry Fox Talbot*, Fox Talbot Collection, British Library, Document 1186.

259 *"thinks it would be a more satisfactory proof"*: Edwin Norris to William Henry Fox Talbot, October 3, 1856, *The Correspondence of William Henry Fox Talbot*.

259 *"the red tape [metaphysical] is all unwound"*: Edwin Norris to William Henry Fox Talbot, January 15, 1857, *The Correspondence of William Henry Fox Talbot*, Fox Talbot Collection, British Library, Document 7353.

CHAPTER SEVENTEEN: THE END OF AN ERA

260 *"certain good spots"*: Hormuzd Rassam, *Asshur and the Land of Nimrod: Being an Account of the Discoveries Made in the Ancient Ruins of Nineveh, Asshur, Sepharvaim, Calah, Babylon, Borsippa, Cuthah, and Van* (Cincinnati: Curtis & Jennings; New York: Eaton & Mains, 1897), 16.

260 *"we heard the sound of the war-cry"*: Ibid.

261 *"rapid march drove in utter confusion"*: Ibid., 17.

261 *"[I]t is a known fact"*: Ibid., 12.

262 *"I was quietly seated"*: Henry Rawlinson, *Personal Adventures*, written January 1870–71, "Sketches of life from 1833 to 1840, adventures told to boys," bound volume, diary 15 Royal Geographic Society, London. RGS Reference number HCR/15.

262 *"[t]he firing did not cease"*: George Rawlinson, *A Memoir of Major-General Sir Henry Creswicke Rawlinson*, 173.

262 *"The whole of the foreign correspondence"*: *Annual Report of the Royal Asiatic Society*, May 1853, xvi.

263 *"a dark, short, thinnish gent"*: C. E. Harle to Edward Hincks, October 24, 1855, in Davidson, *Edward Hincks: A Selection from His Correspondence*, 210.

263 *"Oppert . . . is a young laborious German"*: Henry Rawlinson to Edwin Norris, March 14, 1852, Royal Asiatic Society Collection, III/07/6.

264 *"flippant, offensive [and] . . . untrue"*: Henry Rawlinson to Edwin Norris, May 1, 1852, Royal Asiatic Society Collection, III/07/8.9.

264 *"His kindly thought for others"*: "Death of Dr. Jules Oppert," *Hebrew Standard*, September 8, 1905, 8.

264 *"His worldliness remained"*: *The Times*, excerpted in "Death of Dr. Jules Oppert."

264 *"British hospitality toward strangers"*: Jules Oppert, "On Babylon; and On the Discovery of the Cuneiform Characters and the Mode of Interpreting Them," read March 13, 1856, 1–17.

264 *"He and Fresnel are vegetating"*: Henry Rawlinson to Edwin Norris, July 22, 1852, Royal Asiatic Society Collection, III/7/15.

265 *"inveterate enemy dyspepsia"*: Henry Rawlinson to Edwin Norris, October 15, 1852, Royal Asiatic Society Collection, III/7/21.

265 *"[t]he French have found nothing"*: Henry Rawlinson to Edwin Norris, October 15, 1852.

266 *"The rain began to fall in torrents"*: Matilda Rassam to Austen Layard, April 16, 1850, Layard Papers, Volume XLIX, Correspondence 1849–1850, bequeathed by Lady Layard, British Library Manuscript Collection, Additional MS 38979.

266 *"I am rather astonished"*: Matilda Rassam to Layard, July 5, 1850, Layard Papers, Volume XLIX, Correspondence 1849–1850.

267 *"I will tell you, confidentially"*: Rassam to Layard, July 5, 1850.

267 *"succeeded in uniting the fragments"*: George Rawlinson, *A Memoir of Major-General Sir Henry Creswicke Rawlinson* (London, Longmans, Green, and Co., 1898), 181.

268 *"It was understood, and indeed"*: Rassam, *Asshur and the Land of Nimrod*, 23.

268 *"a beautiful bas relief in a perfect state"*: Ibid., 25.

268 *"men leading dogs for the hunt"*: Ibid., 30.

268 *"inscribed terra-cotta tablets"*: Ibid., 31.

269 *"I placed him in a neck-stock"*: Ashurbanipal, translation of inscription, in the Open Richly Annotated Cuneiform Corpus (Oracc), oracc.museum.upenn.edu—rinap5.

269 *"Arise, go to Nineveh"*: Jonah 1:2, King James Version.

269 *"an exceedingly great city"*: Jonah 3:3, King James Version.

270 *"There shall the fire devour thee"*: Nahum 3:13, King James Version.

270 *"a terrible defeat upon a great people"*: *Babylonian Chronicles*, quoted in Eckart Frahm, *Assyria: The Rise and Fall of the World's First Empire* (New York: Basic Books, 2023).

270 *"great siege"*: Ctesias of Cnidus cited in Diodorus Siculus, *Library of History*,

Book II, Chapters 1–34, Loeb Classical Library (Cambridge: Harvard University Press, 1963).

271 *"built an enormous pyre"*: Ctesias of Cnidus cited in Diodorus Siculus, *Library of History.*

271 *"Nineveh is laid waste!"*: Nahum 3:7, King James Version.

271 *"empire without a mission"*: Eckart Frahm, *Assyria: The Rise and Fall of the World's First Empire.*

273 *"inspired him with the wish"*: S. T. L. Harbottle, "W.K. Loftus: An Archaeologist from Newcastle," offprint from *Archaeologia Aeliana*, Fifth Series, Volume I (Society of Antiquaries of Newcastle Upon Tyne, 1973), 195–217.

273 *"numerous written bricks"*: Felix Jones to Austen Layard, March 13, 1850, Layard Papers, Volume XLIX, British Library Manuscript Collection.

273 *"active, intelligent, and thoroughly in earnest"*: Hormuzd Rassam quoted in Harbottle, "W.K. Loftus," 195–217.

273 *"He will embarrass the operations"*: Henry Rawlinson to Samuel Ellis, Royal Asiatic Society Collection, June 10, 1854, III/11.

274 *"After all that has passed"*: William Loftus to Henry Rawlinson, June 21, 1854, Royal Asiatic Society Collection, III/11/05.

274 *"I think your indignation"*: Henry Rawlinson to William Loftus, June 27, 1854, Royal Asiatic Society Collection, III/11/07.

274 *"a storm in a slop bucket"*: Henry Rawlinson, letter to Edwin Norris, July 13, 1854, Royal Asiatic Society Collection, III/10/13.

275 *"bone had been broken before"*: George Rawlinson, *A Memoir of Major-General Sir Henry Creswicke Rawlinson*, 199.

275 *"on taking the furlough"*: Ibid.

275 *"that we cannot consent"*: Bülent Genç, "Memory of Destroyed Khorsabad, Victor Place, and the Story of a Shipwreck," *Journal of the Royal Asiatic Society* 31, no. 4: 759–74, published by Cambridge University Press, 2021, 765.

276 *"where they had hidden"*: D. T. Potts, "'Un Coup Terrible de la Fortune': A. Clément and the Qurna Disaster of 1855," in *In Context: The Reade Festschrift*, eds. I. L. Finkel and St J. Simpson (Oxford: Archaeopress, 2020), 235–44.

CHAPTER EIGHTEEN: THE UNRAVELED MYSTERY

278 *"calculated to tax to the utmost"*: "Miscellaneous," *National Era*, July 18, 1857, 113.

279 *"I will translate as much as I can"*: Edward Hincks to William Henry Fox

Talbot, April 28, 1857, *The Correspondence of Edward Hincks*, Volume III: 1857–1866, edited by Kevin Cathcart (Dublin: University of Dublin Press, 2008).

281 *"cast-off"*: Edward Hincks to Austen Layard, April 1854, in Cathcart, "Edward Hincks (1792–1866): A Biographical Essay," 18.

281 *"a mass of information"*: Edward Hincks quoted in Mogens Trolle Larsen, *The Conquest of Assyria: Excavations in an Antique Land* (London and New York: Routledge, 1996), 335.

281 *"I have no doubt"*: Hincks quoted in Mogens Trolle Larsen, *The Conquest of Assyria*.

282 *"to enter into scientific intercourse"*: Jules Oppert to Edward Hincks, June 28, 1855, *The Correspondence of Edward Hincks*, Volume II, 1850–1856, ed. Kevin Cathcart (Dublin: University of Dublin Press, 2008), 279.

282 *"I have often felt"*: Edward Hincks to William Henry Fox Talbot, February 1857, Letters of William Fox Talbot, British Library Manuscript Collection.

282 *"I should hope"*: Ibid.

283 *"unpleasant smell"*: Transcriptions of the original files of the Royal Asiatic Society archives, November 13, 1830.

283 *"The four translations have been made"*: John Gardner Wilkinson, "Comparative Translations," *Journal of the Royal Asiatic Society of Great Britain and Ireland*, Volume 18 (1861): 150–219, published by Cambridge University Press, 1861.

284 *"Then I went to the country of Comukha"*: Ibid., 170.

286 *"It is to be regretted"*: Ibid., 153.

286 *"who are understood to have prosecuted"*: Ibid.

286 *"Both as to the general sense"*: Ibid.

287 *"Now that it is done"*: Edwin Norris to William Henry Fox Talbot, May 21, 1857, *The Correspondence of Edward Hincks*, Volume III: 1857–1866, ed. Kevin J. Cathcart, 30–31.

287 *"has now been carried out"*: "Decipherers on their Trial," *The People*, May 30, 1857, 7, reprint of "A Literary Inquest," *The Athenaeum*.

287 *"with its ... arrow-headed character"*: "An Unraveled Mystery," *Chambers's Journal*, collected in *Christian Repository*, August 1858, 243, Nineteenth Century Collections Online.

287 *"a complete triumph"*: Paul Haupt, "Contributions to the History of Assyriology, with Special Reference to the Works of Sir Henry Rawlinson," *Johns Hopkins University Circulars*, vol. VIII, no. 72 (April 1889): 57–62, https://

jscholarship.library.jhu.edu/server/api/core/bitstreams/520cc77c-6bce
-4f2e-bd9e-a889616a8c01/content.

287 *"I have no doubt"*: William Henry Fox Talbot to Edward Hincks, July 5, 1857, *The Correspondence of Edward Hincks*, Volume III, ed. Kevin J. Cathcart, 38.

288 *"After, for seven days"*: The Buried Book.

289 *"On looking down the third column"*: George Smith quoted in *The Treasures of Time: Firsthand Accounts by Famous Archaeologists of Their Work in the Near East*, ed. Leo Deuel (London: Pan Books, 1964), 131.

289 *"We can now see that this greatest"*: Samuel Noah Kramer, *History Begins at Sumer: Thirty-Nine Firsts in Recorded History* (London: Thames & Hudson, 1956), 193.

290 *"There must have been a heritage memory"*: Tom Chivers, "Irving Finkel: Reader of the Lost Ark," *The Telegraph*, January 19, 2014, https://www.telegraph.co.uk/culture/books/10574173/Irving-Finkel-reader-of-the-lost-Ark.html.

290 *"a man all muscle"*: Epic of Gilgamesh, translation excerpt in Robert Macfarlane, "A Fireball from the Sands: Ecocide, Toxic Masculinity, Fear of Death, and More: The *Epic of Gilgamesh*'s Themes Could Be Transcribed from Yesterday's Newspaper," *New York Review of Books*, October 20, 2022, https://www.nybooks.com/articles/2022/10/20/a-fireball-from-the-sands-gilgamesh/.

291 *"Gilgamesh is fascinatingly complex"*: Robert Macfarlane, "A Fireball from the Sands."

292 *"built all the primitive temples of Babylonia"*: Henry Rawlinson in *The Athenaeum*, May 19, 1855, issue 1438.

293 *"It seemed impossible"*: A. H. Sayce, *The Archaeology of the Cuneiform Inscriptions* (London: Society for Promoting Christian Knowledge, 1908), 67.

293 *"the so-called . . . Sumerian people"*: Christopher Johnston, "The Sumero-Akkadian Question," *Journal of the American Oriental Society* 15 (1893): 317–22.

294 *"about the most mundane subjects"*: Author interview by phone with Peter Daniels, October 2022.

294 *"He opened up the holy furrows"*: Ariane Thomas and Timothy Potts, eds., *Mesopotamia: Civilization Begins* (Los Angeles: J. Paul Getty Museum, 2020), 130.

295 *"From behind a pile of dusty old books"*: William Sandys Wright Vaux to Henry Rawlinson, November 1, 1854, *The Correspondence of Edward Hincks*, Volume II, ed. Kevin J. Cathcart.

296 *"What would our friend Hincks say"*: William Sandys Wright Vaux to Henry Rawlinson, November 1, 1854.

297 *"The idea quickly gained acceptance"*: William Dalrymple, *The Last Mughal: The Fall of a Dynasty, Delhi, 1857* (London: Bloomsbury Publishing Plc., 2006), 135.

297 *"punishment parade"*: Suchet Vir Singh, "On This Day in 1857, How 'Punishment Parade' in Meerut Lit Spark of 1st War for Indian Freedom," *The Print*, May 10, 2022.

298 *"trap rock, greenstone, and siennate"*: "Royal Asiatic Society," *Morning Post*, March 24, 1857.

298 *"a reprehensible apathy"*: Stuart Simmonds and Simon Digby, eds., *The Royal Asiatic Society: Its History and Treasures* (Leiden: E. J. Brill, 1979), 67.

298 *"We shall respect the rights"*: Queen Victoria, "The Allahabad Proclamation," November 1857, as inscribed on the wall of The Victoria Monument, Kolkata, India.

299 *"[T]here was a strong sense of embarrassment"*: William Dalrymple, "The East India Company: The Original Corporate Raiders," *The Guardian*, March 4, 2015, https://www.theguardian.com/world/2015/mar/04/east-india-company-original-corporate-raiders.

299 *"He has omitted all mention"*: Edward Hincks, quoted in "A Great Orientalist: Edward Hincks: A Memoir by E. F. Davidson," *Sunday Times*, Issue 5744, May 14, 1933.

299 *"could not understand how anyone"*: Edward Hincks, letter to Edwin Norris.

299 *"One gets the impression"*: E. F. Davidson, *Edward Hincks: A Selection from His Correspondence, with a Memoir* (London: Oxford University Press, Humphrey Milford, 1933).

299 *"I wish I could destroy the impression"*: Ibid., 14.

300 *"Hormuzd . . . writes me that the papers"*: Matilda Rassam to Austen Layard, July 5, 1850, Layard Papers, Volume XLIX, Correspondence 1849–1850, bequeathed by Lady Layard, British Library Manuscript Collection, Additional MS 38979.

300 *"discovered by Rawlinson"*: E. A. Wallis Budge, *The Rise and Progress of Assyriology* (London: Martin Hopkinson & Co. Ltd., 1925), 101.

301 *"brings to a close the long and eventful career"*: "Funeral of Sir Henry Rawlinson," *The Times*, March 11, 1895, 6.

301 *"more startling and exciting"*: "The Late Sir Austen Henry Layard," *Illustrated London News*, July 14, 1894, 35.

302 *"Never was a man of erudition"*: *The Times*, excerpted in "Death of Dr. Jules Oppert," *Hebrew Standard*, September 8, 1905, 8.

302 *"fully convinced . . . of the entire futility"*: William Henry Fox Talbot, letter to Edward Hincks, March 4, 1862, located in H. J. P. Arnold, *William Henry Fox Talbot: Pioneer of Photography and Man of Science*, 303.

302 *"quarter century love affair with Assyriology"*: Mirjam Brusius, "From Photographic Science to Scientific Photography: Talbot and Decipherment at the British Museum around 1850," in *William Henry Talbot: Beyond Photography*, eds. Mirjam Brusius, Katrina Dean, and Chitra Ramalingam (New Haven: Yale University Press, 2013).

303 *"Edward Hincks died . . . a scholar"*: W. R. Le Fanu, "Edward Hincks," *Times Literary Supplement*, no. 1632 (May 11, 1933): 322.

303 *"The church gave him no deanery"*: E. F. Davidson, *Edward Hincks: A Selection from His Correspondence*, 12.

303 *"the Father of Assyriology"*: *Assyrian and Babylonian Literature: Selected Translations* (New York: D. Appleton & Co., 1901), xxx.

304 *"in no way detracts"*: Budge, *The Rise and Progress of Assyriology*, 78.

304 *"a bully"*: Author interview with Irving Finkel, August 2022, at the British Museum.

304 *"It is Hincks, and he nearly alone"*: Peter Daniels, "Edward Hincks's Decipherment of Mesopotamian Cuneiform," in *The Edward Hincks Bicentenary Lectures*, ed. Kevin J. Cathcart (Dublin: Department of Near Eastern Languages, University College Dublin, 1994), 54.

304 *"the archaeological romance of the nineteenth century"*: A. H. Sayce, *The Archaeology of the Cuneiform Inscriptions*, 7.

EPILOGUE

314 *"blew like the onset of a severe storm"*: Sennacherib quoted in Diodorus Siculus, quoted in Eckart Frahm, *Assyria: The Rise and Fall of the World's First Empire* (New York: Basic Books, 2023).

314 *"trembled like reeds in a storm"*: Esarhaddon quoted in Diodorus Siculus, quoted in Eckart Frahm, *Assyria: The Rise and Fall of the World's First Empire*.

INDEX

Assyrian artifacts and, 117
hieroglyphics on artifacts of,
139
interest in Assyria vs., 127–29
Royal Prussian Expedition and,
93
see also Demotic Egyptian
Egyptian hieroglyphics, 53, 305
Akkadian cuneiform and, 5, 6, 145,
152, 201
attempts to decipher, 139–45
in cartouches, 140–43
Hincks's study of, 3, 131, 147–48
on Rosetta Stone, 138, 143–45
Elamite cuneiform, 6, 31, 34, 48,
93–94, 125, 150, 151, 158, 171
Elgin, Lord, see Bruce, Thomas
Elgin Marbles, 178, 219, 310–11, 313
Ellenborough, Lord, see Law,
Edward
Ellesmere, Earl of, 186, 190–91
Ellis, Henry, 237, 247, 273, 295
Elphinstone (warship), 184
Elphinstone, William, 65
England
cultural competition between
France and (see French–English
cultural competition)
First Anglo-Afghan War, 63–65
"Great Game" between Russia and,
60–64, 66, 92, 283
Layard's life in, 70–71, 173–75,
185–87, 228, 230–33
public opinion on Layard's
methods, 182
Rawlinson's life in, 161, 190–92,
196–97, 300–301
view of Irish in, 194, 236–37

view of Turkish Arabian tribes in,
215–17
see also British Parliament
Enki, 294, 295
Enkidu, 290, 291
Enlil, 91–92, 294
Epic of Gilgamesh, 78, 290–91, 302
Esarhaddon, xii, 79, 196, 197, 243, 248,
257, 280, 309, 314
Ethiopians, 36
see also Amharic
Eton, William, 74
Ewuare I, Oba, 310

Fath-'Ali Shah Qajar, 18, 19
Felix, James, 182
Fellows, Charles, 178, 181
Fergusson, James, 246
Fielding, Charles, 251
Figueroa, Garcia de Silva y, 37
Finkel, Irving, 290, 304
First Anglo-Afghan War, 63–65
Flandin, Jean-Baptiste Eugène, 49–51,
83, 109
Flaubert, Gustave, 183
Forshall, Josiah, 174
Forsskål, Peter, 27
Forster, George, 71–72
Frahm, Eckart, 271–72
François-Adolphe de Bourqueney, 111
French–English cultural competition
British Museum and Louvre in, 120,
177–78
Kingdom of Judah campaign
account and, 209
Layard and Botta in, 108–11
over Assyrian artifacts, 182–83
Rassam and Place in, 260–65

IMAGE CREDITS

179 The *Illustrated London News* engraving of a winged, human-headed lion from the palace of King Ashurnasirpal II, wheeled backward up the steps of the British Museum in 1852 (*Credit: Alamy Inc.*)

215 Layard supervises the procession of the bull beneath the mound of Nimrud (*Credit: Alamy Inc.*)

221 Rawlinson's sketch of the Arch of Ctesiphon (*Credit: Royal Geographic Society/Getty Images*)

233 Portrait of Edward Hincks in later years (*Credit: Alamy Inc.*)

254 Portrait of William Henry Fox Talbot taken in 1864 (*Credit: Alamy Inc.*)

265 Plan of the city of Babylon around the fifth century BCE according to Herodotus's description (*Credit: Alamy Inc.*)

ABOUT THE AUTHOR

Joshua Hammer is the *New York Times* bestselling author of six books, including *The Bad-Ass Librarians of Timbuktu*. His writing has appeared in *The New York Times Magazine*, *GQ*, *The Atlantic*, *The New Yorker*, *National Geographic*, *Smithsonian*, and *Outside*. He lives in Berlin.